Ethernet

Building a
Communications Infrastructure

Data Communications and Networks Series
Consulting Editor: Dr C. Smythe, University of Sheffield

Selected titles

Ethernet

Building a
Communications Infrastructure

Heinz-Gerd Hegering
University of Munich

Alfred Läpple
Leibniz Computing Centre

Translated by
Stephen S. Wilson

ADDISON-WESLEY
PUBLISHING
COMPANY

Wokingham, England · Reading, Massachusetts · Menlo Park, California · New York
Don Mills, Ontario · Amsterdam · Bonn · Sydney · Singapore
Tokyo · Madrid · San Juan · Milan · Paris · Mexico City · Seoul · Taipei

Translated from the German edition *Ethernet. Basis für Kommunikationsstrukturen* published by Datacom-Verlag.

Cover designed by Chris Eley
and printed by The Riverside Printing Co. (Reading) Ltd.
Printed and bound in Great Britain by William Clowes Limited, Beccles and London

First printed 1993.

ISBN: 0-201-62405-2

British Library Cataloguing in Publication Data
A catalogue record for this book is available from the British Library.

Library of Congress Cataloging-in-Publication Data is available.

Preface

Computer systems and terminal networks which operate in isolation are largely a thing of the past. With the ever increasing power of PCs and workstations and the ever growing importance of operations based on distributed cooperation, local area networks (LANs) have become an indispensable component of the essential communications infrastructure. More than two million LANs have been installed worldwide. The majority of these are based on Ethernet technology; hence the reason for this book on Ethernet-based communications structures.

However, beyond a consideration of LAN access protocols and physical network structures, the potential benefits of LANs as part of the enterprise network should also receive due attention. The title of the book reflects this emphasis. It is intended to show that, as a basis for in-house communication, Ethernet is still a key technology. By virtue of its widespread use and the large variety of media and protocols supported, Ethernet is more than just another type of LAN. The broad range of applications and the extensive facilities for forming subnetworks and linking to public networks have made Ethernet an appropriate basis for a modern communications infrastructure.

The widespread use of workstations in all commercial and scientific sectors and the new service structures based on client–server concepts, together with the increasing trend towards UNIX, have not only strengthened the position of Ethernet as the predominant type of LAN but have also sharply increased the demand for telecooperation at all levels. The themes of network integration (LAN internetworking) and LAN applications, and as a consequence and a prerequisite that of LAN management, are increasingly important. Thus, in addition to the detailed presentation of Ethernet standards and components, particular emphasis has been given to these topics.

We have more than a decade of Ethernet experience, and are responsible for large production networks based on Ethernet. Thus, when describing this subject area, practical aspects are close to our hearts. Because of the ephemeral nature of many products, we often found it more appropriate to include a basic discussion of the fundamental operating modes of hardware and software components rather than a product-oriented description.

The book is structured such that the initial description of the underlying theory and standards is followed by a discussion of their practical relevance, including examples of typical applications. Thus, the book may be used as both a text and a reference book. Each chapter begins with an introduction describing its structure; these introductions represent both the central theme of the book and a detailed chapter summary. Overall, a certain prior knowledge of data communication terminology and applications is assumed.

A book such as this cannot be written without encouragement from others. Thanks are due to our colleagues at the Leibniz Computer Centre of the Bavarian Academy of Sciences and the Munich Network Management Team: these are the environments in which we have gained most of our experience. We should also like to thank all our other friends and colleagues who have supported us throughout with advice and assistance. We mention in particular, Ingrid Fromm, Dipl.-Phys. for providing us with the IEEE papers, Dr Peter Chylla for his helpful cooperation and valuable preparatory work, and Dr Sebastian Abeck for his many ideas. We also thank our families for their great patience.

Munich, May 1993   Heinz-Gerd Hegering
                                                       Alfred Läpple

Trademark Notice
Apple™, AppleTalk™ and Macintosh™ are trademarks of Apple Computer, Inc.
RFS™ and UNIX™ are trademarks of AT&T.
CRAY™ is a trademark of Cray Research Inc.
DEC™, DECnet™ and VAX™ are trademarks of Digital Equipment Corporation.
HP™ is a trademark of Hewlett-Packard Company.
80X86™, 80286™, 80386™ and 80486™ are trademarks of Intel Corporation.
IBM™, NetBios™, OS/2™, PROFS™, System Network Architecture™ (SNA) and Token Ring™ are trademarks of International Business Machines Corporation.
Microsoft™, MS-DOS™ and Windows™ are trademarks of Microsoft Corporation.
Motorola™ is a trademark of Motorola Corporation.
Starlink™ is a trademark of National Semiconductor Corporation.
DCE™ is a trademark of Open Software Foundation.
NFS™ and SunOS™ are trademarks of Sun Microsystems, Inc.
XNS™ is a trademark of Xerox Corporation.

Contents

Chapter 1

Introduction

- Ethernet LANs as in-house communication systems

- LAN classification based on Ethernet technology within the IEEE LAN standard

- Possible uses of Ethernet LANs

In this first chapter we describe the general classification of Ethernet local area networks (LANs). In Section 1.1 we give a classification of in-house communication systems. Ethernet LANs are local area networks in the narrow sense, the most important representatives being those which satisfy the IEEE LAN standards. In Section 1.2 we describe how Ethernet LANs fit in with this family of standards and outline and compare typical access procedures. A detailed specification is withheld until Chapter 2. Finally, in Section 1.3 we describe possible uses of Ethernet LANs; a detailed discussion is given in later chapters.

1.1 Ethernet LANs as in-house communication systems

It is indisputable that, as a component of corporate information processing, communication both within a company and between companies, has a strategic role to play. However, although it is important, communication is only one of several facilities for coordinating operations based on distributed cooperation.

The design of the information and communication relationships is directly related to the structuring of a company's operation in terms of its structural and sequential organization.

The technical systems which support internal company communication have a corresponding infrastructural importance. Since communication within a company constitutes by far the greatest part of the overall communication requirement, it is sensible to look for technical systems which specialize in this part of the communication, namely in-house communication networks.

The terms 'in-house system' and 'local area network' are not rigorously defined. In general, they could be taken to refer to one of (possibly) many access or switching units (linked by lines) of an existing system which is used to transport information between the attached data terminals (terminals, PCs, hosts). They are characterized by a small spatial coverage (at most a few kilometres, a complex of buildings, a campus, an industrial estate), a relatively simple topology (ring, bus, star, tree) and a private operator (company, organizational unit).

Figure 1.1 shows various ways in which in-house communication may be implemented. This variety is a consequence of the degree of freedom available to the designer of a communications network, for example:

- Support for a preferred application area (e.g. office, production area, computer-centre, scientific area);

In-house networks

Networks with switching centres

Networks from mainframe manufacturers

SNA
TRANSDATA
DECnet
CDCnet

PBX

Telex PBX
Digital PBX
ISDN PBX

Data switch

X.25 subswitching
Private vtx. centres

Local area networks

Transport networks

Other LANs

Cambridge Ring
ARCNet
Hyperchannel
Wangnet
Planet
Libsy
3M network
Omninet
FIBRENET
ULTRANET

PC networks
Networks of workstations

LANs based on IEEE 802

IEEE 802.5
Token Ring

IBM Token Ring

IEEE 802.4
Token Bus

MAP

IEEE 802.3
Ethernet

Net/ONE
Interlan
DECnet
VSLan
TOP

PC networks based on Ethernet

IBM PC network
Sun network
NS8000
EMS 500
NetWare
NFS
Vines
LAN Mgr

Other PC networks

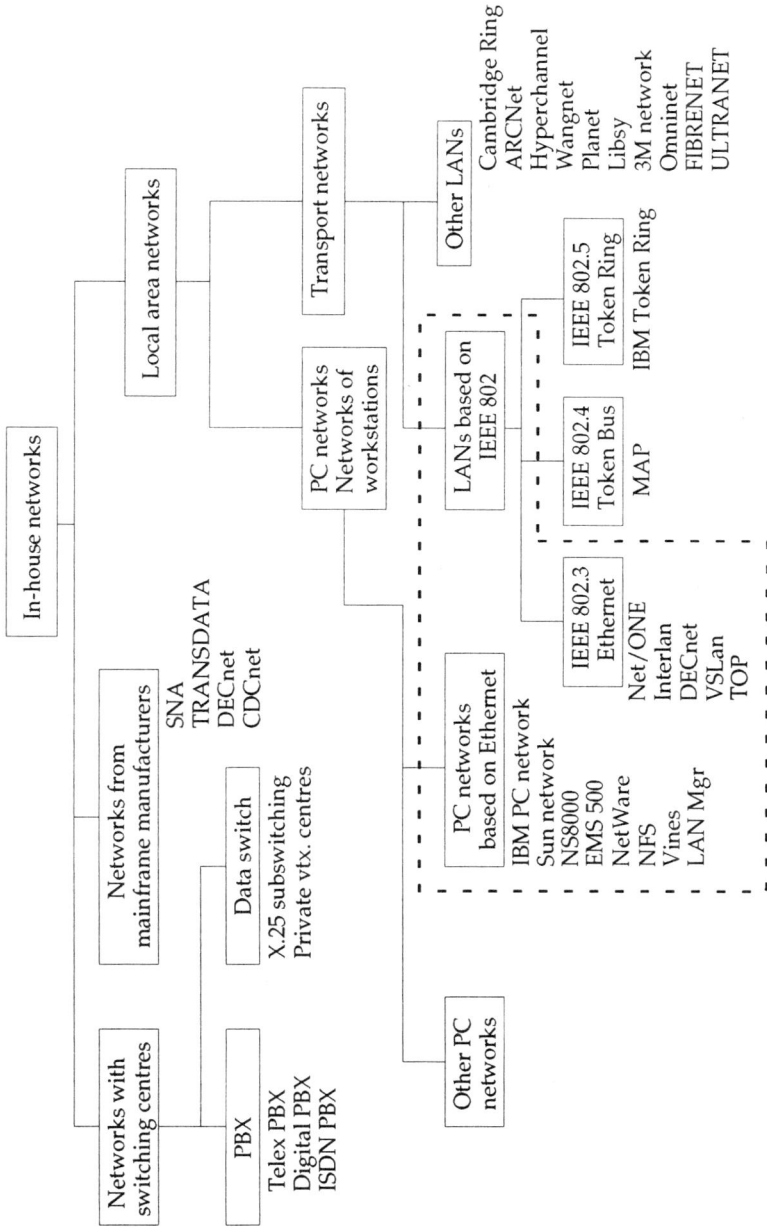

Figure 1.1 Classification of in-house networks, classification of Ethernet LANs.

3

- Support for a preferred type of information (data, text, graphics, facsimile, voice, moving pictures);
- Expected traffic characteristics (continuous/synchronous usage, bursty/asynchronous usage);
- Connection type (switched network, broadcast network);
- Nature of line usage (dedicated, shared usage controlled by access procedure);
- Topology (star, ring, bus, tree, hybrid);
- Transmission media (transmission technology, transmission rate, range);
- Protocol hierarchy and interfaces (manufacturer-specific architecture *de facto* standard, ISO/CCITT/IEEE standard).

The product names used in Fig. 1.1 are intended as examples only, and no attempt is made to be complete. Here, the classical networks of mainframe manufacturers and manufacturers of switching systems do not exhibit any characteristics which would differ from their use in wide area networks (WANs). This applies to the protocol hierarchies, the underlying network architectures and the range of products offered. The technical construction of the PBXs is largely similar to that of public switching systems. In other words, they are primarily optimized for voice communication and provide for data channels with a transmission rate up to 64 kbps, although the range of services provided in the private area is incomparably broader.

The fact that a network is privately owned and has limited coverage means that the underlying network technologies and network services may be freely selected. This leads to network architectures markedly different from those of WANs, namely those of LANs in the narrow sense. In these architectures because of the smaller coverage, more expensive media (affecting sensitivity to noise, data rates, error rates) and simpler topologies (affecting routing algorithms, delays, reliability) may be used and other network operating objectives (for example, line saturation as a minor goal) may be achieved.

The growing demand for local area networks is a result of technical, economic and organizational factors:

- Cost reductions from shared use of information and databases, resources and network services;
- Increased information exchange between an institution's departments. This includes, for example, distributed transaction processing and electronic mail;
- The desire to automate communication and manufacturing processes. Here, we mention computer-integrated manufacturing (CIM) efforts;

- Integration of different information streams (hybrid documents, multifunctional workstations);

- Increasing number and variety of intelligent data terminals, PCs and workstations.

This book does not aim to discuss in-house communication systems in general. For this, we refer the reader to appropriate introductory books (Boell, 1989; Kauffels, 1991). The subject of this monograph is the most important class, namely that of local area networks in the narrow sense.

Of the initial variety of LAN products, only those which are based on standardized protocols and interfaces (such as IEEE 802.x with Ethernet, Token Ring and Token Bus) are important. PCs, workstations and hosts may now be directly connected to all standardized LANs at acceptable prices. A number of network programming interfaces for various operating-system environments have emerged as *de facto* standards, and serve as the basis for distributed applications and server schemes. The standardization of LAN protocols not only allows the LAN planner to construct a heterogeneous LAN using components from different manufacturers, but also permits the manufacturer to specialize in a particular segment of the LAN-component market.

In parallel with the above developments, there has been dramatic development in ever more powerful workstation systems. As a result of the ever increasing cost-effectiveness and performance capability of PCs, workstations, RISC systems, etc., with a correspondingly increasing range of software, the penetration of all commercial and scientific areas by workstation computers is continuously extending. This leads to an increase in the demand for telecooperation, the need to collect originally decentralized information, and the desire for access to more powerful systems or remote databases from workstation systems. Application-oriented LANs are emerging offering value-added services such as electronic mail, multiple database organization, and remote job entry (RJE) and remote procedure call (RPC) mechanisms. Multiprotocol and multiserver support are catchwords which denote a cooperation of heterogeneous systems, and hence a step towards open communication. A jumbled world of DOS, OS/2 and UNIX workstations interwork over the same LANs with servers and mainframe systems. Server concepts support shared and central data organization and security, the shared use of special devices, gateway services to other networks, including PTT services and a central software provision.

Network services also support distributed applications. For example, programs may be developed and their results edited or visualized on a personal workstation computer, although more involved computations such as the processing of a graphics model or database access may be carried out on remote systems such as supercomputers. In this respect, LANs have undoubtedly contributed to distributed data processing, since because of their higher transmission rates, it is increasingly rare for communications networks to form bottlenecks. Thus, certain distributed applications and network services have become sensible for the first time. Examples here include distributed transactions, video communication, the transmission of an extensive series of measurements, the use of a central archiving capacity, the recording of newspaper articles, and the distribution of software.

The appearance of bridges and routers (components for coupling LANs in the lower protocol layers), together with the internetworking of LANs via fibre optic systems and even via satellite links, have removed the restrictions on the coverage of the original LAN technology. There are even examples of the installation of coupled LANs with FDDI rings as a backbone network (a network linking the LANs) which are able to bridge a distance of 100 km and have a transmission rate of 100 Mbps. Filter technology in bridges and routers makes it possible to separate local LAN traffic from LAN internetwork traffic. The classical difference between LANs and WANs, namely their geographical coverage, is increasingly disappearing. The difference now relates more to the protocol hierarchy used and to the difference in transmission rates. The latter has already been reduced by the leasing of fibre-optic links by the PTT. New LAN aspects will also be introduced by the hybrid networks for data and voice communications, currently being planned, in which packet-oriented procedures will be combined with time-slot procedures. Compatibility with narrowband transmission on the one hand and, above all, with broadband ISDN (ATM) on the other hand, are central issues in the current standardization of such networks.

One other thing has changed. For a long time, the transmission medium and the LAN type were closely connected; however, now various types of LAN may be operated on a single type of medium (for example, shielded twisted pairs). Thus, a strategy for a uniformly structured cable system which does not *per se* prejudice the LAN type may be successfully followed. By forming levels of supply (cabling linking buildings or floors, storey or room cabling), it is possible to implement cabling within building complexes with a view to the future. Thus, attention may be given to important operational requirements such as, for example, the different lifetimes of buildings, cable channels, cables and strap connections, support for changing network concepts and transmission procedures, and the creation of subnetworks for technical, organizational or security reasons.

All in all, local area networks are no longer restricted to in-house communication, they no longer form a closed world as far as coverage, protocols, media and services are concerned. More than ever before, they are on the move and gaining ground. The limitations of the LANs of the early days were breached some time ago. Local area networks and internetworks of workstation systems are important infrastructural elements of the overall DP (data processing) provision of companies. Thus, integration aspects relating to overall DP supply structures must be increasingly to the fore in the planning and operation of local area or PC networks.

Of the LANs standardized by the IEEE, Ethernet-based communication systems are *de facto* the most important. This fact justifies this monograph dedicated to Ethernet technology and its possibilities.

Local area networks based on Ethernet technology are networks which use the CSMA/CD technique (described in detail in Sections 1.2.2 and 2.3.1) to access the shared transmission medium. This access technique was originally developed by Xerox in the mid-1970s for a LAN called 'Ethernet' based on coaxial cable with a then revolutionary transmission speed of 3 Mbps. As a result of its simplicity and robustness and the passive attachment of stations, and not least because of its cost effectiveness, this LAN technology caught on to become a market leader. An Ethernet interface is now supplied as standard with many PCs, workstations and hosts. Ethernet technology is no longer restricted to the famous 'yellow cable'. CSMA/CD standards and products exist for the simpler types of coaxial cable, for broadband coaxial cable (e.g. the cable used for television aerials) and shielded twisted pairs (e.g. the IBM cable system), for unshielded conductors (e.g. conventional telephone lines) and fibre optic conductors. A common interface above the different media, which we shall discuss in detail in Chapter 2, provides for the interworking of subnetworks with different media, and thus forms the basis for customized cable systems.

The early standardization of Ethernet and the broad base of products available from a very large number of different manufacturers mean that *de facto* Ethernet LANs permit more open communication in a heterogeneous system environment than do other LAN systems.

1.2 LAN classification based on Ethernet technology within the IEEE LAN standard

In the following, whenever we refer to LANs we mean LANs in the narrow sense (Figure 1.1).

A number of LAN classifications appear in the literature; for example, transport-oriented *versus* application-oriented LANs, front-end LANs *versus* back-end LANs, LANs to transmit speech, data or moving images, etc. Here, we shall use a classification based on the physical nature of the LAN, namely the topologies used in the LAN (bus, ring, star, tree), the media used (twisted pair, coaxial cable, optical fibre), the transmission procedures (baseband synchronous/asynchronous, broadband) and the access procedures (FTDM, CSMA, token passing, etc.).

1.2.1 LAN layer model

An extended *layer model* based on the ISO/OSI reference model is used as a common reference model (RM) for describing LANs (Figure 1.2).

7	Application		Application
6	Presentation		Presentation
5	Session		Session
4	Transport		Transport
3c	Internet		Network
3b	Enhancement		
3a	Subnetwork access		
2b	Logical link		Data link
2a	Medium access		
1	Physical		Physical

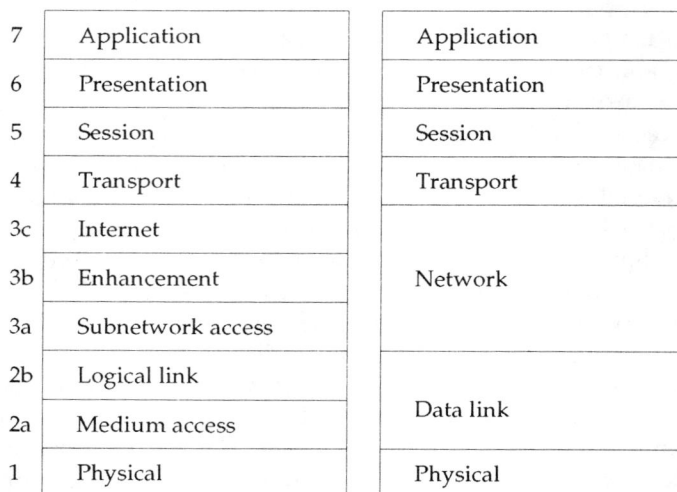

Figure 1.2   Layer model for LANs. The OSI model is shown on the right.

The physical characteristics of individual types of LAN are reflected in a refined subdivision of the three lowest OSI layers.

The *physical layer* is responsible for the transparent transmission of bit sequences over different media. The specification of this layer takes account of the different mechanical (pin layout and configuration), physical (electrical, electromagnetic, acoustic, optical) and functional (e.g. meaning of pin assignments) characteristics of transmission media and interfaces. The different transmission types (e.g. analog/digital, synchronous/asynchronous, modulation, encoding) also belong to this layer.

The *medium access control* (MAC) layer comes into play when the transmission medium is not dedicated to two communications partners, but when (as is normal in LANs) many communications partners (stations) are connected to the same medium. The MAC layer controls the assignment of the shared transmission medium resource using a fixed scheme (e.g. time multiplex, frequency multiplex) or dynamically using so-called multi-access protocols (reservation procedures, stochastic access procedures). The underlying procedure for Ethernet belongs to the class of stochastic procedures.

When the MAC layer allocates the transmission medium for a communications relationship, the medium- and transmission-related securing of the link takes place in the *logical link layer* (LLC), which corresponds to the ISO/OSI data link layer. Layer 2b is responsible for combining bit sequences into blocks (bytes, frames), for block synchronization, for error detection at the block or frame level and, if necessary, for error correction.

The *network layer* has overall responsibility for controlling the path of a logical connection through a network, which is implemented using so-called transit systems (relay systems, switching systems, node computers). Thus, layer 3 is responsible for routing and switching. If a network consists of interconnected subnetworks the routing and switching tasks occur twice: once in each subnetwork (layer 3a) and then again in the internetwork (internetworking, layer 3c). Since the layer 3 procedures used in layers 3a and 3c may be very different, it can sometimes be necessary to adapt the network services; this is carried out in layer 3b. Thus, in a single LAN, layers 3b and 3c are absent and the network layer is provided by layer 3a.

The *transport layer* provides a network-independent transport service between two end systems (end-to-end). It maps the various network services of the network layer onto the transport service using appropriate end-to-end transport protocols. In this sense, there exist typical LAN layer 4 protocols.

OSI layers 5 to 7 are application-related. Since typical LAN applications have taken shape, we shall return to the tasks of these layers later.

In summary the LLC/MAC interface is independent of the medium, the topology and the access strategies used, while the MAC layer depends on the access strategy and the topology, although it is independent of the medium. The medium-specific operations are carried out in the physical layer, in particular, in the medium access units (MAUs). Access strategies are needed because the LAN medium resource is shared by all subscribers to the LAN.

As mentioned in Section 1.1, the most important LANs in the narrow sense are those for which the interfaces and protocols are standardized. Thus, in our classification of Ethernet LANs we shall only consider the most LAN-specific layers 1 and 2a which are characterized by the medium and the access strategy. Moreover, we additionally restrict our attention to those LANs which are covered by the standardization efforts of the IEEE and the ISO.

The LAN standard is defined in the *Local and Metropolitan Area Networks, IEEE 802* standard. As shown in Figure 1.3, this is a family of standards called 802.x which deal mainly with the OSI physical and data-link layers. These standards define various transmission media and technologies together with the associated access procedures, where each procedure is suitable for specific applications or system objectives. The outline structure of the LAN station shown in Figure 1.4 is based on the IEEE 802 standard.

1.2.2 LAN access procedures

Standards 802.3/4/5 are designed for local area networks for the in-house area, the 802.6 standard is for metropolitan area networks (MANs),

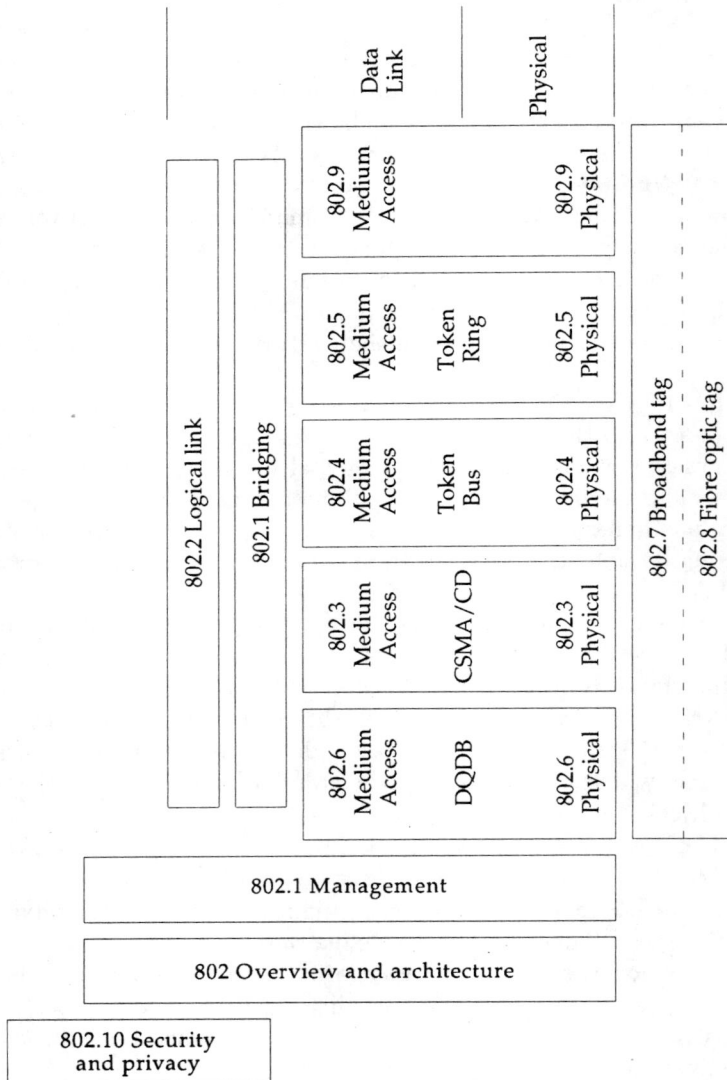

Figure 1.3 IEEE 802 LAN standard.

10

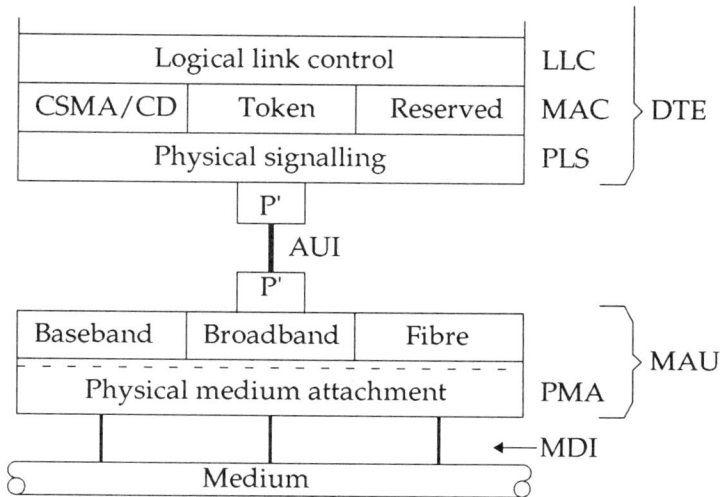

AUI   = Attachment Unit Interface
LLC   = Logical Link Control
MAC   = Medium Access Control
MAU = Medium Access Unit
MDI   = Medium Dependent Interface
PLS   = Physical Signalling
PMA = Physical Medium Attachment

Figure 1.4   Outline structure of a LAN/MAN station based on IEEE 802.

which are larger urban networks suitable not only for carrying asynchronous bursty data traffic but also for isochronous traffic (for voice communication). Corresponding to the network objectives, different strategies exist for the MAC layer. The access procedures defined in IEEE 802 are CSMA/CD (802.3), token passing (802.4/5) and DQDB (distributed queue dual bus, 802.6). In what follows, we outline the two most important access strategies relevant to the Ethernet LAN. MAN access procedures will not be considered further here. We refer readers to the appropriate literature for a detailed treatment of access procedures which are not relevant to Ethernet.

   Token passing procedures are decentralized access procedures which control access to the medium using an authorization to send (represented by the special 'token' bit pattern). The token circulates on the logical ring (consisting of passively connected, suitably numbered stations on a linear bus according to 802.4) or on the physical ring with actively connected adapters (IEEE 802.5). When a station which is ready to transmit receives the free token it may transmit, the receiving station copies the message which is eventually deleted from the ring by the transmitting station. The sender then generates a new token.

The CSMA/CD (carrier sense multiple access with collision detection) procedure used in Ethernet LANs is an access procedure based on collisions which uses a competitive scheme. This involves three subactivities:

- Carrier sensing; in other words, eavesdropping on the medium and listening in to the transmission channel (listen before talking). A station waiting to transmit only does so after sensing the channel and ensuring that it is free.

- Collision detection involves listening to the channel while transmitting (listen while talking), and interrupting one's own transmission if a collision is detected. A collision may occur in a short time interval (collision interval) when, at the previous instant, several stations waiting to transmit determine that the channel is free using carrier sensing and begin to transmit at almost the same time. The collision interval depends on the signal speed for the medium and the distance between stations.

- The backoff algorithm is a strategy for repeating transmissions which are affected by collisions.

The collision parameter K determines the quality of the CSMA/CD procedure:

$$K = \frac{\text{Max. signal propagation time}}{\text{Message transmission time}}$$

$$= \left(\frac{\text{Channel length}}{\text{Signal speed}}\right) \Bigg/ \left(\frac{\text{Message length}}{\text{Channel transmission rate}}\right)$$

For $K > 1$ a transmitter could pass its whole message to the channel before a collision is discovered; thus, CSMA/CD procedures are only practicable for $K \ll 1$. The procedure imposes limits on the distance, the bandwidth and the minimum message length, from which the system parameters referred to in Chapter 2 result. We shall discuss the Ethernet standard in more detail in Chapter 2.

1.2.3 Performance aspects

The access procedures outlined above exhibit different performance features which are characterized by the delays (of transmission and access to the medium), the throughput and extent to which fair access is maintained for different network loads.

The robustness of a system in the presence of faults or noise must form part of the evaluation. Systems based on a contention principle exhibit an inherently greater robustness. Unlike Token Ring systems, CSMA/CD systems do not need a monitor, they are self-stabilizing in the presence of faults and interference (for example, as a result of the connection new stations) affects the access procedure like a normal collision signal or frame error.

A comparison of the performance of LAN systems is beyond our scope here, and we refer readers to discussions of this topic in introductory LAN literature such as Spaniol (1982), Bux (1981), and Hammond and Reilly (1986). The most important results may be qualitatively summarized as follows. The CSMA/CD procedure is advantageous for traffic which is highly variable and irregular in terms of time and volume (bursty traffic), such as that typically found in the office and computer centre areas. When there is a high load (traffic above 60% of channel capacity), the packet transmission delays increase sharply in comparison with the average packet transmission time, as a result of the increased risk of collisions; in other words, it is not possible to guarantee a maximum waiting time. Moreover, the maximum achievable value of the quotient of throughput rate by channel capacity for CSMA/CD buses is smaller than that for Token Rings which exhibit a stable behaviour in terms of throughput and waiting times as the load increases. On the other hand, for lower traffic loads, the waiting times for rings are somewhat disturbing and are greater than those for bus structures. In other words, for a given packet length (e.g. 500 bytes) and traffic load (e.g. up to 50%), the probability of accessing the medium within a time interval T is more favourable for CSMA/CD buses (e.g. 90% of all access under 1 ms).

The results of a performance comparison, as outlined above, follow from theoretical traffic analysis and simulation. In reality, limiting throughput and 'unhealthy' traffic loads scarcely play any part in Ethernet LANs, since they may be countered by timely (and easily executed) reconfiguration. As far as Ethernet LANs are concerned, we do not know of any networks operating in the production area where such critical traffic levels have been reached that limiting behaviour of this type has occurred (except in error situations).

Measurements in large CSMA/CD networks have shown that normally collisions are rare and that, even with a very high network load (greater than 90%), a CSMA/CD system does not fall apart. However, the average network load should not be more than 30–40%, in which case short-lived load peaks of 60% or more are not a problem. Since measurements in a heavily used CSMA/CD office system with more than 100 workstations have shown an average channel load of 5%, this requirement is easy to satisfy.

The differences in the performance characteristics of the access strategies naturally leads to the question 'Which LAN technology is the best?'. Any answer must depend on the traffic characteristics of the network users; in other words, on the distribution of the interactions in terms of time and volume, on the necessity of guaranteed waiting times, and on the priority rules, etc.

Since maximum transmission times may be given for all token passing procedures, and because priority schemes are easier to implement, such procedures are particularly suitable for real-time applications. The Token Ring (IEEE 802.5) is the basis for an IBM product. The Token Bus (IEEE 802.4) is the basis for the MAP architecture (Suppan and Simon, 1986). MAP is a multipart scheme to introduce open communication in an automated manufacturing environment (CIM), which (based on a General Motors project) has currently led to a standardized protocol hierarchy and a number of products.

The application environment which favours the Ethernet technology (CSMA/CD) is largely found in the areas of remote access systems, PC networks, internetworked workstations, client–server structures and office communications. In the office communications area, Xerox and the TOP (technical and office protocols) project in particular have provided impressive demonstrations of the suitability of local area networks based on CSMA/CD. Under the TOP project, Boeing has been trying (analogous to the MAP project) to drive forward the development of networks based on Ethernet technology since the National Computing Conference in 1984. This has led to a standardized protocol hierarchy with a number of products.

For many years, existing Ethernet installations in companies such as Siemens, DEC, HP, National Semiconductor, IABG, ESG/FEG and BMW have demonstrated that Ethernet LANs may be installed not only in the office communications and university areas, but also in software engineering and industrial manufacturing where they represent a sensible and important basis for communication infrastructures. Even in the area of manufacturing automation, the pleasantly low degree of complexity of the essential protocol building blocks of an Ethernet system in comparison with other access procedures, and the availability of a large number of cost-effective state-of-the-art Ethernet LAN components, have led to the acceptance of Ethernet as a network solution. An early example is Siemens's industry bus, SINEC H1.

Finally, we note that discussions of the performance capability of local area networks all too often centre solely on the performance achievable at the lowest protocol levels (medium, signal structure, access strategy), and that comparisons of LANs consider predominantly borderline situations or very special loads. However, those aspects of the network performance visible to the end user (useful data rate, delays) are restricted to a far greater extent by the architecture of the network access unit, the overall protocol hierarchy used, and the constraints on the connection of subscriber systems.

1.3 Possible uses of Ethernet LANs

In this section we give a brief outline of scenarios for using Ethernet LANs which exploit their specific advantages. Of course, not all the scenarios are limited to the use of Ethernet LANs.

The description here is intended as a basic introduction to the use of Ethernet LANs. Later chapters include detailed discussions of the Ethernet components and software modules required in the implementations and the practical effects for in-house communication together with explanatory diagrams.

1.3.1 Decentralized switching system

Remote access networks are systems which provide a variety of spatially distributed data terminals (for example, dialogue stations, remote batch stations (RJE), workstation computers, process computers, etc.) with access to (possibly centrally implemented) processing capacity (host, mainframes) with the aid of a switching system. Unlike networks with central star switching systems (for example, a private X.25 network), because of its topology (rootless tree) and its transmission method, an Ethernet LAN is a direct diffusion network without explicit switching; in other words, all stations are attached to a common medium. A message is transmitted directly to this medium and may be received directly by all stations, although, in most cases, only the destination station interprets the messages. Through this broadcast facility an Ethernet bus system has the effect of a system with switching without the phenomenon of bottlenecks which is associated with central components of switching systems. Furthermore, automatic services such as round calls and group calls are available without the need for switching over several point-to-point links.

1.3.2 Freedom of access by data terminals

Ethernet LANs exhibit a particularly good topology modularity and an excellent reconfiguration behaviour. The former determines the behaviour of the network when it is extended or shrunk; the latter determines the reaction of the network to the breakdown of a station. Because of the passive coupling of stations and the CSMA/CD access strategy, introduction, removal or breakdown of stations is not in any way problematic, and the operation of the network need not be interrupted. A station may be introduced at practically any point of the medium, without the need to reconfigure other stations (as far as the layers relevant to Ethernet are concerned), to carry out new attenuation calculations or to measure signal amplitudes. The latter would be necessary, for example, in broadband installations if the connection outlets were not originally taken into account during network planning. This freedom of connection is particularly important when Ethernet LANs are used in an environment where, because of frequent moves or changes to the spatial layout of production components, the exact positioning of network stations is not constant.

1.3.3 Ethernet for saving cable

Ethernet LANs may be viewed as statistical multiplex systems; in other words, by virtue of the CSMA/CD multi-access protocol it is possible to implement a variety of logical point-to-point links simultaneously, as dictated by the traffic.

Thus, because of the high 10 Mbps transmission capacity of Ethernet, a number of channels with a lower transmission rate may be handled almost simultaneously. In an environment of intense DP usage, the number of installed data terminals gives rise to a serious cabling problem. In such situations, multiplexing channels lead to considerable savings of cable. Here, Ethernet (with its protocols) is used as a transport system which is able to switch virtual lines with very different line procedures through the single medium. This is made possible by so-called terminal servers, discussed in detail in Section 5.1. By a terminal server (network interface unit, NIU), we mean system components (software and hardware) which make available firstly the interface to the Ethernet-cable medium, and secondly the interface to the user terminal (terminal, PC, workstation, host, cluster controller). Thus, the NIU has the role of a protocol converter which converts the LAN protocols into protocols for the attached subscribers or access lines. NIUs may either be implemented as standalone devices or built in to the data terminal device.

When the Ethernet is used to handle various line procedures (for example, TTY, 3270, BSC, 327x SDLC), the protocol data units of the line procedures are transmitted as useful data for the Ethernet LLC protocols in a protocol encapsulation procedure, which is performed by the NIUs in stochastic multiplex mode. A number of such NIUs are currently on the market. However, problems may arise if timer values for the procedures are of the same order of magnitude as the Ethernet network delay.

Another use of Ethernet in order to save cable must be mentioned, namely the situation in which independent subnetworks may be operated over the same shared medium, where the subnetworks satisfy the IEEE 802.3 standard for OSI layers 1–2 but differ in the higher protocol hierarchies. Examples of different higher protocol hierarchies which are normally operated above the Ethernet protocol include DECnet, TCP/IP, XNS and OSI.

When different protocol hierarchies are used there is no cooperation between the subnetworks, a fact which may be used as a possible means of separating user groups. The subnetworks each make inroads into the channel capacity available to the others, although because of the CSMA/CD procedure, no station of any specific subnetwork is given preference. Thus, the subnetworks coexist on the cable, which is a prerequisite for the use of a LAN as a cable infrastructure.

1.3.4 Ethernet for linking computers

For traffic characteristics (bursty traffic, connectionless traffic without real-time requirements) as in the case of sporadic file transfer, office communications or distributed data processing requiring the cooperation of different computers, Ethernet technology is particularly suitable.

Because of its standardized basis, Ethernet technology is primarily used to link heterogeneous computers. However, even in some homogeneous computer worlds (e.g. HP, DEC, CDC), computer coupling is largely based on Ethernet. Coupling of computers via Ethernet is used almost exclusively in environments with TCP/IP protocols and UNIX operating systems.

Since UNIX is the dominant operating system as far as workstations are concerned, Ethernet is also the preferred LAN scheme in this area for the internetworking of workstations.

1.3.5 Use of Ethernet LANs with server schemes

The transmission security, access times and transfer rates of Ethernet LANs are comparable with those of some floppy disk or disk systems. Thus, questions about the functional specialization of computer systems and their interworking based on the division of tasks, in the sense of distributed processing, take on a practical nature.

This led to the idea of servers or systems which provide specific services for *a priori* unknown user systems, where the server and the user (client) run on separate systems. Examples of servers include:

- servers which provide for shared use of resources (file server, disk server, print server, compute server);
- servers for special applications (mail server, database server, calendar, storage and editing of voice documents);
- servers for common system services (name server, time server, authentication server, network monitor, gateway monitor).

In the context of the execution of a task based on distributed cooperation, the individual functions which a client may delegate to a server depend not only on the performance capability of the server, but also on whether for any particular function the required data transfer rate on the data path between the client and the server is achievable. This is why LANs are important for DP supply structures based on client–server schemes.

The use of Ethernet LANs in conjunction with the implementation of server schemes is met in particular in PC networks and in the coupling of workstations. Here, multipoint and broadcast communication, which is automatically supported by Ethernet as a diffusion network, facilitates the implementation of distributed servers.

Chapter 2

The Ethernet standard

- Development of the Ethernet standard

- Data link layer (IEEE 802.2, LLC)

- Medium access control (IEEE 802.3, MAC)

- Physical layer (IEEE 802.3, PLS, AUI, MAU)

- Further development of standards relevant to Ethernet

This chapter is entirely devoted to the Ethernet standard; the specifications as given in the standard documents are given prominence. Statements about products, practical experiences and the like are discussed in later chapters. Readers who do not need to understand the Ethernet specifications may want to skip this chapter.

The specifications relevant to Ethernet cover several hundred pages, and it is not the aim of this chapter to paraphrase these. For non-experts, standards documents are very difficult to understand because they are very formal and rich in detail and have not been adapted for didactic purposes. This chapter provides a basic introduction to the Ethernet standard; we consider only the important stipulations of the specifications which we substantiate and justify.

Section 2.1 gives a brief overview of the existing standards of relevance to Ethernet; these are then described in the following sections. For didactic reasons, the description is based on the LAN layer model, beginning with layer 2 (Section 2.2). We outline the tasks, services and protocols of this layer and its interface to the medium access control (MAC) layer. The MAC layer is described in Section 2.3, in which the characteristic Ethernet CSMA/CD procedure is discussed in detail. Section 2.4 is given over to a description of the physical layer; the individual subsections describe the medium-dependent characteristics of the various Ethernet LAN types, including the standard Ethernet based on thick yellow coaxial cable, Cheapernet with its thin coaxial cable and the twisted-pair LAN based on twisted-pair telephone cables. Section 2.5 describes how more complicated multisegment Ethernet LANs may be constructed from segments of these Ethernet types using repeaters. The remainder of the chapter contains a description of the specifications for other Ethernet LAN types, namely the StarLAN, an Ethernet based on broadband technology and Ethernet LANs based on fibre optic cables.

2.1 Development of the Ethernet standard

The name Ethernet is inseparably linked with the research and development activities of the Xerox Palo Alto research centre. An experimental Ethernet was developed there from 1972 (Shoch *et al.*, 1982) with the following objectives:

- relatively high data rates (1–10) Mbps;
- short delays (no storage or transport logic in the network);
- network diameter around 1 km;
- support for several hundred independent stations;
- very simple algorithms (medium access, addressing);

- high reliability (no central component as a bottleneck);
- efficient use of the shared transmission medium;
- fair distribution of access to all subscribers;
- simple to install and reconfigure;
- high stability under load;
- low costs.

The first results from Xerox were contained in Metcalfe and Boggs (1976). Recognition of the increasing importance of networking workstation computers led to an improved Ethernet design (Figure 2.1) as a result of a joint project between DEC, Intel and Xerox (DIX) in 1980. This specification was later termed Ethernet V1.0. The transmission rate was increased from 3 Mbps for the experimental Ethernet to 10 Mbps for the improved design. The specification was completed and refined with the acknowledged goal of using the specified layers to achieve the compatibility of heterogeneous systems as network subscribers.

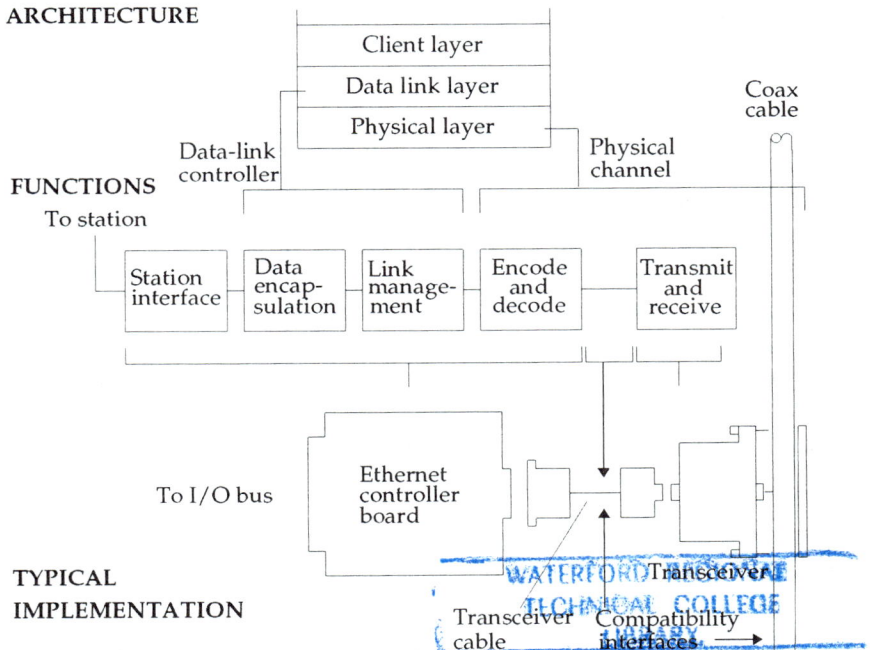

ARCHITECTURE

Client layer

Data link layer

Physical layer

Coax cable

Data-link controller

Physical channel

FUNCTIONS

To station

| Station interface | Data encap-sulation | Link manage-ment | Encode and decode | Transmit and receive |

To I/O bus

Ethernet controller board

TYPICAL IMPLEMENTATION

Transceiver

Transceiver cable

Compatibility interfaces

Figure 2.1 DIX Ethernet architecture and typical implementation.

This specification was introduced to the local network standards committee of the IEEE and published, largely unaltered, with other standard proposals in the first full status report of the IEEE project 802 as draft B in October 1981. At almost the same time, the European Computer Manufacturers' Association (ECMA) began its LAN standardization efforts. The DIX group also continued its work to complete the Ethernet specifications. The specification of the DIX Ethernet V2.0 was published in 1982 as a result of efforts to adapt the version V1.0 to the IEEE proposals.

As explained in Section 1.2.1 using Figure 1.4, the IEEE 802 standard (corresponds to the ISO 8802 standard) represents a whole family of standards and recommendations developed in various subcommittees and working groups:

- **802.1** Overview and architecture of the IEEE 802 standard; management; system load protocol; MAC bridging (coupling of LANs below LLC).
- **802.2** Logical link control (LLC).
- **802.3** CSMA/CD access method and physical layer specifications.
- **802.4** Token Bus access method and physical layer specifications.
- **802.5** Token Ring access method and physical layer specifications.
- **802.6** Metropolitan area network access method and physical layer specifications.
- **802.7** Broadband technical advisory and physical layer topics and recommended practices.
- **802.8** Fibre optic technical advisory and physical layer topics.
- **802.9** Integrated voice/data access method and physical layer specifications (IVD LAN).
- **802.10** Security and privacy access method and physical layer specifications.
- **802.11** Wireless access method and physical layer specification.

Thus, the standardization relevant to Ethernet is contained in IEEE documents 802.1, 802.2 and 802.3. Not all the work of the corresponding committees has led to the release of standards.

Currently, the following official standards relating to Ethernet LANs have been released:

(1) IEEE standard 802.2, 1985. Logical link control.
(2) IEEE standard 802.3, 1985. CSMA/CD access method and physical layer specifications.

      This standard describes the carrier sense multiple access with collision detection (CSMA/CD) access method and the physical layer for a specific transmission medium, namely the well-known thick yellow Ethernet coaxial cable with a transmission rate of 10 Mbps. Since the individual cable segments should not be longer than 500 m and baseband transmission is used, this Ethernet type is known as 'Type 10base5'. The general scheme for type names is:

⟨Data rate,Mbps⟩⟨Transmission technology⟩⟨Max. segment length, expressed in metres/100⟩

(3) IEEE standard 802.3 a, b, c, e, 1988. Supplements to CSMA/CD access method and physical layer standards.

These supplementary standards contain specifications for:

— Ethernet type 10base2, which uses 200 m segments of thin coaxial cable (thin wire).

— Ethernet type 10broad36, which defines a CSMA/CD-compatible broadband transmission.

— Ethernet type 1base5, which is based on standard twisted-pair telephone lines (StarLAN).

— Repeater units for 10base5.

(4) IEEE standard 802.3 i, 1990. Supplements to CSMA/CD access method and physical layer standards. This supplementary standard contains specifications for:

— Ethernet 10baseT, which defines the Ethernet technology for twisted-pair lines up to 100 m long.

— Multisegment CSMA/CD networks.

(5) IEEE standard 802, 1990. Overview and architecture.

This gives an overview of the IEEE 802 family of standards and how it fits in with the OSI reference model.

(6) IEEE standard 802.1 D, 1990. This deals with the coupling of LANs (bridging) below the MAC level service interface.

(7) IEEE standard 802.1 E, 1990. This specifies services and protocols for loading systems over IEEE LANs.

(8) IEEE standard 1802.3, 1991. Conformance test methodology for IEEE LAN/MAN standards. This specifies test methods for proving the conformance of LAN termination cables.

The publication of these standards in no way marks the end of the development of Ethernet. New options and properties are under discussion and will lead to additional standards. Examples of further work of this type include:

• The specification of star-shaped fibre optic networks using the Ethernet access technique (type 10baseF).

- The specification of management characteristics of hubs. Hubs are repeaters and optical star couplers.

- The completion of the specification of conformance test methods.

- The specification of LAN management methods and management objects.

There is thus a considerable variety of network types which operate with CSMA/CD and are specified in IEEE 802 (Figure 2.2).

In the following sections, we shall summarize only the most important statements of the Ethernet specifications. The only standard which is specific to Ethernet in the narrow sense is the 802.3 standard which specifies the CSMA/CD access procedure together with the physical characteristics of the transmission media and their access interfaces. Strictly speaking, the IEEE 802.3 specification should be considered in conjunction with the DIX Ethernet V2.0 specifications. Sometimes in the literature, only the latter are referred to as 'Ethernet' for short. Although the two specifications differ in a number of details (which we shall discuss in depth later), we shall subsume both specifications and the corresponding products under the term 'Ethernet'.

The 802.2 standard applies not only to Ethernet but also to the other standardized access procedures (for example, Token Bus, Token Ring), since the upper part of layer 2, in which the logical link control protocol is described, is independent of the access method. The standard defines an HDLC-like data link protocol and a common service interface (see Figure 1.4). Since this standard is implemented in every Ethernet LAN and the interfaces defined by it are accessible via user software in a number of LAN products, we shall discuss this further.

For didactic reasons, our treatment begins with the data link layer. There then follows a discussion of the CSMA/CD access scheme (MAC layer) and a characterization of the media currently authorized for use with Ethernet (physical layer signalling, PLS). Armed with this knowledge it is already possible to construct multisegment CSMA/CD LANs. Extensions of layer 2 (bridging) or the network layer (layers 3b, 3c) must be considered when linking such LANs into integrated LAN networks. This is discussed in Chapter 4.

The description of the IEEE 802 standard is not intended to be a full restatement of the original text but an explanation of the most important concepts of the protocol architecture and interface specifications. This should enable the reader to understand how the Ethernet components work, and provide him with the ability to refer to the original texts of the standards for detailed specifications. Some of the figures used in this chapter are taken from the IEEE 802.x standards.

Class of services

Token passing

802.3 (CSMA/CD)

Baseband

Unshielded twisted pair	Coaxial cable
	1 Mbps
	5 Mbps
1 Mbps	
10 Mbps	10 Mbps
	20 Mbps

Broadband

Coaxial cable
10 Mbps (18 MHz channel)

802.4 (bus)

Broadband

Coaxial cable
1.544 Mbps (4 MHz and 6 MHz chan.)
5 Mbps 10 Mbps (6 MHz chan.)
10 Mbps 20 Mbps (12 MHz chan.)

Baseband

Phase continuous	Phase coherent
Coaxial cable	Coaxial cable
1 Mbps	5 Mbps
	10 Mbps

802.5 (ring)

Baseband

Shielded twisted pair	Coaxial cable
	4 Mbps
	20 Mbps
	10 Mbps
1 Mbps	
4 Mbps	

802.6

Metropolitan area network

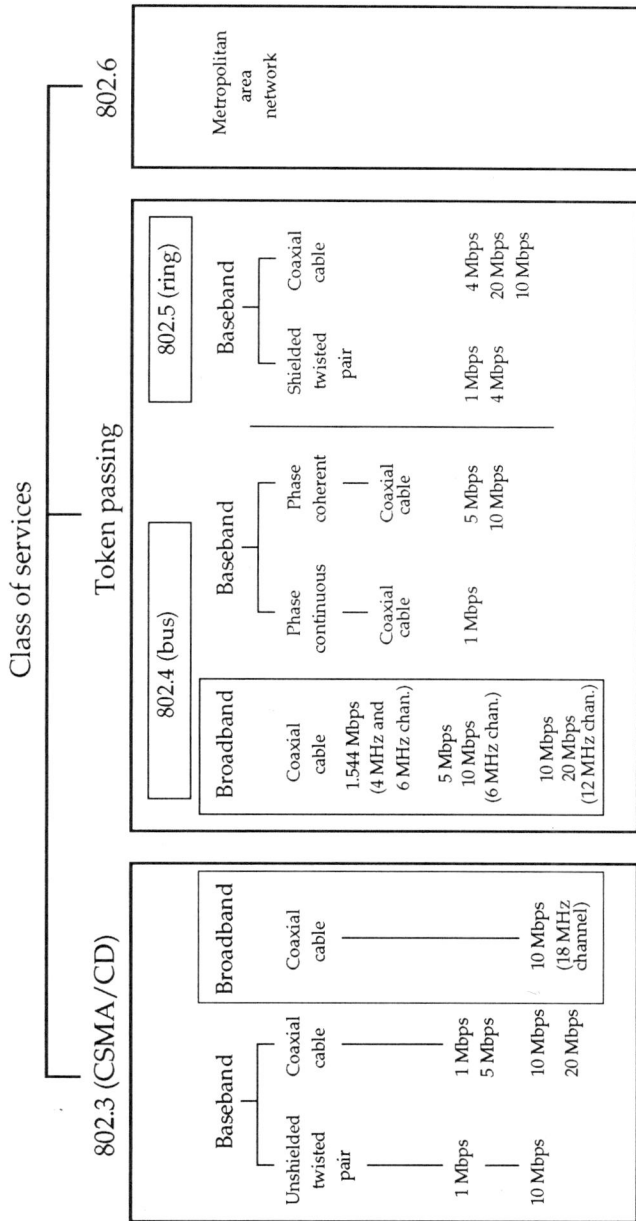

Figure 2.2 IEEE 802.x LAN standards.

2.2 Data link layer (IEEE 802.2, LLC)

2.2.1 Overview

The data link layer is responsible for the error-free transmission of frames (character blocks, bit sequences) over data links; in other words, over communications circuits linking two stations without intermediate switching nodes.

Thus, based on the layer structure of the ISO reference model, typical tasks of data link protocols include:

- Error handling: error detection, error correction where possible or reporting of errors to the overlying layer, acknowledgement services.
- Flow control.
- Sequence control.

The Ethernet LAN is a diffusion network; in other words, every attached station can monitor the signals of all other stations on the LAN without the help of intermediate switching nodes. Thus, it is possible to dispense with an individual network layer (layer 3a). Switching and routing do not arise as network layer tasks, and the provision of connection services can be integrated into the data link layer.

LAN links (OSI layer 2 connections) differ from normal data links as follows:

- The form of multiple access cannot generally be described by a multipoint data link (multidrop), since it involves asynchronous access of peer stations; in other words, no primary nodes are designated.
- A LAN link makes available a number of connection services:
  - Datagram services (transmission of individual self-contained messages).
  - Connection-oriented services (transmission of sequentially ordered sequences of messages over a dynamic logical channel established between sender and receiver stations).
  - Multicast, broadcast (transmission of frames to a group of stations or to all stations).
  - Multiplex (support for several logical channels via a station access line to the LAN).

Corresponding to its architectural embedding, the LLC specification consists of three parts:

(1) Subscriber interface defines the services which the LLC layer makes available to LAN subscribers.

(2) LLC protocol specification.

(3) MAC interface defines the services which the LLC may request from the underlying MAC layer.

2.2.2 LLC services

In the ISO/OSI specifications, a service is usually specified by a triple L_S.E, where L denotes the layer of the architecture (here L = DL (data link), which means the LLC layer), S denotes the service group (for example, DATA, CONNECT, RESET, etc.) and E denotes a service element (request, confirm, indication, response). Figure 2.3 illustrates the use of a service.

LLC distinguishes between three *service types*:

(1) Type 1 refers to a datagram service (unacknowledged connectionless mode service).

(2) Type 2 refers to a connection-oriented service, for which the phases of connection establishment, data transfer and connection release are separated.

(3) Type 3 refers to a confirmed datagram service (acknowledged connectionless mode service, also called a 'request data with reply service' by the PROWAY standardization group).

There are corresponding differences between the service groups and service primitives required for each type of service (see Table 2.1). If type 1 is used, a data unit passed from layer 3 to the LLC is simply passed on to the medium, regardless of whether the receiver station is ready to receive or has accepted

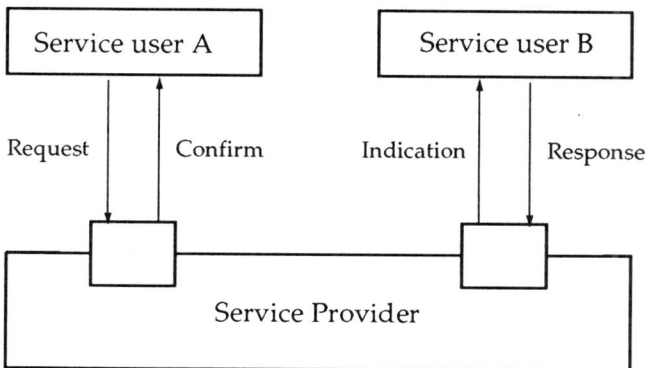

Service user A   Service user B

Request   Confirm   Indication   Response

Service Provider

Figure 2.3   Service model.

Table 2.1 LLC service groups.

Service type	Service group	Service primitive	Use
1	DL-UNITDATA	request indication	Datagram exchange
2	DL-CONNECT	request indication response confirm	Connection establishment
	DL-DATA	request indication	Data exchange
	DL-DISCONNECT	request indication	Connection release
	DL-RESET	request indication response confirm	Re-establishment
	DL-CONNECTION-FLOW-CONTROL	request indication	Flow control
3	DL-DATA-ACK	request indication	Datagram delivery
	DL-DATA-ACK-STATUS	indication	Acknowledgement signal
	DL-REPLY	request indication	Invitation to send
	DL-REPLY-STATUS	indication	Receive indication
	DL-REPLY-UPDATE	request	Advance notice of invitation to send
	DL-REPLY-UPDATE-STATUS	indication	Confirmation of advance notice

previous packets. The LLC type-1 service relies on the presence of suitable software in a higher layer, which ensures that the packets are complete, error-free and in sequence. In the LLC type-2 service, some of these tasks may be carried out in the LLC layer, since a logical link is explicitly established and a call-related status may be maintained. The LLC type-3 service may be used for simple polling of other LAN stations, or to send an acknowledgement of transmission over the network without the complexity of a connection-oriented status.

The three service types are used to define four *classes of LLC operation*. Class I provides only type-1 service, class II provides type-1 and type-2 service, class III provides type-1 and type-3 service, while class IV provides all services. The type-3 service was first specified in Addendum 2 (ISO 8802-2/DAD2, 1990).

The IEEE 802.2 standard includes the following specifications for each service primitive:

- the function in general;
- the parameter list;
- the semantics in detail;
- the time at which it is permitted to be called;
- the effect produced in the receiver;
- other details, as necessary.

Here is an example of a service primitive:

DL-UNITDATA.request(source address, destination address, data, priority)   Here, the addresses define the logical link service access points (LSAPs) as individual or group addresses, 'data' defines the data unit to be transported (data link service data unit, LSDU) and 'priority' defines a transmission priority. The status parameter (confirm, indication) which occurs in other primitives, identifies, for example, successful or unsuccessful execution of the service. In flow control, the parameter 'amount' defines the variable size of data sets permitted at the LLC interface.

2.2.3 LLC protocol

The LLC protocol is based on the bit-oriented HDLC protocol, which is used as a line procedure in X.25 level 2. The frame format is shown in Figure 2.4.

The structure of the control information in the control field and the use of the LLC frame types (layer 2b protocol elements, Table 2.2) is largely identical to HDLC, with the following exceptions:

- LLC uses only the asynchronous balanced mode and, unlike in the normal response mode, does not assume asymmetric configurations. Thus, any station may be a primary node. Connections are opened using the HDLC command, SABME, and released using DISC. Sequence numbers modulo 128 are used.

- LLC supports a datagram service through the use of the unnumbered information frame (UI).

- LLC permits multiplexing at level 2, so that several LSAPs per station are allowed. This supports, for example, the connection of terminal servers to the LAN.

y : 16, if the frame contains a sequence number, otherwise 8.

z : Natural number, the upper limit of which depends on the
MAC strategy

Destination SAP address	Source SAP address	Control field	Information
8 bits	8 bits	y bits	8 * z bits

a. LLC frame, LPDU format

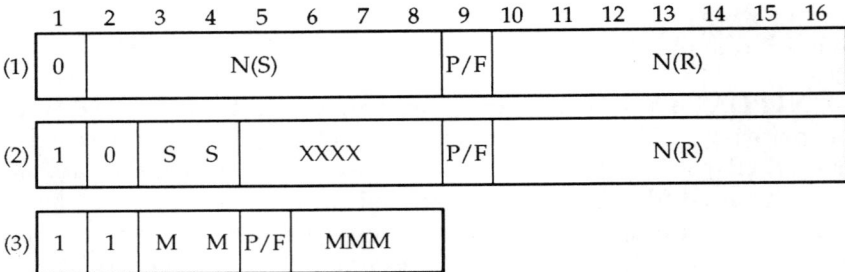

| 1 | 2 | 3 | 4 | 5 | 6 | 7 | 8 | 9 | 10 | 11 | 12 | 13 | 14 | 15 | 16 |

(1)

| 0 | N(S) | | | | | | | P/F | N(R) | | | | | | |

(2)

| 1 | 0 | S | S | XXXX | | | | P/F | N(R) | | | | | | |

(3)

| 1 | 1 | M | M | P/F | MMM | | |

N(S) = Send number
N(R) = Receive number
P/F   = Poll/Final bit
S   = Denotes supervisory function
M   = Denotes modifier function

(1) = Information frame
(2) = Supervisory frame
(3) = Unnumbered frame

b. Structure of control field

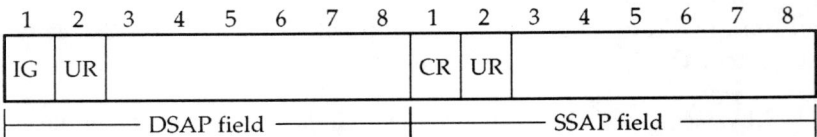

| 1 | 2 | 3 | 4 | 5 | 6 | 7 | 8 | 1 | 2 | 3 | 4 | 5 | 6 | 7 | 8 |
| IG | UR | | | | | | | CR | UR | | | | | | |

|————— DSAP field —————|————— SSAP field —————|

IG   = 0   Individual DSAP
     = 1   Group DSAP

UR   = 0   Free user address
     = 1   Address based on standard

CR   = 0   Command
     = 1   Response

c. Structure of address field

Figure 2.4   LLC frame structure.

Table 2.2 Use of the LLC frame types.

Frame type	Definition	Use
I	Information	Data transfer with sequence numbers
UI	Unnumbered information	Data transfer without sequence numbers
XID	Exchange identification	Determination of service types and window sizes of individual LSAPs
TEST	Test	Loop test on LLC links
RR	Receive ready	Ready to receive I frames; implicit acknowledgement
RNR	Receive not ready	Retarding indication for sender, implicit acknowledgement
REJ	Reject	Refusal to receive I frames, implicit acknowledgement
SABME	Set asynchronous balanced mode extended	Request to open connection with window size 128
UA	Unnumbered acknowledge response	Confirmation for SABME and DISC
DM	Disconnect mode response	Connection release indication
DISC	Disconnect	Connection release request
FRMR	Frame reject	Rejection of frame in case of error
ACn	Acknowledge sequence n	Acknowledgement with alternating sequence number $(n = 0, 1)$

- The address fields have the same length as in HDLC but are encoded differently. The first bit in the destination address field determines whether the address is an individual or a group address. The first bit in the source address field is used to distinguish between commands and responses. This is sensible since, because of the balanced mode, every station has the role of primary node and secondary node. It is also possible to determine whether standard addresses or other addresses are being used. A broadcast message is identified by setting all the destination address bits to 1.

- LLC uses a 32-bit cyclic redundancy checksum. Thus, in a transmission, the probability of residual errors in erroneous bits which are not detected as such falls to the order of 2^{-32}.

Table 2.3   Assignment of LLC frame types to LLC service types.

Operation	Commands	Responses
Type 1	UI	
	XID	XID
Type 2	I	I
	RR	RR
	RNR	RNR
	REJ	REJ
	SABME	UA
	DISC	DM
		FRMR
Type 3	AC0	AC0
	AC1	AC1

- In Addendum 1 of 802.2, LLC provides for flow control via dynamic alteration of the window size. This is intended, in particular, to support flow control in LANs coupled by bridges.

Corresponding to the forms of service at the LLC service interface, LLC supports a type-1 operation (connectionless), a type-2 operation (connection oriented) and a type-3 operation (connectionless acknowledged). Thus, all LANs support type 1. Table 2.3 shows the assignment of the LLC frame types to the LLC service operations. Here, as previously mentioned, the frame types are as defined in HDLC (Table 2.2); we shall not describe the execution of the LLC protocol in any further detail.

2.2.4 LLC/MAC interface

In order to execute its tasks, the LLC layer (2b) can only access the services of the MAC layer (2a) using the following three service primitives:

- **MA-UNITDATA.request** (source address, destination address, data, priority, service class)
- **MA-UNITDATA.indication** (destination address, source address, data, reception status, priority, service class)
- **MA-UNITDATA-STATUS.indication** (destination address, source address, transmission status, provided priority, provided service class)

In the first two, an LLC frame is transferred as a MAC service data unit from the source station to one or more destination stations. Here, the indication service elements only have a meaning local to the station.

The above service primitives of the MAC layer are identical for all underlying MAC-layer types (one such, Ethernet–CSMA/CD is of interest here). This fact is important because it forms the basis for LAN coupling over so-called MAC bridges which we discuss in detail in Section 4.2. We shall not discuss the individual parameters of the service primitives. There is naturally some dependence on the type of the MAC layer, in other words, on the access strategies used in layer 2a. We note that the interface is designed in such a way that every type of LLC data may be delivered to any type of MAC layer (and thus to any LAN type).

2.3 Medium access control (IEEE 802.3, MAC)

2.3.1 CSMA/CD access procedure

The IEEE 802.3 standard defines not only the specifications for layer 1 (physical layer, physical signalling, medium attachment), but also and in particular, the multiple access methods for accessing the shared transmission medium. In other words, it defines the MAC (medium access control) layer (layer 2a), which is a sublayer of OSI layer 2. The access method defined for Ethernet LANs is the carrier sense multiple access with collision detection (CSMA/CD) method. Amongst the possible CSMA variants, the standard specifies the 1-persistent protocol, in which when there is a free channel, transmission takes place with probability 1 (see below).

This procedure controls the channel allocation as follows:

(1) The station that wishes to send, monitors the channel (carrier sensing, listen before talking).

(2) If the channel is free, the transmission is initiated, not less than 9.6 microseconds (interframe gap) after the channel has become free.

(3) If the channel is busy, the channel is again monitored until it is free. Transmission then begins immediately.

(4) The channel is sensed during the transmission (listen while talking).

(5) If a collision is discovered, the transmission is immediately broken off and a special jam signal (see below), is sent to the channel.

(6) After the jam signal has been sent there is a waiting period (backoff, see below), after which a new attempt at the CSMA transmission is begun, starting at step (1).

This procedure is summarized in Figure 2.5.

Here are some brief comments on the above rules. Rules 1–3 greatly

```
        ┌─────────────────┐              ┌──────────────────┐
        │ Station is ready │  New attempt │ Wait according   │
        │ to send         │◄─────────────│ to backoff strategy│
        └─────────────────┘              │ (6)              │
                 │                        └──────────────────┘
                 │               Channel           ▲
                 ▼               busy              │
              ◇ Sense ◇          (3)              │
              ◇ channel ◇──────────┘              │
              ◇ (1) ◇                             │
                 │                                 │
          Channel free                             │
          (2)                                      │
                 │                                 │
        ┌─────────────────┐  Collision detected ┌──────────────┐
        │ Transmit data   │────────────────────►│ Transmit     │
        │ and sense       │                     │ jam signal   │
        │ channel         │                     │ (5)          │
        │ (4)             │                     └──────────────┘
        └─────────────────┘
                 │
          No collision
```

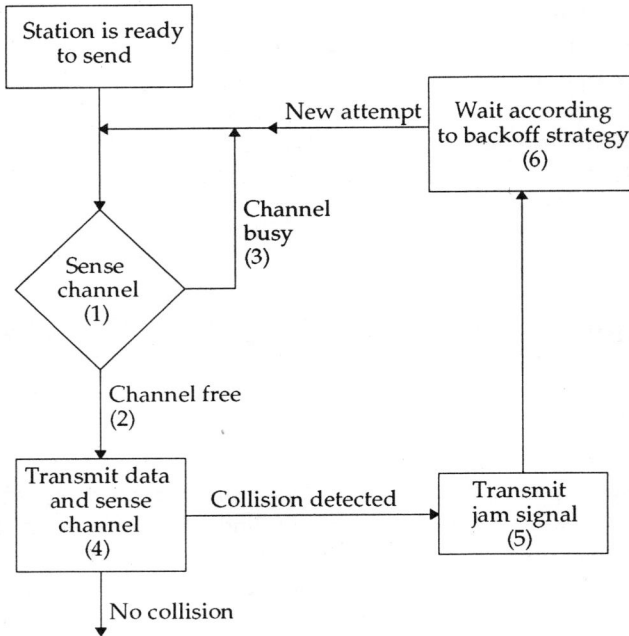

Figure 2.5   CSMA/CD access procedure.

decrease the probability of collision in comparison with transmission at arbitrary points in time for all stations. It is sensible to detect collisions when the collision parameter K (see Section 1.2.2) is less than 1; otherwise, the sender delivers the whole message to the medium before a collision is detected. CSMA avoids collisions, but does not exclude them. Collisions occur when a station i finds the medium free and begins to transmit during the period it takes a signal to propagate between stations i and j (i not equal to j) after station j has started to transmit.

The smaller the collision parameter K is, the smaller this dangerous period is and the lower the probability of collision. The collision parameter may be decreased by shortening the signal propagation time (for example, by decreasing the diameter of the network), decreasing the channel capacity or enlarging messages (increasing the frame length). Since a collision cannot be excluded, rule 4 is sensible. Without rule 5 the channel would remain unusable until the messages garbled in the collision had been transmitted in full. The amount of channel capacity wasted, particularly in the case of long messages, would be large (in comparison with the signal propagation time).

Thus, rule 5 reduces the time wasted to the time taken to detect the collision. The collision detection times may differ for different stations. In baseband systems, in the most unfavourable case the detection time is twice the maximum signal propagation time determined by the length of the medium. For a single- or dual-cable broadband bus the detection time is four times the distance from the station to the headend, unless special remodulators are installed at the headend to detect collisions. Rule 5 may be sensibly modified further:

(5′) The first station/stations to detect a collision transmits/transmit the jam signal (4–6 bytes of arbitrary data). Thus, the length of the jam signal is well below the shortest permissible Ethernet packet length of 64 bytes. As soon as the jam signal is detected, all current transmissions are aborted.

Assuming a collision parameter with a value less than 1, rules 4 and 5 distinguish the CD version of CSMA from simple CSMA procedures in which collisions are only detected when an acknowledgement is outstanding and transmission of an erroneous message is completed.

Rule 6 mentions a waiting time before a new attempt to transmit. This time is calculated according to the 'truncated binary exponential backoff procedure'. The actual delay time for the nth attempted repeat of a given message is i times the slot time where the slot time corresponds to the time taken to transmit 64 bytes. The number i is a uniformly distributed random number in the interval $0 \leq i \leq 2\exp(k)$, where $k = \min(n, 10)$. After ten failed attempts to transmit, the backoff interval is not increased any further, and after 16 failed attempts an error message is generated. Thus, the algorithm attempts to adapt to increasing network load, where new applicants for the right to send have the advantage. Since the transmission attempts of new applicants are added to the retransmission attempts, it is clear that for a high traffic load the collision overheads represent an additional load which increases the probability of collision.

2.3.2 MAC layer tasks

The following tasks fall within the MAC layer:

(1) Frame preparation on transmission (encapsulation):
- Receipt of data from the LLC layer.
- Padding of the data with PAD bits in order to exceed the minimum frame size if the data length is too small for Ethernet.
- Calculation of the cyclic redundancy check (CRC) checksum and entry of this into the frame-check-sequence (FCS) field.

   (2) Frame preparation on receipt (decapsulation):

      — Execution of the CRC check.

      — Checking of the destination addresses in the frame to see whether they agree with the service access identifiers of this station.

      — Delivery of the data to the LLC layer.

   (3) Delivery of the frame to the access management (transmitter side):

      — Delivery of the serial bit sequence (= frame) to the physical layer.

      — Delaying transmission if the channel is busy.

      — Stopping transmission if a collision is detected.

      — Calculation of the time point for a retransmission attempt.

      — Generation of a jam signal.

   (4) Receipt of a frame from the access management (receiver side):

      — Receipt of bit sequences from the physical layer.

      — Removal of sequences which are shorter than minimum frames.

The physical layer is then left with the tasks of data encoding and decoding; in other words, the conversion of the bit sequences into sequences of signals on the medium, including the synchronization of the stations, the physical carrier sensing and the collision detection.

    The mode of operation of the MAC layer is based on the cooperation of five processes:

- Frame transmitter
- Frame receiver
- Bit transmitter
- Bit receiver
- Deference

The interworking of these processes and the details of the individual processes may be read directly from Figures 2.6a to 2.6c (taken from the IEEE 802.3 standard) using the descriptions of the CSMA/CD procedure (Section 2.3.1) and the frame structure (Section 2.2.3). The exact algorithms are specified in the IEEE 802.3 standard in Pascal notation.

    In this representation, the services which the MAC layer offers the LLC layer are the transmit and receive frames. The services of the MAC layer which are made available at the interface with its underlying layer, the physical layer, are called receive bit, transmit bit and wait.

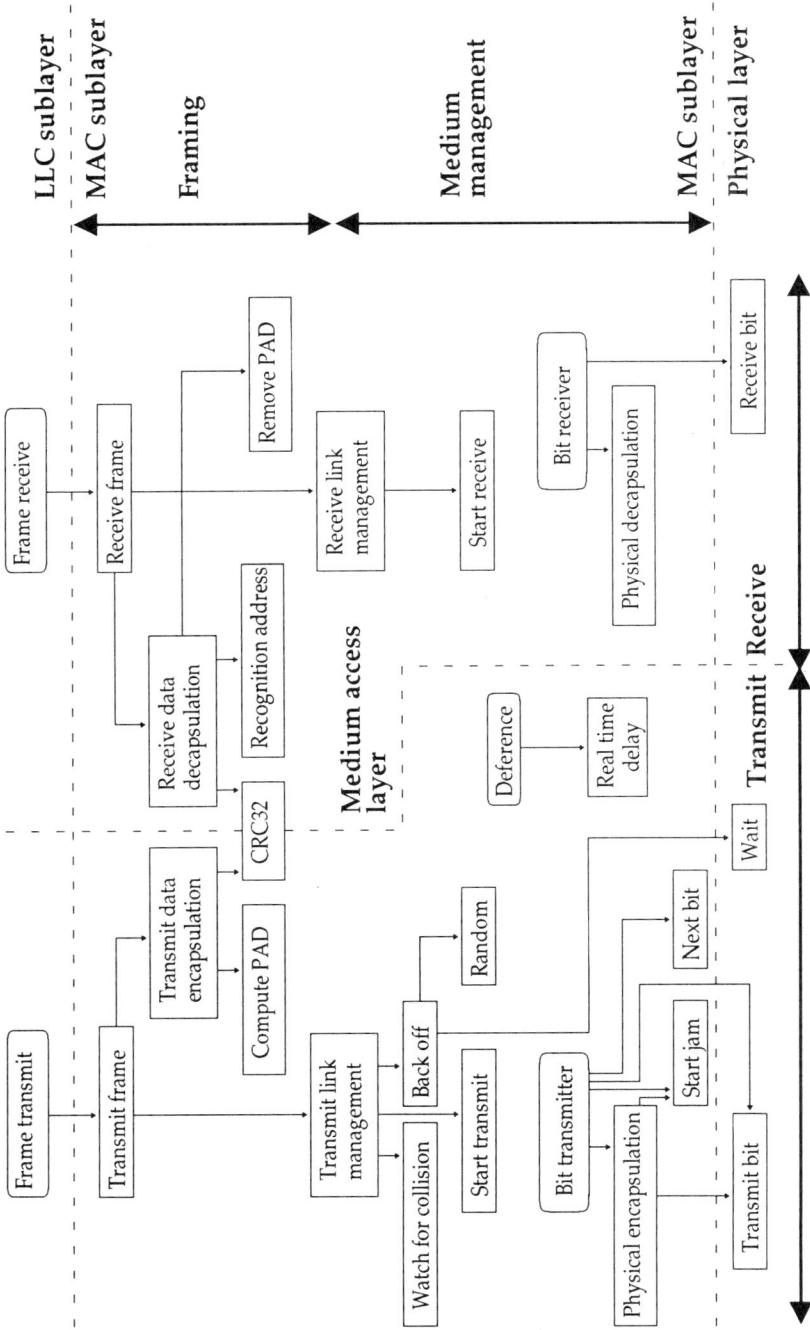

Figure 2.6a Interworking of the CSMA/CD subfunctions.

37

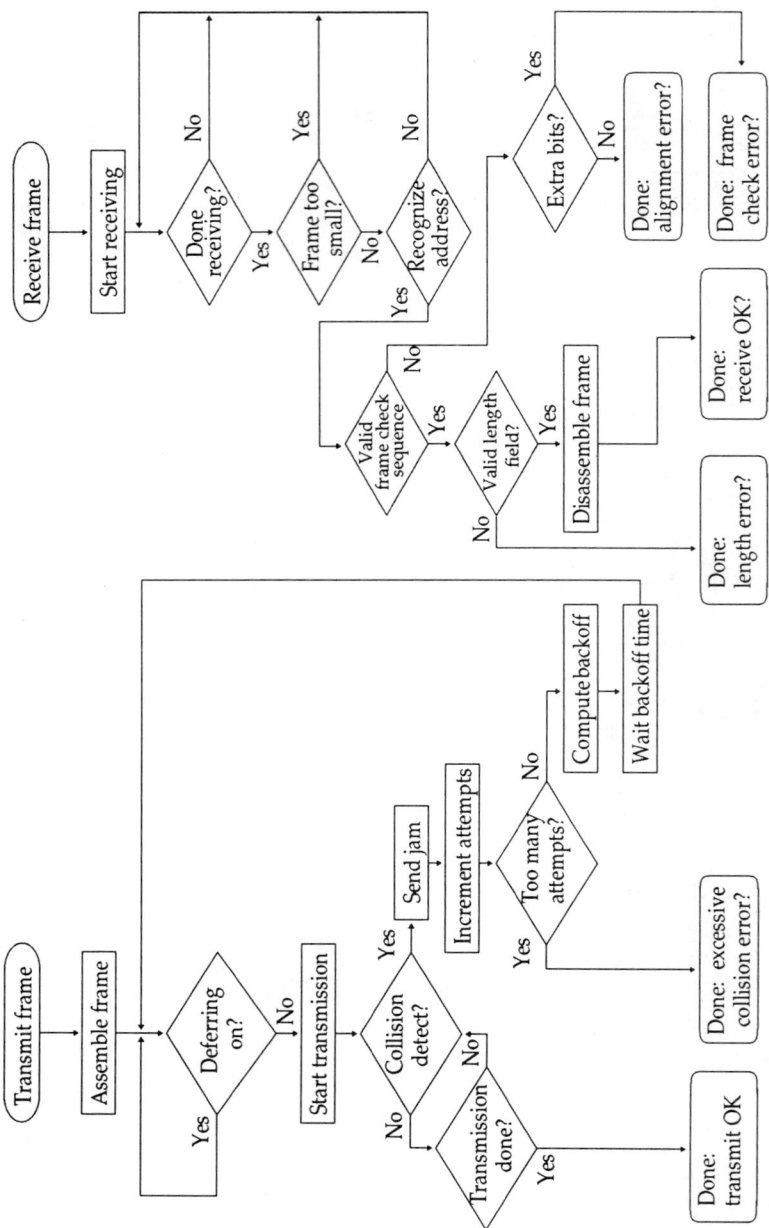

Figure 2.6b Interworking of the CSMA/CD subfunctions.

Bit receiver process

Bit transmitter process

Deferring process

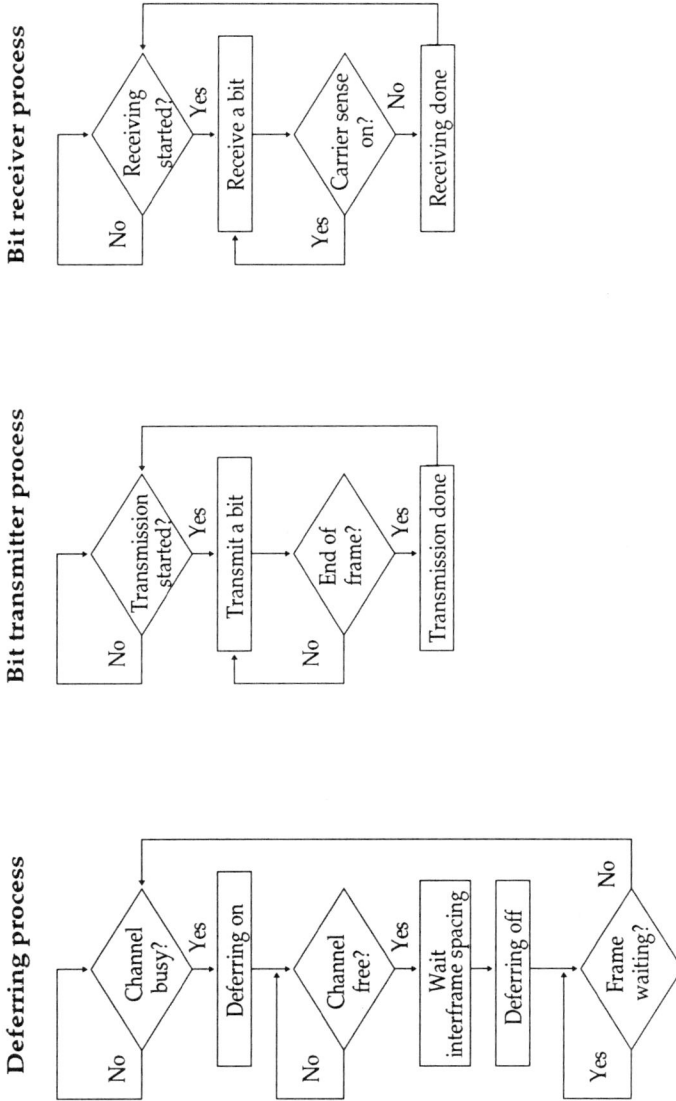

Figure 2.6c Interworking of the CSMA/CD subfunctions.

39

The slot time is a critical parameter for the CSMA/CD access procedure. This determines the collision interval, the transmission time for a minimum packet and the waiting time for retransmission attempts. In Ethernet, this corresponds to approximately twice the maximum signal propagation time, in other words around 512 bit times.

Thus, collision detection takes place in the first slot time of a MAC frame (see Section 2.3.3), possibly even during the preamble. Here too, in order to force all other stations to detect a collision, the transmission is not immediately stopped but instead the jam signal (a random 32-bit pattern) is sent to the channel.

2.3.3 MAC frame structure

The IEEE MAC CSMA/CD frame structure is shown in Figure 2.7:

(1) The receiver uses the *preamble* to achieve bit synchronization and to locate the first frame bit.

(2) *Start frame delimiter (SFD).* The bit pattern 10101011 identifies the beginning of a frame.

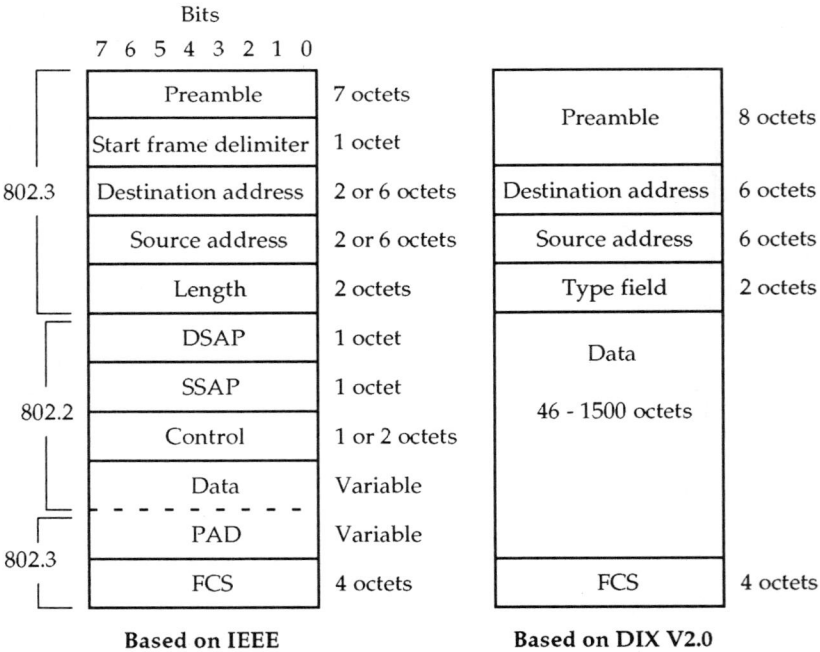

Figure 2.7 MAC frame structure.

(3) *Source address and destination address.* These are 16- or 48-bit addresses (the length is constant throughout a LAN). The first bit is used to distinguish between individual and group addresses while the second bit is used to distinguish between local and global addresses (see also Figure 2.8).

(4) The *length* defines the number of octets (eight-bit bytes) in the LLC data field.

(5) *LLC data* contains the data which is generated in the LLC layer and delivered to the MAC layer. All bit sequences are permitted. The longest permissible length of LLC data (in octets) is:

Max. frame size $-(2*$ address size $+48)/8.$

(6) *PAD* contains an arbitrary number of filler bits to achieve the minimum frame length necessary for reasonable operation of the CSMA/CD procedure (see the discussion of the collision parameter in Section 1.2.2). Thus, the number of PAD octets depends on the LLC data. If the LLC data is n octets long, the PAD length in bits is given by

$$\max(0, \text{min framesize} -(8*n+2* \text{ address size } +48)).$$

PAD is included in the checksum calculation.
The maximum frame length is implementation dependent as is the minimum frame length. The values for implementations of type 10base5 are given in Subsection 2.4.2.3.

(7) *Frame check sequence (FCS) field.* The CRC procedure based on the polynomial

$$\begin{aligned} G(x) \;=\; & x^{32} + x^{26} + x^{23} + x^{22} + x^{16} + x^{12} + x^{11} + x^{10} + x^8 + x^7 \\ & + x^5 + x^4 + x^2 + x + 1 \end{aligned}$$

is applied to the bit sequence, beginning with the address fields, up to and including the PAD field. The result of the calculation (residue after polynomial division) is entered as checkbits in the FCS field.

A frame is deemed to be invalid if:

• the frame length is inconsistent with the length entries;

• the frame length is not a multiple of 8 bits;

• the CRC indicates errors.

Invalid MAC frames are not passed to the LLC layer.
In Section 2.1, we mentioned that in addition to the Ethernet standard for Ethernet LANs there is also the DIX standard. This uses a

| Byte 1 | Byte 2 | Byte 3 | Byte 4 | Byte 5 | Byte 6 |

16-bit or 48-bit address (IEEE, receiver side)

I/G = 0   individual address
I/G = 1   group or multiple address

16-bit or 48-bit address (IEEE, transmitter side)

U/L = 0   universal address
U/L = 1   local address

Manufacturer ID   Node ID
                               (Manufacturer assigned interface no.)

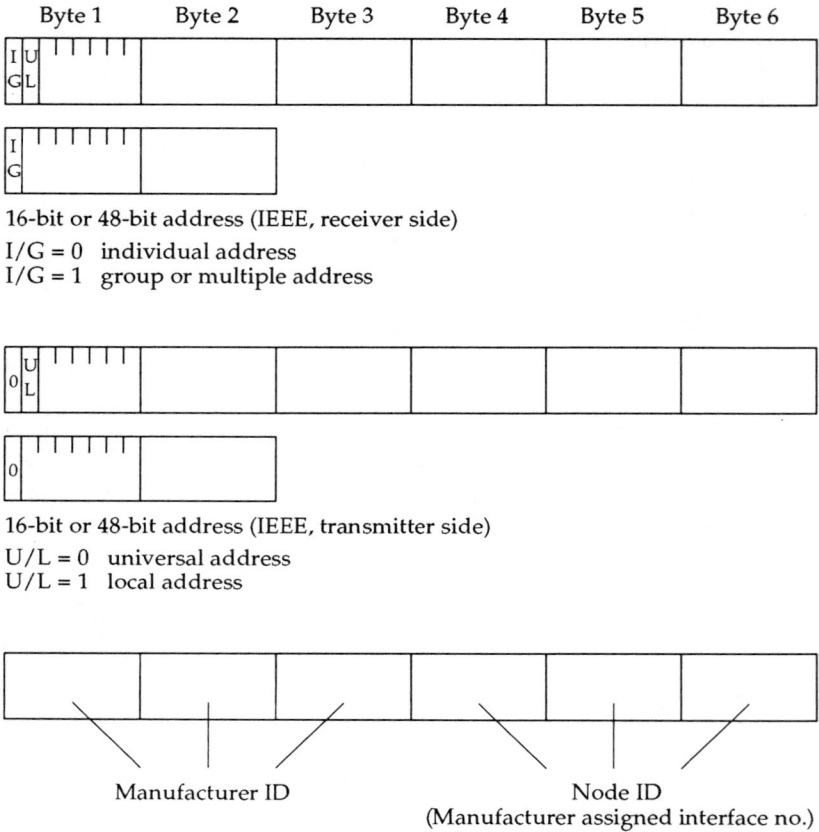

Figure 2.8   Ethernet addressing.

different MAC format (Figure 2.7). The DIX format does not support a length field and permits only one type of address field. The DIX Ethernet does not provide for a fixed LLC service interface; in other words, different user protocols could be used above layer 2a. Thus, the type field is used to determine the (higher) protocol family for which this MAC frame is intended. The encoding of the type field is coordinated by Xerox. For example, the hexadecimal code 0600 denotes the XNS protocol hierarchy while 0800 denotes the TCP/IP protocol family. This is in some ways a copy of the IEEE SAP concept. A DIX Ethernet itself only provides a single service which corresponds to the LLC type-1 operation. Thus, the specifications of the DIX Ethernet do not explicitly distinguish between layers 2a and 2b.

The address structure (see Figure 2.8) is flat, so the address bits do not provide any location information. In other words, the station address is globally unique and independent of the actual location of the station. If the global management is considered, the address assignment is oriented towards the allocation of Ethernet licences by Xerox. Thus, the first 3 bytes of the address identify the manufacturer of the Ethernet component; for example, the manufacturer 3Com is identified by 02608C (hex) while Tandem is identified by 00DD00. The remaining 3 bytes of the address identify the node. Using this scheme, it is easy to implement manufacturer-specific logical subnetworks on a single medium since, despite the multivendor environment, unique Ethernet addresses are guaranteed.

2.4 Physical layer (IEEE 802.3, PLS, AUI, MAU)

2.4.1 Overview

The medium-specific processing takes place in the OSI physical layer; in other words, the layer-1 specifications contain definitions of physical, mechanical, functional and procedural characteristics of the physical connections:

- The physical characteristics include, for example, the signal level, the signal edges, resistances and frequencies in the case of electrical transmission or wavelengths, apertures and refractive indices in the case of optical transmission.

- The mechanical characteristics include, for example, the pin layout and the geometrical arrangement of the pins in plugs together with the cable structure.

- The functional characteristics include, for example, the meaning of the pin assignment in plugs and the bit encoding.

- The procedural specifications define the execution of the layer-1 protocol and include, for example, the clock generation for synchronization and watchdog functions, carrier sensing protocols, collision detection, generation of the frame preamble, bit-stream transmission and medium tests.

For the LANs covered by the 802 standard, the physical layer (Figure 2.9) is described by a number of sublayers with corresponding interfaces.

This subdivision provides for:

- The possibility of using a common scheme to describe the various layer-1 characteristics of different implementations. As mentioned in Chapter 1, the Ethernet specifications cover a range of network types, using different media, transmission technologies and data rates but an identical MAC layer.

OSI
REFERENCE MODEL
LAYERS

LAN
CSMA/CD
LAYERS

| Application |
| Presentation |
| Session |
| Transport |
| Network |
| Data link |
| Physical |

Higher layers

| LLC Logical link control |
| MAC Medium access control |
| PLS Physical signalling |

DTE

DTE
(optional,
no AUI)

AUI

| PMA |

MAU

Medium   MDI

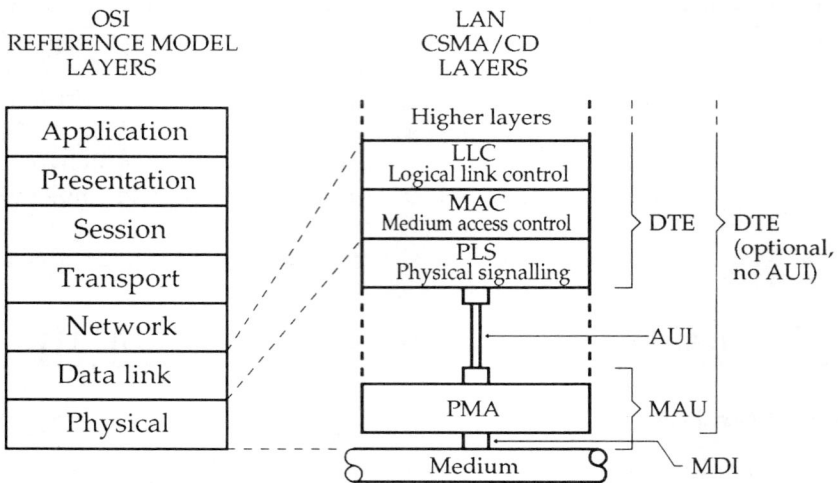

AUI = Attachment Unit Interface
MAU = Medium Attachment Unit
MDI = Medium Dependent Interface
PMA = Physical Medium Attachment

Figure 2.9   Subdivision of the physical layer.

- The creation of an implementation reference model permitting the implementation of LAN direct access in a modular fashion via various hardware components, which may be produced by different manufacturers since their interworking is guaranteed by the interface definitions.

The following decomposition is provided for by IEEE 802.3:

Physical signalling sublayer, PLS   This is the part of the physical layer which is located in the data terminal equipment (DTE) and is responsible for the logical and functional coupling of the MAC layer of the DTE to a (possibly separate) medium attachment unit (MAU).
PLS has five service primitives:

- PLS-DATA.request
- PLS-DATA.confirm
- PLS-DATA.indication
- PLS-CARRIER.indication
- PLS-SIGNAL.indication

The first three are used for peer-to-peer communication, in other words, for the traffic between stations. The last two have a local meaning and are used for interface communication within a station. PLS-CARRIER forwards the activity status of the medium from the PLS to the MAC layer. PLS-SIGNAL informs the MAC of the PLS physical signal quality.

Attachment unit interface, AUI   If the DTE and the MAU of a station have a modular structure (in other words, are standalone components), the AUI must be used to guarantee interworking. The AUI consists of the circuit logic, the connection cables and the connector units which are needed to connect the MAU and the PLS. Whilst the AUI is naturally specific to each LAN type, it has the following characteristic properties:

- The AUI must support one or more specific data rates.
- It must be operable with connection cables of length up to 50 m.
- The AUI must support a DTE test of the AUI itself, the AUI cable, the MAU and the Ethernet medium.
- It must be possible to connect MAUs based on different transmission technologies.

Medium attachment unit, MAU   The MAU is the coupling module between the LAN DTE and the LAN medium. The AUI is the interface in the DTE direction; in the LAN direction, the medium-dependent interface (MDI) is used. In normal Ethernet implementations most of the AUI and MAU logic is contained on DTE–Ethernet interface cards. The MAU contains the electronics for transmitting and receiving the encoded physical signals which are superimposed on or filtered out from the LAN medium.

Physical medium attachment, PMA   This is the part of the MAU which contains the functional circuit logic of the MAU.

Medium-dependent interface, MDI   This is the physical (electrical, optical) and mechanical interface between the Ethernet medium and the MAU. The Ethernet medium is sometimes also called the *trunk cable*, in contrast to the station connection cable which is called the *branch cable* or *drop cable*.

Other specifications of the physical layer relate to:

Repeaters   Repeaters are amplifier units which regenerate the signal course, signal level and timing. Repeaters may be used to weaken or remove restrictions on length, topology or interconnectability arising from the segment-related specifications for the physical medium.

The following subsections contain information about the most important physical-layer specifications for the individual Ethernet network types. These are:

- *10base5*. Ethernet with thick coaxial cable. Baseband.

- *10base2*. Ethernet with thin coaxial cable. Baseband.

- *10baseT*. Ethernet with twisted-pair cable. Baseband.

- *1base5*. Ethernet with twisted-pair cable. Baseband.

- *10broad36*. Ethernet with TV cable. Broadband.

- *10baseF*. Ethernet with fibre optic cable.

In this section, we shall only consider the standard specifications. Later chapters discuss the most important component properties, product structures, installation-related hints and operational experiences relating to the practical use of networks.

2.4.2 Standard Ethernet, IEEE 802.3 type 10base5

2.4.2.1 AUI

The main components of 10base5 are shown in Figure 2.10. This network type represents the original Ethernet (standard Ethernet). Figure 2.11 shows a typical 10base5 configuration.

As mentioned in Section 2.4.1, the specification of the AUI provides for a physical separation between the transceiver component (MAU) and

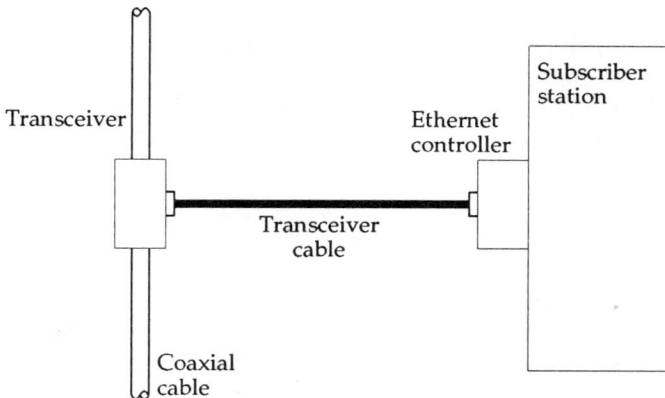

Figure 2.10   Main components of an Ethernet connection.

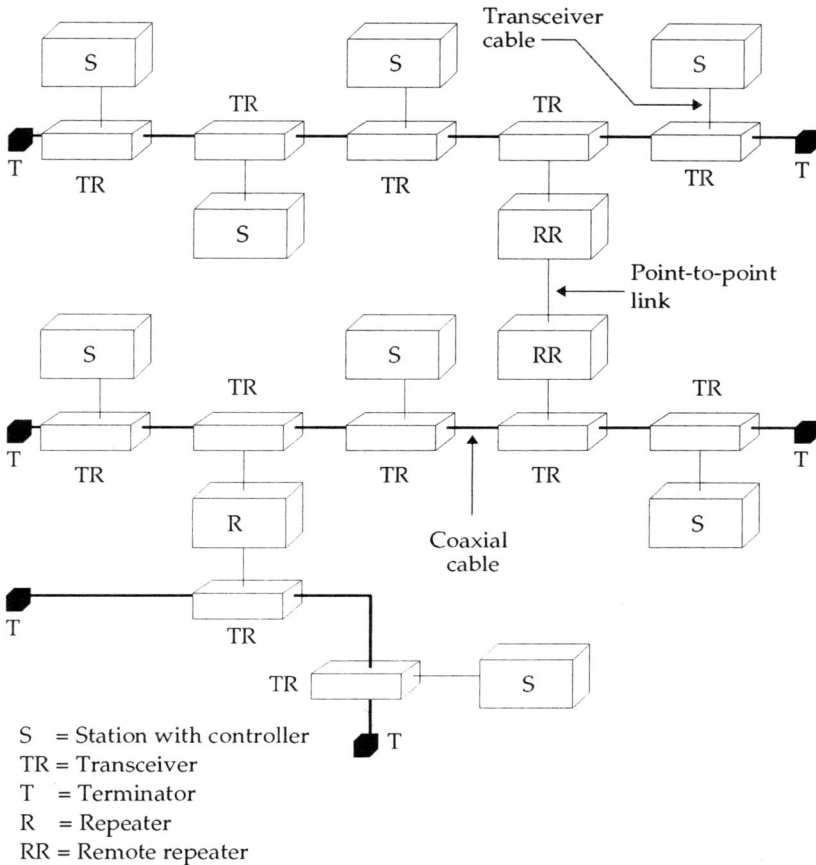

Figure 2.11   Typical 10base5 configuration.

the Ethernet controller (PLS/MAC in the subscriber station). The AUI represents an abstraction from the physical properties of the medium and the transmission technology which makes a common interface available to the controller. The interface is structured so that:

- Up to four data rates may be supported, namely 1, 5, 10 and 20 Mbps.

- Connection cables up to 50 m in length may be used. The physical separability of the transceiver and controller provides for a greater degree of flexibility as far as the arrangement of the Ethernet stations is concerned, since the transceiver may only be a few centimetres distant from the Ethernet cable. This often occurs in installation channels which are hard to access.

- The station (DTE) is able to test the AUI, the drop cable and the MAU (transceiver) in an operational 'monitor mode'. Thus, interference which occurs in these parts can be distinguished from signal interference (for example, collisions) on the Ethernet medium.

- Transceivers for various media are supported.

On the station side, the sublayer driving the AUI is the PLS (physical signalling) as described in Section 2.4.1. PLS only communicates with the MAC sublayer of its own station (local MAC) using the service primitives PLS-CARRIER.indication and PLS-SIGNAL.indication; in this way the MAC sublayer receives the information needed for executing the CSMA/CD mechanism. If the MAC layer wishes to send a CSMA/CD frame (cf. Section 2.3.3) to the MAC layer of another station, it uses the service primitive PLS-DATA.x to inform the MAC layers of all Ethernet-LAN stations.

The AUI consists of data- and signal-line pairs. The cable ends of the 78 Ω interface cable consist of 15-pin connectors, with pin assignment as shown in Figure 2.12, where the jack is on the transceiver side.

The Manchester encoding procedure is used to encode the signals on the data lines. This encoding guarantees a transition (jump in the signal voltage level) in the middle of each bit (Figure 2.13); the bit time is 100 ns. The Manchester code is a so-called 'self-clocking code'.

The synchronization and the implicit transmission of the transmitter bit timing are provided for by transmission of each bit in inverted form in

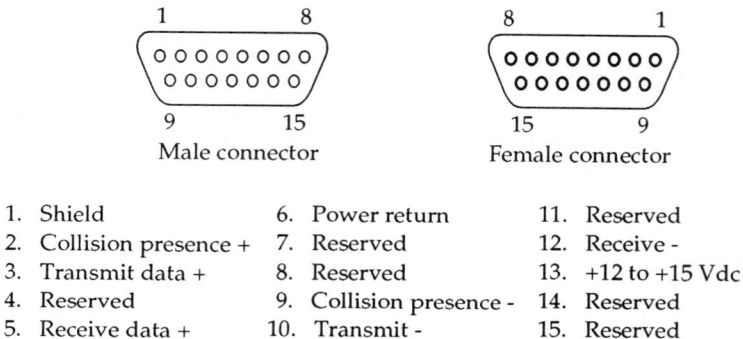

1. Shield
2. Collision presence +
3. Transmit data +
4. Reserved
5. Receive data +
6. Power return
7. Reserved
8. Reserved
9. Collision presence -
10. Transmit -
11. Reserved
12. Receive -
13. +12 to +15 Vdc
14. Reserved
15. Reserved

Figure 2.12   Transceiver-cable pin assignment (Ethernet V2.0).

High = "1" =   0 mA = 0 V
Low = "0" = -82 mA = -2.05 V

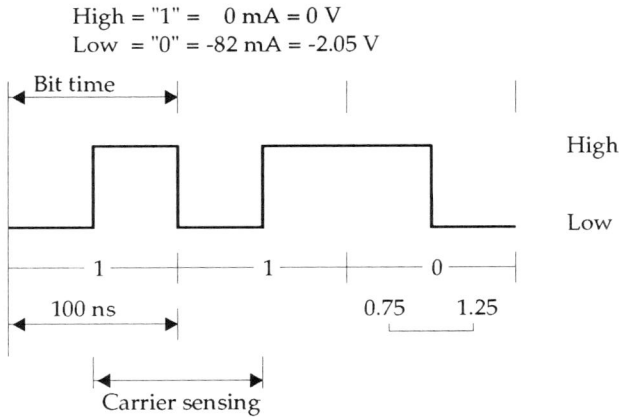

Figure 2.13   Manchester encoding.

the first half of the bit-transmission time. Thus, the bit rate corresponds to half the baud rate. A bit time of 100 ns gives a data rate of 10 Mbps. The presence of the carrier, in other words of activity on the cable, is indicated by the presence of jumps in the signal voltage level. If no new jump in the signal voltage level occurs in the interval corresponding from 0.75 to 1.25 bit times, the carrier is absent.

PLS has to convert the AUI signals into PLS service primitives. The corresponding PLS function modules here are: input, output, operational mode, error monitoring, collision monitoring and, of course, an initialization part.

The protocol between the PLS and PMA sublayers (in other words, between the DTE (controller) and MAU (transceiver) components) is very simple. It contains interface data units for input and output, idle indication, error and collision indication (signal quality error) and for switching to monitor mode (used for test purposes, see above). We shall not describe the encoding of these AUI signals here. The AUI frame structure is shown in Table 2.4.

The transceiver cable consists of five separately shielded twisted conductors. As outlined above, two of these carry data and two carry control information; the fifth provides the supply voltage for the PMA electronics. The control line is also bi-phase encoded, thus self-clocking. The control line to the coaxial cable is optional. It is only used to check the signal quality and so may be utilized for collision detection. Good signal quality is represented by the idle signal on the AUI control line. The idle signal on data lines is used, for example, to detect the end of a frame.

Table 2.4 AUI frame structure.

(silence)(preamble)(sfd) (dat)(etd)(silence)	Means
(silence):	Idle state Min. duration = interframe gap
(preamble):	A sequence of alternating 1s and 0s which is at least 56 bits long and ends with 0. Used to synchronize the receiver.
(start-of-frame delimiter)	Bit sequence 10101011
(data)	A number of octets containing the CSMA/CD–MAC frame
(end-of-transmission delimiter)	The IDLE signal with which the transmitter turns the transceiver off. Minimum signal duration = twice bit time, no transition.

2.4.2.2 MAU and Ethernet cable (10base5)

The MAU consists of the transceiver and its connection to the Ethernet cable.

The transceiver contains the transmit and receive logic, is responsible for monitoring the cable occupancy and for collision detection, and has certain test facilities.

The transceiver must meet certain very strong implementation rules. Thus, the coaxial driver must have controlled signal ramp and fall times of 25 ± 5 ns with only 1 ns deviation and no more than 2 ns drift, while the coupling impedance on the 50 Ω Ethernet coax cable should be no greater than 4 pF. High requirements are also imposed on the driver current, noise filtering, dielectric strength and collision detection. The tasks of the transceiver as a protocol entity are largely outlined by the description of the AUI. The basic architecture of a transceiver is shown in Figure 2.14 (Crane and Taft, 1980).

A transceiver may be attached to the LAN medium Ethernet cable in two ways:

Standard N connectors Here, the Ethernet coaxial cable at the interface point is cut in two and the two ends and the transceiver contacts are linked together via a coaxial cable coupling (screw connections).

TAP connectors This method of connection does not require interruption of the LAN operation. In TAP connection (TAP = terminal access point) (see Figure 2.15, after ECMA) a pointed probe is pressed into

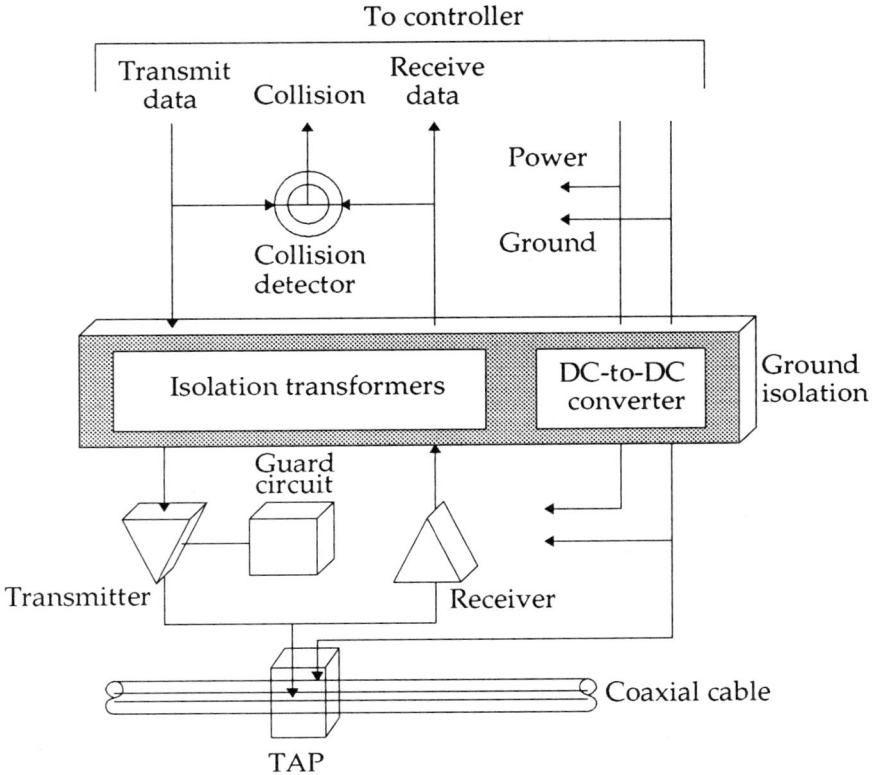

Figure 2.14   Ethernet transceiver.

the inner conductor of the coaxial cable (Figure 2.16) while at the same time contact with the outer conductor is established via a clamp. The probe and the clamp are linked to the transceiver.

The basic structure of the Ethernet coaxial cable is shown in Figure 2.16. The copper inner conductor has a diameter of 2.17 mm, then follow the dielectric and shielding layers (with a diameter between 6.15 and 8.28 mm) and a plastic outer jacket (teflon, FEP, PVC) which satisfies the corresponding fire-retardation regulations. Overall, the 9.525-to-10.287 mm thick, yellow Ethernet cable with markings every 2.5 m should permit a bending radius of 25 cm when laid.

Other characteristics of the cable include its impedance of 50 ± 2 Ω. Correspondingly, every segment must be terminated with a 50 Ω terminator. On cable segments longer than 500 m, the attenuation should not

Button head
socket screw
(secure with
hex wrench)

Clamp
assembly

Probe
assembly

Application tool
(socket wrench end)

Pressure
block

Cable
channel

Braid
terminator

Tap
body

Nut

PC board

Attach PC board
with suitable
hardware

Probe
assembly

Screw

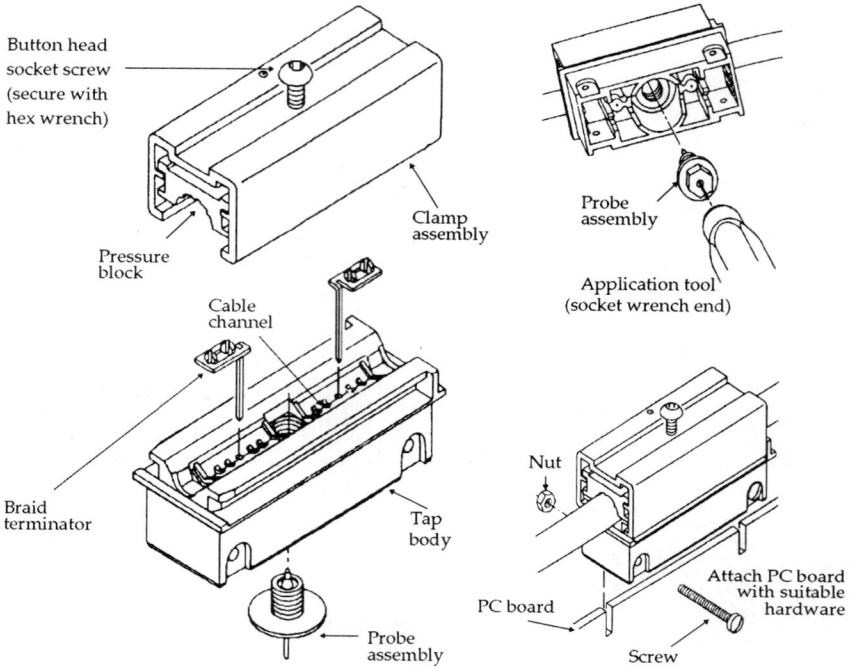

Figure 2.15 TAP connection.

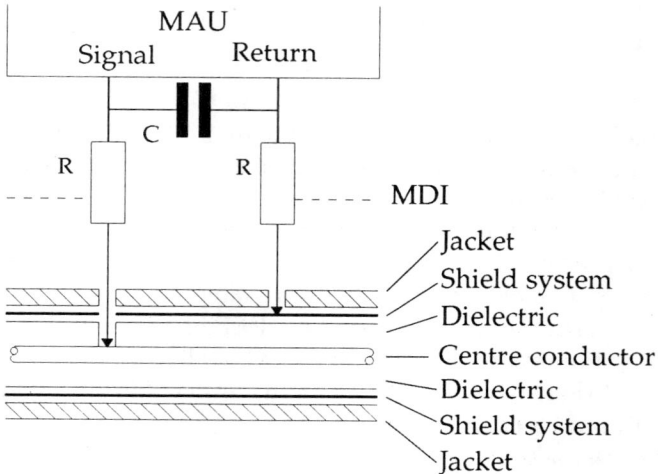

MAU

Signal   Return

C

R   R

MDI

Jacket
Shield system
Dielectric
Centre conductor
Dielectric
Shield system
Jacket

Figure 2.16 Ethernet coaxial cable structure and TAP connection.

exceed 8.5 (6.0) dB at 10 (5) MHz. The signal propagation speed should be at least 0.77 c. For other specifications, we refer readers to the standard.

The driver requirements for transceivers and cable are such that coaxial cable segments of up to 500 m long may be operated without repeaters. However, for the distances of, for example, larger Ethernet LANs, repeaters are needed. We shall discuss this in more detail in Section 2.4.5.

Repeaters are amplifiers operating in the physical layer which regenerate the signal course, level and timing; they may be used to link LAN segments.

2.4.2.3 Characteristic parameters of Ethernet LANs of type 10base5

Various Ethernet LANs may be configured using the components, interfaces and protocols described in the previous paragraphs. Regardless of special configuration structures, the Ethernet standard implicitly defines system characteristic quantities which are mandatory for all Ethernet LANs of type 10base5 and which determine maximum configurations:

(1)   A coaxial cable segment cannot be longer than 500 m and must have a 50 Ω/1 W terminating resistor. At most 100 MAUs may be installed with a minimum separation of 2.5 m. The signal propagation speed is at least 0.77 c and the propagation delay is at most 2165 ns.

(2)   The maximum transceiver cable length (AUI cable) is 50 m. The minimum signal speed is 0.65 c and the maximum propagation delay is 257 ns.

(3)   Repeaters (local or remote repeaters, see Section 2.4.5) may be used to combine segments together into a multisegment LAN, representing a single area for collisions. To keep the network collision parameter small, the formation of multisegment LANs is subject to other rules, which we describe below. A maximum route between two stations, beginning with the corresponding AUI on the Ethernet LAN, involves five segments and four repeaters (including remote repeaters). Of the five segments, up to three are coax segments, the others may be link segments or links between remote repeater 'halves'. Thus, the maximum distance between two stations is 2500 m while the minimum distance is 2.5 m.

(4)   The link segment (point-to-point link) of a remote repeater should have an end-to-end delay time of less than 2570 ns. Repeaters may be connected anywhere to an Ethernet cable segment; they count as MAUs as per (1). The standard provides for a maximum link length of 1000 m.

(5)   As far as the collision parameter K, introduced in Section 1.2.2, is concerned, the parameter specifications of this and the previous

paragraphs lead to the worst case value of around 0.21, if we assume the largest permissible network length and the smallest permissible packet length. Thus, a very good value for K is achieved.

(6) The MAC parameters are listed in Table 2.5.

Figure 2.17 shows examples of possible Ethernet LAN configurations. Other configurations will be discussed in later chapters. In particular, we shall show that 10base5 may be combined with other Ethernet network types and that larger maximum distances between two Ethernet stations may be achieved using LAN coupling components.

In Section 2.1 we mentioned that there are currently three Ethernet specifications, namely V1.0, V2.0 and 802.3, where V1.0 is only listed for historical completeness. While systems based on these three specifications may coexist on the same cable, it is impossible to achieve data exchange between systems based on the DIX specifications and those based on the IEEE specifications. The Ethernet specifications V1.0 and V2.0 are upwards compatible. It is important to be aware of this point when acquiring network components, and also when 'mixing' components. Table 2.6 gives a comparative overview. There is also a difference in the frame format as described in Section 2.3.3.

We note that there are a number of products which, according to the product information meet the 802.3 specification, but which in fact obey the DIX rules.

Table 2.5 MAC parameters.

Parameter	Value
Slot time	512 bit times
Interframe gap	9.6 μs (minimum)
Attempt limit	16
Backoff limit	10
Jam size	32 bits
Max. frame size	1518 octets
Min. frame size	64 octets (512 bits corresponds to 51.2 μs)
Address size	48 bits

Table 2.6   Comparison of 802.3 and DIX.

Subject	802.3	DIX V2.0	DIX V1.0
Preamble, bit times	56	64	
Preamble bits consumed by DTE, max.	18	16	16
Carrier sense inhibit function:			–
Minimum time to clear the carrier sense signal after loss of carrier presence (receive and collisions), bit times	–	1.6	–
Carrier inhibited period, μs	4–8	4–9.6	–
Data rates supported, Mbps	1–10	10	
Transceiver cable driver:			
AC signal levels, mV	450 min. – 1315 max.	550 min. 700 nom. 1200 max.	– – –
Idle (IDL) levels, mV	0 ±40	0	700
Time for returning to IDL state following last positive-going transition of the frame	200 ns – 8 μs	300 ns – 2 μ s	–
Voltage presented to the transceiver cable by the driver during return to IDL time	100 mV differential		–
Jabber control	Auto reset by absence of transmit signal 0.5 sec ±50%	No auto reset. Must be ready to transmit within 100 ms of fault determination	
Input bias current	+2 – −25 μA	–	50 mA
Collision (SQE) to jam delay of repeater, bit times	6.5	–	–
Propagation delay through repeaters, bit times	7.5	6	8
Worst case round trip signal propagation delay, bit times	499	464	465

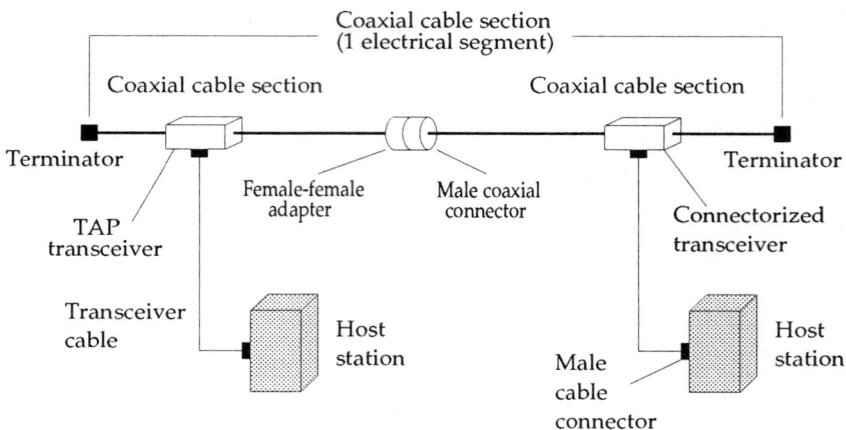

a. Minimum configuration

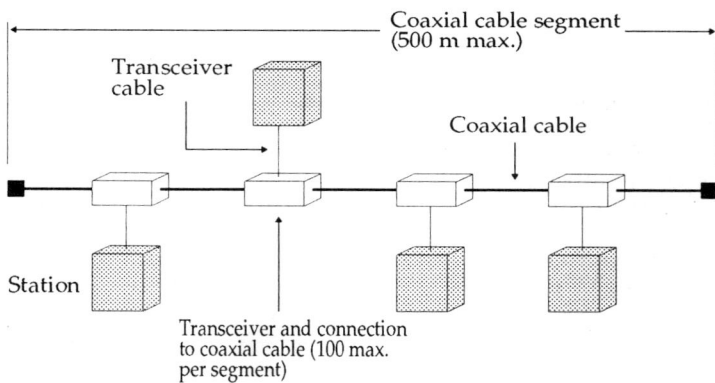

b. Small configuration

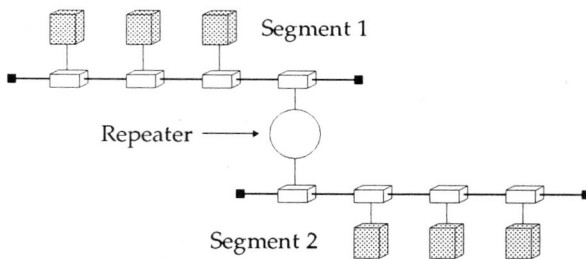

c. Medium configuration

Figure 2.17 Possible Ethernet LAN configurations.

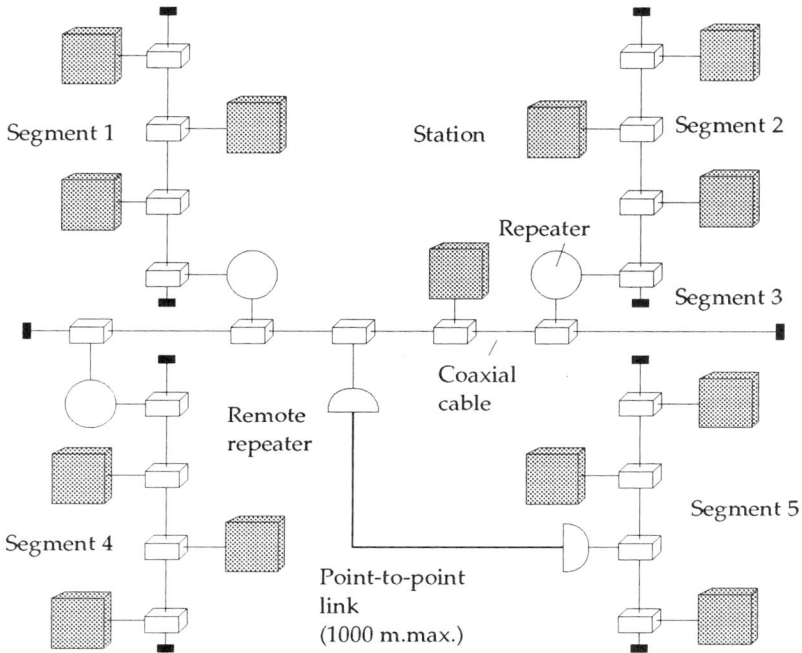

d. Large configuration

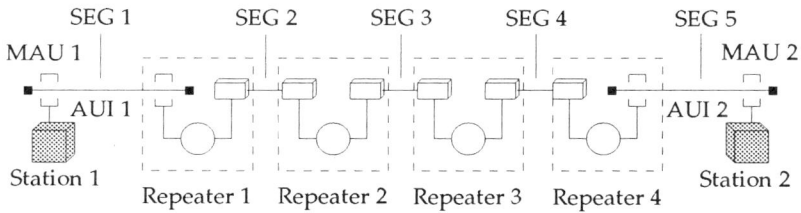

e. Maximum configuration

Figure 2.17 *(continued)*.

2.4.3 Cheapernet, IEEE 802.3 type 10base2

The Ethernet network type 10base2 represents a less expensive CSMA/CD 10 Mbps LAN with a smaller maximum coverage. It is suitable for local area networks which are limited to a single storey, several rooms, etc. It can, of course, be linked to the standard Ethernet. According to the architectural principles given in Section 2.4.1, we only need to describe the MAU and

RG 58A/U cable, segment length $\leqslant 185$ m

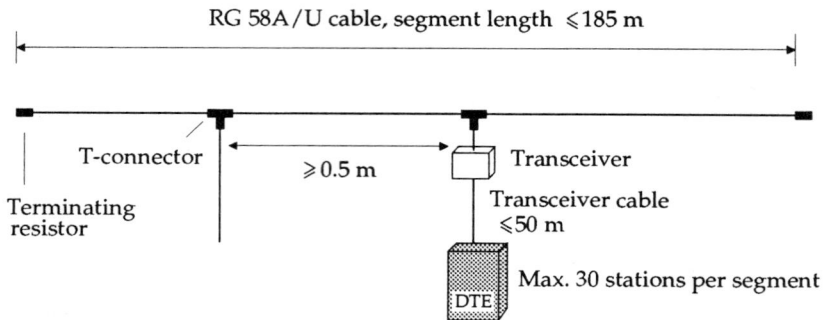

Figure 2.18 Cheapernet configuration.

the medium of this Ethernet network type (known as Cheapernet). The 10base2 MAU has the following characteristics:

(1) The PLS sublayer, as described in Section 2.4.1, may be directly coupled to the Cheapernet MAU.

(2) A 10 Mbps data rate is supported in the baseband transmission technology. A linear bus topology is supported.

(3) It cannot operate cable segments longer than 185 m without repeaters. The industry-standard RG58 A/U or RG58 C/U (Thin Ethernet) coaxial cables are used with standard BNC connectors.

(4) It supports the CSMA/CD procedure described in Section 2.3.

(5) It supports the operational 'monitor mode'.

(6) It is generally implemented within the subscriber-station (DTE) casing so that there is no equivalent to the transceiver cable of 10base5 LANs. Thus, the transceiver is no longer implemented externally on the cable but on the DTE Ethernet controller card. The card also contains a T connector or a BNC jack for connection to thin coaxial cable.

(7) Repeaters with a functionality similar to the 10base5 repeaters are permissible. Repeaters are not DTEs in the Cheapernet sense.

(8) The bit error rate should be less than 10^{-7} in the physical layer and less than 10^{-8} in the data link layer.

Since Cheapernet only differs from the standard Ethernet (type 10base5) in the physical layer, and is thus protocol compatible in the other LAN layers and uses the same data rate, a normal Ethernet segment may be linked to a Cheapernet using a suitable repeater.

The existing 802.3a standard of 1988 for the 10base2 Ethernet type includes a detailed specification of:

- the MAU functions (transmit, receive, collision presence, jabber);
- the encoding of the signals at the MAU/DTE interface;
- the electrical and mechanical characteristics of the cable, including the connectors.

Here are some examples of these specifications:

- The coupling impedance on the coaxial cable should not be greater than 8 pF, the line resistance should be greater than 7.5 Ω in the range 0–4 V.
- Signal ramp and fall times of 25 ± 5 ns are specified at 10 Mbps.
- The current drawn by a MAU should be less than 0.5 A.
- Coaxial cable impedance: 50 ± 2 Ω; attenuation on a 185 m segment less than 8.5 (6.0) dB for 10 (5) MHz; signal speed 0.65 c; maximum segment signal propagation time 950 ns.
- 'Thin wire' cable structure: braided inner conductor of tinned copper with diameter 0.89 ± 0.05 mm, dielectric, shielding beginning with a diameter of 2.95 ± 0.15 mm of tinned copper, PVC or fluorpolymer outer jacket with external radius 4.9 or 4.8 mm (respectively). The cable should be marked in metre lengths. The smallest permissible cable-laying radius is 5 cm.
- A cable segment may have at most 30 MAUs (or 29 MAUs and a repeater). The minimum permissible distance between MAUs is 0.5 m.
- A maximal communications route between two DTEs/MAUs is limited to five segments and four repeaters. These five segments may include at most three coaxial cable segments, the other segments may be link segments with remote repeaters. Using repeaters, a pure Cheapernet may have a total length of up to 925 m (see also Section 2.4.5).
- Hybrid combinations of Ethernet LAN segments of type 10base2 (Cheapernet) and segments of type 10base5 (standard Ethernet) may be formed (see Figure 2.19, IEEE). In this case, Cheapernet segments should not be connected to more than one standard Ethernet segment; Cheapernet segments should be used as peripheral segments in the hybrid network and the standard Ethernet should at the same time be configured as a backbone network.

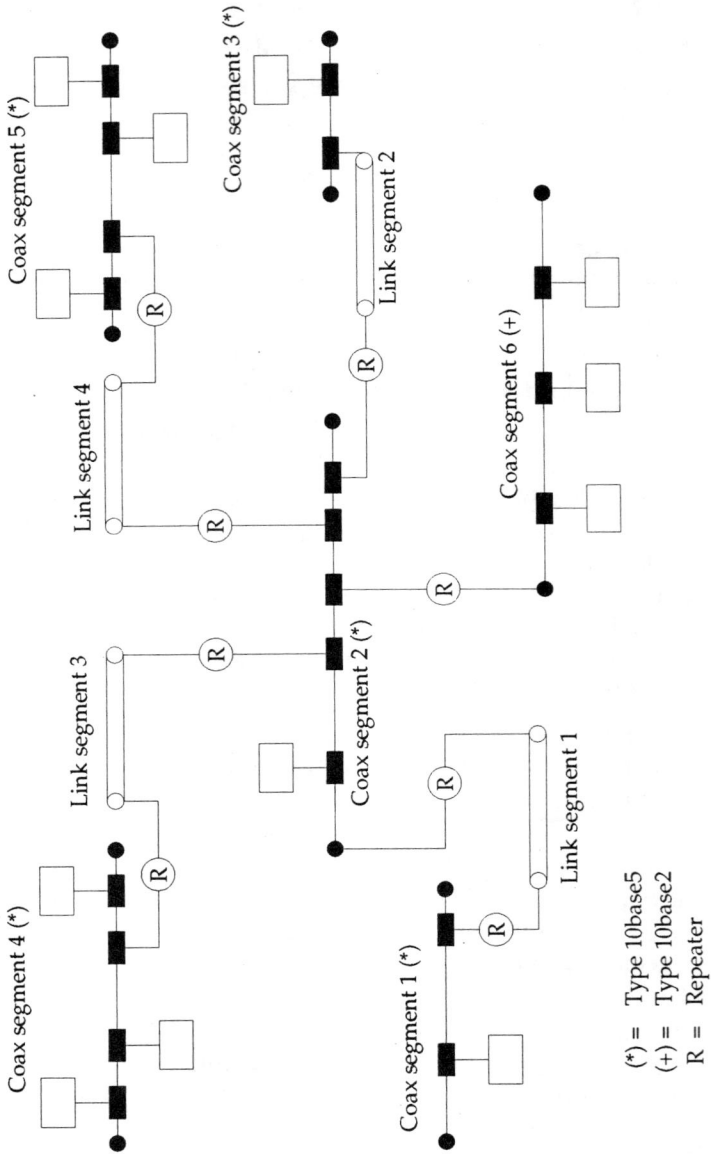

Coax segment 5 (*)

Coax segment 3 (*)

Link segment 2

Link segment 4

Coax segment 6 (+)

Link segment 3

Coax segment 4 (*)

Coax segment 2 (*)

Coax segment 1 (*)

Link segment 1

(*) = Type 10base5
(+) = Type 10base2
R = Repeater

Figure 2.19 Example of a hybrid configuration.

2.4.4 Twisted-pair LAN, IEEE 802.3, type 10baseT

Twisted-pair conductors are an inexpensive and widely used transmission medium, which has been in use for a long time in the form of telephone cable and, for example, V.24 data cable. Thus, it is appropriate to investigate whether this cable, which is installed almost everywhere, can be used as the basis for local area networks with higher data rates. At a very early stage, Synoptics marketed a product which implemented an Ethernet on unshielded twisted-pair conductors.

As of October 1990, the IEEE 802.3 standard for Ethernet networks of type 10baseT specified a 10 Mbps CSMA/CD LAN with unshielded twisted-pair (UTP) conductors.

Unlike the two Ethernet coaxial networks which are based on a bus topology, UTP forms a point-to-point cable scheme and, overall, the 10baseT LAN which is based on this represents a star topology. The cable length between the Ethernet controller and the so-called *repeater hub* (a cable concentrator, see below) may be up to 100 m. In this network type, as in 10base2, the transceiver may be implemented directly on the controller card. Unlike in 10base2, in the twisted-pair LAN the network stations are not concatenated on the same medium; here, every participating station is individually connected directly to the repeater unit hub (Figure 2.20). We note that the hub is the point where the access problem occurs in 10baseT; in other words, where the CSMA/CD procedure comes into effect. There is no competition for the DTE–hub link since this involves a dedicated point-to-point connection. There is competition for a source–hub–sink link, where for all source–sink connections the hub is the same shared resource, which also guarantees the broadcast properties of an Ethernet. This explains the position of the AUI in Figure 2.21a. If several DTEs transmit simultaneously to the hub, the hub generates a collision signal which is transmitted to all attached DTEs; the latter then move to the 'collision present' state.

A 10baseT Ethernet with its star topology is in some ways easier to manage than a bus Ethernet. A fault on the link cable between DTE and hub (repeater) only affects this DTE, while a bus fault affects all LAN stations. This occurs because the standard for 10baseT contains a so-called 'link integrity test' which is implemented in the repeater module. The latter transmits test signals to the Ethernet controller of the station in order to check the link. If there is a fault, this station is logically removed from the 10baseT network. The monitor then continues to test the link periodically until it is operational again, so that the logically-deactivated station may then be reattached to the remaining network. These monitor actions are executed without operator intervention.

Figure 2.21a illustrates the layer-1 specifications for the twisted-pair LAN.

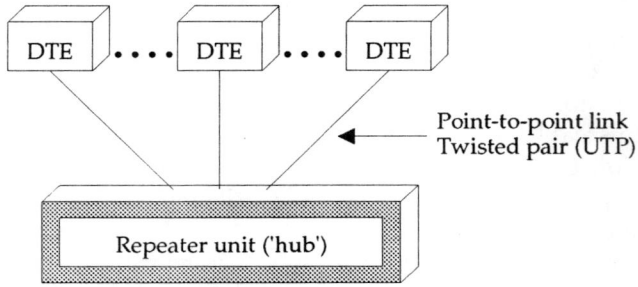

a. Star topology

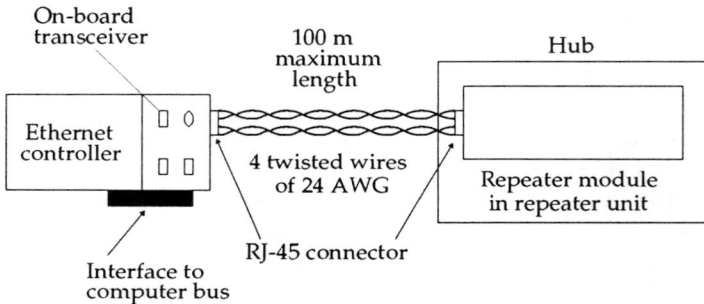

b. Implementation of point-to-point link

Figure 2.20   Ethernet 10baseT configuration.

The MAU has the following properties:

- It provides for a connection of the DTE PLS sublayer to a baseband UTP link.
- It supports a transmission rate of 10 Mbps on the UTP over a distance up to at least 100 m without repeaters.
- It supports test functions on the DTE or the repeater side.
- It supports point-to-point links between MAUs or, if multiport repeaters are used, star topologies.
- It is generally implemented on a built-in card for the DTE or the repeater.
- The bit-error rate at the PLS interface should be at most 10^{-8}.

OSI REFERENCE MODEL

ISO/IEC 8802-3 CSMA/CD LAN LAYERS

OSI REFERENCE MODEL
Application
Presentation
Session
Transport
Network
Data Link
Physical

Higher Layers

Logical Link Control (LLC)

Medium Access Control (MAC)

Physical Signalling (PLS)

Physical Signalling (PLS)

DTE

DTE

AUI

DTE (AUI not exposed)

AUI

MAU   PMA   MDI

PMA   MDI   MAU

Medium

Twisted-pair link segment

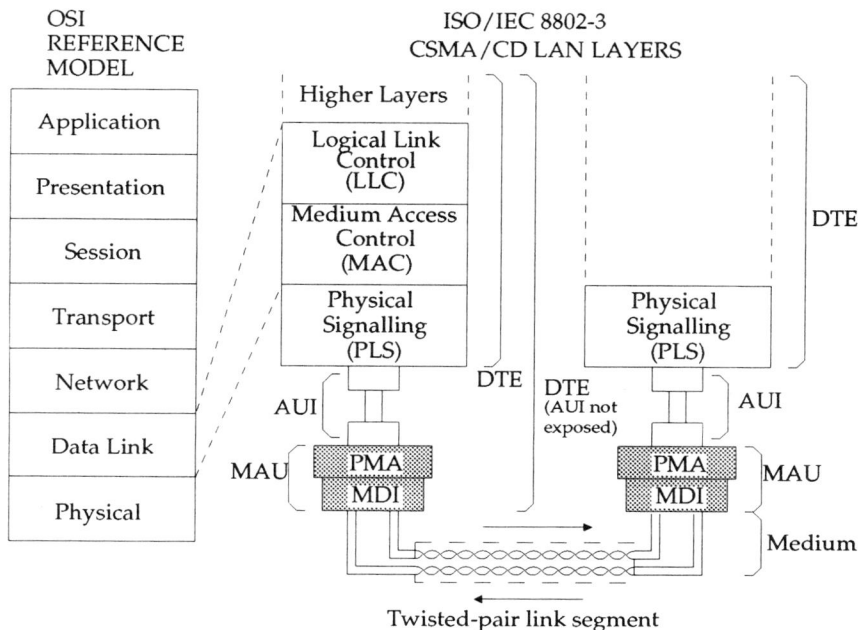

a. 10baseT: relationship with the LAN reference model

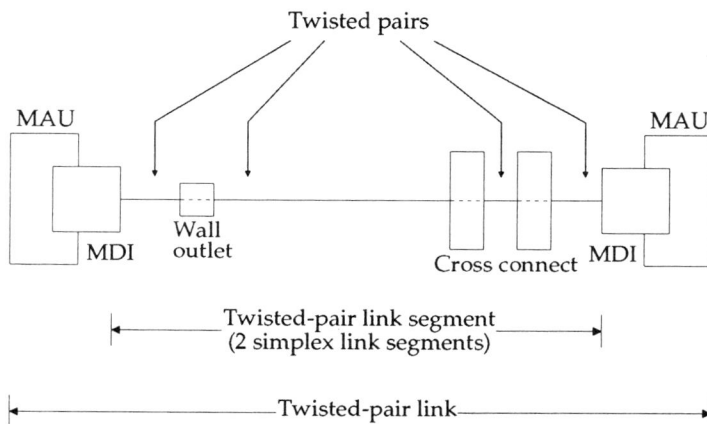

Twisted pairs

MAU

MAU

MDI   Wall outlet

Cross connect   MDI

Twisted-pair link segment (2 simplex link segments)

Twisted-pair link

b. Twisted-pair link

Figure 2.21   Physical layer for 10baseT.

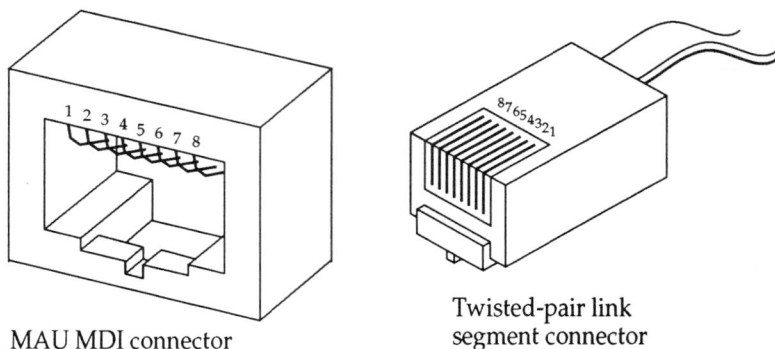

MAU MDI connector

Twisted-pair link
segment connector

Figure 2.22 Plug connection for twisted-pair Ethernet.

The repeater unit has no DTE functions and thus imposes slightly different requirements on the MAU assigned to this unit. For example, the latter must be capable of executing the so-called auto-partition/reconnection algorithm.

A twisted-pair link includes a 'twisted-pair link segment' and the two attached MAUs. The segment itself consists of two 'simplex link segments'. Each simplex segment is implemented using a 2-wire conductor (UTP). Thus, a 4-wire cable is used on the link segment, which may be contained in a cable cord (multipair UTP). The conductors have a diameter of 0.4 to 0.6 mm (26–22 AWG). Figure 2.21b shows the position of the wall outlet and the cross connect within a link segment.

The performance characteristic is defined in such a way that it is usually met by 100 m of twisted-pair telephone cable with diameter 0.5 mm. The cable resistance in the range 5–10 MHz should be between 85 and 111 Ω; the attenuation (insertion loss) for this frequency range should not be greater than 11.5 dB on each simplex segment. The minimum signal speed should be 0.585 c and the signal delay on a link segment should be less than 1000 ns.

Eight-pin plugs (type RJ 45) are specified as MDI connectors (Figure 2.22), where only four pins are used by 10baseT, namely pins 1 and 2 for transmit data and pins 3 and 6 for receive data.

2.4.5 Repeaters and multisegment LANs

Repeater sets are components which may be used to extend LAN topologies and lengths beyond the medium-dependent limits specified for a LAN segment. Table 2.7 gives examples of these limits.

Table 2.7 Segment characteristics for 10 Mbps Ethernet.

Segment type	Maximum number of MAUs per segment	Maximum segment length (m)	Minimum signal speed (c)	Maximum delay in a segment (ns)
Coax 10base5	100	500	0.77	2165
Coax 10base2	30	185	0.65	950
Link FOIRL	2	1000	0.66	5000
Link 10baseT	2	100	0.59	1000
AUI	1 MAU/1 DTE	50	0.65	257

Thus, repeater sets may be used to couple segments within the physical layer. Figure 2.23 shows the repeater set for a coax-to-coax configuration. A repeater set consists of the repeater itself (repeater unit) together with the associated MAUs. MAUs and repeaters may be designed as multiport repeaters. In particular, a repeater hub of Section 2.4.4 is a multiport repeater for twisted-pair link segments.

A repeater uses two transceivers to link together two different Ethernet segments. It combines these into one logical channel by regenerating and amplifying signals which are propagated in both directions in such a way that the repeater is transparent to the remainder of the

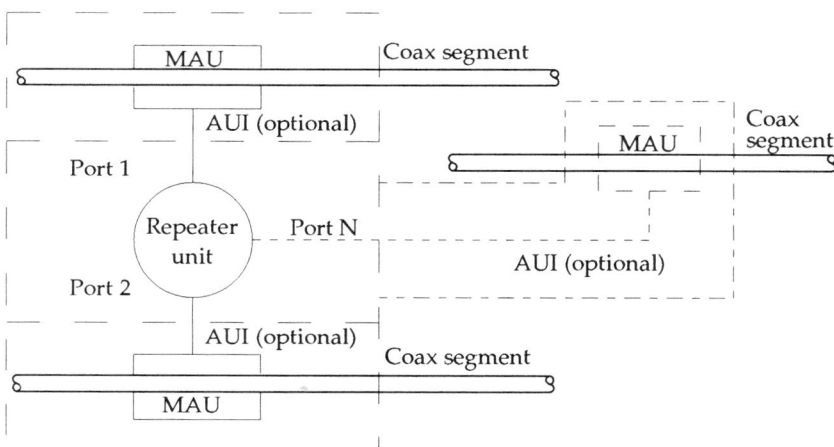

Figure 2.23 Structure of a repeater set.

system. Thus, stations on different segments may collide in the sense of the CSMA/CD procedure; consequently, repeaters must be able to detect and handle cross-segment collisions.

The use of repeaters increases the signal propagation time in the Ethernet LAN. This time is the sum of the signal propagation times for the individual segments plus the delays due to the repeaters and should, for example, be less than 8 bit times. The tasks of a repeater include:

- Carrier sensing
- Synchronized signal regeneration
- Collision detection
- Generation of the collision signal (jam)
- Generation of the frame preamble
- Extension of frame fragments to at least 96 bits
- Adherence to the delay conditions
- Support for the operational 'monitor mode'
- Separation of faulty segments (for example, in the case of protracted collisions due to the lack of a line terminating resistor).

Repeaters may be implemented in two different ways, namely as local or as remote repeaters. Local repeaters link two coaxial segments directly. Remote repeaters are used to link two coaxial segments over a point-to-point link (link segment). Typically, optical fibres are used to implement link segments because these are able to bridge longer distances between two coaxial segments. Link segments may not be used to connect user stations. The implementation of a link segment requires two repeaters, often referred to in product descriptions as the 'repeater halves' of a remote repeater.

If the repeater unit consists of two 'halves', the circuit between these is called the inter-repeater link (IRL). The operation of a repeater should be transparent to LAN subscribers and to the access strategy; in other words, it should not violate the fairness criterion and should not be addressable. It should only permit a topology extension over a coax segment in the CSMA/CD framework. Thus, particular attention should be paid to the contribution of these components to the delay. Packet forwarding, collision, jam notification, transmit recovery and carrier recovery all contribute to the delay.

The proposed text for section 9.9 of the Ethernet standard (IEEE standard 802.3d, released in 1987), which specifies a manufacturer-independent fibre optic inter-repeater link (FOIRL), is still unpublished. Thus, both the characteristics of the optical fibre and the fibre optic MAU (FOMAU) remain to be defined (Figure 2.24).

The FOMAU interworks with type 10base5 (standard) or 10base2

To 10base5 or 10base2 network

Repeater
unit

PMA

MDI

FOMAU

Optical fibre
link segment

Vendor-
independent
FOIRL

Repeater
unit

To 10base5 or 10base2 network

AUI   = Attachment Unit Interface
FOMAU = Fibre Optic Medium Attachment Unit
MDI   = Medium Dependent Interface
PMA   = Physical Medium Attachment
FOIRL = Fibre Optic Inter-repeater Link

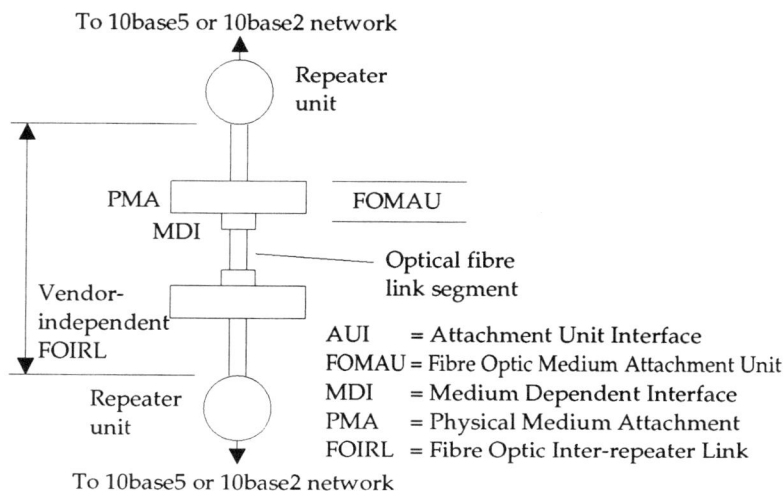

Figure 2.24   Optical-fibre – repeater connection.

(Cheapernet). The MAU has the usual functions of transmit, receive, collision detect and jabber. In addition, another function, 'low light level detection' is specified. This ensures that a bit error rate of 10^{-10} can be achieved on the link segment. An MTBF of 100 000 hours is specified for the FOMAU.

The optical transmitter has a central wavelength between 790 nm and 860 nm and a spectral width of 75 nm (FWHM). The optical signal ramp and fall time should be within 10 ± 3 ns for signal levels from 10% to 90%.

The FOMAU may be used with several different types of fibre. The recommended fibre characteristics are as follows:

- Core diameter: 62.5 ± 3 μm
- Cladding diameter: 125 ± 3 μm
- Core/sheath concentric deviation: 6%
- Numerical aperture: 0.275 ± 0.015
- Attenuation: 4 dB/km
- Bandwidth–length product: at least 150 MHz km for wavelength 850 nm
- Connectors: as per IEC 86 B/36.

An optical link segment consists of two directed fibres of the above

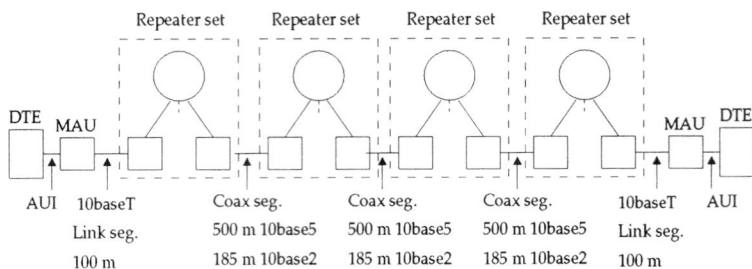

Figure 2.25   Maximal multisegment network.

type, which may be composed of several fibre subsections. The fibre link attenuation should be no more than 7 dB, the bandwidth must be at least 150 MHz. The overall contribution to the delay provided by optical segments on a data path between two Ethernet stations (DTEs) should be less than 5140 ns.

As previously stated, multisegment Ethernets form a single collision domain. With a view to achievable values of the collision parameter K, overall restrictions on the number of repeaters permitted in a network configuration must be followed.

The following rules hold for multisegment Ethernet LANs:

(1)   Repeaters are needed to create multisegment networks.

(2)   MAUs as components of repeater sets also count as MAUs in the sense of the maximum number of MAUs permitted per segment.

(3)   An overall maximum communications route between two network stations (DTEs) may consist of up to five segments, four repeater sets (possibly including AUI circuits), two MAUs and AUI circuits.

(4)   If a communications route consists of five segments and four repeater sets, up to three segments may be coax segments and the remaining segments must be link segments. In the case of five segments, any FOIRL segment should be no longer than 500 m.

(5)   In a network consisting of three repeater sets and four segments, the FOIRL segments may have a length of up to 1000 m.

Figures 2.25 and 2.26 show various multisegment configurations.

2.4.6 StarLAN, IEEE 802.3 type 1base5

The Ethernet extension described below is defined in the 802.3e 1988 standard (IEEE, StarLAN). This is entitled 'Physical signalling, medium

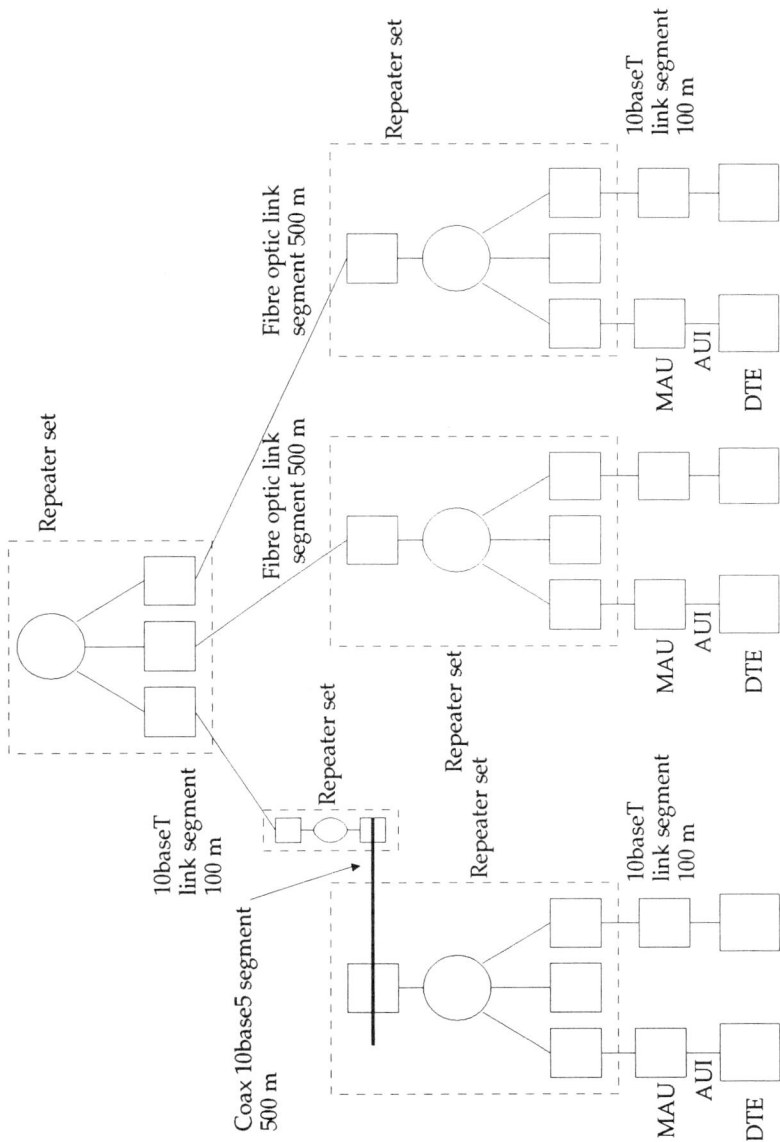

Figure 2.26 Multisegment network with various media.

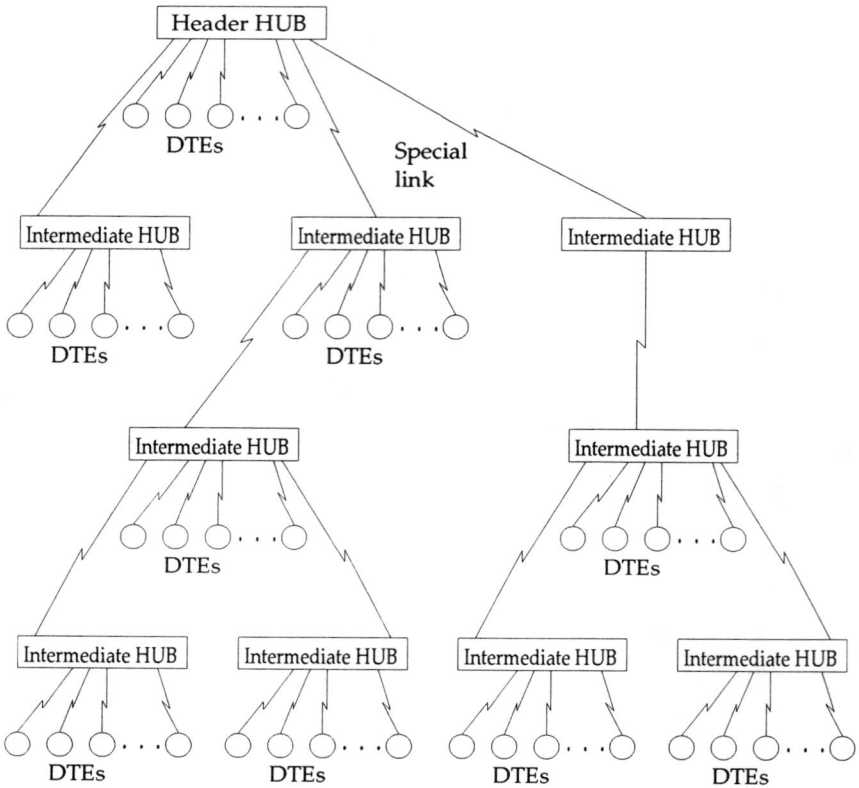

Figure 2.27 Four-level StarLAN network.

attachment and baseband medium specifications, type 1base5'. For reasons which we describe below, 1base5 is also known as StarLAN. StarLAN is an inexpensive 1 Mbps CSMA/CD network based on twisted-pair copper wiring. Each station (DTE) is linked in a star shape via a double pair cable to a switching node called a hub. Hubs may be cascaded so that a tree topology may occur.

Within such a topology (Figure 2.27), one component lies at a higher level relative to another, if for example, in the cascading it is nearer to the root of the tree. If a hub receives packets from an attached DTE, it sends them to the higher-level hub if such a hub exists; otherwise, the hub sends the packets back to all directly attached DTEs and the attached lower-level hubs (broadcast). Similarly, a hub transmits packets which it receives from a higher-level hub using the broadcast procedure. If several DTEs or lower-

Reference model	LAN model					
Higher layers	Higher layers					
Session	LLC					
Transport	MAC					
Network	PLS		HUB PLS			
Data link	PMA	Port PMA	. . .	Port PMA	Upper PMA	
Physical	MDI	Port MDI	. . .	Port MDI	Upper MDI	

Optional
connection
to higher-
level
HUB

Connection to
other stations or
lower-level HUBs

LLC = Logical Link Control
MAC = Medium Access Control
PLS = Physical Signalling
PMA = Physical Medium Attachment
MDI = Medium Dependent Interface

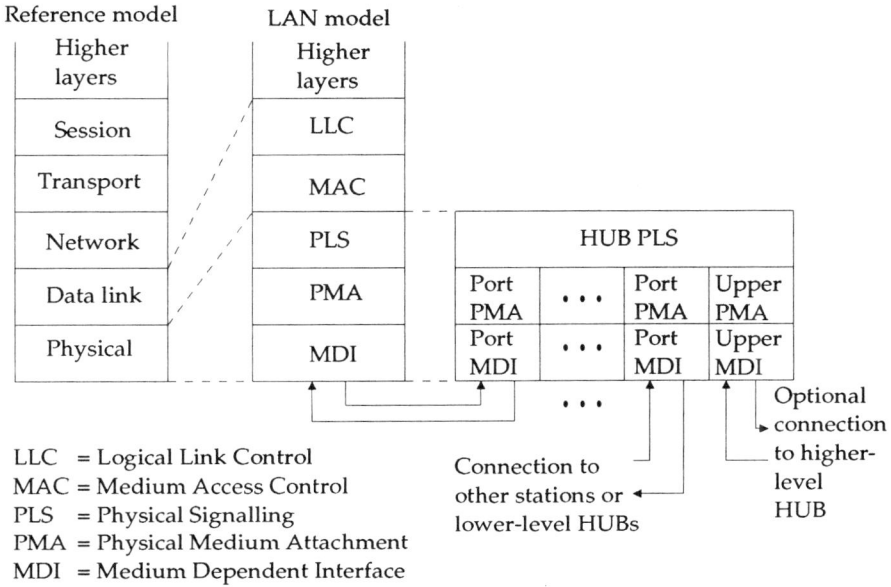

Figure 2.28 Relationship between type 1base5 (StarLAN), the OSI model and IEEE 802.3.

level hubs transmit simultaneously to a hub, the receiver hub generates a collision signal. This signal is sent to the transmitting DTEs, which move to the 'collision present' state, and it is forwarded via the higher-level hubs to the header hub (root of the tree). The header hub transmits the signal to the whole tree topology using the broadcast procedure. The collision signal is encoded in such a way that it is detected by the DTEs as a faulty Manchester coding.

Figure 2.28 (IEEE) shows the relationship between 1base5 and the previous IEEE 802.3 CSMA/CD standard. StarLAN (1base5) has the following properties:

(1) Twisted-pair cable as the medium (0.4–0.8 mm), 1 Mbps transmission rate, Manchester coding, attenuation 6.5 (13.8) dB at 1 (2) MHz, delay less than 4 μs.

(2) DTEs are linked to hubs over point-to-point connections, one wire pair is required for each of the transmit and receive directions. The wire pairs may run inside telephone trunk cables.

(3) DTE/hub and hub/hub connections are terminated electrically at both ends. Up to five levels of hubs are permitted in a tree-like

structure. The maximum cable length for a DTE/hub or hub/hub connection is 250 m. Special links (optical fibre) may extend these lengths up to 4 km.

(4) Hubs are used as repeaters.

(5) Hubs should have an MTBF of at least 45 000 hours of operation.

(6) The frame (packet) structure on the segments corresponds to that of the standard Ethernet (Figure 2.7). The bit time is 1 μs. The minimum frame length is 512 bits. The data is encoded using Manchester coding.

(7) The bit error rate is less than 10^{-8} in the physical layer and less than 10^{-9} in the data link layer. False collision detection should occur with frequency 10^{-2} for a DTE and 1.5×10^{-3} for a hub.

The execution of protocols in the PLS layer of the DTE is very similar to that for the standard Ethernet. Of course, the signal conditions for collision detection are different.

The hub specifications are also different. On the one hand, a hub has an amplifier function, whereby ingoing signals are regenerated in terms of time and amplitude. On the other hand, collisions between transmissions from various hub ports and the broadcast signal to all stations must be detected. Thus, each hub may be decomposed into an upward part and a downward part in order to carry out the tasks within the possible tree structure. This decomposition is reflected in the port addresses and in the different message headers. Each hub may have several downward ports but only one upward port.

Packets from below may be combined in a message stream leading towards a higher level, while messages entering a single hub input channel from above are forwarded unaltered (possibly regenerated) through all output channels.

To achieve a certain fairness in the network, all input ports have a timeout facility, which may be used to suppress excessively long transmissions.

Like other physical layer standards, this supplement also contains specifications related to the transmit/receive diagram, the electrical characteristics of the cable, shielding, signal and time conditions, propagation times and delays for individual network components. Because of the overall delay budget, the minimum frame length is fixed at 512 bits.

It is reasonable that because of the medium used, other special requirements relating to crosstalk exist and must be specified.

As demonstrated in Figure 2.28, the specifications described in Sections 2.2 and 2.3 also apply to StarLAN networks.

StarLAN was the first published standard for Ethernet LANs based on twisted-pair conductors. In the meantime, the type 10baseT has been standardized (see also Section 2.4.4). Since considerably higher transmission rates of 10 Mbps are now achievable, StarLAN is of little practical importance and will not be discussed in the remainder of this book.

2.4.7 Broadband Ethernet, IEEE 802.3 type 10broad36

2.4.7.1 Introduction to broadband technology

The Ethernet versions described up to this point are based on the baseband transmission technology, in which electrical signals are transmitted on the cable without (frequency) modulation. In baseband transmission the digital message signals transmitted via Ethernet range (at least theoretically) down to a frequency of 0. The use of baseband transmission is not new: (analog) telephone signals are also transmitted without modulation (at least in the subscriber-line area).

Data transmission using the baseband transmission technology has the advantage that no components are needed to carry out carrier modulation and demodulation (modems). This makes the procedure less expensive than broadband technology. On the other hand, a medium used in baseband technology has only one transmission channel. However, by means of various mechanisms in a type of time multiplexing, this channel may be used in such a way that several subscribers are able to transmit quasi-simultaneously (also on Ethernet). This method is not suitable for arbitrary applications such as, for example, a mixture of various network access procedures or shared use of the medium to transmit pictures, voice and data. For these reasons broadband data transmission is important.

This transmission method is essentially based on two technologies:

Modulation In modulation, a message signal is overlaid on a sine-shaped carrier (continuous time) or a pulse-shaped carrier (discrete time). According to the nature of the carrier signal, we speak of amplitude modulation, frequency modulation, phase modulation, etc. In a digital transmission of an analog signal a digital signal is first generated by sampling and quantization and encrypted into code words.

Multiplexing This refers to the multiple use of a transmission medium for several communication relationships. The multiplexing procedure may be executed either in the frequency domain or in the time domain (frequency division or time-division multiplexing) and thus makes several channels available. Another degree of freedom is whether the channel assignment is fixed or based on need.

Historically, today's broadband networks developed from cable television (CATV) networks. In these networks, the information flow was in one direction only from a transmitter (head station) to a number of receivers. In such cases, frequency modulation was used, in which typically, a television channel occupied a 6 MHz band. The network topology was

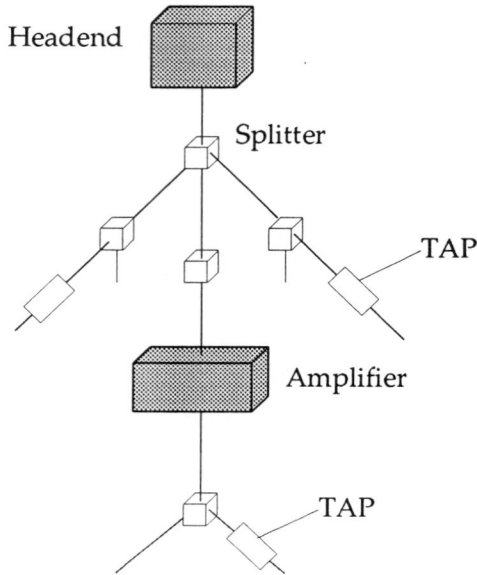

Figure 2.29 Components in the broadband system.

tree-shaped with various branches outwards from the head station using splitters and amplifiers (Figure 2.29).

The requirements on data communications technology are somewhat different because, potentially, any subscriber should be able to communicate with any other. This means that the unidirectional flow of the CATV network is insufficient.

There are two known ways of solving this problem. The first possibility involves replacing the transmission cable by two (parallel) cables, one for each transmission direction. Such a solution leads to the 'dual cable system' (Figure 2.30b). In many cases (existing cable infrastructure) this could lead to new cabling. The second possibility involves logically dividing the existing cable or the transmission frequencies used into two separate cable systems. Such a solution leads to a 'single cable system' (Figure 2.30a). In this case, a special frequency range is used for transmissions in the direction of the head station (transmit direction), while a non-overlapping frequency range is used for transmissions in the direction away from the head station (receive direction). The head station then has the special task of converting incoming signals in the transmit direction to corresponding frequencies in the receive direction (frequency shift). Such systems are known as subsplit, midsplit or highsplit systems, according to the division

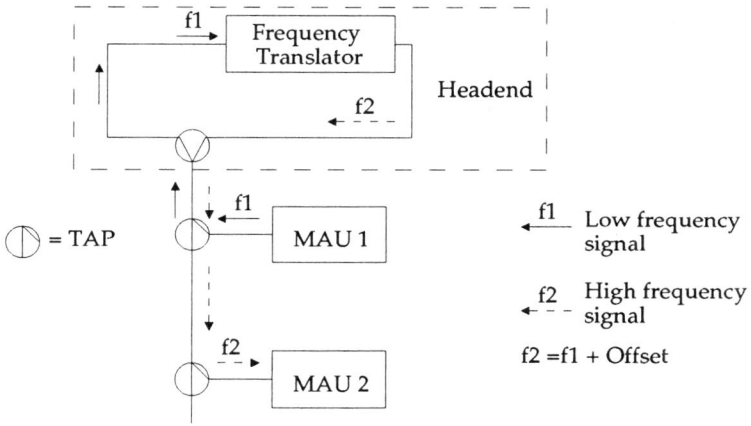

a. Single cable system

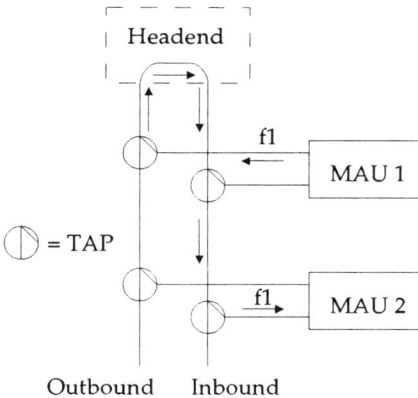

b. Dual cable system

Figure 2.30   Broadband cable system.

of the frequency range. The amount by which the frequency of the transmit direction must beshifted for conversion to the frequency of the receive direction is called the frequency offset. Typically, at present, a 400 MHz bandwidth of frequencies is used by broadband networks; within this, the lowest frequencies of a few MHz are unused because of the susceptibility of this band to noise.

When implementing broadband data communication networks as single cable systems, it is advisable to choose the midsplit system because this provides the same bandwidth of frequencies for the transmit and the receive directions. In any broadband system, modulated signals are transmitted on the cable. The modulation and demodulation is carried out by a modem at the cable system interface point. The signals transmitted in this way are subject to attenuation which depends on the cable type, length, branches, etc. Amplifiers may be incorporated to raise the signal level. To summarize, the configuration and dimensioning of a broadband network should only be carried out with great care by a professional.

The advantage of broadband networks is that several mutually independent transmission channels may be used. For example, in addition to data, analog speech and video signals may be transmitted. There is an extensive range of corresponding components which we shall not discuss further here.

One application for broadband networks involves the provision of an independent frequency range to facilitate the creation of an Ethernet compatible with the standard transceiver interface. An Ethernet based on broadband technology has been available from DEC for a number of years now. During this period, standard specifications have been produced for such an Ethernet version.

2.4.7.2 Specifications for 10broad36

The specifications for a broadband version of Ethernet are contained in the IEEE standard 802.3b, 1988 'Broadband medium attachment unit and broadband medium specifications'. This type is defined to be a 10 Mbps LAN with a distance of up to 3600 m between two connected stations. The corresponding topology is an irregular tree with arbitrary branching; the headend is the common root.

The standard specifies the broadband MAUs in such a way that the standard AUI remains unaltered and Ethernet controllers are unaffected. In other words, a baseband MAU is emulated (except for signal delays). For each transmission direction the MAU requires a frequency range of 18 MHz, 14 MHz for data and 4 MHz for its own signalling channel which transports the collision signal. This separate signalling channel is needed because the baseband collision detection techniques (monitoring of the DC level) are not directly applicable to broadband technology (AC coupling, carrier modulated). Thus, if the MAU detects bit errors when comparing receive and transmit data, or the receive time window (UMD timer) is exceeded, or there is a discrepancy in the times of the AUI output signal and receipt from the coaxial cable, the MAU generates an 'RF collision enforcement signal' on the separate channel. On a broadband network, collisions may occur independently in the transmit and receive channels. However, the specifications are designed so that collision detection takes

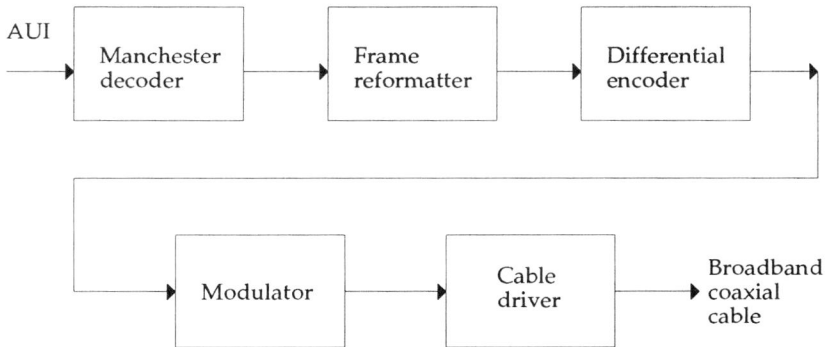

Figure 2.31   Subfunctions of a broadband MAU.

place within the same time span as that prescribed for the baseband Ethernet. Overall, according to the IEEE standard, a bandwidth of 36 MHz is required for a broadband Ethernet; this corresponds to six 6-MHz television channels.

Like the standard MAU, the broadband MAU has four basic functions: transmit, receive, collision detect and jabber (thus, it has the facilities for timeout and interruption). Because of the special broadband cable medium, these functions must also take account of the modulation aspect. For example, the transmit function consists of the following subfunctions (Figure 2.31). The Manchester encoded frame which is sent by the Ethernet controller is received via the AUI and decoded. Its preamble is modified and a postamble is added (broadband end of frame delimiter). In other words, instead of the AUI frame ⟨Preamble SFD DA SA Data FSC⟩, a frame ⟨Preamble UMD Seed DA SA Data FCS Postamble⟩ is transmitted on the broadband medium. UMD is the 'unscrambled mode delimiter'; all the bits between the UMD and the postamble are scrambled using a CCITT V.29 scrambler. In order to avoid intermodulation products, NRZ (non-return-to-zero) encoding is used on the coax cable instead of the Manchester code. The binary-phase-shift-keying (PSK) procedure is used for the carrier modulation (to generate the RF signal). Figure 2.32 shows the frame format at the AUI/coax cable interface.

A 75 Ω (CATV) television cable with F-connectors is used for the coax cable (broadband medium). Both single-cable and double-cable installations are supported. For single-cable systems, midsplit or highsplit technology with a frequency offset of 192.25 MHz is recommended; older systems with offset 156.25 MHz are also supported. Table 2.8 shows the frequency band divisions for the single cable system. The preferred subband is 53.75–71.75 MHz.

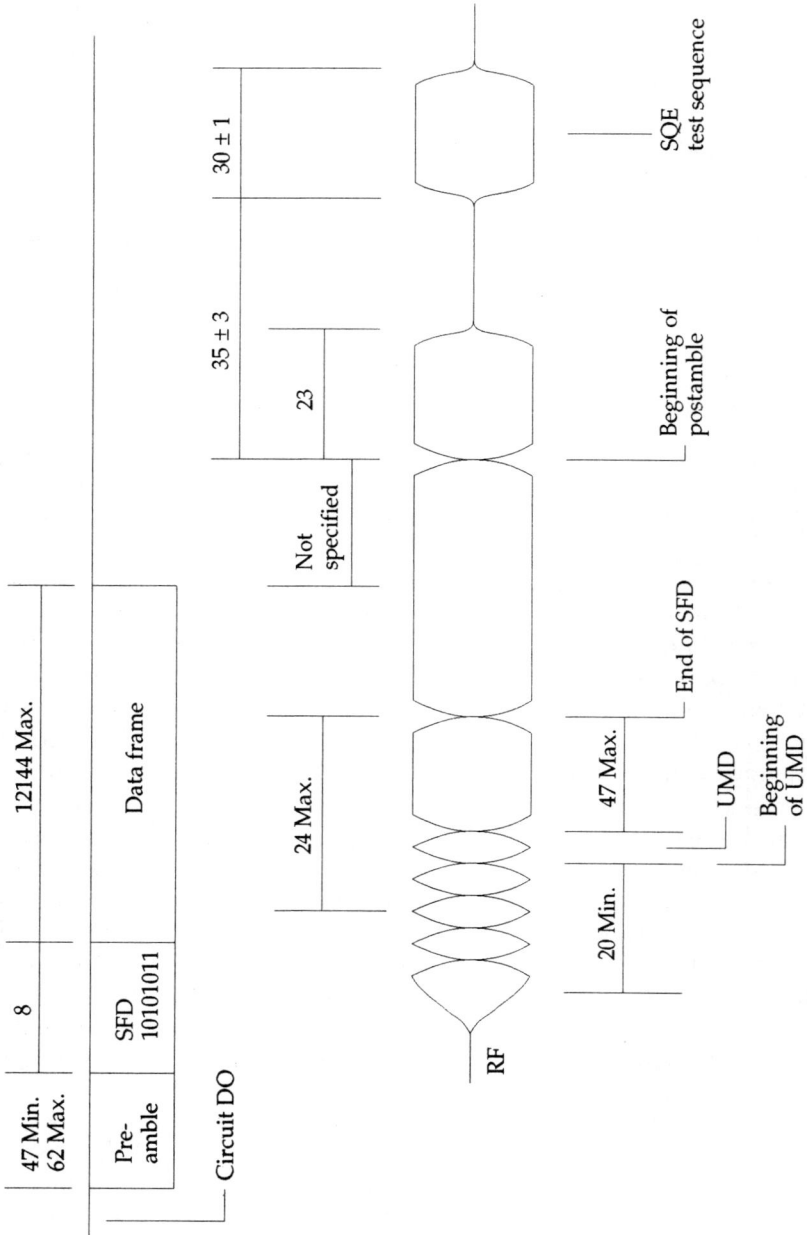

Figure 2.32 Frame format at the AUI/coax interface.

Table 2.8   Single cable system: frequency allocation.

Transmitter			Receiver	
			Offset 156.25 MHz	Offset 192.25 MHz
Data carrier	Coll enf Centre freq	Transmit band	Receive band	Receive band
43	52	35.75–53.75	192–210	228–246
49	58	41.75–59.75	198–216	234–252
55	64	47.75–65.75	204–222	240–258
61	70	53.75–71.75	210–228	246–264
67	76	59.75–77.75	216–234	252–270
73	82	65.75–83.75	222–240	258–276

The various delay-time diagrams for the conversion of an AUI signal into an RF signal (for transmitter and receiver), for the line test (signal quality error test) and for the collision detection (collision enforcement signal) are also specified. The bit error rate should be less than 10^{-8} with a maximum attenuation of 26 dB, the MTBF of a MAU should be greater than 1 million hours.

The signal speeds are specified as 3.83 ns/m for the 75 Ω trunk cable, 4.27 ns/m for the drop cable and 5.13 ns/m for the transceiver (AUI) cable. With the corresponding length restrictions of 1800/25/50 m the maximum distance between two DTEs is 3750 m, where a MAU may be up to 1800 m from the headend station.

This corresponds to maximum overall round trip delays of 140 bit times in the cable system from DTE to DTE (including delays in the headend). As far as these delays are concerned, the configuration may vary (time contributions from trunk cables, drop cables, AUI cables, TAPs, splitters, amplifiers and collision detection). The distance values apply to the cable specified, but there may be changes if cable with other signal propagation times is used.

As mentioned in Section 2.4.7.1, 10broad36 enables Ethernet-compatible use of a frequency subband of a cable on which other subbands may or must be used for other communications purposes. Because of the complicated transmission technology and the expensive connection components (including the requirement for multifrequency modems in the high-frequency area), broadband Ethernet LANs are relatively rare. Their use is most often associated with interesting large-size objects such as, for example, in the BMW factory in Regensburg, Germany. Because this type of Ethernet LAN is uncommon, we shall not discuss it further here.

2.4.8 Ethernet based on fibre optic conductors, IEEE 802.3 type 10baseF

2.4.8.1 Introduction to fibre optic technology

As a result of the enormous progress of fibre optic technology in recent years (and the decreasing costs), fibre optic systems are now very strong competitors for classical coaxial cable systems. Thus, it is not surprising that suppliers of Ethernet-compatible fibre optic systems have been represented in the market for some time, and that the IEEE has developed corresponding standards.

Fibre optic technology involves the transfer of signals using optical transmission. In the transmitter, the signal to be transmitted is digitally encoded and used to control the corresponding light source (light on, light off). The light source is either a laser diode (LD) or a light-emitting diode (LED). The light pulses are injected into the fibre optic conductor (glass or plastic fibre). In the receiver, the light entering from the fibre optic conductor is received by an optical decoder (photodiode). This converts the optical signals into electrical signals, which then must be amplified, regenerated and decoded. There are differences in the fibre optic technology relating to the use of the fibre optic cable, the optical transmit and receive facilities and the technology used to link the fibre optic cables.

Here is a brief summary of the advantages of this technology:

- Fibre optic conductors do not cause interference effects (emission of radiation) in other components.

- Fibre optic conductors are themselves immune to electromagnetic or high-frequency irradiation.

- Fibre optic conductors exhibit high security against difficult to detect physical intrusions, such as eavesdropping.

- Fibre optic conductors offer considerably higher transmission rates at considerably lower costs over longer distances than coax systems.

- Fibre optic cables are considerably thinner, more flexible and lighter than thick, standard Ethernet cable.

Glass fibres consist of a glass core surrounded by a glass sheath. The glass material usually consists of silicon oxide. Additives are used to give the glass core and the glass sheath different refractive indices. Light waves which are incident at a very small angle to the axis of the fibre, are reflected at the boundary between the fibre core and the fibre sheath so they remain in the fibre core. There are three different types of glass fibre depending on the profile of the refractive index between the glass core and the glass sheath.

Multimode fibres These have a homogeneous core and sheath with different refractive indices. Here, the light describes a zig-zag path within

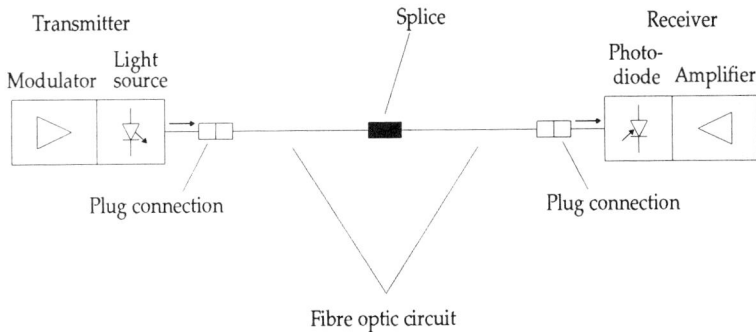

Figure 2.33   Optical message-transmission circuit.

the optical fibre. As a result of different angles of reflection, the individual modes acquire different time delays.

Graded-index fibres   Here, there is no discontinuity in the refractive index in the core/sheath area which decreases steadily (parabolic profile) from the centre of the fibre. The individual modes are carried in the core in the form of waves.

Monomode fibres   Here, the diameter of the core is similar to the wavelength of the light to be transmitted. The modes are carried rectilinearly within the medium.

The individual fibre types differ in the following ways:

- In the profile of the refractive index. For stepped-index fibres, the refractive index of the core and the sheath is constant. For graded-index fibres, the refractive index is a (usually quadratic) function of the distance from the core axis. The refractive index of the core is always greater than that of the sheath.

- In the geometric structure. The core diameter, the sheath diameter and the numerical aperture may vary.

- In the wave propagation. These relate to differences in the propagation times of the individual light beams within the medium, the pulse distortion and mode dispersion (shape preserving, little/much spreading), the desired bandwidth/range product and the material dispersion.

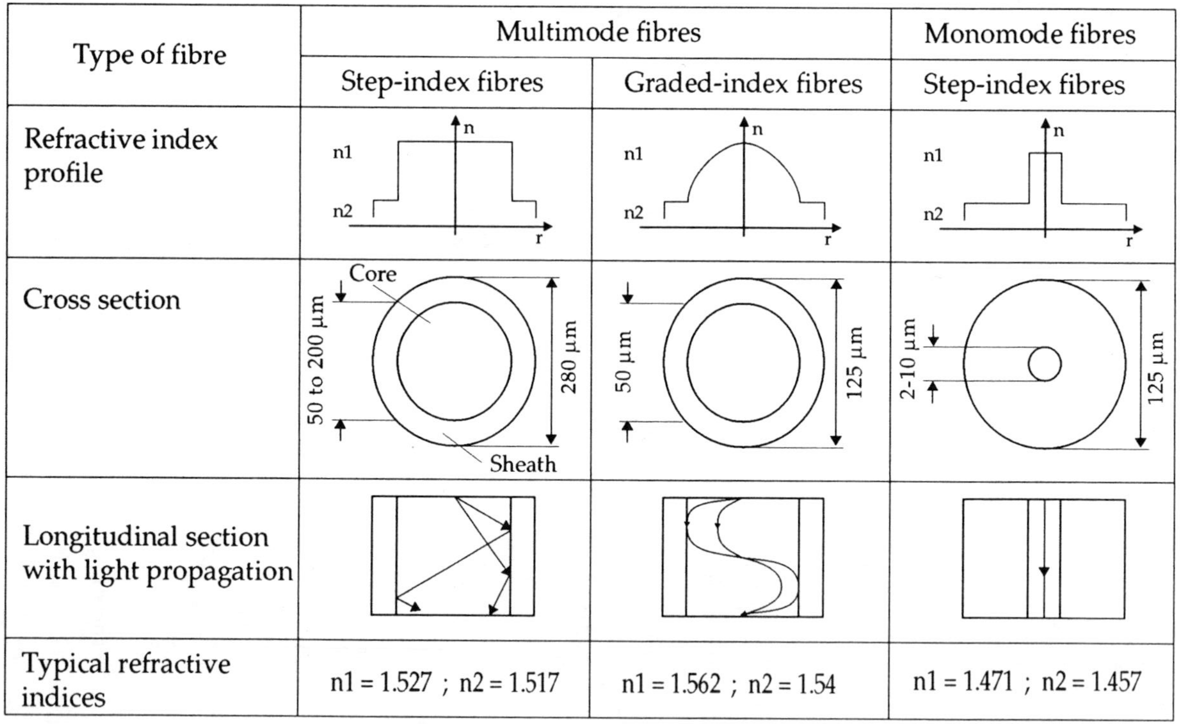

Type of fibre
Multimode fibres
Monomode fibres
Step-index fibres
Graded-index fibres
Step-index fibres
Refractive index profile
n
n1
n2
r
Cross section
Core
Sheath
50 to 200 µm
280 µm
50 µm
125 µm
2-10 µm
125 µm
Longitudinal section with light propagation
Typical refractive indices
n1 = 1.527 ; n2 = 1.517
n1 = 1.562 ; n2 = 1.54
n1 = 1.471 ; n2 = 1.457

Figure 2.34 Optical-fibre types.

2.4.8.2 Specifications for the fibre optic Ethernet

The IEEE specifications for fibre optic Ethernet appear as draft supplements to the overall Ethernet standard, and they are largely contained in the following three sections:

- Section 15: Fibre optic medium and common elements of medium attachment unit and star, type 10baseF.
- Section 16: Passive star and medium attachment unit, type 10baseFP
- Section 17: Active star and medium attachment unit, type 10baseFA.

The specification is again oriented in the well-established way towards the corresponding physical layer implementation reference model (Figure 2.35).

Outwardly, in other words, at the AUI the system behaves like a normal Ethernet. This means that subscribers to the LAN may use the same Ethernet controllers as in the standard Ethernet. However, the network topologies for optical fibres are not of the bus type but form a star network, often with several levels see Figure 2.36.

At the node points, there are so-called star couplers from which point-to-point duplex links (optical link segment) lead to the optical transceivers of the next stars or subscribers. Thus, a star has a distribution function. As far as the access problem (which is solved in Ethernet LANs using CSMA/CD) is concerned, in optical networks of type 10baseF the star plays the same role as the hub in 10baseT LANs (see Section 2.4.4). There are two different types of star coupler:

Active stars   These link two or more optical link segments. The optical signals received from the input ports are converted into electrical signals and are forwarded to all output ports (except the output port corresponding to the input port which was active immediately beforehand) where they are again converted into optical signals. Ports which are able to process FOIRL-compatible signals (see Section 2.4.5) are called asynchronous ports. Synchronous ports can only process optical signals which are synchronized using the 'active idle signal' timing defined for 10baseF. The link segments between active stars must pass through synchronous ports.

Passive stars   In a passive star, the optical signals received from the input ports are directly distributed, to all output ports (including that leading to the sender) as equally as possibly by optical means, . To a first approximation, the attenuation in such couplers consists of the distribution-related attenuation and the insertion-related attenuation (transition to the optical fibre).

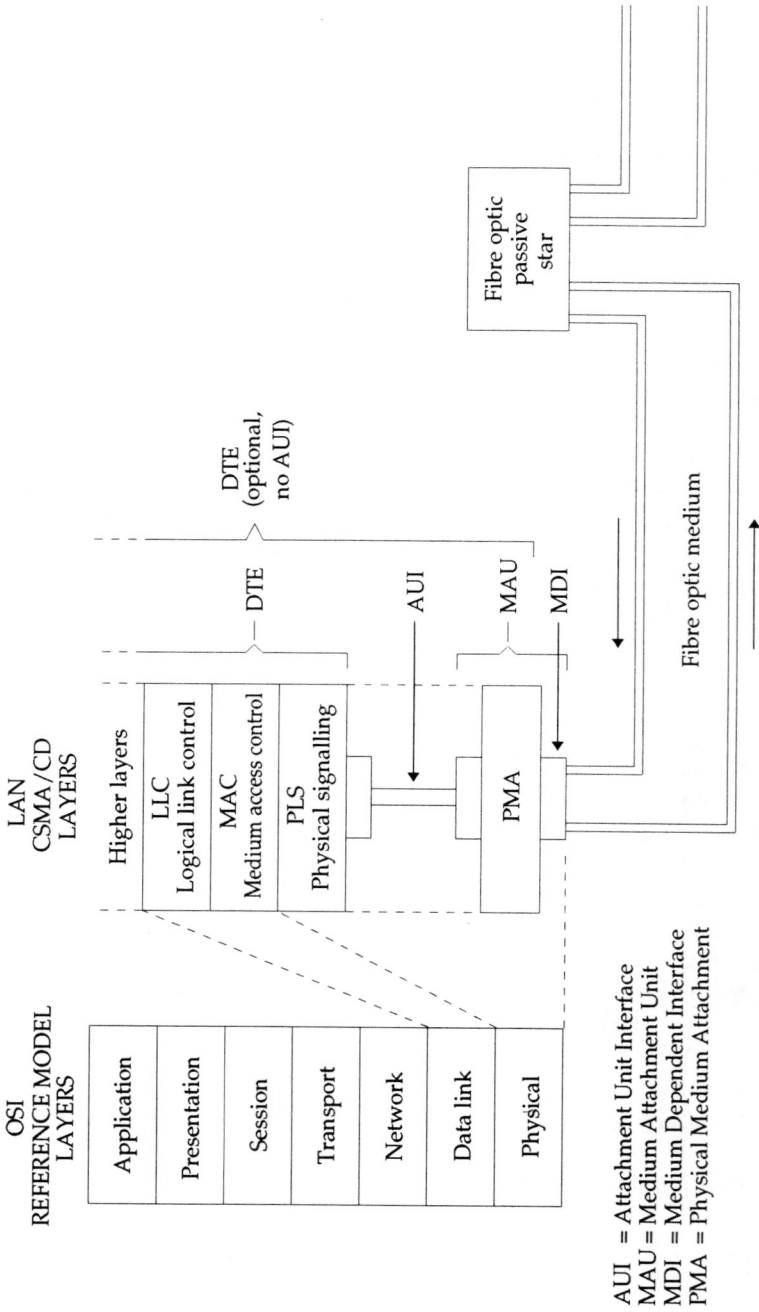

Figure 2.35a Physical layer for 10baseF: a – 10baseF passive star.

AUI = Attachment Unit Interface
MAU = Medium Attachment Unit
MDI = Medium Dependent Interface
PMA = Physical Medium Attachment

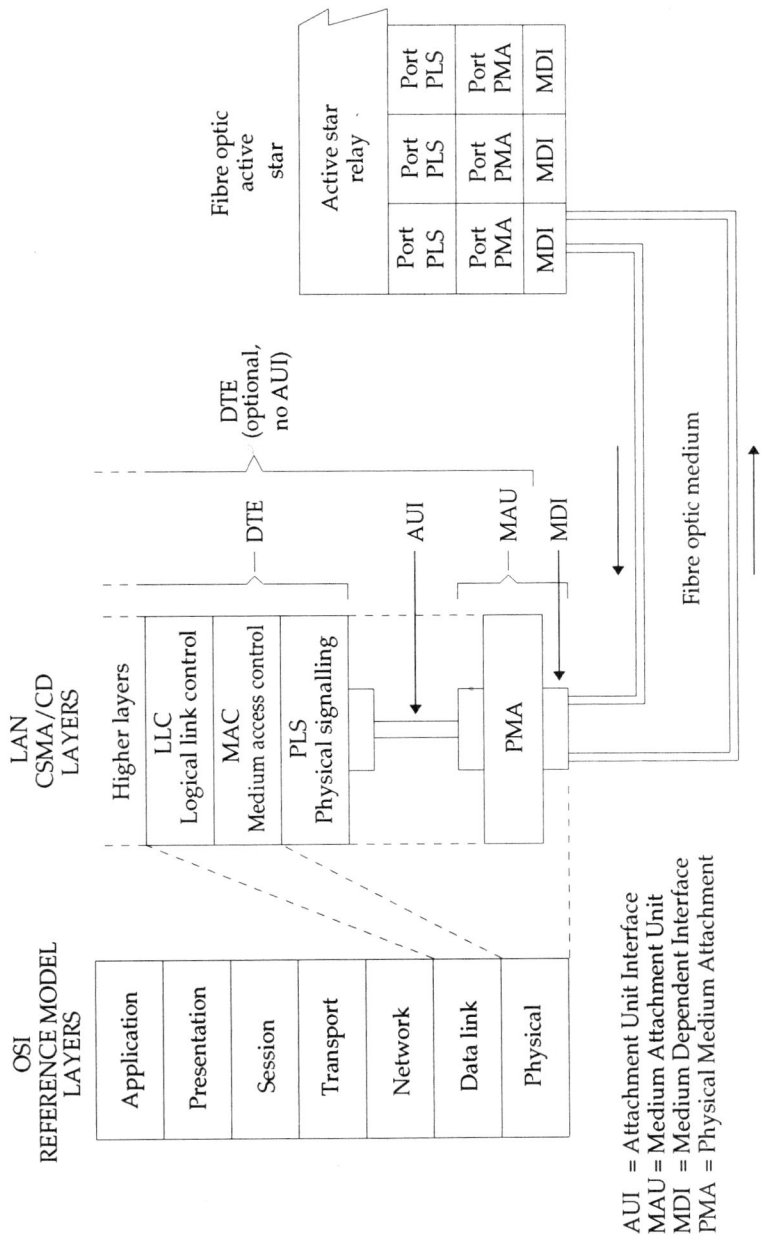

Figure 2.35b   Physical layer for 10baseF: b – 10baseF active star.

AUI = Attachment Unit Interface
MAU = Medium Attachment Unit
MDI = Medium Dependent Interface
PMA = Physical Medium Attachment

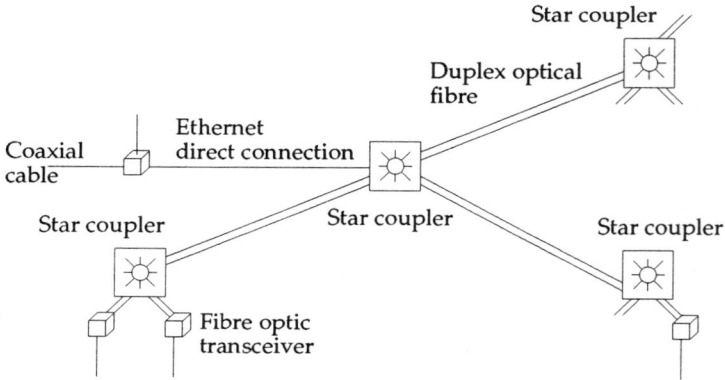

Figure 2.36   Fibre optic Ethernet.

The wavelength of the light used in optical LANs lies between 800 and 900 nm in a spectral bandwidth of 75 nm. The optical performance values are −15 dB/m for the active star (tolerance ±3 dB) and −12 dB/m for the passive star (tolerance ±1 dB). The recommended fibre optic conductor is a 62.5/125 μm fibre as described in the specification IEC 793-2 Type A1b. For a wavelength of 850 nm, this has a maximum attenuation of 3.75 dB/km and a module bandwidth of 160 MHz for a 1 km reference length and wavelength of 805 nm. The signal speed is at least 0.67 c. The IEEE standard also contains values for other fibre optic systems; however, the above system is preferred. Connectors (fibre optic conductor terminators) of type BFOC/2.5 are designated (according to the specification IEC 86B) for which the maximum insertion loss is 1 dB. The signal rate should be 10 Mbps ±0.0005%.

Optical link segments, which form the point-to-point links between an active star coupler and an active MAU, two active couplers or two active MAUs, are called active fibre optic segments (AFOSs). A segment which may be linked to more than two MDIs (see Figure 2.35) is called a passive fibre optic segment (PFOS). Different specifications are available for the optical MAUs, corresponding to the different segment and star types.

A *passive MAU* has the following properties:

- It supports a star-shaped network topology using passive couplers.

- It connects a station (DTE) or a repeater (Section 2.4.5) to a PFOS, where a data rate of 10 Mbps is supported.

- It permits a fibre optic conductor with length 500 m between the passive MAU and the passive star.

- It supports a DTE test of the MAU to check the availability and the correctness of the collision detection (SQE test).

- It generates a new preamble before frames are transferred to the MDI so that collision detection is also permitted in passive systems. The preambles of received frames are also recoded. Preambles to be transmitted (recoded) contain a so-called Manchester violation (MV) signal, which is encoded in such a way that the signal level LOW occurs in both halves of a bit cell (Figure 2.37).

The recoding of the preamble relates to the first 40 bits. They are replaced by the synchronization pattern 1010, a packet header CVR containing the MV signal, and the 'unique word'. The latter is a 32-bit pattern which uniquely identifies the MAU (20-bit unique MAU number, 12-bit manufacturer ID).

The standard does not recommend the number of input/output ports for a passive star. However, the insertion loss for an arbitrary pair of input/output ports should lie in the range 16–20 dB with an input sensitivity of −27 to −41 dB. The loss due to the medium and the connection structure should be between 0 and 6 dB. The ratio of the desired optical signal to all undesired signals resulting from reflection at a passive MAU MDI should be greater than 27 dB.

An *active MAU* has the following properties:

- It supports a star-shaped network topology using active couplers.

- It connects a station (DTE) or a repeater (Section 2.4.5) to an AFOS, where a data rate of 10 Mbps is supported.

- It permits a fibre optic conductor with segment length up to 2000 m between the MAU and the active star coupler.

- It supports a DTE test of the active MAU to check the operational readiness (loopback test) and the correctness of the collision detection (SQE test).

- It provides for synchronous data transmission.

The active star coupler functions as described above. Its advantages arise from the full regeneration of the optical power and from the simple, branch-free point-to-point links (due to every port of the coupler having its own PLS, PMA and MDI circuits). The nature of the message distribution (to all ports except that associated with the active input) provides for a simple and reliable collision detection. Thus, a collision occurs in the optical transceiver when it receives data while in the process of transmitting. If more than one active input port is detected, the outgoing transmission of the data stream is stopped, and in its place a jam signal is sent to all output ports. In idle periods, an IDLE signal is transmitted

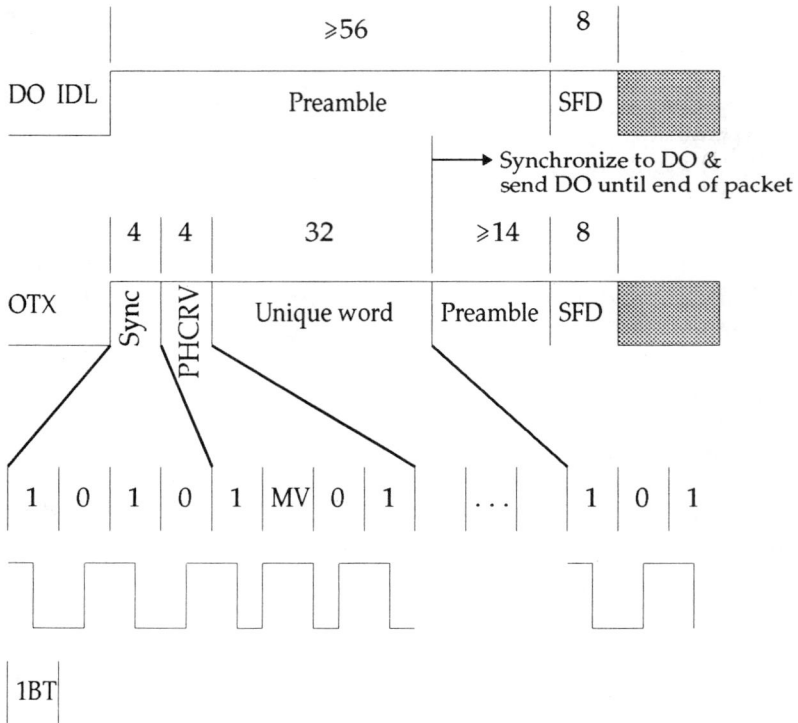

Figure 2.37   Preamble for passive stars.

to monitor the circuits and to ensure that the receiver electronics remains active. This is also used to monitor input levels and transmission times. Of course, the active MAU must contain functions which facilitate sensible interworking with the overall system.

An active coupler (also known as a hub) must have at least two asynchronous ports to enable it to connect to corresponding repeater link segments (FOIRL, see Section 2.4.5). It must not be possible to connect FOIRL segments to synchronous ports.

The IEEE standard for optical Ethernet LANs defines the exact mode of operation for DTE MAUs and star couplers via a precise specification of the process automata, including all time conditions attached to the individual subfunctions. A more detailed discussion of this is beyond the scope of this book.

2.5 Further development of standards relevant to Ethernet

Work on the IEEE LAN standards remains incomplete. The following developments are awaited:

Ethernet type 10baseF   The current specifications for optical Ethernet LANs have yet to be completed and published as a mandatory standard.

Ethernet management   In the original development of the ISO reference model and in the specification of Ethernet LANs, the importance and the necessity of network management standards was not realized. Neither was there a common understanding of a network management architecture. In the meantime, ISO standards for an OSI network management architecture have been produced. These assign the complete management task to the systems management (responsible for the overall management of cooperating systems in a network), the layer management (responsible for functions, services and protocols which are specific to a layer and do not require the services of higher OSI layers), and the protocol management (layer operation, management-related elements within normal communications protocols).

In addition, the OSI standard incorporates an information model which may be used to describe network resources which are to be managed (managed objects). The work of the IEEE takes account of this. In addition, individual network components are described as management-object classes. One example is the planned section 19 of the Ethernet 802.3 standard, called 'Layer management for hub devices'. Here, hub devices are baseband repeaters in the sense of our description in Section 2.4.5 and active star couplers as described in Section 2.4.8. Another example is the Ethernet-related IEEE standard 802.3h, 1990, called 'Layer management', which mainly describes the relationships between CSMA/CD protocol entities and the layer-management functions in formal terms.

Conformance test   A large number of products are claimed to be 802.3 compatible. In fact, many products do not conform to the Ethernet specifications V1.0 and V2.0 or to the 802.3 specifications. As a result, standards for 802.3 conformance tests are under development; to be more precise, abstract test suites for AUI, MAC, PLS and MAU are to be specified.

Furthermore, a new series of standards, called IEEE 1802.3 'Conformance test methodology; CSMA/CD access method and physical layer specifications', was initiated in 1991. To date, only section 4 'AUI cable' has been published. While these are retrospective specifications, the stipulations of the specification of the optical Ethernet which are relevant to conformance tests already accompanied the system specification. In other words, proposals exist for PICS (protocol implementation conformance statements) proforma which include statements for all system parameters indicating whether they are mandatory, optional or conditional for a conformal implementation. Lists of their expected values are also provided.

802.2 standard The additions to the 802.2 standard, namely flow control techniques for LANs coupled via bridges and the type-3 LLC operations (see Section 2.2), still have the status of an ISO draft addendum.

802.1 standard The 802.1 standard applies to all IEEE LANs, in particular, to Ethernet LANs. The following have been published:

- Architectural overview (IEEE standard 802, 1990).
- Specifications for MAC bridges (IEEE standard 802.1D, 1990).
- Specifications for the system load protocol (IEEE standard 802.1E, 1990).

The models for LAN/MAN management (IEEE draft standard 802.1B, July 1991) and the guidelines for the development of layer management standards (IEEE draft recommended practice 802.1F, May 1991) are available as draft standards. Here, in view of the importance of the subject, we may expect an early release of the standards. We shall discuss the contents of these draft standards later, concentrating on their relevance to the construction of larger LAN structures involving Ethernet LANs.

Chapter 3

Components and media for constructing Ethernet multisegments

- Standard Ethernet

- Cheapernet

- Fibre optic systems

- Twisted-pair systems

- Wireless systems

- Multimedia access centre

Currently, Ethernet is certainly the most common technology for local area networks. There are many Ethernet component manufacturers, some have concentrated exclusively on this market sector. The development of Ethernet and its related components did not come to a halt when the original standard was issued. For some time, techniques have been available for bypassing a number of the restrictions of the original scheme, while retaining compatibility with the standard Ethernet. Many of these techniques are reflected in the form of additions and extensions to the IEEE 802.3 standard. This standard is described in detail in Chapter 2.

In this chapter, we attempt to give a didactic/pragmatic approach. Starting from the principles and the components of the original standard Ethernet, we attempt to explain the practical importance of various new techniques.

Section 3.1 contains a brief description of the standard components, and we discuss a number of questions and problems which arise in connection with the construction of Ethernet networks based on these components. This section aims to describe the conditions under which it is sensible to deploy extended Ethernet techniques. The other techniques all have one thing in common, there are no changes at the interface between the transceiver and the Ethernet controller. Consequently, from the point of view of the Ethernet controller, it makes no difference which of the following techniques is used to implement the communication route between two LAN stations.

The main part of this chapter describes the extended Ethernet technologies in more detail (Cheapernet, fibre optic Ethernet, twisted-pair Ethernet). Operational experiences are described and advice is given on the installation of the associated components. Sections 3.5 and 3.6 (wireless systems and multimedia access centre) are devoted to more recent developments which have already led to products, but for which no standards have been released to date.

Table 3.1 lists the questions and problems which often arise in connection with Ethernet. For each problem, we indicate the technologies or the components which may be used to provide a solution. In this chapter, we only consider components and media for building multisegment Ethernet LANs (in other words, network structures which may be formed from various segment and repeater types). More complicated structures, such as integrated networks with bridges and routers, are discussed in Chapter 4.

3.1 Standard Ethernet

The following components should be included with the standard Ethernet (Figure 3.1):

- 50 Ω coax cable, 0.4 inch.
- Transceiver for connection to Ethernet controllers.

Table 3.1   Standard Ethernet and extensions.

Problem	Associated technology
A large number of Ethernet direct connections have to be realized in a small space. A complete Ethernet has to be installed in the least possible space.	Multiport transceivers.
Direct connection to the standard cable via transceivers is too expensive.	Online transceivers for Cheapernet/twisted-pair cable.
The cable to be laid will be used for other purposes in addition to Ethernet.	Broadband Ethernet/twisted-pair cables.
All or some of the cabling area is affected by high external electrical interference. The cable paths should be made more secure against eavesdropping.	Fibre optic Ethernet.
Two Ethernet segments on the same site and up to 1000 m apart are to be linked together.	Remote repeaters.
A large, highly ramified, integrated Ethernet network is to be built, but most of the traffic is very local. The required throughput rate is greater than 10 Mbps. In principle, subscribers can eavesdrop on all data traffic for all users. An attempt should be made to separate traffic (as far as possible) to ensure that data traffic is local. The maximum number of subscribers (directly attached terminals) should be increased.	Bridges/routers.
New cabling should be avoided.	Use of telephone cables, twisted-pair Ethernet.
Ethernet is to be installed in an existing IBM cabling-system environment.	Components for twisted-pair cables.
The Ethernet range has to be extended to lengths over 1500 m whilst retaining the 10 Mbps transmission speed.	Fibre optic Ethernet, broadband Ethernet, bridges/routers.
The danger of interference due to defective transceivers or end-subscribers (for example, blockade, traffic overload), should be decreased. The cabling bus topology is too insecure against cable faults and interruptions.	Star structures such as fibre optic Ethernet or twisted-pair cables.

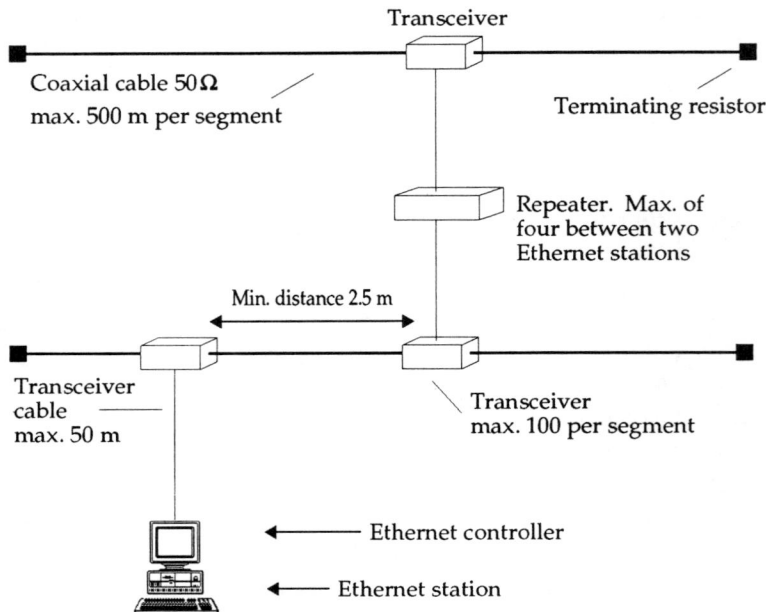

Figure 3.1   Ethernet standard components.

- Transceiver cable to link transceivers and controllers.
- Repeaters to link two coax cable segments.

These components may be used to build networks consisting of several cable segments which are linked together via repeaters. Here, according to the IEEE 802.3 standard, the route from any point in the network to any other point should not pass through more than four repeaters. In Ethernet V2.0, this is reduced to two repeaters, where a remote repeater pair counts as a single repeater. A cable segment may be at most 500 m long. The least permissible distance between two transceivers is 2.5 m and the transceiver cable may be at most 50 m long. In addition, at most 100 transceiver connections per coax segment are permitted.

3.1.1 Ethernet cable

The central transmission medium, the so-called Ethernet cable, is a shielded 50 Ω coaxial cable of type RG 8A/U. Typically, it has a yellow PVC jacket. However, this version cannot be installed in the air shafts of an air-conditioning system for example, because of the risk of creating poisonous gases that would be rapidly circulated by the air-conditioning system in the event of a fire. In this case, the considerably more rigid and more expensive teflon cable should be used. If possible, an Ethernet cable should be (but need not be) laid in a single piece. However, it may be divided into shorter pieces which can be linked using cable connectors. In order to ensure that the signal reflections which then occur are kept as small as possible, the IEEE standard specifies the length of the shorter pieces as 23.4, 70.2, 117, 257.4 and 500 m.

Each cable segment should be terminated at both ends with a terminating resistor. The cable may only be earthed at one end of the segment.

Most of the available cables are marked throughout their length by rings separated by a distance of 2.5 m. This is because the distance between two transceivers should be an integer multiple of 2.5 m. Thus, the colour marking is an excellent installation aid. All the recommendations serve to minimize signal reflections.

These recommendations were not adhered to at the Leibniz Computer Centre, with the exception of the minimum distance of 2.5 m between transceivers. During the operation of the extensive Ethernet (over 20 000 m of Ethernet coax cable), no problems have occurred to date which can be traced back to signal reflections.

3.1.2 Transceivers and transceiver cables

One important point when choosing transceivers which is, however, of decreasing significance as times goes by, is an awareness of small differences between Ethernet V2.0 and the IEEE 802.3 standard. These differences have an effect on the design of transceivers and Ethernet controllers and mean that, normally, controllers and transceivers must belong to the same generation (in other words, implement the same standard). There have been problems with networks based on Ethernet V2.0 which were subsequently extended. These problems relate to the so-called collision test signal or 'heartbeat'. In Ethernet V2.0, the transceiver generates a signal at regular intervals (SQE or heartbeat) to signal to the controller that the transceiver is operational. The IEEE 802.3 standard, on the other hand, uses this signal to indicate a fault. If an 802.3 transceiver is connected to an Ethernet V2.0 controller, the controller interprets the lack of an SQE signal as meaning that the transceiver is defective. In the converse case, the controller thinks that there are constant faults, which the transceiver signals at regular intervals. In more recent transceivers, it is possible to specify the behaviour of the transceiver by switching the SQE signal on or off. The use of transceivers corresponding to different versions of the standard within a network may also give rise to difficulties.

Other major differences between transceivers relate to the way in which they are installed. Many transceivers are of the vampire type. In this case, whilst the network is in continuous operation the Ethernet cable may be drilled using a special drill, and the transceiver may be inserted. There are also transceivers for which the installation procedure involves interrupting the cable (leading to an interruption of the overall network operation on this coax cable). While in this case later removal of the transceiver requires the cable to be coupled using connectors, in the case of the first transceivers, the hole left in the cable may be sealed using a paste.

It remains to be noted that transceivers from different manufacturers may be used within a network without problems (except when different versions of the standard are involved, see above). Often, in addition to price, the size of transceivers plays an important role in the choice, since they are usually installed in very narrow cable conduits or shafts. In the meantime, transceivers which are smaller than the associated adapter unit (tap) (that is, about the size of a matchbox or a cigarette packet) are now available.

An Ethernet controller is connected to a transceiver over a so-called transceiver cable. This consists of four twisted-line pairs with a teflon or PVC sheathing. It is terminated by a 15-pin subminiature connector or jack. The connector and the jack are fastened together, according to the standard, by a sliding lock mechanism. In practice, however, this has proved susceptible to malfunction so screw connections are also available. The maximum length of this cable is 50 m. Since it is relatively rigid and inflexible to lay (permissible bending radius 20 cm, external diameter 11.5 mm), thinner versions of the cable are also available (office transceiver cable). Because the line diameters are lower, the electrical characteristics are also poorer. Thus, the maximum length of this cable is correspondingly less (up to 10 m, depending on the manufacturer).

It is relatively uncomplicated to attach connectors, couplers and terminal resistors to the normal Ethernet cable using clamping claws and this can be done in about 10 minutes. During this period, network operation on the coax cable is not possible. A coax type-N connector (IEC 169/16) must be attached to the cable segment end. The impedance resistor (50 Ω) or the N-barrel connector is then screwed on.

It is possible to assemble transceivers without interrupting the continuous operation of the network by using an assembly kit. After the connection bracket has been attached, a hole is drilled into the cable core. When the transceiver is screwed on to the bracket, the contact pin of the transceiver tap slips into the cable core and establishes the connection. It takes approximately 15 minutes to assemble a transceiver. After a transceiver is removed, the hole cannot be re-used. A new transceiver may be inserted at a distance of about 3 cm.

3.1.3 Multiport transceivers

In many cases there is a requirement to connect several Ethernet terminals to the network within the same room. Normally, for the standard Ethernet,

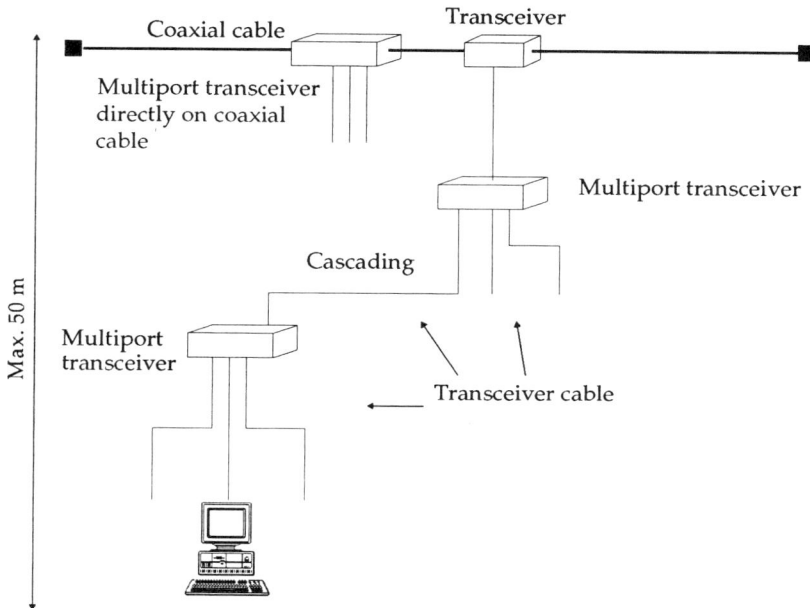

Figure 3.2 Multiport transceiver.

one transceiver per terminal is needed. Since there must be a minimum distance of 2.5 m between transceivers, it used to be necessary in many cases, to lay additional coils of cable to allow for these distances.

Multiport transceivers help to solve this problem. They act as transceiver multiplexers and, typically, may be used to connect several terminals over the normal transceiver cable. There are two options: either the multiport transceiver (two or four ports) is attached directly to the coaxial cable, or the multiport transceiver (up to 16 ports, fan-out unit) is itself attached to the coaxial cable via a transceiver cable and a single transceiver. As far as the rule '100 transceivers to an Ethernet segment' is concerned, a multiport transceiver of the latter type counts as one transceiver. Thus, many more Ethernet controllers may be connected to a coax segment. It is questionable whether this is sensible in practice because of the high traffic volume.

It is also possible to increase the number of connections by cascading multiport transceivers. Here, the overall length of the transceiver cable up to the coax cable must be less than 50 m.

A multiport transceiver need not necessarily be attached to an

Ethernet cable. In so-called 'standalone operation', it may be used to construct a standalone mini Ethernet (for example, within a room).

Some of the available multiport transceivers of the fan-out type (for example, DELNI from DEC) require their own power supply, others draw the necessary current from the controller interface.

A multiport transceiver in no way reduces the transmission speed for the individual attached terminals. Thus, it does not form an additional bottleneck.

In addition to eliminating the need for additional coils of cable to provide for sufficient separation between transceivers in the case of a high terminal density, a multiport transceiver has another positive side effect. It reduces the proportional connection costs per terminal. This effect only comes into play when the multiport transceiver is almost fully occupied.

3.1.4 Repeaters

Repeaters connect two cable segments and are used when these are less than 100 m apart. The repeater is then attached to each cable segment using a transceiver cable of a maximum length of 50 m and a transceiver for each cable segment. The transceiver for the repeater may be placed at any point of the coax segment. A repeater regenerates and repeats all signals from each of the segments and forwards them to the other segment. Most repeaters have a self-test function and detect erroneous signals on a segment. These are not then forwarded to the other segment. This means that errors are to some extent kept local.

The signal delay time due to a repeater corresponds approximately to the propagation time over 500 m of Ethernet cable.

Repeaters must be installed in such a way that they do not create ring or loop configurations. There must be a unique route through the Ethernet system between two Ethernet controllers.

3.1.5 Remote repeaters

Even when two Ethernet segments are separated by (up to) 1000 m, it is also possible to form a single Ethernet. This is done using so-called remote repeaters.

The overall repeater function is implemented by two repeater halves linked together by a duplex fibre optic cable. The maximum cable length of the link is 1000 m. In most available products several types of fibre optic cables may be used: 50/125 μ, 62.5/125 μ and 100/140 μ multimode fibre optic conductors are currently the most popular.

The total link, including both halves, has the effect of a single local repeater as far as the network layout is concerned. If a repeater half detects erroneous signals on its cable segment, it stops transmitting them to the other side, thus providing additional reliability.

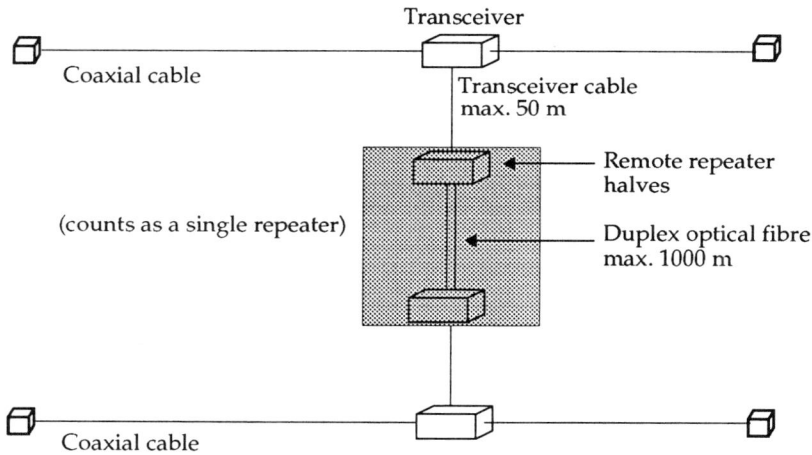

Figure 3.3   Remote repeater.

Many manufacturers/suppliers of Ethernet networks have such devices in their programme. Normally these do not adhere to the standard and so cannot be mixed. Moreover, use of these devices is declining as the products described in Section 3.3 become increasingly popular for fibre optic cabling.

3.2 Cheapernet

Cheapernet is a less expensive and more flexible coaxial cable than standard Ethernet. The connection procedure, using on-board transceivers and pre-mounted connection points (sockets or T pieces), may be somewhat different. Connection to the classical Ethernet and to other Cheapernet segments involves the use of multiport repeaters. In contrast to the standard Ethernet, the permissible segment length and number of stations are substantially less.

3.2.1 Cheapernet cable

10base2, which is defined in IEEE 802.3, represents a considerably less expensive type of Ethernet, which is easier to lay because of the flexibility of the cable. This version of Ethernet is also known as Cheapernet or thin Ethernet (Figure 3.4). An RG 58A/U or C/U (50 Ω) cable is used (see Section 2.4.3). One disadvantage of this cable type is that it exhibits considerably greater attenuation than the standard cable. Thus, the layout possibilities are also different. The following values are specified for Cheapernet:

- Individual cable segments may have a maximum length of 185 m.
- Thirty transceivers are permitted per cable segment.
- The minimum distance between two transceivers is 0.5 m.

While some manufacturers (for example, Schneider and Koch) guarantee longer cable lengths for individual Cheapernet segments (for example, 300 m) provided controllers from only these companies are used, it is imperative when laying the Cheapernet cable to adhere to the prescribed length of 185 m in order to avoid problems should controllers from other manufacturers be added at a later date.

Table 3.2 lists the major differences between standard Ethernet and Cheapernet.

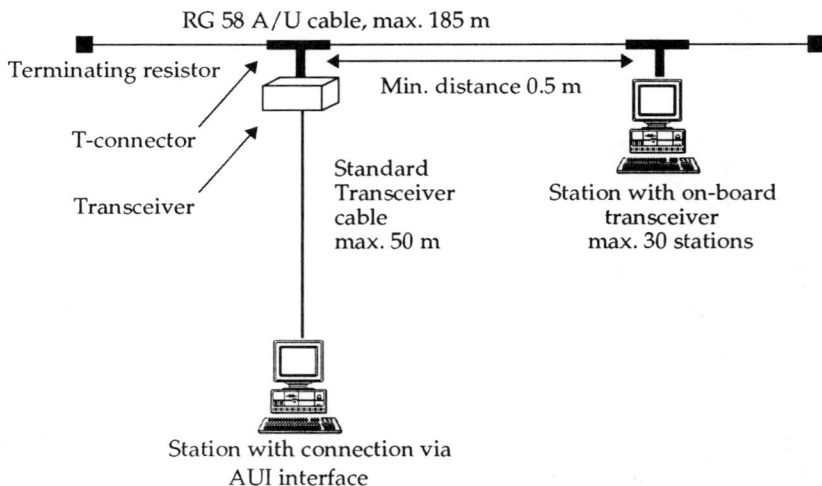

Figure 3.4 Cheapernet components.

Table 3.2 Comparison of standard Ethernet and Cheapernet.

Parameter	Standard Ethernet	Cheapernet
Data rate	10 Mbps	10 Mbps
Segment length	500 m	185 m
Transceiver distance	2.5 m	0.5 m
Cable diameter	10.3 mm	4.7 mm
Bending radius	20 cm	8 cm
Laying	Costly, since rigid	Simple, since more flexible

3.2.2 Transceivers

In the case of the standard Ethernet cable, a new transceiver may be connected at any time during continuous operation (at least for transceivers with vampire clips, provided the minimum length between transceivers is preserved). This is not the case for Cheapernet cable. Here, if necessary, transceivers are attached directly to the cable. For this, the cable must be cut and BNC connectors attached. Then a T piece is inserted between the two ends and the transceiver is attached to this. The latter has a tap which was specially developed for Cheapernet. The installation cannot be carried out whilst the network is operational (interruption to the network is required for the full assembly time). Thus, when laying Cheapernet, a different strategy should be chosen; it is best to know the requisite points in advance, since T pieces can already be inserted in the cable at these points at the time of laying. These T pieces need only be equipped with a transceiver when a terminal is to be connected. However, in this case, the T piece must always be fitted with a terminating resistor to avoid interference effects during network operation. Thus, one possible strategy when laying Cheapernet is a blanket pre-cabling of all rooms, including insertion of the T pieces. However, the cost savings of this strategy as compared with standard Ethernet are not very important. Cheapernet transceivers currently cost just as much as standard transceivers. While the price of the cable used in Cheapernet is only a third of that of the standard cable, the laying costs (which are the main component) will be similar in both cases (with the slight advantage that Cheapernet cable is more flexible and so easier to lay).

3.2.3 Sockets

The above techniques for pre-installation of the T pieces have recently been improved to permit interruption-free connection of additional stations. Instead of a T piece, it is possible to install a socket which provides a through

Wall socket

Cheapernet cable

Special cable

T-connector

Station with Ethernet controller
and on-board transceiver

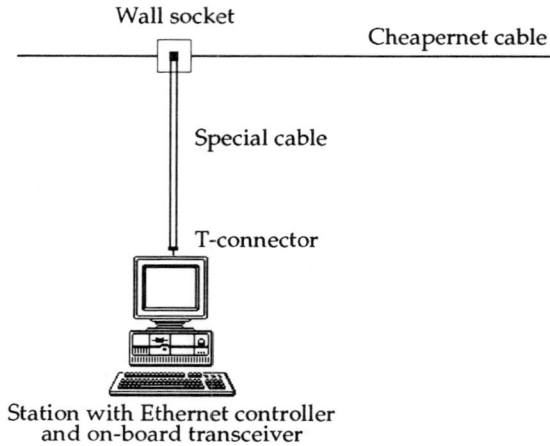

Figure 3.5   Cheapernet wall socket.

connection for the Cheapernet bus when it is not used as a connection point. When installing a station, either a transceiver is inserted in the socket without interrupting the network (for example, Zellner Data Technology), or the bus is extended to the station using special connection cable (for example, Easy Connect, DEC Connect, Ackermann, Belden). The use of a transceiver does not affect the length of the Cheapernet. However, if the option of connection with a special cable is chosen, in length calculations, twice the length of this cable must be added to the length of the existing Cheapernet. Thus, the maximum length of 185 m is easily reached and exceeded. Moreover, because of the increased attenuation, the installation of sockets may reduce the number of attachable devices.

3.2.4 On-board transceivers

One advantage of Cheapernet is the use of ready-made Cheapernet controller cards. These cards have a so-called on-board transceiver. This transceiver is implemented directly on the card and is thus considerably less expensive to manufacture than a standalone transceiver.

The on-board transceiver requires a different cabling technique to that of standard Ethernet because the Cheapernet cable must now lead directly to the controller, since the BNC jack of the on-board transceiver must be attached directly to the Cheapernet T piece or to the special cable (in the case of the socket solution). Using this technology, one avoids not only the standalone transceiver, but also the relatively expensive transceiver connection cable.

3.2.5 Multiport repeaters

Two Ethernet segments are normally connected via a repeater. This must access each cable segment via a transceiver. As far as Cheapernet is concerned, there is now a solution which, under certain conditions, provides a more cost-effective way of coupling cable segments. This solution involves the use of a so-called multiport repeater. Typically, the ends of up to eight Cheapernet segments (without additional transceivers) may be attached to such a repeater and linked together. This gives rise to a star-shaped structure of the linked Cheapernet segments. In addition, an AUI is available and may be used to implement a connection via a transceiver to a standard Ethernet or a fan-out unit. Currently, a multiport receiver with four Cheapernet ports is inexpensive; thus, it is already less expensive to couple two Cheapernet segments with a standard Ethernet in this way than using standard repeaters.

Since at the interface to the Cheapernet cable the multiport receiver has the function of a transceiver, at most 29 stations may be connected to the attached Cheapernet segment. The multiport repeater may also be used in standalone mode.

Examples of such components include DEC's DEMPR-AB and Cabletron's MR-X000C series, which offer repeaters with 1, 4 and 8 Cheapernet ports.

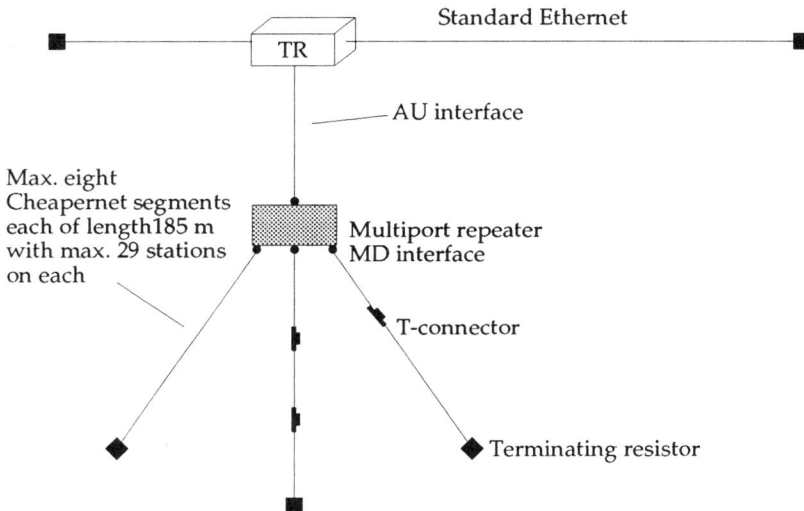

Figure 3.6 Multiport repeater.

3.3 Fibre optic systems

A brief introduction to fibre optic technology is given in Subsection 2.4.8.1. This section contains further technical details. The components of the optical message transmission system are (see Figure 2.33):

- the transmitter, with modulator and light source;
- the fibre optic circuits with plug and splice connections;
- the receiver with photodiode and amplifier.

The signal to be transmitted is modulated in the transmitter and used to control the corresponding light source (light on, light off). The light pulses are then injected into the fibre optic conductor. In the receiver, the light arriving from the fibre optic conductor is received by an optical decoder, amplified and decoded. Here, differences may occur depending on:

- the fibre optic cable used;
- the optical transmitter and receiver used;
- the connection technology used for the fibre optic cable.

3.3.1 Fibre optic cables

Nowadays, fibre optic cables are usually made from glass fibres. Because of the high attenuation levels, it is currently only possible to use plastic fibres in local area networks under certain circumstances, since the distances which can be bridged are still less than 50 m. The glass fibre itself consists of a glass core with a high refractive index and a surrounding glass sheath with a small refractive index. The glass material usually consists of silicon oxide. Additives are used to give the glass core and the glass sheath different refractive indices. Incoming light waves, which are incident at a very small angle to the axis of the fibre in the fibre core, are reflected at the boundary between the fibre core and the fibre sheath, and thus remain within the fibre core. As mentioned in Subsection 2.4.8.1, the profile of the refractive index between the glass core and the glass sheath is used to distinguish between two types of optical fibres:

- multimode fibres which may be stepped-index or graded-index fibres;
- monomode fibres.

Graded-index fibres are usually distinguished by the thickness of their light-conducting core. The following rule of thumb applies: the thicker the fibre core is, the greater the attenuation is (the loss of energy per route section). The attenuation also depends on the wavelength used (850 nm or 1300 nm). The losses on injection of the light into the cable are correspondingly lower

Table 3.3   Typical values for various optical fibres.

Fibre	G 50/125	G 62.5/125	G 100/140	E 9/125
Type	Multimode graded index			Monomode
Core diam., μm	50	62.5	100	9
Sheath diam., μm	125	125	140	125
Fibre diam., μm	250	250	260	250
Attenuation in dB/km – at 850 nm – at 1300 nm	< 3.0 < 1.0	< 3.5 < 1.5	< 4.0	< 1.0 < 0.5
Bandwidth for 1 km, in MHz, at 850 nm	> 400	> 160	> 100	> 800
Numerical aperture	0.20	0.27	0.29	0.40

for the higher wavelength. Moreover, plug connections for thicker fibres exhibit smaller losses and are less sensitive as far as their exact adjustment is concerned. Despite these advantages of a thicker fibre, thinner graded-index fibres are the most widely used. There are currently three important types of graded-index fibre:

100/140 μ fibre   The notation 100/140 μ refers to the core size (100 μm) and the overall diameter (140 μm), respectively. These fibres are mainly used by American LAN manufacturers. They include, for example, fibres belonging to IBM's in-house cabling-system family and fibres from Hewlett-Packard and Ungermann Bass. Use of these fibres is declining.

50/125 μ fibre   This is a fibre specified by CCITT. It is used (if monomode fibres are not already used) by many European PTTs and the European market is oriented towards this fibre.

62.5/125 μ fibre   This type of fibre is common in North America. It has been accepted as a reference fibre by all important standardization bodies (IEEE 802.3, IEEE 802.5, ISO 9314-4 (FDDI)). Its performance capability is comparable with that of the 50/125 μ fibre. The FDDI standard recommends the use of this type of fibre although 50/125 μ fibres are permissible. IBM bases all its products on this type of fibre.

There is only one type of monomode fibre in use, which has the dimension 9–10/125 μ. The German Telekom now lays and supplies exclusively monomode fibres because of their ability to cover considerably greater distances (up to 50 km) without amplifier components. Table 3.3 gives typical values for the various optical fibre types.

Currently, in the LAN area, graded-index fibres are predominantly used for cabling in companies and university campuses, since this connection technology is less expensive and because the advantages of monomode fibres for long line lengths do not come into play for a small area measuring only a few kilometres across.

The costs vary, depending on the nature of the outdoor cable. There are steel-armed cables, cables with protection against gnawing by rodents, cables that are cross-sectionally or longitudinally watertight, mono- and multimode fibres in one cable, etc. When fibre optic cables are used, the number of fibres chosen should not be too small because later applications (for example, FDDI, Token Ring, connections to PBXs, image transmission) may need to share them. Moreover, the additional cost of increasing the number of fibres is negligible when compared with the laying costs.

The specification sheet for fibre optic cable typically includes the following entries (based on the example of an 8-fibre outdoor cable from the company LAPPKABEL):

- Optical data
  - Fibre: G 50/1125
  - Fibre type: Multimode/graded index
- Mechanical data
  - Cable weight: 85 kg/km
  - Permitted tension: 2000 N
  - Cable diameter: 10.5 mm
  - Permitted bending radius: 20 × cable diameter
  - Laying temperature: −5 to +50° C
  - Operating temperature: −20 to +60° C

- Standard: DIN VDE 0888 part 3.

3.3.2 Optical transmission systems

In addition to the cable, the optical transmission system (electro-optical conversion) also plays a role. First the wavelength of the light which is used for transmission must be determined. The attenuation pattern for fibre optic conductors over the wavelengths of light has marked minima in areas around certain wavelengths. These wavelengths are 850 nm, 1300 nm and 1500 nm (invisible infrared light). Currently, the first two 'windows' are primarily used for optical message transmission.

The following requirements are placed on the optical transmitter:

- High light power
- Good efficiency

- Light wavelengths in a suitable window
- Directed light emission
- Modulable with the highest possible frequencies
- Linear characteristic curve of modulation.

Light-emitting diodes (LEDs) and (semiconductor-) laser diodes (LDs) are distinguished by their fundamentally different modes of operation.

LEDs are available for all three windows, have longer lifetimes (one million hours), are simpler to construct and have low costs. However, their usable optical power is only in the micro- to milliwatt area. Thus, LEDs can only be used to bridge distances of between three and at most five km.

The advantage of laser diodes is that their power lies in the milliwatt to watt area, which means that they can be used to bridge considerably greater distances. On the other hand, they have a relatively short lifetime (100 000 hours), exhibit a strong dependence on temperature and are very expensive compared with LEDs. Laser diodes are mainly used in conjunction with monomode fibres, since LDs can emit almost monochromatic light. For all these reasons privately operated networks in the LAN area with speeds up to approximately 50 Mbps mainly use LEDs.

The following conditions are imposed on the receiver element (optoelectrical converter):

- High optoelectrical efficiency.
- Low noise.
- Most higher modulation frequencies are processed.
- Linear characteristic curve for conversion.
- Uncomplicated attachment of fibre optic cable.

There are also two different receiver elements, the PIN diode and the AP diode. All three windows can be received with these diodes. The PIN diode is largely used because of its robustness, the low supply voltage and its low cost. The AP diode with its considerably greater optoelectrical efficiency is substantially more expensive. A description of how these systems work and the differences between them is beyond the scope of this book.

3.3.3 Connection technologies

Another factor which determines the performance of fibre optic systems is the way in which connections and plug assembly are implemented. Here, we distinguish between two basic technologies: splices and plug connections.

In (mechanical or thermal) splices two fibres are linked together insolubly. This is carried out either using an immersion adhesive (mechanical, now almost of no importance), or by thermal welding with an arc lamp (fusion splicing). The additional attenuation resulting from splicing amounts to between 0.1 and 0.3 dB. However, this technique requires relatively expensive tools and skilled personnel. Splicing is usually carried out by third-party companies.

Another form of connection involves the fitting of mechanical plug connectors. With these, a connection may be released at any time. The fibre is adjusted in the connector and fixed, and the cable stress relief is clamped round the plug stem.

In addition to precision connectors (which cannot usually be assembled locally), other connectors and simple assembly kits are available to meet the highest requirements. Either the connectors are assembled by the company carrying out the installation or, as decided in the Leibniz Computer Centre, a staff member must be trained in the task of assembling connectors. This requires an assembly box. The training in the assembly of connectors takes approximately five hours. The assembly itself, including extra work, takes around one hour per connector. After the optical fibre is exposed, it must be positioned exactly in the connector case, adjusted and fixed; the adhesive must be hardened using a hot-air device. The connector is then connected to the fibre optic cable sheath using a contracting tube. Finally, the optical fibre surface protruding from the plug must be polished until it is smooth, and the polished surface should be inspected with a microscope. An error rate of approximately 5% may be predicted. The attenuation is 0.5 to 2 dB per connector. Another version involves splicing the plugs already assembled by the manufacturer (fibre pigtail with measuring protocol) to the end of the fibre. Thus, low attenuation is achieved, since factory-assembled connectors are associated with considerably less attenuation than those assembled locally. In this case, the additional splice does not play an important role. Fibre optic lines may be connected together using connectors and couplers or with splices. Connection using two connectors and couplers results in attenuation of 1 to 4 dB, connection with splices gives an attenuation of at most 0.3 dB.

There are several connector types. Two of the most commonly used are the F-SMA and the ST connectors. Connections with the SMA connector use screws and are more robust against mechanical effects than those using the ST connector. However, the ST connector, with its bayonet catch, provides a specific contact force, a protection against torsion and thus a reproducible attenuation. It is suitable for instances in which the fibre optic conductors are frequently rearranged. The SMA connector should only be used for fixed connections which do not change often.

The connectors and fibre optic lines should, if possible, come from a single manufacturer in order to achieve as high a cabling quality as possible. After the installation is complete, attenuation and reflection should be measured for each fibre in a circuit. The measured values should be less than or equal to the values computed from the standards (dB values for connectors and splices, fibre optic cable lengths). In addition, the cable routing in buildings and sites must be documented (if possible using computer aided design (CAD)).

3.3.4 Ethernet-compatible fibre optic systems

The following applies to all available Ethernet-compatible fibre optic systems.

At the electrical AUI between transceivers and controllers the system behaves like a standard Ethernet. This means that the network subscriber may use the same Ethernet controller as in coax systems.

As described in Subsection 2.4.8.2, there are two versions of this system which have different star couplers (passive or active). In the passive star coupler, the ingoing optical signal is forwarded on all output lines without regeneration; in the active star coupler, the signal is amplified before it is forwarded. Although passive star couplers may be more fail safe, they do have disadvantages, such as limited extensibility of the network, which are so serious that these systems still play only a subordinate role in the market. We shall not consider them further in this book.

Hirschmann provides a representative example of a system with active star couplers. The system cabling topology is not of the bus type but forms a (usually multilevel) star network. At the node points, this has so-called star couplers from which duplex fibre optic conductors lead to so-called optical transceivers. The latter convert the optical signal in the electrical AUI transceiver interface.

The Hirschmann system uses active star couplers which regenerate incoming signals before these are forwarded on the output lines. In this way, a maximum distance of 4500 m may be bridged where the distance between transceivers and star couplers without add-on components may be up to 3000 m (for multimode fibre optic cables).

The Hirschmann system may be used to construct an Ethernet consisting of up to 350 star couplers. At most five star couplers may be cascaded; in other words, there may be at most five star couplers between any two points of the system. This value is calculated from the maximum permissible signal propagation time of 51.2 μs.

A star coupler consists of a basic casing of various sizes (possibly with a double electric supply-line) into which various adapter cards may be inserted. Naturally, these include (among others) adapter cards for the optical transmission circuits which support various duplex multimode fibres ($50/125\ \mu$, $62.5/125\ \mu$, $85/125\ \mu$ and $100/140\ \mu$); they have an LED as transmitter, a PIN diode as receiver and the transmit power can be set. A circuit attenuation of at least 17 dB must be bridged (for $100/140\ \mu$). The largest casing is capable of holding up to 19 such cards. In addition, an optical card for monomode fibre optic circuits is available which operates with laser diodes. This may be used to bridge distances greater than 4.5 km.

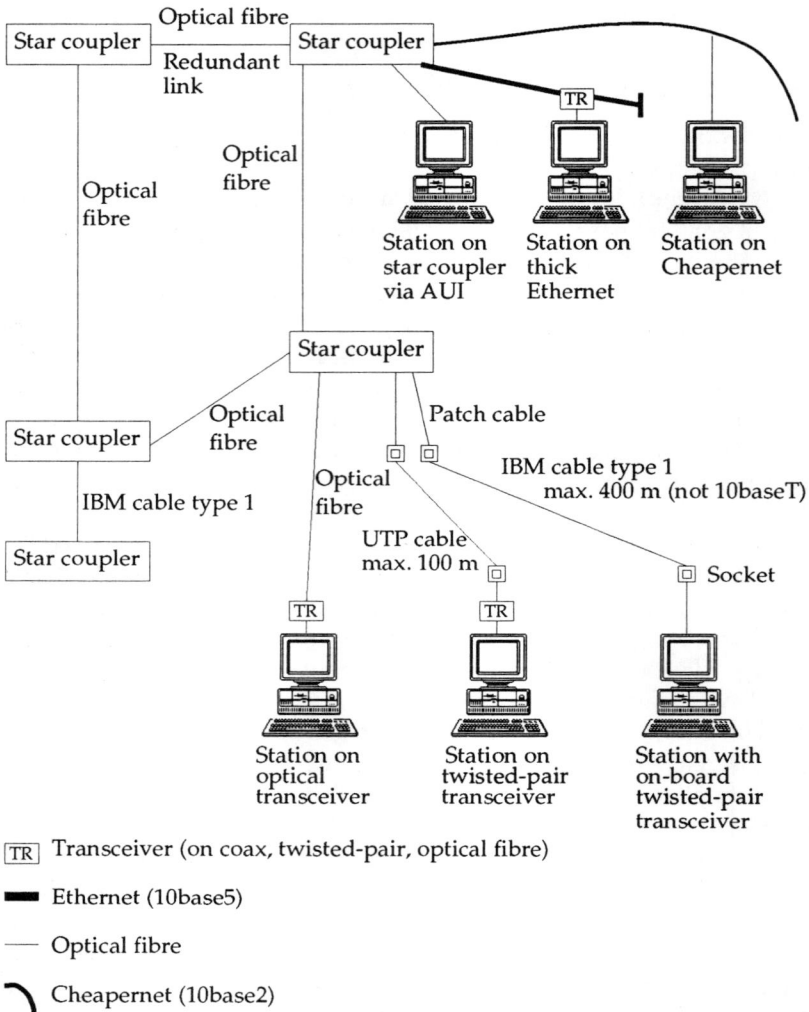

Figure 3.7   Ethernet based on optical fibres (Hirschmann system).

Another adapter card permits direct connection of up to 500 m of standard-Ethernet cable or 185 m of Cheapernet cable via type-N or BNC jacks, respectively. Other cards provide for the direct access of two transceiver cables and the operation of Ethernet over twisted-pair lines (see next section). Moreover, a diagnostic card with an SNMP agent may be built in to the star coupler so that the star coupler can be integrated into a network management system. A so-called retiming card enables the installation of redundant circuits between star couplers and a considerable extension of the network in terms of the number of star couplers and coverage.

Either an optical star coupler or an optical transceiver may be attached at the end of a fibre optic circuit. This converts the optical signals to electrical signals and provides the standard transceiver interface for connecting arbitrary Ethernet controllers with no modifications.

3.4 Twisted-pair systems

Because of the existing wire infrastructures in buildings and the wide dissemination of the Ethernet standard, an attempt was made to implement this system on twisted-pair lines. Synoptics was one of the first companies to bring such a (then unstandardized) system to the market. In the meantime the Ethernet version 10baseT for UTP cable has been standardized (see Section 2.4.4). 10baseT is based on a joint proposal from Hewlett-Packard, Synoptics Communications and Wang. The recommended architecture is based on a star-shaped wire cabling. In the centre of the star is an amplifier (hub); at each end there is a wire transceiver which makes the well-known AUI available to end subscribers. Since Ethernet-compatible wire systems are also available for cables other than UTP, we shall first discuss the various line types.

3.4.1 Cable types

The most important cable parameters for twisted-pair copper cables are:

- impedance
- attenuation
- crosstalk.

The impedance of the cable and all other components of the system (for example, jumper and connection cables) should be constant over the frequency area to be used to avoid the need for adapter units (baluns).

The cable attenuation is frequency dependent and determines the maximum transmission speed and the range for data communications.

Crosstalk occurs because the current in a conductor produces a magnetic field which may be received as electromagnetic waves (emission) but also induces an unwanted voltage in neighbouring lines (crosstalk). There are various ways of minimizing the emitted radiation (larger distance to sources of interference, coax cable, twisted-pair conductors, earthed shields). If twisted-pair conductors are used, the outward and the return line are as close together as possible and radiate the same signal with the opposite polarity, then the amplitude of the emitted radiation is reduced. Moreover, for twisted-pairs the transmitted signal also has opposite polarities over each twisted length so that it annihilates itself almost completely. More recent developments reduce crosstalk further by increasing the twisting rate and using different twisting rates for individual wire pairs.

In the standard, 10baseT is defined for UTP cable. This is often used as telephone cable, particularly in the USA. It consists of twisted pairs and has an impedance of 100 Ω. Neither the cable jacket nor the cable pairs are shielded. In Europe, on the other hand, UTP also refers to cable with a shielded cable jacket. In this way, the stricter European requirements on irradiation and emission are easier to satisfy; however, the electrical properties of a UTP, such as attenuation and impedance, remain the same. One variant with an impedance of 100 Ω is a cable which also has shielding around the cable jacket, but a different twisting, namely so-called quad-stranding. This is called the star quad.

Shielded twisted pair (STP) cable is primarily used in the IBM cabling system as type-1 cable. This two-pair cable has shielding around the twisted-pairs of wires and around the cable sheath. Its impedance is 150 Ω. Table 3.4 gives a comparison of the UTP and STP cable types.

The use of wire cable with high data rates, such as that provided by Ethernet, raises a number of questions.

STP   UTP
Shielded twisted pair   Star quad   Unshielded twisted pair

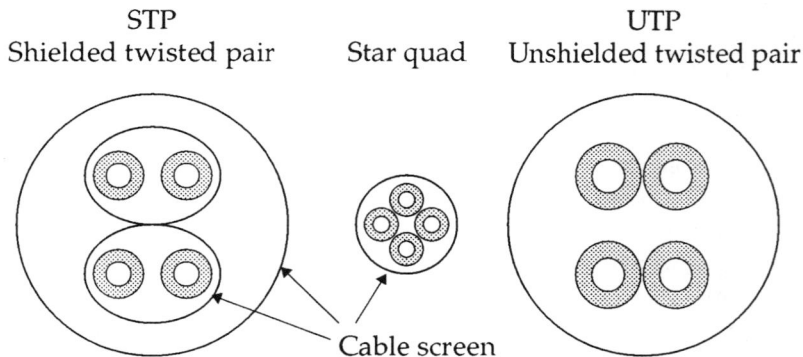

Cable screen

Figure 3.8   Cable structure: UTP, star quad, STP.

Table **3.4**   Comparison of UTP and STP.

Cable parameter	UTP	STP
Impedance, Ω	100	150
Attenuation at 10 MHz	< 70 dB/km	< 40 dB/km
Crosstalk, 0–16 MHz	> 45 dB	> 70 dB

Shielding of the cable

Are the cables constructed (shielding, twisting) in such a way that no relevant electromagnetic radiation is emitted? Are the emissions tolerated by the PTT? Are the components authorized?

Crosstalk

Is the crosstalk so little that links via the same cable are not affected? Can such links be passed through distribution systems? Can cable with a large number of wire pairs be used without interactive effects?

To avoid these problems, the type-1 cable of the IBM cabling system (or cable of a similar quality) should be used, because this prevents both outgoing emission and crosstalk. However, this cable has an impedance of 150 Ω while most twisted-pair systems operate with 100 Ω. Moreover, it is also quite thick and rigid, which may affect the size of the cable conduit.

Currently, the so-called star quad is also a good solution. Here, only one application should be run on the same cable (thus, there can be no voice and data communications at the same time).

Test devices are available which may be used to test whether existing laid lines are suitable for this system. In any case, even if the lines do not correspond fully to the specification, a test should always be carried out. For example, at the Leibniz Computer Centre it was possible to use existing non-twisted 16-wire V.24 lines of a length up to 50 m for 10baseT. With a clever choice of wires, it is even possible to implement two 10baseT links in a single cable.

Copper cables are primarily used in the so-called storey area of a cabling structure to achieve a star-shaped cabling based on a network wiring cabinet located in that storey. The active component (hub), which links the attached lines to an Ethernet, is then implemented in this cabinet. Other types of networks (for example, Token Ring, V.24) may also be implemented on these wire lines provided the corresponding components are implemented in the cabinet.

3.4.2 Hub

The hub is the central element of an implementation of Ethernet based on twisted-pair lines. At the centre of the star, it links all the twisted-pair lines attached to it to an Ethernet. The links between the hub and DTE may be up to 100 m long in the 10baseT standard. However, some companies and users report considerably longer achievable line lengths (up to 350 m for UTP cables and up to 400 m for STP cables). The hub operates like a repeater and may be connected to a thick coax cable (via AUI) or a thin coax cable (via BNC jacks). Of course, it can also be operated as a standalone unit. Moreover, as in the case of multiport repeaters, cascading is also possible.

The hub for 10baseT Ethernet usually has RJ 45 jacks or a 50-pin twisted-pair port for a Telco connector. This connector divides the 50-pin interface in the hub into twelve patch connections with RJ 45 connectors. These may then be led directly to the associated patch field, for example, in the network wiring cabinet. Other types of connectors (such as sub D9) may also be used, for example, with non-10baseT hubs (e.g. STP cable).

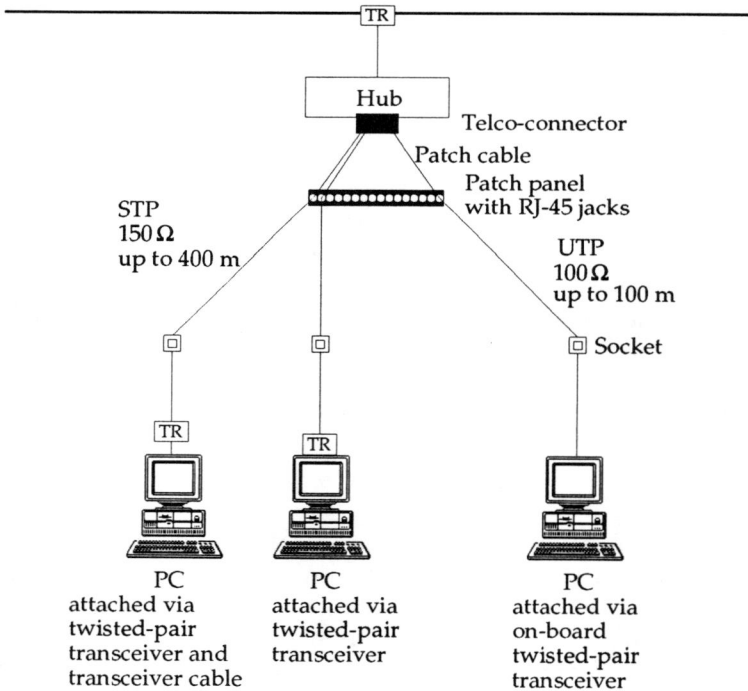

Figure 3.9   Hub for twisted-pair Ethernet.

The individual connections to the DTEs are automatically disabled in the case of faults (for example, 30 consecutive collisions, collision of an inadmissible duration, excessively long data packets), and automatically re-enabled after error recovery. If network management functions are implemented in the hub, the enabling and disabling of connections to the DTEs may also be carried out by operator intervention. The star-shaped implementation of the Ethernet scheme provides a considerably improved error isolation and network management facility when compared with the bus-based Ethernet.

The functionality of Ethernet on twisted-pair lines is provided either by compact devices (workgroup concentrators) with this interface alone, or by so-called multimedia access centres into which individual slot-in cards for this Ethernet version are inserted. We shall discuss multimedia access centres in more detail in Section 3.6.

3.4.3 Twisted-pair transceivers

On the DTE side, as with Cheapernet, there are two possible connection procedures, namely the conventional procedure of connection via a special twisted-pair transceiver or connection via an on-board transceiver. Here too, the RJ 45 connector is predominantly used in 10baseT.

The twisted-pair transceiver is almost as small as a matchbox and has an RJ 45 jack on one side and the AUI interface to the transceiver cable on the other. Thus, all controllers with AUI interfaces may be attached to 10baseT. Another version, which saves on transceiver cable, is a twisted-pair transceiver which can be connected directly to the AUI of the station's Ethernet controller.

A number of companies now provide controllers with on-board transceivers for 10baseT with the RJ 45 interface. Such transceivers are no more expensive than those for Cheapernet. There are even slot-in cards for PCs with three possibilities for Ethernet connection (AUI, BNC and RJ 45 interfaces).

The components for the 10baseT standard (hub, transceiver, Ethernet controller) may be intermixed. The picture is different if a non-standard wire Ethernet is used (for example, STP cable) when the components must all be from the same manufacturer.

3.5 Wireless systems

Communication via wireless systems (for example, satellite, radio relay) has been available for some time in the trunk area. Increasingly, wireless systems are becoming available for the local area. This trend is also reflected in the creation of an IEEE 802.11 working group in November 1990, charged with the development of network standards for wireless LANs. It is hoped to issue a preliminary standard by mid-1993.

Wireless systems currently use four technologies: radio frequencies, infrared light, microwaves and ultrasound. The advantage of wireless systems over wire-based systems is their greater flexibility and their short installation times. They could be used, for example:

- in listed buildings which would be disfigured by the installation of cable conduits;
- when cable conduits are full;
- for temporary purposes when installation and deinstallation of a wire-based system is too expensive.

The disadvantage is the current lack of a standard for the frequencies. Above all in the RF area, in which the national PTTs have a very strong say, there are no recommended and reserved frequencies for radio LANs.

In addition, installation may give rise to acceptance problems since the effects of RF waves on health are not yet clear. Discussions of the use of low-emission screens in the workplace may be connected.

Products available in the RF area include NCR's WaveLAN and Olivetti's Sixtel. Products in the infrared area include BICC's InfraLAN together with CBL's System Laserlink 2000 which operates as a LAN connection for bridges.

Motorola's Altair system is a representative radio LAN, which permits wireless communication of devices with Ethernet capabilities. The system operates in the 18 GHz area which, because of its costs, was previously unattractive for commercial use. The only interference factor, as far as the use of this system is concerned could be due to radio relay systems which by chance pass over the site of the installation. 18-GHz waves are able to penetrate walls of a light construction in the interior of buildings, but are blocked by thicker reinforced concrete walls or floors. The range is around 15 m; thus, the frequency area is reusable at a distance of 40 m.

A unit (micro cell) of the Altair system (Figure 3.10) consists of a control module (CM) and user modules (UM). From a user module, it is possible to connect, via a BNC jack, to a Cheapernet which may contain up to six devices with Ethernet capabilities. The control module is attached to the wire-based Ethernet backbone and functions as a bridge. It is able to manage up to 32 devices with Ethernet capabilities and may be integrated into a network management system using an SNMP agent. The distance between user modules and control modules should not be greater than 15 m.

Wireless transmission between user and control modules takes place at 15 Mbps. However, this transmission rate must be shared between all the devices managed by the control module. This means that, in comparison with the standard Ethernet, there may be an additional delay of around

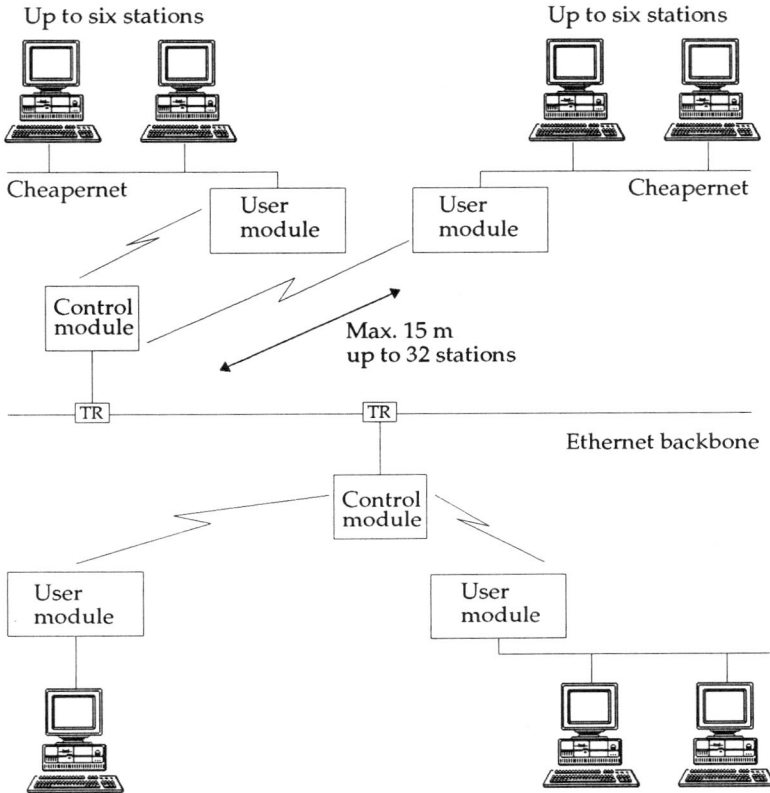

Figure 3.10   Motorola's Altair system.

8 ms between two stations. In some applications, this may have a negative effect on the transport rate and the response time.

3.6 Multimedia access centre

Since Ethernet is now implemented on many media, it is sensible to market new components which provide for integration of these media within a single device in an Ethernet. All available systems are essentially similar. At central points (star coupler, hub) the various media on which Ethernet is implemented are combined using the repeater functionality. The central points are linked together via appropriate media into a network. The interfaces for each medium are implemented in the interface cards of hubs or individual star couplers, which may, for example, be exchanged without interrupting the network. Interface cards are available for the following media (not from all manufacturers):

- Standard Ethernet
- Cheapernet
- Multimode fibre optic cables of various diameters with various connector types
- Monomode fibre optic cables
- Twisted-pair lines, 100 Ω (for example, UTP)
- Twisted-pair lines, 150 Ω (for example, STP)
- AUI (transceiver) interfaces.

The interface cards are linked together over a bus system. The incoming signals are amplified and regenerated (as in the repeater). If the interface card detects a fault in the attached medium (for example, constant collisions, data packet too long), the corresponding port is disconnected from the remainder of the network for the duration of the fault. Moreover, in some products when lines are interrupted, it is possible to activate parallel back-up lines. With the integration of cards with additional functions (for example, network management functions, bridge functions, router functions, gateways between networks of different types such as Ethernet, Token Ring and FDDI), these star couplers may be turned into powerful communications nodes. Readers are referred to the product literature of the relevant companies (for example, Ungermann Bass, 3Com, Chipcom, BICC, Cabletron, Allied Telesis, Hirschmann, Synoptics, AEG) for further details.

Whilst it is technically fascinating to install all interface cards at the same time in a single star coupler, this has no advantages as far as the network operation is concerned since, for example, fault-tracing devices for all these media must be provided at this point. Moreover, this contradicts the basic principle of structured cabling which provides, if possible, for the use of only one medium in a given area. Nevertheless, the various media with the products from a single manufacturer may be connected to an Ethernet where the Ethernet is implemented on different media in different buildings. Thus, it may easily happen that one building or part of a building was cabled with standard Ethernet when the Ethernet was first installed, while the next building or part of a building was cabled with Cheapernet, and finally, further twisted-pair cable was installed.

Chapter 4

Integrated networks of LANs, gateways

- The gateway problem

- Bridges

- Routers

- Planning LAN internetworks with bridges and routers

- LAN–WAN gateways

- Planning backbone networks for LAN interconnection

In recent years, local area networks have been so extensively installed in many companies for in-house communication that the limits of LAN-specific restrictions on their coverage and on the maximum number of subscribers have been reached. As a result, there is a requirement for components which help to overcome such restrictions. This involves solving the problems of how to create subnetworks of a too large network and an integrated network of LANs from subnetworks.

Until now, the most complicated LAN structures, which we described in Chapter 3, were multisegment LANs constructed from individual segments using repeaters. Multisegment LANs form a single collision area; in other words, the repeaters are layer-1 coupling elements. This chapter is concerned with LAN interconnection at higher levels. Thus, integrated networks of LANs may be formed from homogeneous or even heterogeneous subLANs. In the latter case, and also on the transition from LANs to WANs, the necessary adaptations to the various protocol worlds must be made using components called gateways.

Section 4.1 gives a general introduction to the gateway problem and classifies the coupling elements of the various layers. Section 4.2 describes the IEEE specifications for LAN coupling in layer 2a using so-called bridges. Section 4.3 describes the basic mode of operation of coupling elements for interconnecting LANs at layer 3 (known as routers) which are compared with bridges. Bridges are specified within the IEEE 802 standard, routers are not. There are as many different routers as there are variants of LAN transport systems. The recent development of bridges and routers has been chaotic, and an interesting range of products is now available. While Sections 4.2 and 4.3 are concerned with fundamental descriptions and specifications, Section 4.4 is practice- and product-oriented, and includes a detailed discussion of the choice and use of bridges, routers and brouters.

Section 4.5 is concerned with protocol structures for LAN transport systems and fundamental gateway approaches for LAN–WAN coupling in layer 4. Finally, Section 4.6 describes so-called backbone networks, or transit networks, for interconnecting local area networks.

4.1 The gateway problem

The tendency towards integrating networks is clearly discernible. Functional integration (at the level of the workplace, at the level of network services and applications), together with transmission-related integration (for example, cabling structures), demand that communications networks, including LANs, should be combined into a communications infrastructure. This infrastructure should be based on subnetworks which have developed independently in isolation as a result of organizational and spatial subdivisions, application-specific grounds or different DP hierarchies. In

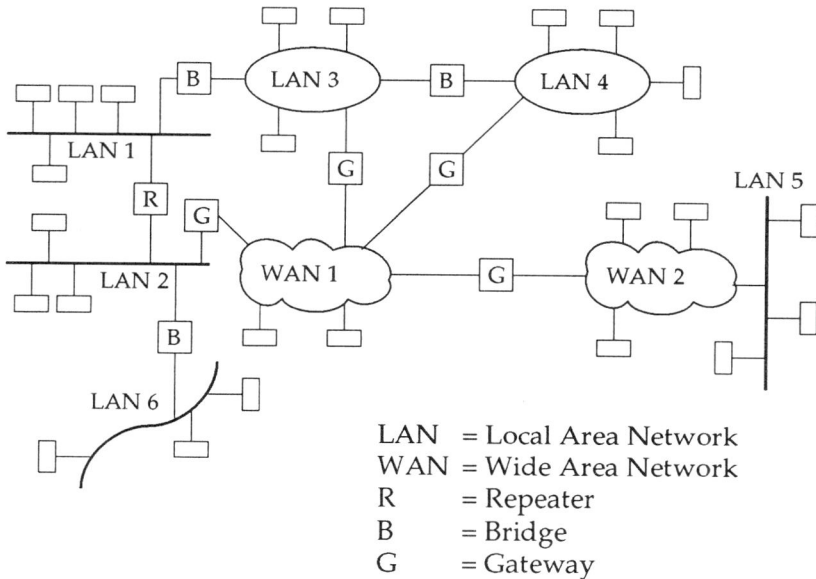

Figure 4.1   Example: LAN–WAN scenario.

addition, access to external partners and services requires connection to public telecommunication services and external networks over these subnetworks. Since the networks are not all based on the same schemes, adaptation services are required in an overall scenario (Figure 4.1). Typically, such services are used in the interworking of several departmental LANs in a company, or for communication between companies.

These adaptation services are provided in gateways. Gateways, with their hardware and software components, are used to implement the interface between coupled networks. In general, gateways map protocol and service hierarchies of network architectures on to one another. A mapping system is called a *level-N gateway* if the mapping is possible within layer N; in other words, if above layer N the same protocols and services are provided in the networks to be coupled. Here, it may be necessary for one of the networks to provide a service interface layer (enhancement/de-enhancement) if the service elements of the $(N-1)$ layers of the two networks cannot be mapped on to one another (Figure 4.2).

Some level-N gateways have names. For example, level-1 gateways are called *repeaters*; we described these in Section 2.4.5. Repeaters provide coupling at level 1, the physical layer, permit the formation of *multisegment LANs*, regenerate the medium-specific signals and act

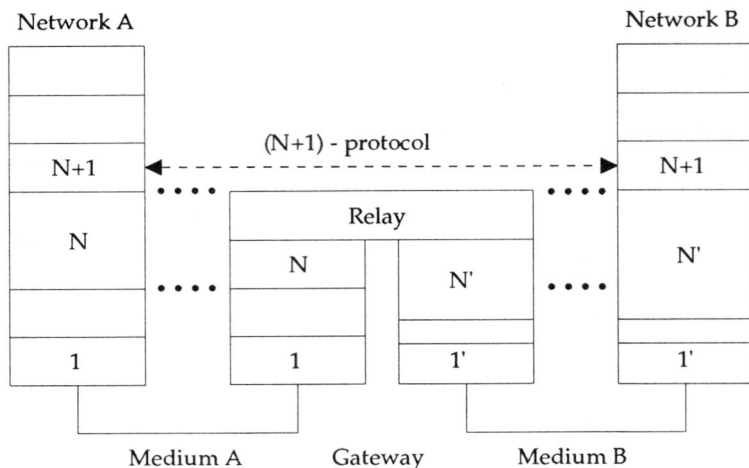

Figure 4.2   Level-N gateway .

as store-and-forward components for the individual bits. Local repeaters and remote repeaters with an intermediate inter-repeater link are not addressable. Since they lie below the MAC level, the delays which they cause must satisfy the Ethernet/CSMA-CD time conditions for collision detection (cf. with the collision parameter). Multisegment Ethernets form a single collision area. Possibilities for extending the topology using repeaters are very restricted, and the number of repeaters on a transmission circuit is very limited (see Chapter 2).

Level 2 gateways are called *bridges* (Figure 4.3). The structure of the IEEE standard suggests the design of a common level 2a (MAC level) gateway for the various types of LANs (Ethernet, Token Ring, Token Bus). This coupling facility is extremely important for the formation of Ethernet internetworks so we shall return to it a number of times (Sections 4.2 and 4.4).

ISO's preferred coupling level is the network layer. Coupling at level 3 means that subnetworks, with possibly different protocols and services in layers 1 to 3, must be adapted so that the resulting LAN internetwork provides a globally valid network service. This suggests a specific architectural structure for a level-3 gateway (often called a *router*), which is achieved by a corresponding division of layer 3 into three sublayers (Figure 4.4).

Layer 3a denotes the subnetwork-specific layer 3 tasks. Layer 3c denotes the LAN-internetwork global layer-3 tasks (for example, LAN

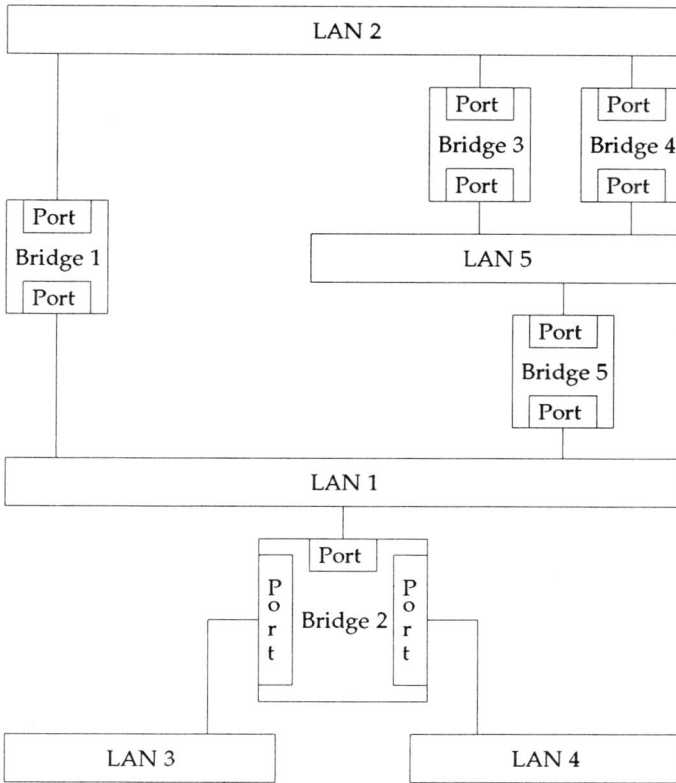

Figure 4.3   LAN internetwork using bridges.

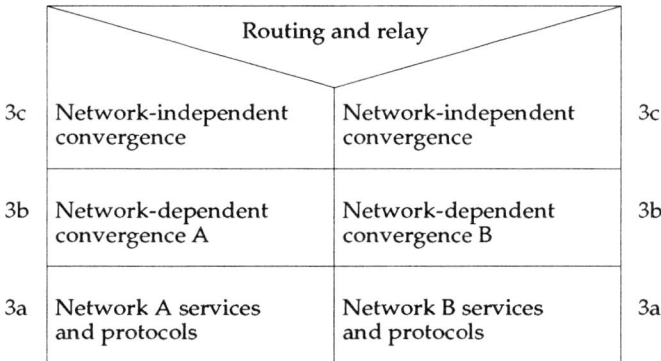

Figure 4.4   Router architecture.

internetworking, routing) which may be implemented by internet protocols or hop-by-hop relaying. Layer 3b provides the necessary service adaptations.

In Section 4.5, we shall describe how level 4 gateways are also used for LAN–WAN interconnection. Completely incompatible transport systems (for example, non-standardized manufacturer architectures) must be linked together at the application level (level 7 gateway). In this connection, appropriate network interfaces (see Chapter 7) play a role as common programmer interfaces (for example, NetBios, application programming interfaces (APIs)). If a gateway functions as a subscriber system for all layers in both of the networks to be connected, it is called a dual node gateway. Such gateways are often used as communication servers.

In general, the tasks of a gateway involve:

- Addressing over network boundaries and address mapping because the subnetworks of a LAN internetwork generally have different addressing schemes, involving different name and address structures for end systems and different address directories.

- Adaptation of messages in terms of format (syntax structure), length (fragmentation/blocking) and sequence.

- Adaptation of network access mechanisms (network interfaces and access protocols).

- Tuning of protocol parameters (for example, window sizes, timeouts, flow control).

- Adaptation of error-handling mechanisms and signalling mechanisms (status report).

- Mapping of services (for example, connection-oriented service, datagram service) and adaptation of service-quality parameters.

- Mapping of different routing strategies in subnetworks onto an adaptive global routing scheme.

When communications partners from two similar networks are linked together via a third network (transit network), complicated mappings are often unnecessary and the technique of *encapsulation* may be applied. The protocol data units of the end networks are delivered as user data to the transit-network access protocol, and transmitted unaltered (transparently). Of course, this procedure must take account of time-related boundary conditions of the end-network protocols, the timeouts for which, for example, should not be less than the network delay of the transit network. A similar consideration applies to frame sizes.

A general discussion of the gateway problem is beyond the scope of this book; we refer the reader to the appropriate literature for a comprehensive introduction.

4.2 Bridges

4.2.1 Overview

The structure of the IEEE LAN/MAN standard facilitates an as uniform as possible MAC service interface for use by the LLC layer. This includes the possibility of a level 2a gateway or (MAC) bridge (see Figure 4.5).

A bridge, as a coupling component between two LANs, provides for:

- communication between subscriber stations attached to LANs with different access strategies (for example, Ethernet, Token Bus, Token Ring);

- a division of an overall network into separate subnetworks to facilitate monitoring and maintenance (for example, by separating traffic and filtering out subscriber relationships).

MAC bridges are specified in the IEEE standard 802.1D, 1990, published in 1991, which is almost 180 pages. This describes:

- The embedding of the bridge functions into the architecture of the MAC layer.

- The 'bridging' subfunctions in the form of processes and entities.

- The protocol which is executed between bridges in order to configure a bridged LAN and to facilitate routing, including the associated encoding of bridge protocol data units.

- The requirements on the bridge management and the interface to the LAN system management. This includes the specification of management objects and operations which form the basis for the ISO/OSI network management architecture.

- The performance requirements (delays, timers, change mechanisms, operation of filters).

- The filter function.

- The relay function.

Of course, there must also be a statement about the MAC service in a bridged LAN (Figure 4.3) since it should be possible to forward messages (frame relaying) over different types of MAC layers. According to the standard, the bridges operate in such a way that the MAC service primitives, MA-UNITDATA.request and MA-UNITDATA.indication (see Section 2.3), are only available as unconfirmed services; no confirmed services between end subscribers are provided.

As far as communication between two LAN stations and the behaviour of individual LANs is concerned, a bridge behaves transparently.

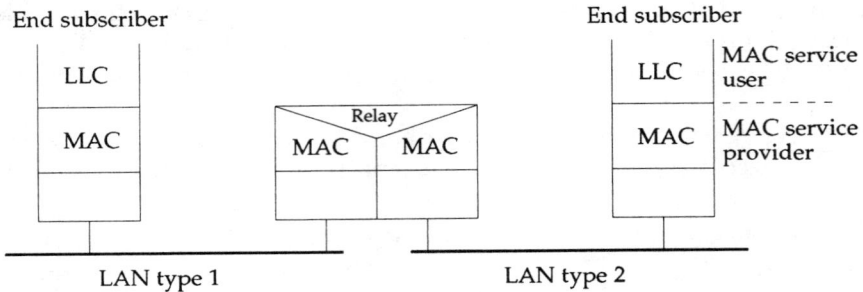

Figure 4.5   LAN MAC bridges.

This means that:

- A bridge is not addressed directly from LAN stations (except for management purposes); in other words, the MAC frames contain the destination address of a station which may also lie in another LAN. As a consequence, all the addresses in a LAN internetwork (in this section this always means a bridged LAN) must be globally unique. The usable MAC addresses are not restricted by the topology of the LAN internetwork; however, a common address scheme must be selected for each individual subnetwork (either 16-bit addressing or 48-bit addressing, see Section 2.3.3).

- The quality of service of the LAN internetwork should not be noticeably worse than that of the individual LANs. This relates to the following service-quality parameters:
    - service availability;
    - frame loss;
    - frame duplication;
    - frame lifetime;
    - maximum frame size;
    - residual error rate;
    - transmission delay;

— priority;

— throughput.

Of course, there are conflicting objectives. On the one hand, to improve the availability of the internetwork there should be explicit support for several physical routes; in other words, there should be more than one bridge between two LANs. On the other hand, the preservation of message sequences calls for a unique route and requires a corresponding routing protocol. Unique routes are guaranteed by calculating an 'active topology' (see below). Frame loss may occur in several ways (errors in layer 1, buffer overflows in the bridge, frame size too large for a subnetwork, timeout, etc.).

- Every bridge must be capable of storing at least one MAC frame in intermediate storage. This is necessary because MAC bridges are based on the store-and-forward principle. Moreover, frame format conversion must take place on transition to a different type of LAN subnetwork in the LAN internetwork; this may mean the removal or even the automatic introduction of frame fields or whole frames (Figure 4.5). If, for example, a Token Ring and an Ethernet are linked together via a bridge, so-called Token Ring control frames (for example, the beacon and the monitor present frame) will not be transmitted by the bridge because Ethernet LANs do not recognize frames of this type. In particular, the bridge recalculates the checksum (FCS).

- Figure 4.6 illustrates that in order to guarantee the operation of a bridge as a coupling element between two different LAN types, further internal service interfaces must be defined within the bridge (for example, the transition between the two independent MAC entities and the relay entity). The service elements are largely identical with those described in Section 2.2.4; however, they have extra parameters which are used to carry out the above protocol conversions. These include, for example, the frame type identification, the FCS and a parameter for controlling the MAC entities.

The most important bridge operations are the relay and filter function and the management of the associated database for routing and filtering out frames. The relay function includes the following subtasks, the execution of which depends on the individual subLANs involved:

- Frame receipt and frame checking.
- Destruction of a frame if the FCS is wrong, an illegal frame type is present or the maximum frame length permitted in the LAN internetwork is exceeded.

Table 4.1 Comparison of frames in IEEE LANs.

Field	If defined, length entry in bytes for:		
	802.3 (Ethernet)	802.4 (Token Bus)	802.5 (Token Ring, 4 Mbps)
Preamble	7	Variable	–
Start delimiter	1	1	1
Access control	–	–	1
Frame control	–	1	1
Destination address	2/6	2/6	2/6
Source address	2/6	2/6	2/6
Length	2	–	–
PAD	Variable	–	–
Data	Variable	Variable	Variable
Frame check seq.	4	4	4
End delimiter	–	1	1
Frame status	–	–	1
Max. frame length	1518	8191	2048

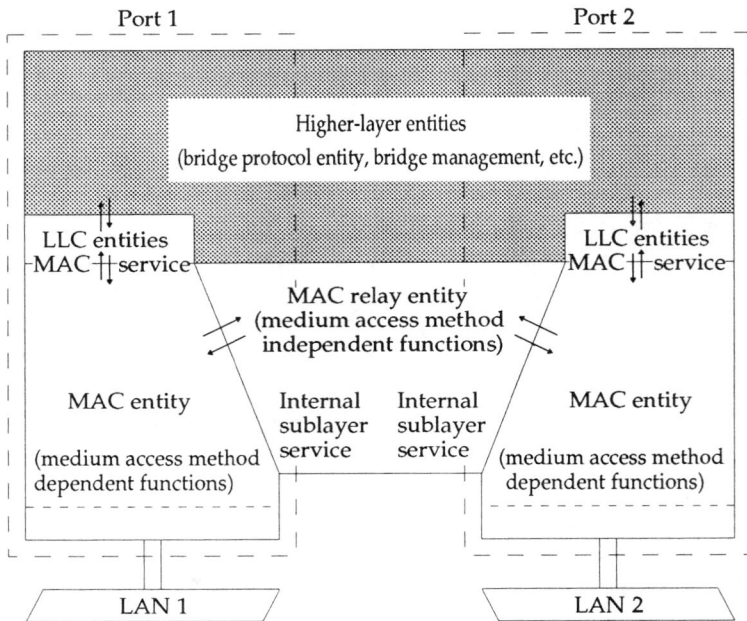

Figure 4.6 Bridge architecture.

- Destruction of a frame if decreed by the filter function (see below).

- Destruction of a frame if the bridge load would otherwise increase to a point where the maximum permissible contributions to the delay from the bridge would be exceeded.

- Delivery of certain frame information to the learning process (see below).

- Delivery of the frame to the determined bridge output port.

- Choice of the correct output priority, construction of the interface formats for the service primitive, recalculation of the FCS checksum.

- Transmission of the frame to the destination LAN.

In the following sections we describe the routing, filter-function and bridge-management aspects.

4.2.2 Active LAN-internetwork topology

At the physical level, IEEE LANs (such as Ethernet LANs) may be coupled into an overall network with an arbitrary topology (not restricted to bus, tree or ring). However, in order that the MAC services may be provided, this arbitrary physical topology must be given the form of an appropriate 'active topology'. This is carried out dynamically by calculating the minimum spanning tree using the *spanning tree algorithm* (STA). The active topology determined in this way has no data loops and thus no associated faults such as alteration of sequence order and packet duplication. It is guaranteed that there is only one route between any two stations in the LAN internetwork, which passes through at most eight bridges. The specified procedure permits a certain fault tolerance by automatically carrying out a sensible reconfiguration if several physical routes exist. The algorithm ensures that the active topology is uniquely defined and reproducible. For this, bridges need only know their own MAC addresses and a generic MAC group address. They do not have to be configured because they use an adaptive learning procedure to remember which subscriber addresses are in which LAN segments. Thus, bridges only transmit frames which are exchanged between end subscribers in different segments (or LANs).

The bridge uses backward learning, with flooding as a back-up strategy. Backward learning is based solely on locally available information, and thus requires a full traffic observation and a memory capacity (routing database) in the bridge.

The following are prerequisites for the STA:

- A unique MAC group address which is recognized by all bridges in the LAN internetwork and which is used to identify the protocol entities of all bridges attached to the individual subnetworks.

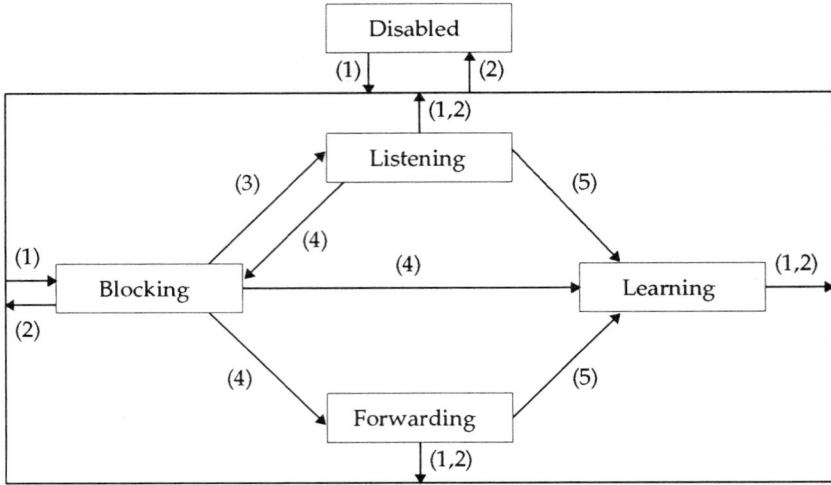

(1) Port enabled, by management or initialization
(2) Port disabled, by management or failure
(3) Algorithm selects as Designated or Root Port
(4) Algorithm selects as not Designated or Root Port
(5) Protocol timer expiry (forwarding timer)

Figure 4.7   States of a bridge port.

- A bridge ID which is globally unique within the LAN internetwork. This is determined from the (Ethernet) hardware address of the bridge and its priority.

- A unique port ID for bridge ports.

- If two LANs are coupled via several bridges, bridge priorities should be assigned to the set of bridges in the LAN internetwork.

- Bridge ports should be assigned a port priority and a path cost. For example, the interface delays or the data rates supported by the bridge interfaces could be used to determine the path costs.

- The bridge with the lowest bridge ID is defined to be the *root bridge*. During the algorithm it becomes the root of the calculated logical topology tree over the physical topology.

- The port of each bridge with the lowest path cost is called the *root port*.

- All ports have various port states, as shown in Figure 4.7.

- The bridge of each subLAN with the lowest path cost to the root bridge (root path cost, RPC) is called a designated bridge. If there are several designated bridges in the subLAN, the one with the lowest identity is chosen.

For the STA to operate, it is necessary to ensure that the required topology information is actually known to the bridges in the LAN internetwork. The *bridge protocol* is used for this, and in particular, the configuration BPDU protocol element, often called the 'hello packet'; see Figure 4.8.

After a bridge is switched on, a hello packet is first transmitted via all output ports. The start value for the root bridge parameter is initially the bridge's own identity. When a bridge receives a hello packet with 'better' information than that already known in the bridge, the information in the bridge is updated and a corresponding hello packet is sent to all networks for which the bridge is a designated bridge. On receipt of a hello packet with 'worse' information, a bridge forwards its own hello packet.

The STA operates as follows:

(1) Choice of the root bridge, in other words, the bridge with the smallest bridge ID.

(2) Choice of the root port within each bridge (except the root bridge).

(3) Choice of the designated bridges with their corresponding ports.

(4) Activation of all root ports and designated ports and blocking of all other bridge ports.

Figure 4.9 shows an example of an active topology for the LAN internetwork of Figure 4.3. In the STA calculation, bridge 1 is chosen as the root and is thus the designated bridge for LAN 1 and LAN 2. Bridge 2 has this role for LAN 3 and LAN 4, while the bridge 4 is the designated bridge for LAN 5.

The STA is also forced to reconfigure the network if a bridge is removed or added or the network administrator alters relevant parameters. If a bridge detects a change in the topology a 'topology information notification' is transmitted via the root port and finally received by the root bridge, which then informs all other bridges correspondingly using broadcast. While the STA is running, the bridge is in the learning state. User data is not forwarded until another loop-free active topology is calculated. The learning process is also used to obtain data for the filter database. It is possible that, after a reconfiguration of the active topology, a LAN station may initially disappear from the LAN internetwork as far as a bridge is concerned; however, as a result of the continuous learning process, it will reappear at some stage.

So much for the spanning-tree algorithm to calculate a cycle-free logical topology, the so-called active topology. This method is specified in the IEEE standard. However, we note that for many LAN internetworks, in particular those containing Token Ring LANs, a different procedure is used, particularly in IBM's Token Ring products. Here, the *source routing* procedure is used, which differs from the usual Ethernet-internetwork-transparent transmission of frames over bridges. In the source routing

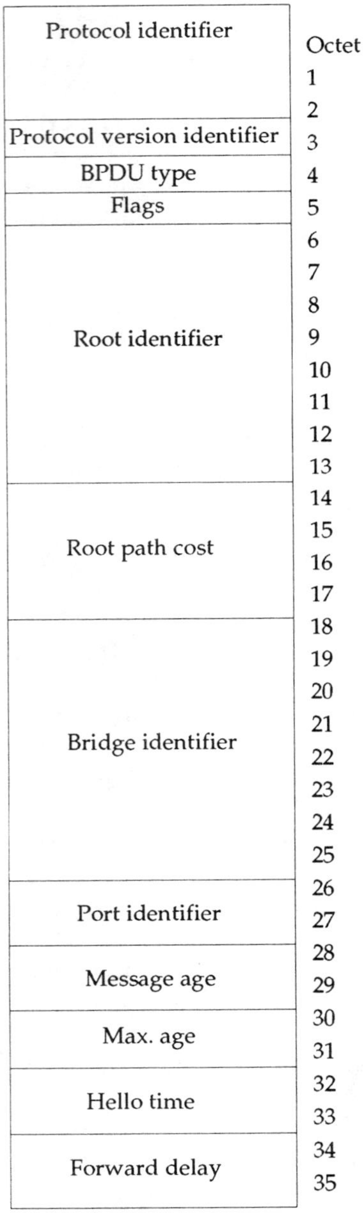

	Octet
Protocol identifier	1
	2
Protocol version identifier	3
BPDU type	4
Flags	5
	6
	7
	8
Root identifier	9
	10
	11
	12
	13
	14
Root path cost	15
	16
	17
	18
	19
	20
	21
Bridge identifier	22
	23
	24
	25
	26
Port identifier	27
Message age	28
	29
Max. age	30
	31
Hello time	32
	33
Forward delay	34
	35

Figure 4.8 Format of a configuration BPDU (hello packet).

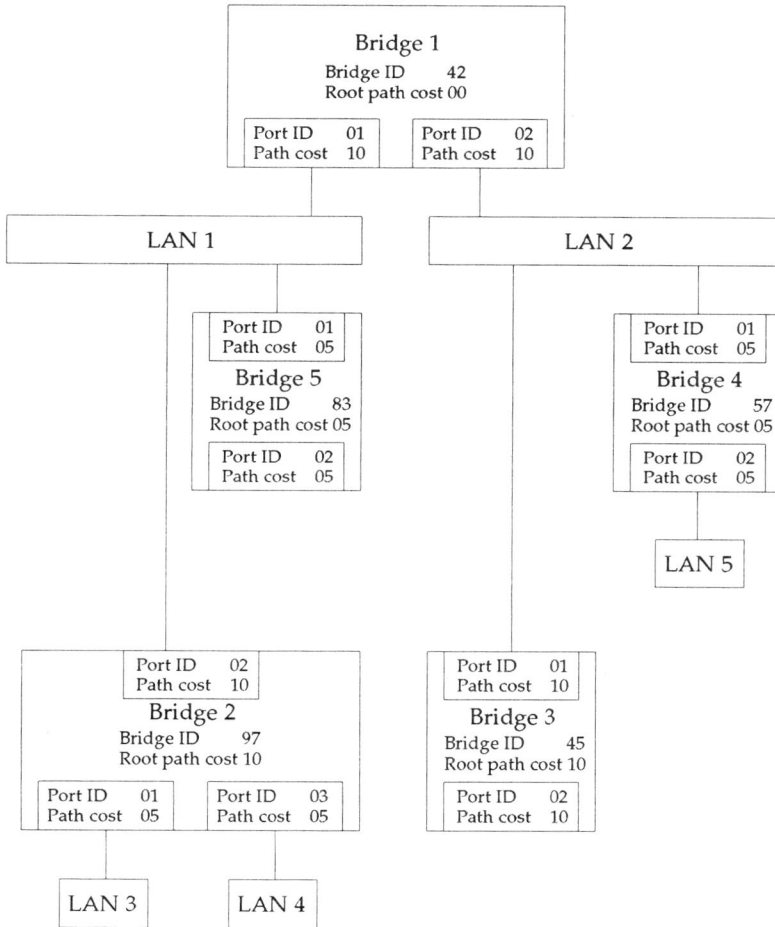

Figure 4.9 Spanning tree as active topology.

procedure each frame also carries information about the transport path so that the routing information is stored in the DTEs. A routing information field in a Token Ring frame may contain up to 18 bytes corresponding to eight ring numbers. A bridge based on the source routing principle must handle every packet of all LAN systems attached to it. If a frame routing indicator indicates that no routing information is present, the frame is a frame for the local LAN subnetwork and the LAN-internetwork relay function will not be activated. The optimal routes for source routing are determined by broadcast transmission of an explorer frame.

IBM uses source routing for its Token Ring products. However, there are other manufacturers (for example, VitaLink, Novell) who use the STA in the Token Ring world. In any case, the latter is preferred in the Ethernet world.

There are already proposals for an alteration to the standard, to enable bridges to use information contained in a frame to decide which of the two mechanisms should be used to forward the frame over a LAN internetwork. Such a hybrid bridge is called a *source routing transparent* (SRT) *bridge*.

4.2.3 Filter functions

A filter function is the ability of store-and-forward coupling elements to transmit only certain frames from one subLAN to another. Several reasons make it sensible to use this facility:

- Network traffic which only affects two subscribers to the same subLAN need not be transported across all segments. This reduces the overall network load in the other segments.

- Certain subscribers can be prevented from transmitting frames beyond their own subLAN.

- To ensure data security, it is possible to prevent subscribers on other subLANs from eavesdropping on the network traffic of a subLAN, if certain network traffic is only held locally within a subLAN.

The filter function is executed in the bridge by the so-called forwarding process using the filtering database. The filtering database contains the filtering information, which identifies the MAC addresses to which the forwarding process should not forward frames. The database entries may be updated either by explicit configuration with a management action or automatically using the results of the learning process described in Section 4.2.2. Filter entries may be static or dynamic. The database may be accessed by the local bridge management entity and may be manipulated from outside (remotely).

4.2.4 Bridge management

The IEEE specifications for bridge management are oriented towards the OSI network management architecture schemes. This applies to the specification of network management functional areas and the way in which managed objects are described.

Managed objects (the objects of management operations) include the bridge management entity, the various MAC entities of a bridge, the forwarding process, the filter database and the bridge protocol entity. The following management functions are specified:

- identification of bridges;
- resetting and initialization;
- setting of the priority;
- control of the frame transport;
- statistics relating to performance and traffic analysis;
- elementary accounting functions.

The above functions are activated using GET, SET and ACTION operations, similar to those of the OSI network management CMIS/CMIP schemes. The corresponding specifications are contained in the IEEE standard 802.1B. We shall return to this later.

4.2.5 Performance aspects

Two performance measures are crucial for a bridge, namely the guaranteed port filtering rate and the guaranteed bridge relaying rate. These two quantities may be used to calculate the throughput in a given time interval. However, the standard does not specify these quantities.

As we shall see later, MAC bridges may be bottlenecks in a LAN internetwork. However, since MAC bridges are transparent to all protocols above layer 2, they have no means of protecting themselves against overloading. Their only defence mechanism is to throw away frames which they can no longer handle (for example, because the internal buffer is insufficient). Such a loss of frames must be detected by a higher-level protocol and corrected by a frame repetition. Typical current transport protocols (TCP, XNS-SP) guarantee this. However, it should be borne in mind that MAC level bridges may form a bottleneck and decrease the overall throughput of an Ethernet.

On the other hand, careful planning of the points at which bridges should be used means that bridges may contribute to raising the overall throughput of an Ethernet internetwork to over 10 Mbps. This is possible due to the network hierarchy which may be created using MAC level bridges. By way of a simple example, we consider a sequence of three Ethernet LANs coupled via MAC level bridges. We use the following notation:

- $V(1)$, $V(2)$ and $V(3)$ denote the average traffic rates in Ethernets 1, 2 and 3, respectively.
- $V(1,2)$, $V(2,3)$, $V(2,1)$ and $V(3,2)$ denote the traffic rates between the given Ethernets.
- $F(1,2)$ and $F(2,3)$ denote the maximum filter rates of the MAC level bridges between Ethernets 1 and 2 and 2 and 3, respectively.

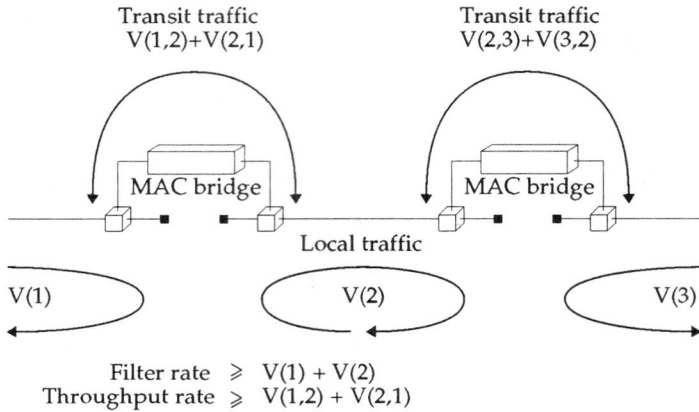

Figure 4.10 Determination of traffic quantities when using MAC level bridges.

The filter rate is the number of frames per period of time which may be handled by a bridge without frames being lost.

- $D(1,2)$ and $D(2,3)$ denote the maximum throughputs of a MAC level bridge between networks 1 and 2 and 2 and 3, respectively.

To determine configuration parameters for the above networks and bridges so that for the given traffic rates no frames are lost, the following conditions must be satisfied:

(1) Bounds for the filter rates. We must have:

$$F(1,2) \geq V(1) + V(2)$$
$$F(2,3) \geq V(2) + V(3)$$

(2) Bounds for the throughput rates. We must have:

$$D(1,2) \geq V(1,2) + V(2,1)$$
$$D(2,3) \geq V(2,3) + V(3,2)$$

It is quite clear that both characteristic quantities, the filter rate and the throughput rate, must be considered when judging the performance of a MAC level bridge. The filter rate indicates the maximum permitted value of the sum of the traffic rates for the two coupled networks. If the traffic between two networks was sufficiently low and the throughput of the bridge was completely adequate, the filter rate would determine the performance of the bridge. Thus, it is only sensible to consider the throughput rate when the condition for the filter rate is satisfied.

The less traffic there is between two networks, the more sensible it is to use a bridge. Among other considerations, a bridge should be installed when it is desirable to keep the traffic local as far as possible. The more localized the traffic is, the higher the overall throughput of the integrated network may be (and this extends far above the limiting speeds of 10 Mbps for Ethernet). In Section 4.4 we discuss practical questions relating to the formation of LAN internetworks and the creation of subnetworks using bridges.

4.3 Routers

4.3.1 Mode of operation

Routers or *network-layer relays* are layer 3 gateways; in other words, network components which may be used to connect networks which use the same layer 3c protocol. They are important building blocks for the implementation of *internetworking*, namely the interconnection of subnetworks which are not necessarily of the LAN type. Thus, one speaks of *internet gateways*. This type of coupling means that the networks involved in the internetwork may have their own layer 3 (Figure 4.4) so that different switching techniques and routing strategies may be used in the subnetworks. In the internetwork an independent protocol, which uses a globally unique addressing, is usually transacted at the internet level (layer 3c).

Usually, a hierarchical address scheme is used which is able to distinguish between addresses of subscriber stations and network addresses. A router may use this to logically divide the internetwork into various subnetworks. As we shall see later, the subnetworks may be viewed as logical independent management domains. Routers do not impose any particular restrictions on the internetwork network topology (for example, bus, tree, ring); in other words, routers can also cope with redundant paths (active loops).

Internetworking requires routing tables. The routing tables in the routers contain network IDs and identifiers for the stations of the subnetworks, but they do not contain the specific addresses of the end stations in a subnetwork. Unlike bridges, routers take a packet-related routing decision. Unlike a bridge, even for normal packet switching, a router may be addressed directly from subscriber stations (source address) or other routers in the internetwork. Depending on the identification of the subnetwork and the information in the routing table, the router chooses the next subnetwork, etc. Thus, packet forwarding is from router to router (hop-to-hop). Possible criteria for the routing (cost function) include the number of hops on the route, the delay time, etc.

Static and dynamic routers are distinguished by the way in which the routing tables are updated. In the first case, changes in the internetwork topology are associated with an explicit alteration of the routing tables by a network manager. In the second case, the routers inform one another about changes in the configuration using appropriate routing protocols. In particular, dynamic routing procedures are preferred in large internetworks where there are frequent or unplanned changes to the configuration.

4.3.2 Comparison of bridges and routers

4.3.2.1 Bridges

The principal mode of operation is summarized in Figure 4.11.

- Bridges are layer 2a relays.
- Bridges are invisible to subscriber stations. Bridges only talk to bridges via the bridge protocol. Normal stations do not require extra software in a bridged LAN.
- LANs may be physically coupled over redundant bridges; however, in Ethernet internetworks only the active topology, calculated using STA, is used for the frame transport.
- Bridges take relatively simple relay decisions using the filter database. Thus, they are simpler than routers and result in smaller delay contributions.
- Bridges are relayed in a network component (local bridge) or by components connected by links (remote bridge).

4.3.2.2 Routers

The principal mode of operation is summarized in Figure 4.12.

- Routers are layer 3c relays.
- Routers are not transparent in the internetwork. The stations in the network must support an internet protocol.
- Routers support multiple routes between end stations. Routing is by packets. Usually, broadcast packets from subnetworks are not forwarded.
- Routers permit various packet sizes; if necessary, packets are fragmented.
- Routers are altogether more complicated but also make good use of the logical separation of subnetworks for management purposes (load balancing, traffic separation).
- Routers may also be implemented as remote routers.

Packet received

Is learning disabled ?
— No →
— Yes ↓

Does source address match routing table source address entry ?
— Yes →
— No ↓

Is source address a permanent entry ?
— Yes →
— No ↓

Enter source address and originating network in routing table

Update time stamp and originating network

Is SrcExplicit-forwarding enabled ?
— Yes →
— No →

Is source address a permanent entry in routing table ?
— No → Discard packet
— Yes

Has packet forwarding been disabled ?
— Yes → Discard packet
— No ↓

Can destination address be found in routing table ?
— Yes →
— No ↓

Is destination network the same as that from which the packet originated ?
— Yes → Discard packet
— No ↓

Should the packet be filtered ?
— Yes → Discard packet
— No ↓

Is destination address disabled ?
— Yes → Discard packet
— No ↓

Should the packet be filtered ?
— Yes → Discard packet
— No

Does packet meet all conditions of any log ?
— No →
— Yes ↓

Update log counter

Forward packet to appropriate network(s)

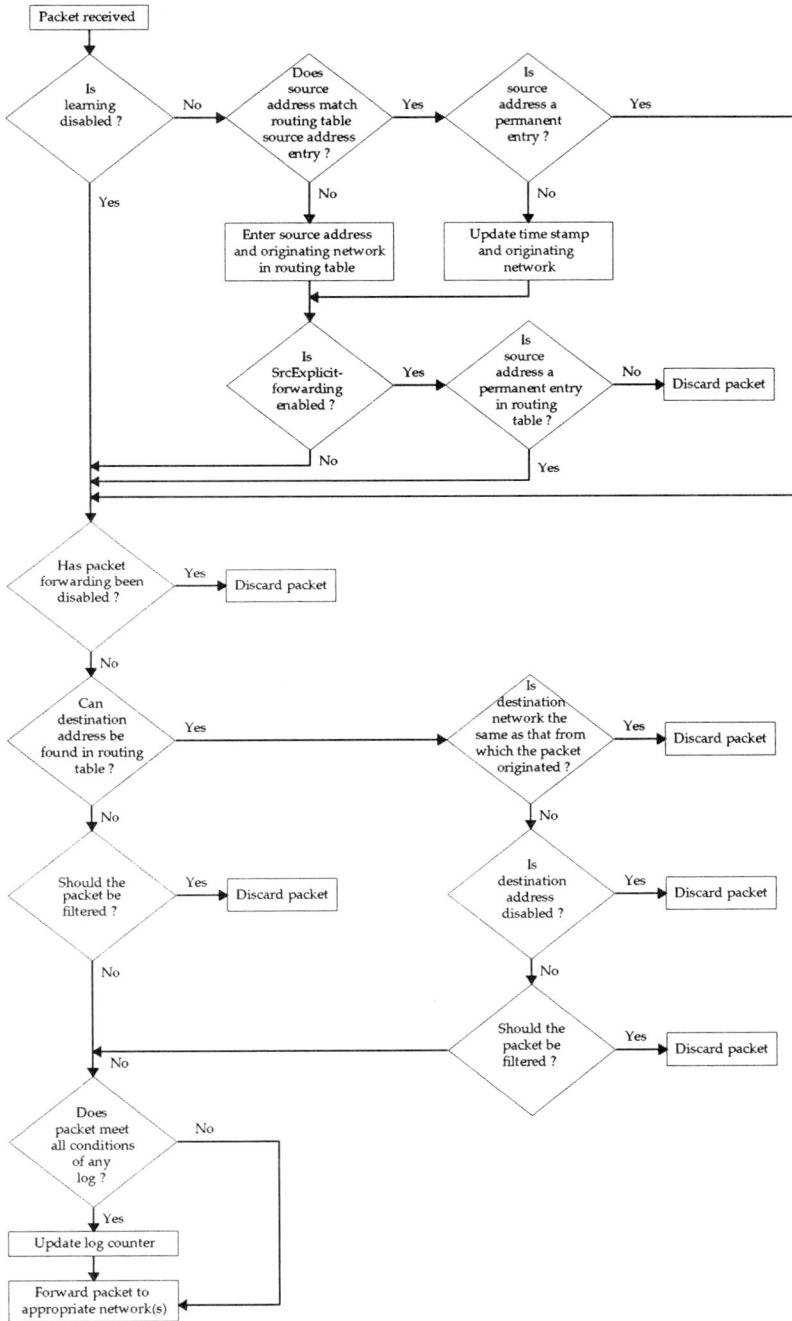

Figure 4.11   Mode of operation of a bridge (3Com).

Packet received from network

Valid header ?

No

Yes

Attached net table lookup based on destination network number

Found ?

Yes

Dest Host = this host ?

Yes

No

Broadcast packet ?

No

Yes

Pass packet to client

Hopcount = 15 ?

Yes

No

No

Increment hopcount and recalculate Checksum

Is destination net directly attached ?

Yes

Use MAC address from packet header and port number from the attached net table

No

Routing table lookup based on destination network number

Found ?

No

Discard packet

Yes

Use port number and MAC address from routing table

Send packet to link layer to be transmitted on network

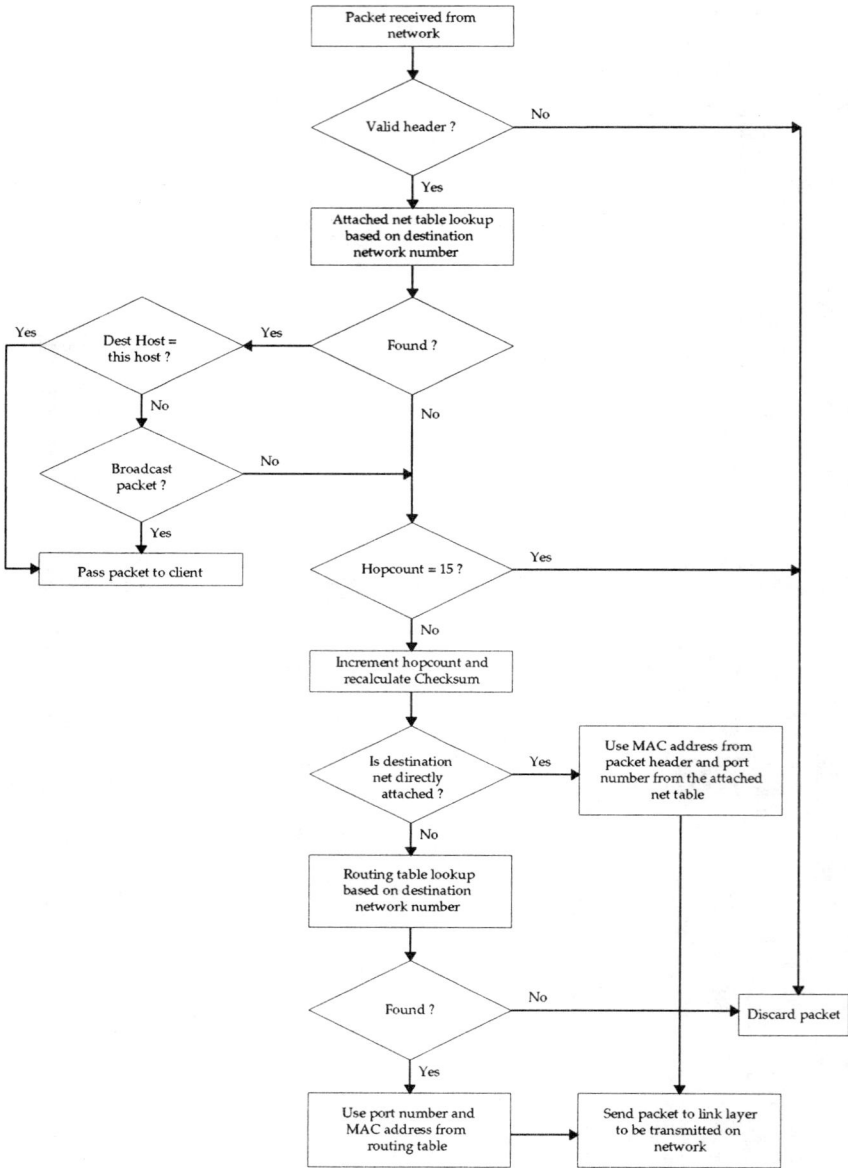

Figure 4.12 Mode of operation of a router (3Com).

There are now routers which can transact more than one internet protocol (multiprotocol routers) and network components which implement both router and bridge functions (brouters). We shall return to this later.

4.3.3 Internet protocols

There are various internet protocols which each developed in the context of a whole family of protocols. Examples include:

- **ISO IP**. This is the protocol standardized by OSI, which is not very common in the LAN area.

- **Internet Datagram Protocol (IDP)**. This comes from Xerox's XNS protocol family.

- **Internet (IP)**. This is the datagram-oriented internet protocol of the TCP/IP or ARPA protocol family.

- **X.75**. This is a connection-oriented internet protocol for an internetwork of X.25 subnetworks which usually uses fixed routing.

As far as Ethernet internetworks are concerned, the IP is the current market leader, although IDP is also common. We shall briefly describe both protocols here.

4.3.3.1 XNS Internet Datagram Protocol (IDP)

The task of the IDP within the family of XNS protocols is to transport datagrams (data packets) over an internetwork from local area networks.

The internet protocol is a connectionless protocol: datagrams are transported as self-contained independent data units. There is no guarantee that datagram sequences will be preserved and no guarantee against loss. The receipt of datagrams is not acknowledged. The XNS internet protocol is related to layer 3 of the ISO/OSI reference model or, more precisely, to layer 3c.

The mode of operation of the internet protocol makes the following assumption about the internetwork: several local area networks are linked together either directly, via point-to-point links, or via packet-switched networks. The coupling elements are called routers. Every internet datagram is transmitted from its source hop-to-hop via several routers to the destination. Datagrams are not fragmented (unlike with the internet IP). Thus, every subnetwork must be able to transport datagrams with a maximum length of 576 bytes.

Addressing   The addressing of the end partner is carried out at the internet level using 96-bit addresses. These are statically subdivided as follows: 32-bit network address; 48-bit host identifier; 16-bit socket number (port).

Hosts attached to several networks thus have several internet addresses. In the case of an Ethernet, the 48-bit host identifier in the internet address is identical to the Ethernet address of the host.

The socket number identifies a process within a host system. Some socket numbers are specified as fixed, for example: 1 routing protocol entity, 2 echo protocol entity, 3 router error.

Broadcast   The XNS family of protocols was specially developed for use in LAN internetworks (more precisely, Ethernet internetworks). At layer 2, Ethernet LANs have a broadcast facility, which enables them to transmit a data packet to all attached subscribers in the same LAN. This possibility is also open to users of the XNS internet protocol. A broadcast datagram is indicated by filling the host address completely with 1s. This is then interpreted by all protocol entities of all hosts to be delivered to all the corresponding sockets. Broadcast in the whole internet is not supported.

Multicast   The physical Ethernet address of each subscriber is usually derived from the 48-bit host address. In addition, each host may have one or more multicast addresses; in other words, a group of different hosts is assigned a single 48-bit host address. Datagrams with this destination address are then delivered to all members of this group.

Hop count   All datagrams have a so-called hop-count field. This is set to 0 by the sender. Whenever a router is passed through, the hop count is increased by 1. As soon as the hop count contains the value 16, the datagram must be discarded by a router. This prevents datagrams from circulating endlessly (for example, because of routing-related faults).

Datagram lifetime   Currently, the lifetime of a datagram is not explicitly defined. However, in order to place an upper bound on the maximum lifetime of a datagram, there is an agreement that every internet protocol entity should discard datagrams which have waited more than six seconds for forwarding.

Datagram types   A number of different higher protocols may be used above the internet protocol. To enable a protocol entity receiving an internet datagram to carry out the local forwarding, the identification of the appropriate higher protocol is contained in a particular field of the datagram. This 8-bit field is called the packet type. Some packet types for other protocols of the XNS family have a fixed definition: 1 routing information, 2 echo protocol, 3 error protocol, 4 packet exchange protocol, 5 sequenced packet protocol.

The datagram header of an IDP protocol data unit has the structure shown in Table 4.2. Generation of checksums is not mandatory; if no checksums are generated, this is indicated by a corresponding identifier.

Table 4.2 Structure of an IDP datagram header.

Byte no.	Bit	Definition
1–2	16	Checksum
3–4	16	Length
5	4	Hop count
6	8	Packet type
7–10	32	Destination network
11–16	48	Destination host
17–18	16	Destination socket
19–22	32	Source network
23–38	48	Source host
29–30	16	Source socket

As described in Section 4.3.1, when internet datagrams are transported over an internetwork, each successive internet router (the interface between two networks) decides which route a datagram should take. The protocol which is responsible for providing the router with the appropriate routing table entries is called the routing information protocol (RIP). To ensure that this routing table is always kept up to date (it may alter during the network operation, for example, because of line failures or overloading), two processes are active in each router. The first is called the requester. This is responsible for incorporating into its routing table the most recent information about routes in another network. The other process is called the supplier; it supplies all requesters in a subnetwork with new routing information. The routing information protocol of the XNS protocol family is not suitable for arbitrary networks, but includes certain assumptions about the network characteristics, namely:

- The whole network consists of at most a few hundred subnetworks; thus, the individual subnetworks may be identified without generating a special hierarchy.

- The majority of the networks are based on Ethernets (or similar local area networks with cost-effective broadcast mechanisms) which are linked together via point-to-point links or via public switched networks.

- The number of hops is the criterion used by the routing procedure to determine the most favourable route between two end systems; in other words, the number of different networks (or internet routers) which lie between these systems. It is important that two end systems should not be separated by more than 15 hops.

The routing information protocol lies above the internet datagram protocol.

Structure of the routing table A routing table in a router consists mainly of the following entries for each relevant destination network (more exactly, for each directly reachable destination network):

- The address of the destination network.
- The number of hops to the destination network.
- Which subnetwork should be chosen next.
- Which internet router should be next to take control.
- A timer, which is described below.

The routing table in an internet router must contain information about all existing subnetworks (global overall view).

Updating of the routing table A supplier (typically, every internet router) uses the routing information protocol (RIP) to send so-called response packets containing its entire routing table every 30 seconds to all routers in adjacent subnetworks. This enables each recipient to compare the information with its own and to update the latter if necessary. The criteria for implementing updates are as follows:

- No entry for a destination network currently exists but a connection to that network is to be established.
- The existing entry for the destination network is already more than 90 seconds old (this is determined from the routing table timer mentioned above).
- A shorter route to the destination network is given.

Independently of the transmission of these unrequested periodic updates, it is of course possible for an end system (strictly speaking, via its requester) to broadcast a request packet requesting this information from a supplier. This is used, for example, when an end system wishes to transmit a packet to a destination network for which its local routing table has no information, or when an end system is started up. The packet format of the routing information protocol is relatively simple because only two packet types are supported:

- Operation code = 1 (16 bit): request
- Operation code = 2 (16 bit): response

In addition, a packet contains an arbitrarily long sequence of pairs of the form:

- Destination network (32 bit)

●   Number of hops to reach it (16 bit).

In a request packet the number of hops has no meaning. If a requester wishes to use a request packet to obtain information about all destination networks it sets the field for the destination network to 0.

This is the case when an end system is started; in particular, the end system is able to determine the address of its own network from the corresponding response packet because the number of hops in this case is 0.

Remarks on the implementation   Basically, only internet routers are obliged to keep routing tables (complete tables containing all destination networks). End systems, on the other hand (terminal servers or hosts), need only know the address of the network to which they themselves are directly attached; all other network addresses may be requested using a request packet as required. However, this requires one request per packet which is transmitted to a foreign network, and is certainly not efficient. Thus, it is recommended that routing information about the most commonly used foreign networks at least be held in cache memory.

Another problem arises when public networks (for example, packet-switched networks) are involved. In particular, if the traffic between two subnetworks coupled in this way is very sporadic, then the exchange of routing information (every 30 seconds) may be very expensive. In this case, a change to the procedure is recommended.

4.3.3.2 ARPA Internet Protocol (IP)

The task of the internet protocol (IP) of the TCP/IP or ARPA protocol family is to transport data packets from a sender across several networks to a recipient. Thus, it is related to layer 3 of the ISO/OSI reference model, or more precisely, to layer 3c (see Figure 4.13). IP provides an unprotected connectionless data transfer service.

The IP data packets are called datagrams. These are transported by IP as mutually independent data packets (even for identical senders and recipients). IP does not guarantee that the datagram sequence will be preserved, or that datagrams will be delivered to the recipient. In other words, datagrams may be lost, for example, because of overloading of the network. There are no acknowledgements at the IP level.

Since every participating network may have a different maximum datagram length, IP includes a fragmentation facility; in other words, a transmitted datagram may be divided into several subdatagrams by IP and reassembled by the recipient. Individual IP modules are used as so-called gateways (routers) at the interfaces between two different networks. These are responsible both for the traffic between the networks and for the appropriate routing. The algorithm for constructing and maintaining the

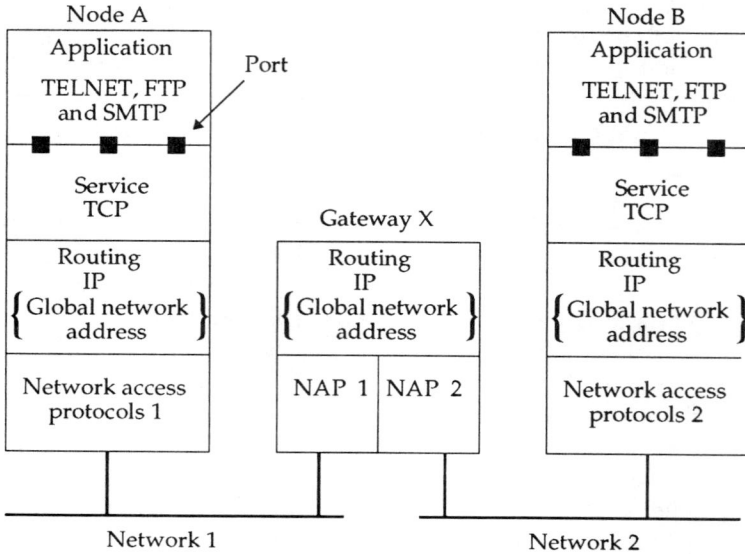

Figure 4.13   Internetworking with TCP/IP protocols.

routing tables is not a component of IP. Individual protocols, operating between the gateways, exist for this purpose.

Addressing   IP uses 32-bit addresses to identify senders and recipients. There are three different classes of addresses, as shown in Table 4.3.

Class A uses a 7-bit network address and a 24-bit host address, the corresponding values for class B are 14/16 and for class C 21/8. Thus, an internetwork may consist of a few large subnetworks (class A) or a large number of small subnetworks (class C).

The internet address is always of the form p.q.r.s where each field of the address is an 8-bit binary number. Whether the address is of class A, B or C may be determined from the first bits of the network address (1, 10, 100, respectively).

The mapping of names on to these addresses is not a component of IP; this task falls to the name server protocol. Thus, the name mapping on to internal binary addresses may be requested from the domain name server. However, the addresses used must be unique in the internetwork as a whole. It is the task of the IP module to map these names on to the local network address of a recipient or gateway.

Table 4.3 IP addressing.

Class	Network			Host		
	No. bits	Octets	No. addresses	No. bits	Octets	No. addresses
A	1 + 7	p	126	24	q.r.s	16.777.214
B	2 + 14	p.q	16.382	16	r.s	65.534
C	3 + 21	p.q.r	64.547	8	s	254

Fragmentation When a datagram is transported over several networks, fragmentation is necessary if the datagram length is greater than the maximum length in one of the networks. The corresponding IP module decomposes a datagram into a sequence of several datagrams. These are then transported independently of one another, although they are given identifiers to show that they belong together:

- All datagrams in this sequence are given the same identifier, for which the datagram header provides a 16-bit field.

- The sequential number of the subdatagram is indicated in a special field (fragment offset).

- The last subdatagram is given a last fragment flag.

In addition, there is an agreement that each IP module must be able to receive datagrams of up to 576 bytes long. The general structure of an IP packet is shown in Figure 4.14. This also shows that the length field (16 bits) provides for a maximum datagram length of 65535 bytes, which is rarely supp

St. Faustina and Divine Mercy ..

Lif...ed by a sender carries
wit...etime. The lifetime is
me...possible lifetime is 255
sec...now has to evaluate the
pro...act this value from the
rer...fter this the remaining
lif...s a result, in overload
sit...etwork, no datagram is
ke

S...n identification by its
s...the importance of the
d

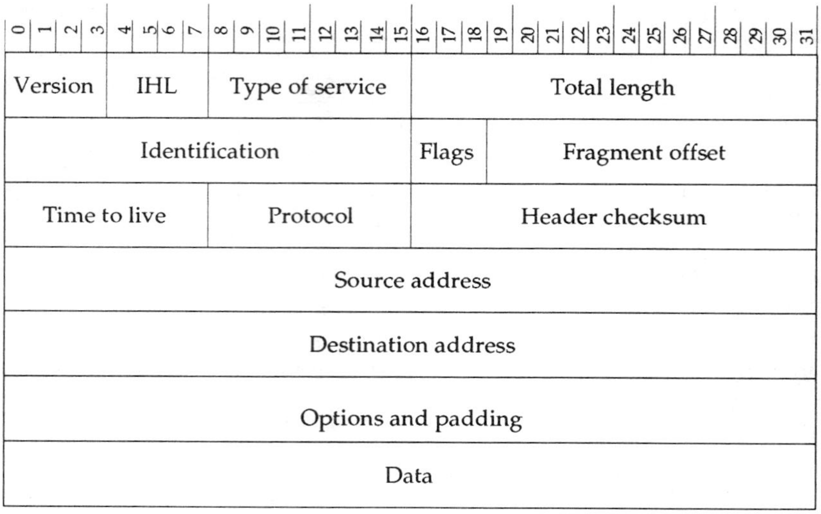

0	1	2	3	4	5	6	7	8	9	10	11	12	13	14	15	16	17	18	19	20	21	22	23	24	25	26	27	28	29	30	31
Version				IHL				Type of service								Total length															
Identification																Flags			Fragment offset												
Time to live								Protocol								Header checksum															
Source address																															
Destination address																															
Options and padding																															
Data																															

Figure 4.14 Structure of an IP packet.

- Desired delay class.
- Desired degree of reliability of delivery.
- Desired degree of protection (security class).

Among the options which may be given in the IP packet, those relating to routing and time stamping are worth mentioning. These may be used to record or prescribe the route (record route, source route) and the times at which the packet is processed by routers may be determined (time stamp).

Thus, it is possible for IP modules to develop strategies which take into account these datagrams (priorities, special treatment, etc.). The IP description does not state how this should be done.

IP routing The IP routing is usually based on the use of IP routing tables in which destination networks (usually) and destination systems (host specific route) may be entered. The routing mechanism in an IP router is as follows:

- Read the destination address Z from the IP datagram.
- Calculate the network address N of the destination network.
- If N is the network address of a network which is directly attached to the router, transmit the datagram to this network (in other words, after Z is reduced to a physical address). Jump to end.

- If a host-specific route is entered for Z, choose this. Jump to end.
- If N is in the routing table, choose a corresponding route. Jump to end.
- If a default route is specified, choose this, otherwise signal a routing error.
- End.

Router management The management of the routing tables is not carried out by the IP protocol but by the router management, which uses a suitable management protocol of its own. The same applies to error management. Here, the TCP/IP world provides a number of mechanisms:

- **Internet Control Message Protocol (ICMP).** This is an error signalling mechanism with which gateways (internet routers) transmit error or control messages to other gateways or hosts, these messages being transported using IP datagrams. Examples include: host/network/port unreachable, addresses unknown, service not available, refusal to accept, fragmentation required, alternative routing, circular route, etc.

- **Exterior Gateway Protocol (EGP).** Exterior gateways are pairs of gateways which belong to separate autonomous networks but are adjacent in the internetwork. EGP may be used to establish such adjacency (neighbour acquisition), and test the availability (alive test). EGP supports tree-like internetwork topologies.

- **Interior Gateway Protocol (IGP).** Routers within autonomous internetworks are said to be interior. IGP is not a single protocol but the collective term for the protocols between interior gateways. The most commonly used IGP is the routing information protocol (RIP). This is an extension of the corresponding protocols of the XNS protocol family (cf. Subsection 4.3.3.1). Here too, the hop count metric is used as a cost function. The hello protocol is an example of an IGP which uses the network delay as a cost function for routing decisions. The hello messages use time stamps. Route D is the UNIX implementation of RIP. Gate D is a UNIX program which implements RIP, hello and EGP.

- **Open Shortest Path First Protocol (OSPF).** The routing update protocols described above are so-called locally adaptive procedures (vector distance routing) which have certain weaknesses, such as the danger of routing cycles or slow propagation of routing information. OSPF uses the SPF algorithm which requires a global knowledge of the topology but does not have the weaknesses of the other procedures. OSPF permits a 'type of service routing', in which different routes may be used between two subscribers, depending on the service. The internetwork may be divided into domains (domain area routing); thus, separation of traffic is supported. Redundant routes and authentication for the use of routes are also supported. Thus, for example, OSPF may be used to construct management hierarchies, and it contains the functionality of EGP and IGP, although the associated OSPF database is naturally more complicated than a simple routing table.

Service interface levels 3/4   The interface between the IP module and the corresponding transport protocol module is relatively simple and is associated with two service primitives:

- SEND requests the IP module to transmit a datagram (various parameters such as addresses, protocol type, service type, fragmentation advice, lifetime, etc. are given).
- DELIVER specifies a buffer in which an incoming datagram should be placed and passes on a number of parameters.

Comparison of IP and IDP   Table 4.4 gives a comparative overview of IP and IDP. The internet protocols of the two families appear very similar; there are no serious differences. However, judgement should not be based purely on a comparison of the internet protocols; the whole set of the attendant protocols related to router management should be considered. The ARPA protocol family is plainly the more important when considering the associated protocols and the distribution of products.

Table **4.4**   Comparison of IP and IDP.

Feature	XNS/IDP	TCP/IP
Broadcast/multicast at internet level	Yes	No
Fragmentation/assembly of internet packets	No	Yes
Typical packet length, bytes	576	576
Length of packet header	30	20
Length of address field, bits	96	32
Support for datagrams of different service classes	No	Yes
Datagram lifetime control	Yes	Yes

4.4 Planning LAN internetworks with bridges and routers

We shall use the theoretical considerations of the previous sections as a basis for a discussion of practical aspects in the implementation of LAN internetworks with bridges and routers. In addition to possible uses, we shall also consider additional functions, performance criteria and operational questions.

4.4.1 Possible uses

In the practical planning of networks, the pressure to use components such as bridges and routers, which have both separating and connecting properties, arises for the following reasons:

Removal of length restrictions

Local area networks are defined with a limited physical coverage (e.g. Ethernet coax segments – 500 m). If these values are exceeded, for example, when connecting two local building networks on a company site, the whole LAN must be connected using components which overcome these restrictions on the segments.

Removal of restrictions on the number of stations

The number of stations which may be attached to a LAN is limited (e.g. 1024 for Ethernet 10base5). If this limit is exceeded suitable components must be used to divide the network into subLANs. The maximum number of stations is then again permitted in a subLAN (if this is sensible).

Separation of faults

The more stations attached to an individual LAN, the greater is the probability that a fault with adverse effects on all attached stations will occur, since LANs are usually based on the broadcast principle. Separation by suitable components permits the erection of fire walls which limit faults (for example, hardware faults, broadcast storms) to individual subnetworks. The nature of the components used determines which faults can be brought under control.

Separation of local traffic

The larger a LAN is, the more likely it is that there will be areas in which most of the communication is local (for example, in a department). Components may be used to keep this traffic in the relevant subLAN without placing a load on the network as a whole. A large LAN without separation of local traffic could in many cases not cope with the overall load of all subLANs.

Structuring of the network

For organizational or operational reasons, it may be necessary to divide a large LAN into subnetworks, since fault location and network management become more complicated as the size of the network increases. Such a subdivision into subLANs using suitable components then permits distributed management and separate analysis of faults.

Connection of LANs via WANs

LANs within a company, parts of which are located at a large distance from one another, must and should be brought together into an overall LAN. These remote LANs may also be connected over WAN circuits (using suitable components) provided by the PTTs.

Security

With the broadcast feature, LANs are essentially information distribution systems. Using suitable components, it is possible to separate the critical data traffic and control access to computers which are at risk.

Each of the above requirements may be satisfied to a greater or lesser extent, depending on the components used (bridges or routers).

4.4.2 Criteria for selecting components

4.4.2.1 Additional bridge functions

The basic functionality of bridges, including the bridge learning and filter mechanisms and the spanning tree algorithm which is executed between bridges, was discussed in Section 4.2. In what follows, we shall describe individual extensions and refinements which could affect the selection of a bridge.

Learning mechanism   After a bridge is brought into operation, tables are constructed by learning on the basis of source and destination addresses, which may then be used to decide whether or not the packet has to be transported to another subLAN.

In some manufacturers' devices this learning mechanism can be switched off after a given time. This has the consequence that the data traffic of newly added stations is not transported further by the bridge, since the

```
                        ┌─────────────────┐
                        │ Frame received  │
                        │   at port X     │
                        └─────────────────┘
                                 │
                                 ▼
                        ╱─────────────────╲          Yes
                       ╱  Source address   ╲──────────────────┐
              Learning ╲  with Port X in    ╱                 │
                        ╲     table ?      ╱                   │
                         ╲────────────────╱                    │
                                 │ No                          │
                                 ▼                             │
                        ┌─────────────────┐                    │
                        │  Entry in table │                    │
                        └─────────────────┘                    │
                                 │                             │
                                 ▼◄────────────────────────────┘
                        ╱─────────────────╲          No
                       ╱   Destination     ╲──────────────────────┐
                       ╲   address with     ╱                      │
                        ╲  Port X in table ?                       │
                         ╲────────────────╱                        │
                                 │ Yes                             │
             Yes                 ▼                                 │
        ◄──────────────╱─────────────────╲                        │
                       ╱  Source port =    ╲                       │
                       ╲ destination port ? ╱                      │
                        ╲ Port X in table ?                        │
                         ╲────────────────╱                        │
                                 │ No                              │
             Yes                 ▼                    No           │
        ◄──────────────╱─────────────────╲──────────────────────►│
                       ╲ Filter condition  ╱                       │
                        ╲   effective ?    ╱                        │
                         ╲────────────────╱                         │
                                                                    │
        ┌─────────────┐                          ┌─────────────┐
        │   Ignore    │                          │  Transport  │
        │    frame    │                          │    frame    │
        └─────────────┘                          └─────────────┘
```

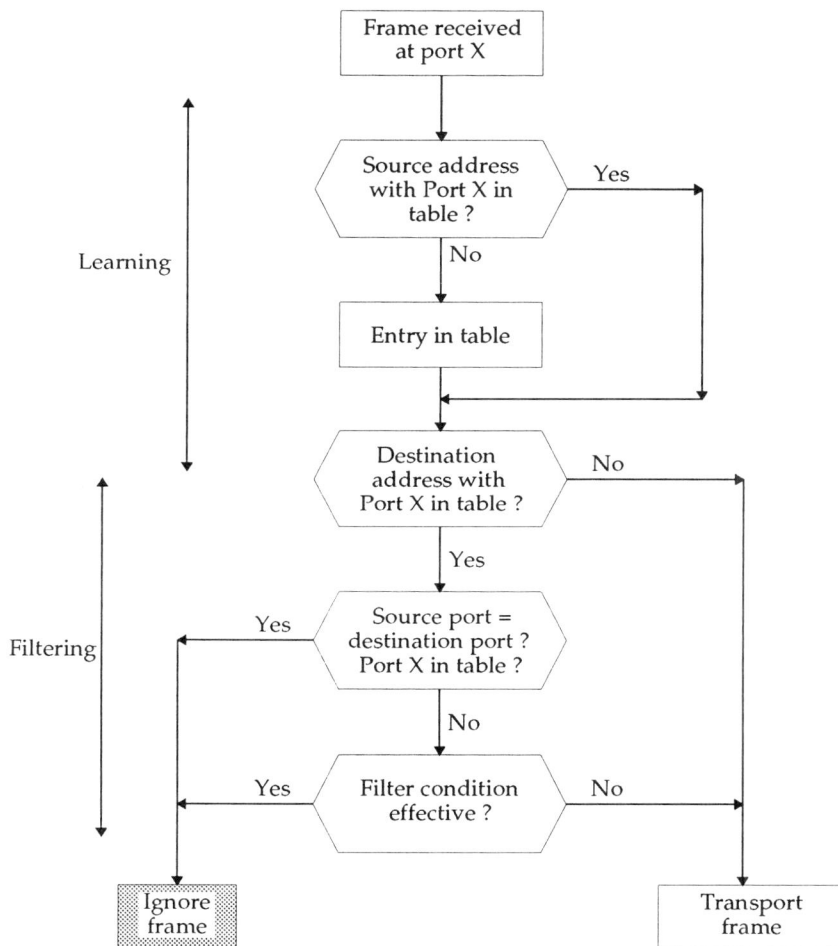

Figure 4.15   Bridge learning and filter mechanism.

new address does not appear in the address table. This may make it more difficult to connect further stations without being noticed or supervised, since communications for a new station are restricted to its subLAN. Another variation involves subsequent correction of the address tables after the learning mechanism has been switched off, or the manual generation of tables by a network administrator.

In many devices, it is possible to install an ageing mechanism which deletes stations that are no longer active from the address tables after a given time. Firstly this keeps the length of the address table short (reduced search times), and secondly it permits changes to the configuration (for example, a station may move from one subLAN to another) without the need for additional manipulation of the address tables in the bridge.

Filter mechanisms   In addition to the check of the address field in the frame, other fields or freely definable masks down to the bit level in the frame may be examined, so that in the case of agreement the frame will be transported to another subLAN (positive filter) or blocked (negative filter). The possible filter settings, and the fineness of filters and how they are combined, are different for every bridge manufacturer. Filters are sensible and conceivable for:

- the type field of an Ethernet packet;
- the source address or the destination address of an Ethernet packet;
- the packet length;
- broadcast packets and multicast packets.

The type field of an Ethernet frame (Figures 2.7 and 2.8) may be used, in conjunction with the filter mechanism, to construct manufacturer- or organization-specific logical subnetworks (for example, for management purposes) within a complicated and heterogeneous Ethernet configuration, as shown in Table 4.5. Other filters and combinations of filters are also possible, according to the application.

Spanning tree algorithm   Redundant routes should not occur in an Ethernet structure consisting of bridges, since were they to occur, bridges would generate continuously circulating packets which would not be detected. Thus, algorithms have been developed to prevent this for redundant network layouts (see Figure 4.3).

Using the spanning tree algorithm, after the exchange of protocol information (every one to ten seconds) between bridges, a unique route (tree structure) is determined. Ports which are not required and connection lines (transceiver cables for a local bridge or WAN circuit for a remote bridge) are logically blocked and deactivated (they are only reactivated if the regular route fails). A separate spanning tree protocol is transacted between the bridges. This protocol is standardized either according to IEEE 802.1 Part D (Section 4.2.2) or, in the case of older products, according to company standards (for example, DEC, Vitalink). Thus, when bridges are deployed, attention should be paid to the spanning tree protocol; the protocol standardized by IEEE should be preferred. Such a bridge is also called a routing bridge because it carries out certain routing functions.

Table 4.5   Type-field values for an Ethernet frame.

Type field	Company/protocol
0600	XNS internet
0800	DoD internet
0801	X.75 internet
0802	NBS internet
0803	ECMA internet
0804	CHAOSNet
0805	X.25 level 3
0806	Ethernet ARP
0888 to 088A	Xyplex
6010 to 6014	3Com Corporation
7020 to 7029	LRT
8006	Nestar
8008	AT & T
8013 to 8016	Silicon Graphics
8019	Apollo Computer
802E	Tymshare
802F	Tigan
8035	Stanford University
8036	Aeonic Systems
8044	Planning Research Corp.
8046 to 8047	AT & T
8049	ExperData
805B to 805C	Stanford University
805D	Evans & Sullivan
8060	Little Machines
8062	Counterpoint Computers
8065 to 8068	University of Mass. at Amherst
8067	Veeco Integrated Automation
8068	General Dynamics
806A	Autophon
806C	ComDesign
806D	CompuGraphic Corporation
806E to 8077	Landmark Graphics
807A	Matra
807C	University of Michigan
807D to 8080	Vitalink Communications
8081 to 8083	Counterpoint Communications
809B	Kinetics
809C to 809E	Datability
809F	Spider Systems Ltd.

Table **4.5**   *(continuation).*

Type field	Company/protocol
80A3	Nixdorf Computers
80A4 to 80B3	Siemens Gammasonics Inc.
80C0 to 80C3	Digital Comm. Assoc. Inc.
80C6	Pacer Software
80C7	Applitek Corporation
80C8 to 80CC	Intergraph Corporation
80CD to 80CE	Harris Corporation
80CF to 80D2	Taylor Instrument
80D3 to 80D4	Rosemount Corporation
80DD	Varian Associates
80DE to 80DF	Integrated Solutions
80E0 to 80E3	Allen–Bradley
80E4 to 80F0	Datability
80F2	Retix
80F3 to 80F5	Kinetics
80F7	Apollo Computer
80FF to 8103	Wellfleet Computers
8069	AT & T
807B	Dansk Data Electronic A/S
8130	Waterloo Microsystems Inc.
8131	VG Laboratory Sys.
8137 to 8138	Novell Inc.
8139 to 813D	KTI
0101 to 01FF	Experimental
9000	Loopback

Not all the bridges available on the market implement the spanning tree algorithm. This is actually only necessary when, because of increased failsafe requirements, the network is operated with redundant routes. Simple coupling of two local area networks via a bridge does not require a bridge with the spanning tree algorithm.

Remote bridges   Remote bridges connect LANs via PTT trunk lines (WANs). A variety of possible interfaces are provided by the manufacturers (for example, X.21, X.25, ISDN, G.703). The lowest speed of a connecting circuit between two LANs should be 64 kbps. Remote bridges often have several possibilities for LAN connection (multiport bridge) and require a larger buffer to equalize the capacity differences between LANs and WANs. In addition, some devices use compression algorithms which achieve a compression factor of up to 4. If a standardized protocol (such as X.25) is not used on the WAN circuit, bridges from the same manufacturer must be used on both sides.

In many products, it is possible to run parallel lines between two remote bridges. Unlike in the spanning tree algorithm, these lines may both be used simultaneously, since from the point of view of the spanning tree algorithm, they are treated as one circuit.

One example of this is the simultaneous use of a 2 Mbps and a 64 kbps circuit between two bridges. Normally, the load is divided proportionately over the two circuits according to their transport capacity. Should one line fail, all the traffic is automatically switched to the other intact line. Another variant is the automatic activation of a switched connection (for example, Datex L or ISDN) when an existing dedicated line fails.

4.4.2.2 Additional router functions

The basic function of a router was described in Section 4.3. Routers connect networks at the level of the network layer; moreover, the protocols of transit networks may differ from those of the networks to be connected. In particular, this is the case for connecting networks in the WAN area and the backbone area. Thus, most routers on the market have a variety of WAN interfaces (for example, X.21, X.25, ISDN, G.703) and interfaces to high-speed LANs (for example, FDDI, DQDB, ATM, Frame Relay).

Since there is no common protocol for the network layer (every protocol family has its own layer 3 protocol) a separate routing mechanism must be transacted per protocol family; thus, each protocol family to be supported requires a separate router. However, this would lead to a large number of different routers if more than one protocol family were used on a LAN. Protocols with their own layer 3 and routing protocols include: DECnet, TCP/IP, IPX/SPX (Novell), XNS, AppleTalk and OSI. These circumstances have very rapidly led to routers which are able to route several protocol families simultaneously (multiprotocol routers).

Many protocol families have no protocols at all for layer 3a since they were designed for networks which did not require connections via transport networks (for example, LAT). If it is required to support these protocols over transit networks, then bridges are the only suitable components. In addition, so that transactions may be carried out with all protocol families which may occur on a LAN, the bridge functionality must also be built into the multiprotocol router. The artificial term brouter (bridge and router) is also used to describe hybrid devices of this type.

Figure 4.16 summarizes the various forms of products. The evolutionary trend is clearly towards increasing functionality. In the meantime, these devices are undergoing functional extensions which could turn them into universal network nodes within a network. For example, they

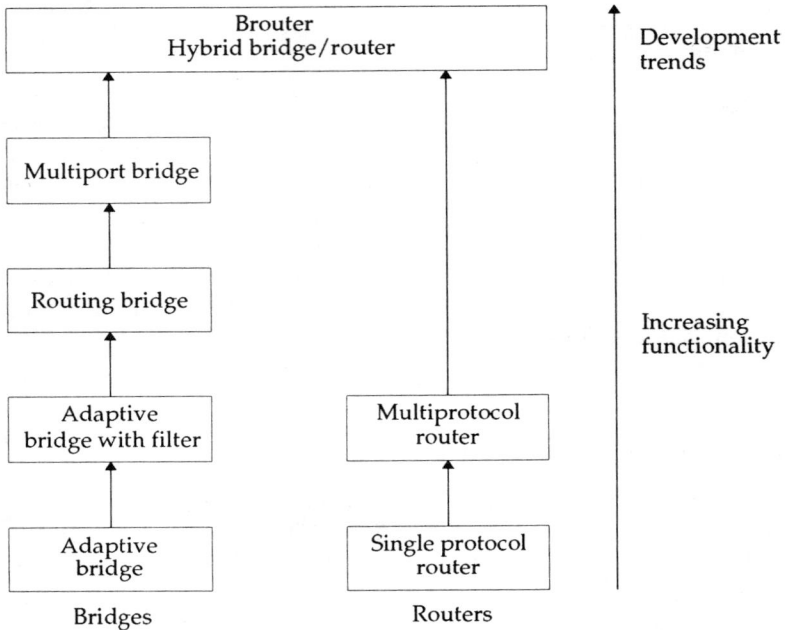

Figure 4.16 Classification of bridges and routers.

have the functionality of X.25 switching subsystems and are able to support SNA connections transparently.

4.4.2.3 Performance criteria

Bridges and routers should be dimensioned in such a way that even when the LAN load is the maximum conceivable the components remain functional. Since the two types of components must receive, manipulate (routers only) and transport packets, the maximum number of packets per second which may be transported on the different types of LAN is important when judging the performance capability. The number of packets depends on the packet size (see Table 4.6).

If an Ethernet component performs at the 100% level, every individual interface may be required to process the maximum number of packets (14880) of minimum packet length. However, the maximum number of packets is only a theoretical value which in practice, because of the CSMA/CD procedure, is never attained.

Most bridge manufacturers give values for the filtering and

Table **4.6**   Maximum number of packets for different LANs.

LAN	Speed, Mbps	Packets of minimum length		Packets of maximum length	
		No. per sec.	Bytes	No. per sec.	Bytes
Ethernet (802.3)	10	14880	64	813	1526
Token Ring (802.5)	4	21700	23	112	4096
Token Ring (802.3)	16	83333	23	112	17000
FDDI	100	416667	22	2772	4500

forwarding of packets, although it is often unclear whether the values given refer to the total throughput of all ports or to individual ports. In the case of bridges, one should also note that the filter rate may decrease considerably as the size of the address tables and the complexity of the filter increase, since lengthy search and compare operations must be executed for each Ethernet packet. This may mean that, because of overloading of the bridge, a packet to be transported is lost. If this happens only once the effect is not significant since the fact that the packet is missing is detected during end-to-end monitoring in the higher layers and the packet is retransmitted. If, however, packet loss becomes regular, the bridge (or possibly, in the case of a remote bridge, the connecting line) is under-dimensioned, as far as performance is concerned.

Untransported packets have a particularly serious effect in dialogue applications. The connection is not interrupted because of missing packets; instead, missing dialogue responses or entries must be repeated several times by a higher layer, without the user being aware of the true reasons for this. Often, such phenomena are blamed on the high loading of the dialogue computer and not on under-dimensioning of the connecting components, since in batch communication (for example, file transfer) longer transport times are not as noticeable. Per port values of 10 000 packets per second for filtering and around 6000 packets per second for forwarding may be considered to be satisfactory performance data for a bridge.

The performance requirements on a router are rather different. Here too, a packet must be received; however, the packet to be transported is addressed to the router directly. The latter must interpret the layer 3 control information and alter the packet (for example, time stamp, address conversion, checksum). Despite the fact that the number of packets to be processed is often considerably smaller, the overall load on a router is higher (50 to 250 instructions per packet). Thus, in the case of a router, the number of packets to be transported is also an important measure.

If routing and bridging functions are implemented in a brouter, possibly together with additional network management functions and connections to a high-speed backbone (for example, FDDI), devices with high-performance bus systems (for example, transport rates up to 800 Mbps) and additional processors on each LAN interface card (for example, M68040 or RISC processors) are required.

4.4.2.4 Operational aspects

In Section 4.1 we showed that it is necessary to use bridges and/or routers in large and/or very remote LANs. We shall now discuss operational aspects which may influence the choice of routers and bridges.

Handling of broadcast storms   In addition to the fault separation facilities of a bridge, routers may be used to avoid so-called broadcast storms. A broadcast storm may occur when, for example, a broadcast frame with a request to delete the name of a wrongly configured station is duplicated time and time again in the LAN. This gives a LAN load of around 3%, which on its own does not give cause for concern. However, the attached Ethernet controllers are often overloaded since they must analyse every broadcast message to see whether it is intended for that particular station. Usually, normal data communication then becomes impossible. Since broadcast frames use a general address the bridge must transport these frames. However, a router only transports frames which are addressed directly to it. Thus, a possible broadcast storm stops at the router in the subnetwork in which the broadcast was first transmitted.

Central monitoring facility   With the separation of faults and local traffic streams the central monitoring facility of the LAN as a whole is lost. Before the installation of bridges or routers it was possible to monitor all traffic on the LAN using a LAN analyser, however, this is now no longer possible. Only values relating to the network loading (percentage loading, number of packets etc.), error situations (for example, collisions, short packets) and communication relationships for the subLAN to which the analyser is attached are supplied. Thus, either analysers interworking with the central analyser must also be installed in the other subLANs (so-called PODs) or the bridges or routers must supply this management information. However, this is only possible for a small fraction of the available components.

Management of the components   A bridge in its simplest form (self-adaptive bridge without filter facility) does not need to be configured. It may be inserted like a repeater as a black box between the two LANs. However, if filter facilities, statistical queries, etc. are required, the bridge must be manageable. On the other hand, a router must always be configured and thus also managed.

The necessary management of these components may take place via a V.24 port to which either an ASCII terminal (local access) or a terminal server (remote access) may be attached. Remote access is also possible via the Telnet protocol (TCP/IP protocol family) or via SNMP (also in the TCP/IP protocol family) (see Section 6.3.6).

Another difference between the components relates to the provision of new software (new versions, changes to the configuration). In addition to local storage and introduction of software, software may also be supplied over the network. More details of this are given in Chapter 8. When more than one component is used, a central management facility is always preferable; of course, this requires appropriate remote access to decentralized components.

Management of the stations   Since the bridge transports all higher protocols transparently in the LAN, the attached stations do not notice the existence of a bridge, except possibly because of time delays. Bridges connect subLANs to a LAN internetwork where, in the case of Ethernet, each subLAN forms an individual collision area for CSMA/CD.

The situation is different for routers. Routers connect independent LANs via transport networks. According to the choice of a protocol family which the station will use for its communications, the station must be assigned an associated router which transports its data traffic to other networks. Thus, configuration changes must be executed in the station. If dynamic routers are used, these stations must be incorporated into the information network.

Installation procedure   The installation of routers in an existing LAN is not straightforward. The existing overall LAN is divided by the installation of the router into logically independent LANs. The communication between these logically independent LANs is at this point through routers only. Thus, routers must be installed at the same time as all the stations are reconfigured. If there is a large number of stations, this leads to significant coordination costs.

These costs are slightly less if brouters are used, since here the installation may involve several steps. First, the brouters are installed with the bridge functionality only; the stations are not affected by this change in the network. Then, at a given time, the routing for the individual protocol families is added. The stations affected by this are those which use the protocol family for which the routing facility is added. This whole process of installing brouters may stretch over several months in a large network.

Use of redundant components   A LAN internetwork of Ethernet LANs linked via bridges requires a unique route between two stations, even when the layout of lines or bridges is redundant. Thus, the spanning tree algorithm was developed. However, this leaves back-up lines and back-up bridges inactive. The situation is different for routers. Because of the routing

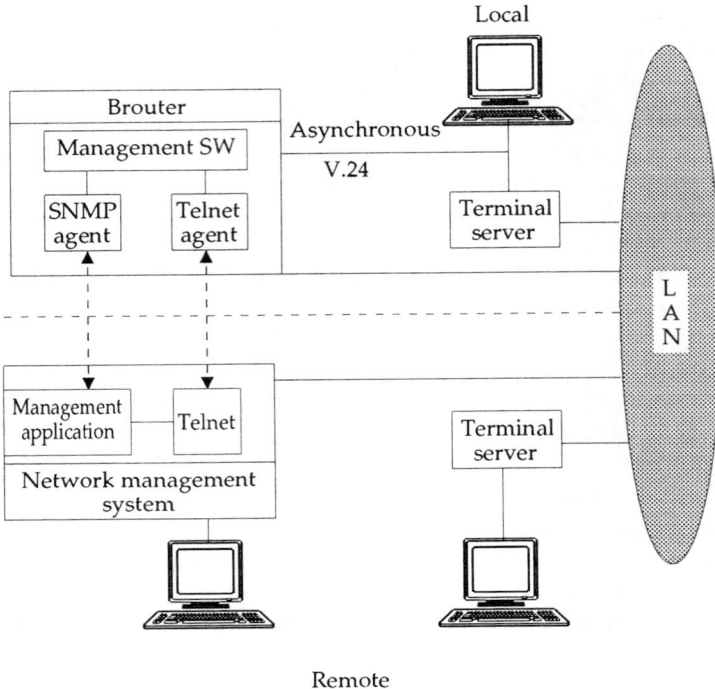

Figure 4.17   Facilities for accessing a brouter.

algorithms an intelligent routing with active back-up lines and redundant components is possible. Thus, the back-up components are not used only in case of faults.

4.4.3 Criteria for forming subnetworks

In addition to the decision as to whether to use bridges, routers or brouters as a means of forming subnetworks or linking the networks, the location of the components also plays an important role. Here, the objective for bridges and routers (which is almost impossible to translate into practice) is that the components should be positioned to obtain the greatest possible separation of the load with a minimum transport of data between the subLANs.

Furthermore, the following influencing factors should be taken into account:

- the number of stations;
- the communication relationships between the stations;

- the protocol families used;
- security requirements;
- redundancy requirements;
- the independence of the subLANs;
- the requirements on network management.

A subLAN will be provided, for example, by a company department or a university institute. The organizational entities between which a large proportion of the traffic transactions take place must themselves formulate the requirements (for example, security, redundancy, independence) on the components which connect them to the remaining subnetworks.

However, the possible locations for bridges and routers are more strongly influenced by the physical structure of the network.

The subnetwork desired by a department cannot always be built if, for example, not all of the department is located in the same building, on the same floor or in the same area. Thus, a subnetwork formed by bridges or routers often coincides with the storey of a building or with a building itself, although the ideal subnetwork from the organizational point of view should extend over several buildings or storeys. More refined subnetworks are often better formed using a star-shaped cabling structure with the 10baseT version of Ethernet. We shall discuss this in Chapter 8.

If there are several subLANs, these should not be connected in a row one after the other, but via a so-called backbone (Figure 4.20). This reduces

Division according to traffic load

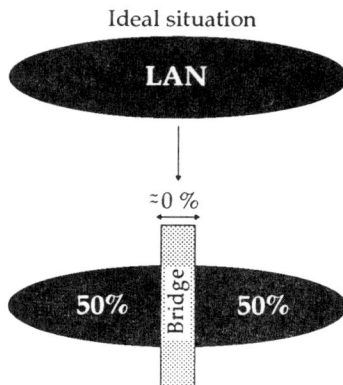

Ideal situation

Figure 4.18 Positioning of bridges or routers.

Coaxial cabling
One subnet per coax

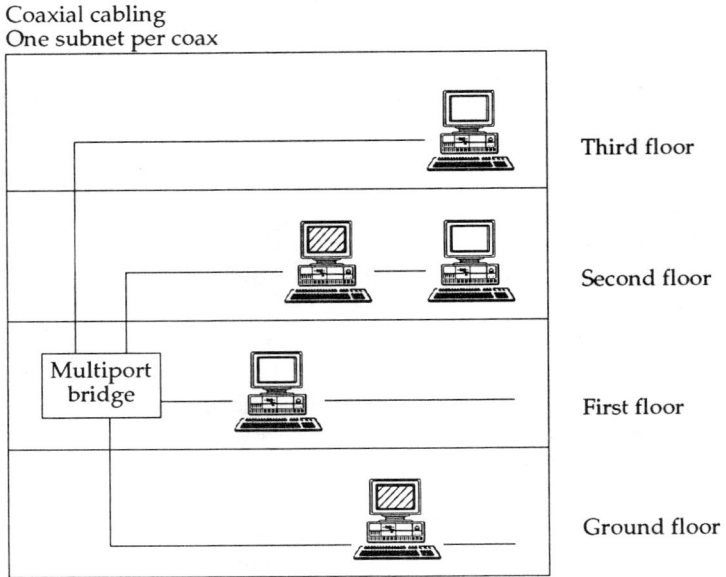

Third floor

Second floor

Multiport
bridge

First floor

Ground floor

Twisted-pair cabling (star wired)
Arbitrary formation of subnetworks

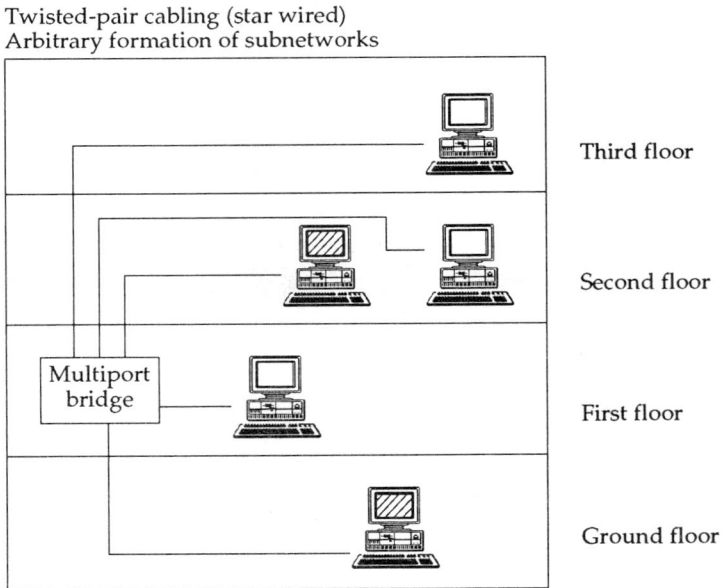

Third floor

Second floor

Multiport
bridge

First floor

Ground floor

Figure 4.19   Formation of subnetworks and the physical network structure.

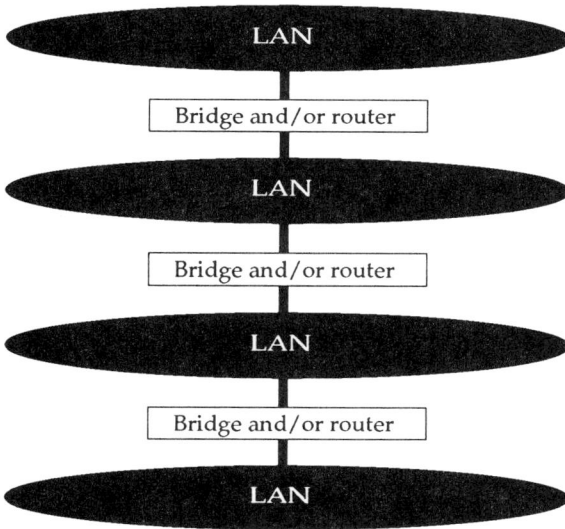

a) Chained subnetworks

Ethernet (10 Mbps)
Token Ring (4 or 16 Mbps)
FDDI (100 Mbps)
DQDB (140 Mbps)

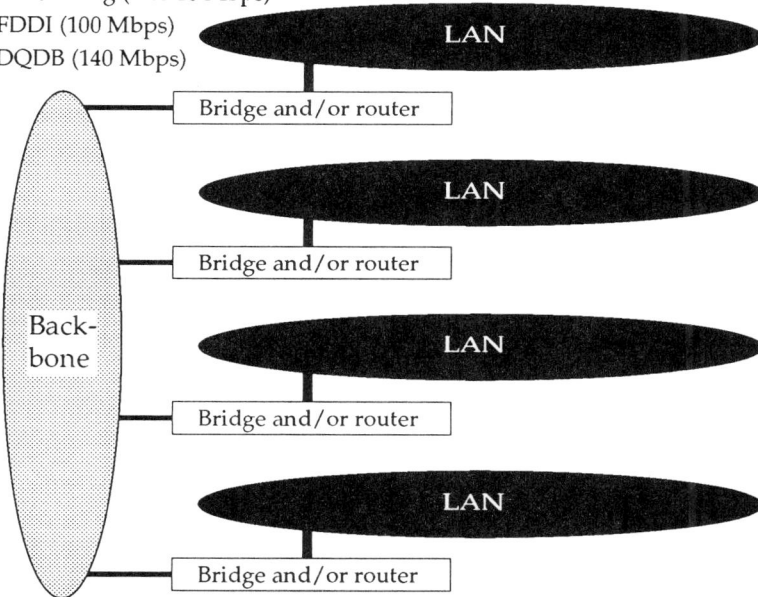

b) Subnetworks linked by backbone

Figure 4.20   Connection of subnetworks via a backbone.

the number of components to be passed through between two stations, which should be kept small because of the delay times in the bridges and routers. However, this increases the number of components to be installed. It is possible to increase the transmission speed of the backbone at a later time without major rearrangements of the network (see Section 4.6).

4.5 LAN–WAN gateways

The cooperation of parts of a company located in different places is only one example to show that local area networks must be connected together via wide area networks. Here, initially, wide areas networks include both public networks and also proprietary network architectures (such as SNA networks). In any case, because of the different protocols worlds, the gateway problem must be confronted. This section is concerned with LAN–WAN gateways; only standardized protocols for the WAN world are considered.

4.5.1 Protocol profiles for LAN transport systems

There are two main forms of transport system implementation which are typically represented by WAN (wide area network) and LAN (local area network) technology.

We stress that the typical difference between LANs and WANs is no longer apparent in the choice of a particular technology. The classical definition of LANs and WANs in terms of their geographical coverage is also of decreasing importance.

Today, Ethernet networks are already linked by satellite and installed as LANs with a worldwide coverage. On the other hand, in the local area there is an increasing tendency towards the use of packet-oriented switching subsystems and digital PBXs suitable for computer communication; thus, connection technology which is traditionally typical for WANs is being brought to the end system.

In this sense, the terms LAN and WAN should no longer be defined in terms of geographical properties, but as specific transport systems over the corresponding 'historically evolved' protocol architectures. In what follows, we describe the most important LAN transport system profiles; the layer-4 protocols referred to are described in Chapter 6.

The basis for telematic development was a transport system which was typically intended to facilitate trunk area communications and was thus recommended by CCITT and adopted by ISO. This is the so-called *telematic profile* (Table 4.7).

This consists of the X.25 connection protocol of the lower layers up to the network layer and T.70 (corresponds to the ISO transport protocol class 0) in the transport layer. It is not sensible to use a multiplexing transport protocol (for example, ISO transport protocol class 2) in a packet-switched network except where justified by tariffs (saving of connection-establishment and time-related costs).

According to CCITT recommendations X.3/X.28/X.29, the dialogue belongs, strictly speaking, to the application system; however, for completeness we describe it here. The telematic profile is not important for pure LANs but is important for the transition from LANs to public networks.

A transport profile for LANs in the narrow sense was developed as part of the MAP/TOP activities. The MAP/TOP protocol profile (Table 4.7) was also proposed by other interest groups (ECMA, SPAG) and has been accepted as a European prenorm (ENV 44101/41102). It will be referred to in what follows as the ISO TP4 profile. Here, the network layer may be empty (within a LAN there is usually no switching necessary in this layer) or it may be a connectionless network service, for example, between

Table 4.7 LAN transport system profiles.

Telematic protocol profile

X.29 dialogue	Class 0 (T.70)
X.25 packet level	
HDLC LAP B	
X.21 (V.24)	

MAP/TOP protocol profile

ISO class 4 transport	
Inactive subset	ISO internet 8473
LLC type 1 (conn. less)	
MAC (e.g. CSMA/CD)	

TCP/IP protocol profile

User datagram protocol (UDP)	Transmission control protocol (TCP)
Internet IP	
LLC type 1	
MAC (e.g. CSMA/CD)	

XNS protocol profile

Packet exchange protocol	Sequenced packet protocol
Internet Datagram Protocol (IDP)	
LLC type 1	
MAC (e.g. CSMA/CD)	

X.25/LAN protocol profile

ISO class 0/1 transport
X.25 level 3
LLC type 2
MAC (e.g. CSMA/CD)

ISO TP0/LAN protocol profile

ISO class 0/1 transport
Inactive subset
LLC type 2
MAC (e.g. CSMA/CD)

several LANs, implemented by the ISO internet IP network protocol.

According to the ISO proposals, transport class 4 is generally provided for all communication systems with a network layer that is very susceptible to faults. It contains functions for multiplexing and must be 'downgradable' to transport class 2 when requested during connection establishment.

Many products also support the *X.25/LAN protocol profile*. This is of interest when Ethernet- and X.25-based communications networks exist within a company and a common network service interface is to be provided. In addition, this profile makes it possible to superimpose some interesting application systems such as FTAM and X.400. This protocol profile is specified in ISO 8881.

The *TCP/IP profile* is important for UNIX systems and Ethernet LANs. It is probably the most common profile. The XNS protocol family is still of some importance in the Ethernet world. In addition, there are also proprietary protocol hierarchies within closed network solutions.

4.5.2 Gateway approaches for LAN–WAN coupling

There are two important but very different ways of looking at LAN–WAN coupling. Firstly, the LAN and the WAN may be viewed as two subnetworks of equal status in an overall internetwork. The internetwork topology looks identical for the second approach, but logically the LAN functions as a (distributed) DTE on the WAN.

4.5.2.1 LAN and WAN as subnetworks

LANs and WANs are subnetworks in the sense of the OSI reference model; in other words, as far as the internetwork (global network) is concerned they have common protocols from the transport layer upwards and subnetwork-specific protocols up to the network layer. Each individual LAN station and each subscriber in the WAN are thus end systems in the global network. This type of linkage requires the definition of a global network layer for LANs and WANs. An alternative is shown in Table 4.8.

Table 4.8   LAN–WAN coupling via ISO internet.

Class 4 transport	
ISO internet	
ISO type 1 (conn. less)	X.25 (packet layer)
MAC (CSMA/CD)	HDLC LAPB
	X.21

Table **4.9** LAN/WAN coupling via X.25.

Class 0 transport	
X.25 (packet layer)	
LLC type 2 (conn. oriented)	HDLC LAPB
MAC (CSMA/CD)	X.21

Here, the left side corresponds to the data link layer of the typical LAN architecture while as an alternative, as illustrated on the right, the X.25 connection protocol may be implemented in the WAN. Thus, the connectionless ISO network protocol IP lies above the connection-oriented and flow-controlled X.25 connection protocol which is now resident in the data link layer. The former provides the connectionless ISO network service, which is in turn supervised by the connection-oriented transport protocol ISO TP4 which provides the connection-oriented ISO transport service.

Another alternative way of combining formerly typical WAN and LAN protocol profiles was first used in the British Joint Academic Network (JANET) (Table 4.9).

Here, the left side corresponds to the lowest two layers of typical LAN architectures with additional functionality in layer 3. The implementation of X.25 (packet layer) above the LLC, according to the ISO standard, may be over LLC type 1 (connectionless) or over LLC type 2 (connection oriented). CEPT favours the protocol version X.25 over LLC type 2 since it seems to permit a simpler implementation of the layer 3 protocol. Since, in any case, an X.25 packet layer which provides a connection-oriented ISO network service is sufficiently well protected, the implementation of the very simple ISO transport protocol TP0 will be sufficient to provide a secure connection-oriented ISO transport service in LAN architectures also. This profile version will be used where WANs (for example, Datex P, Datex L) have to be connected to LAN gateways.

One important possibility for various application systems involves bringing the connection-oriented network layer (for example, X.25 in a WAN) into the LAN. End systems in the LAN and end systems in the WAN may then be uniformly addressed according to X.21.

From the outside, such a LAN then looks like a conventional X.25 switching subsystem. One important advantage is that the services in the WAN (for example, X.29 communications protocols) may also be available unaltered in the LAN terminals. In many cases, it may be undesirable or impossible to relinquish a certain transport system which is only needed within the LAN. Thus, in order to be able to provide a computer system networked over a LAN with the ISO transport protocol class 0 above the

```
┌─────────────────────┐
│   TP0 Transport     │                    ┌─────────────────────┐
├─────────────────────┤                    │    X.25 Mapping     │
│    X.25 Mapping     │                    ├──────────┬──────────┤
├─────────────────────┤                    │X.25 S.L. │          │
│  X.25 Support layer │                    ├──────────┤          │
├─────────────────────┤                    │Transport │  X.25    │
│  Transport class 4  │                    │          │          │
├─────────────────────┤                    │          │          │
│      IEEE 802       │                    │          │          │
└─────────────────────┘                    └──────────┴──────────┘
        │                                              └── Datex P
     LAN
```

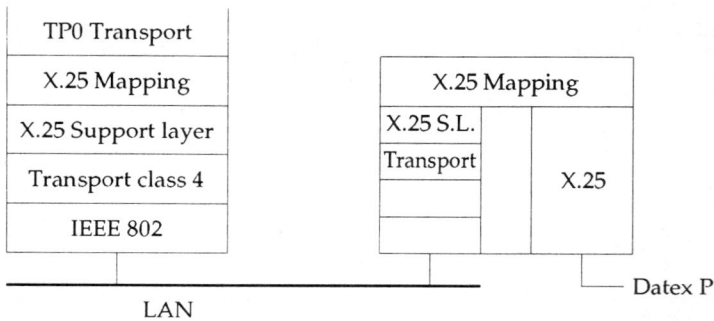

Figure 4.21   Layer 3 gateway above the LAN transport system.

X.25-based network layer, complicated architectures must be designed. For example, an X.25 support layer may be defined for this which transfers X.25 protocol elements to and from the gateway, above the existing LAN transport system, as if the LAN system were directly attached to an X.25 network (for example, Datex P) (Figure 4.21). Above this, it will then be possible to transact the T.70 transport protocol on which the common LAN/WAN application is based. The form of this protocol is unimportant to the gateway (still layer 3).

Such a structure may well be used as a pragmatic transitional solution between a TCP/IP LAN and a X.25/T.70 WAN, and may simplify later steps in the migration towards ISO transport systems. The transport system in the LAN is then characterized in layers 3 and 4 as follows: IP (internet ARPA), TCP (transmission control ARPA), X.25 support (packet level), TP class 0 (ISO transport).

Earlier, we noted that, according to the situation, the *encapsulation* technique may also be used in internetworking. This is the case when two subnetworks intercommunicate over a third subnetwork; in other words, the communicating stations are in the first two networks only and the third network functions as a pure transit network. Figure 4.22 shows such a situation. Here, two LANs intercommunicate via an X.25 WAN (in this example, station A on LAN1 intercommunicates with station B on LAN2).

A and B support a common transport protocol, in this case, the TCP protocol of the ARPA family which is widely used in the Ethernet world. Suppose that the common layer-3c protocol is the internet IP. A's transport data is packed into an IP datagram with destination address the globally unique IP address of B. The IP datagram is packed according to the LAN1-specific protocol and transmitted to the X.25 gateway where the LAN1 header is removed and the datagram is packed in an X.25 packet, etc.

Host/NIU A   Host/NIU B

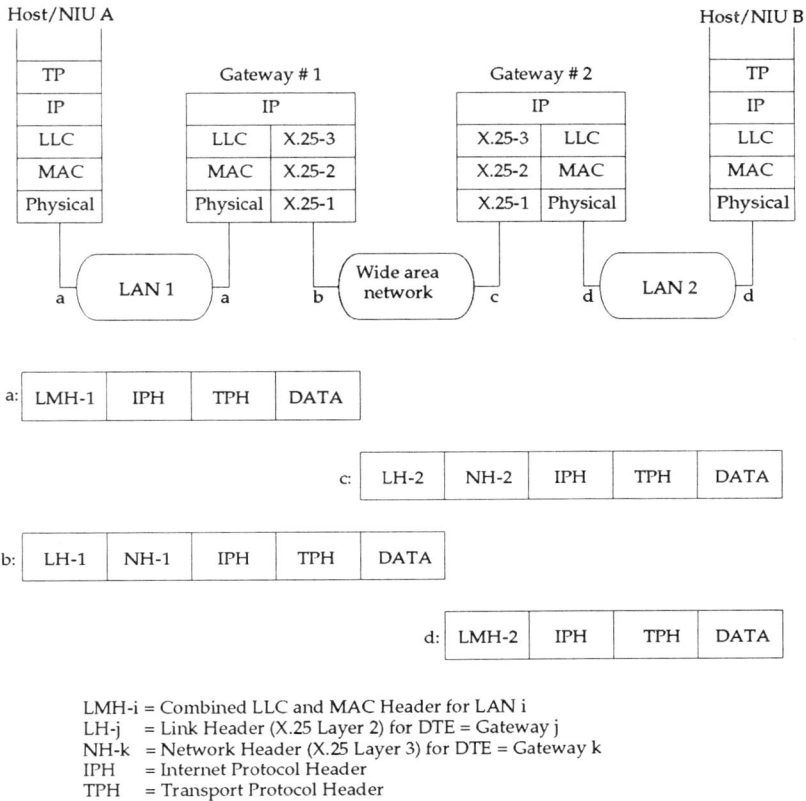

LMH-i = Combined LLC and MAC Header for LAN i
LH-j = Link Header (X.25 Layer 2) for DTE = Gateway j
NH-k = Network Header (X.25 Layer 3) for DTE = Gateway k
IPH   = Internet Protocol Header
TPH   = Transport Protocol Header

Figure 4.22 Internetworking by encapsulation.

The encapsulation technique is not expensive, though it is possible that the internet packet may have to be fragmented. The transit network is transparent to the higher layers, in this case TCP. Thus, care should be taken to ensure that the time conditions of such a protocol are not violated by the use of transit networks.

4.5.2.2 The LAN as a distributed end system

In this approach, from the point of view of the WAN, a LAN is considered as a single subscriber system, which is, however, distributed; in other words, individual LAN stations are not all direct network subscribers on the WAN, but the distributed system interworking unit (DSI) is the coupling unit that contains a transport layer relay function. From this ECMA point of view, the LAN–WAN coupling is a level 4 gateway (Figure 4.23).

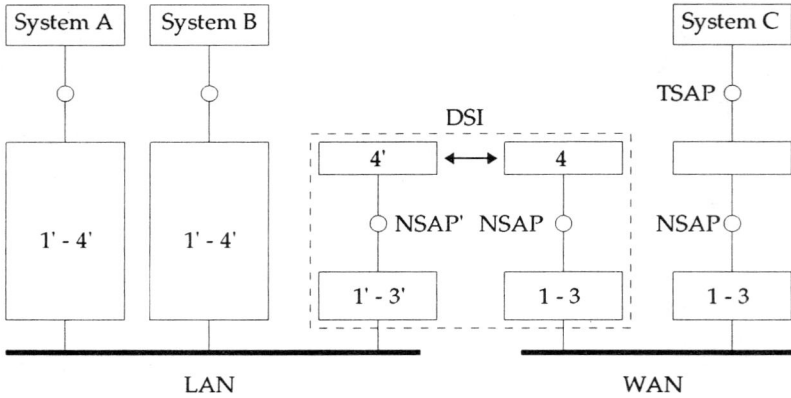

TSAP = Transport Service Access Point
NSAP = Network Service Access Point
DSI = Distributed System Internetworking Unit

Figure 4.23 The LAN as a distributed end system.

LANs are often linked to mainframe manufacturer networks according to this point of view. In this case, the gateway is implemented on a host computer (mainframe) as a dual-node gateway (Figure 4.24) which also has WAN monitor functions. Thus, existing software for access control, accounting, statistics, etc. may be used. Often the same host is used as a network access point to PTT services for LAN subscribers. In this case, the protocol conversion also affects higher OSI layers.

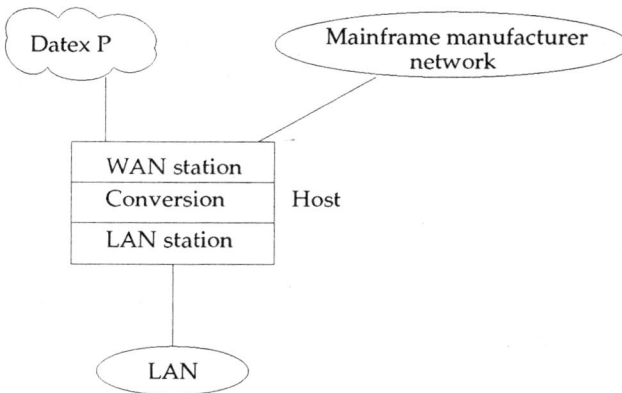

Figure 4.24 The host as a dual-node gateway.

4.5.3 LAN gateways to the WAN world

In addition to the coupling of LANs via WANs with bridges or routers which use the WAN as a pure transit network, direct gateways from the LAN into the WAN are available which provide for communication between LAN and WAN stations. The corresponding protocol profiles and gateway approaches were discussed in Sections 4.5.1 and 4.5.2. The connection-oriented WAN world must be linked to the connectionless LAN world. We shall consider two possibilities, the X.25 gateway and X.25 over Ethernet.

4.5.3.1 X.25 gateway

An X.25 gateway is currently the most common way of interconnecting computers from the WAN and LAN worlds using the triple-X protocol (X.3, X.28, X.29). This permits dialogue and a primitive proprietary file transfer. Computers in the LAN may use the X.25 gateway to reach computers with X.29 capabilities in the WAN (for example, the German public switched X.25 network Datex P, WIN) and conversely, computers in the WAN can reach computers in the LAN. Figure 4.25 illustrates these possibilities.

We note that the user normally has to execute two calling procedures: firstly at the level of the LAN to call the gateway server, and secondly at the X.25 level to call the host in the WAN. The user interface may, if necessary, be simplified to a single calling procedure by clever nomenclature and suitable configuration.

The possibility of reverse access to the LAN via worldwide public networks based on X.25 is interesting, particularly for individual terminals or remote terminal clusters which are linked using PADs.

When choosing gateway products, a number of questions arise which may affect the planning and the operation of the network. Here are some examples of questions in the case of the X.25 gateway.

- Interfaces:
    - Which interfaces to the WAN are supported (V.24, X.21, V.35)?
    - What speeds are possible?
    - How many logical links are possible?
    - Which versions of the X.25 network are supported (for example, Telenet, Tynmet, Datapac, Datex P)?
    - Does there exist a ZZF (Zentrale Zulassungsstelle Fernmeldewesen, the German central authorization authority for telecommunications) authorization for using the gateway with Datex P?

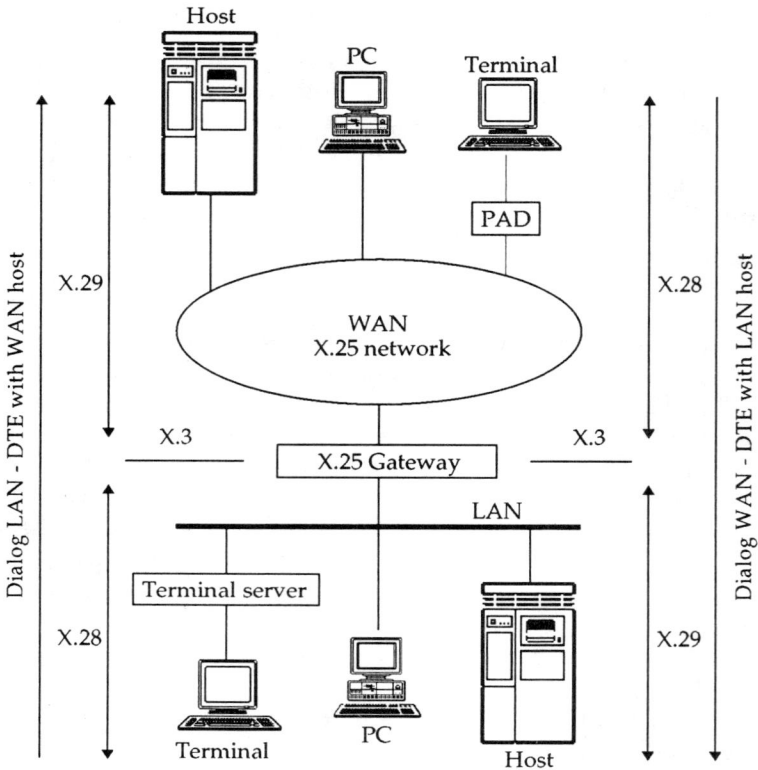

Figure 4.25   Possible use of an X.25 gateway.

- Operation:
    - Do there exist aids for breaking down Datex-P bills with respect to individual users?
    - Is there access protection for outgoing calls on the gateway?
    - Are Datex-P addresses or symbolic names used for subscriber addressing?
    - Are PVCs supported? Which X.3 PAD parameters are supported?
    - For incoming calls, how are LAN ports addressed (subaddresses, user data field)?
    - Is password-protected access possible?

It is no secret that currently the accounting and control mechanisms in many gateway servers leave much to be desired. This has led to the development of so-called X.25 accounting boxes which take on the above accounting and control mechanisms for the gateway servers.

4.5.3.2 X.25 over Ethernet

X.25 is the most common protocol for the WAN area, at least in Europe. It is a secure connection-oriented protocol, the suitability of which for high speeds currently used in LANs has yet to be demonstrated. The idea of using the X.25 protocol in local area networks (X.25 layer 3 on LLC2 layer 2) permits a common protocol and network structure in the WAN and LAN areas, as far as the higher layers are concerned (Figure 4.26). For example, FTAM could be installed on all computers. If one makes full use of the available parameters of X.25, for example, by setting the window size to 128 bytes and the packet length to 4096 bytes, transmission rates in the high-speed area may also be achieved (theoretically).

This protocol stack has been used in the British research network JANET for some three years. In the meantime, some manufacturers now supply this X.25/LLC2 protocol stack for their products (Table 4.10).

The X.25/LLC2 protocol stack is even available for higher speeds, for example, for FDDI. In particular, the fact that this protocol stack, like the TCP/IP protocol stack is to be a fixed component of UNIX 4.4 BSD and may thus spread rapidly, should be noted.

In the area of switching systems between LANs and WANs the number of products for this protocol stack is also not inconsiderable (Table 4.11). Even suppliers of classical X.25 switching subsystems and (thus also) of routers in the LAN area provide such products.

On the WAN side, speeds currently go up to 8 Mbps with the G.703 interface, on the LAN side FDDI is available at 100 Mbps. First measurements at the university computer centre in Erlangen (Holleczek and

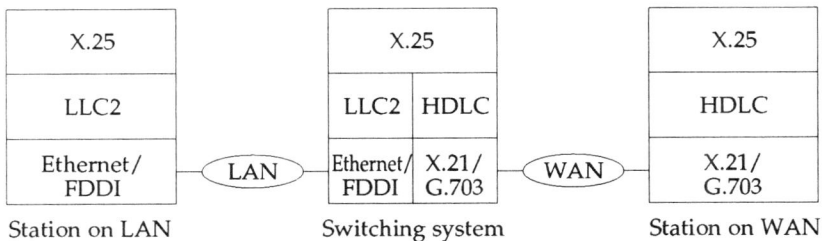

Figure 4.26 Common protocol interface in the LAN and WAN areas.

Table 4.10   X.25/LLC2 products for end systems.

Computer/network operating system	Service	Status
PC/BICC Rainbow/ DOS	X3 dialogue FTAM	Available In preparation
Sun/Sunlink V.7 UNIX	X3 dialogue FTAM X.400	Available Available Available
DEC/VAX/VMS PSI V.5 & DEC/ULTRIX	X3 dialogue FTAM X.400	Available Available Available
Cyber/CDCNet NOS VE 1.5.3 & CDC/EPIX	X3 dialogue FTAM X.400	Available Available Available
Convex/OSI WAN/ Convex OS (UNIX)	X3 dialogue X.400	Available Available
UNIX 4.4 BSD	X.3 dialogue VT FTAM X.400 X.500 X-Window	In preparation In preparation In preparation In preparation In preparation In preparation

Kleinöder, 1991) showed that this protocol stack is unquestionably suitable for transmission rates of 2 Mbps in the WAN area and 10 Mbps in the LAN area. Limiting factors at the present time include the processors in the end and switching systems and the limited facility for setting optimal window sizes and packet lengths. Using RISC systems for file transfer (with a single virtual link) achieves a throughput of around 650 kbytes/s, which equals an Ethernet load of around 60%.

The spread of this European protocol stack will be very closely associated with its availability on as many systems as possible. X.25 is an alternative to the connectionless network service and is a homogeneous network solution for the LAN and WAN area which also has administrative advantages.

Table 4.11   Switching systems with the X.25/LLC2 protocol stack.

Manufacturer	*WAN (HDLC)*		*LAN (LLC2)*		*Status*
	X.21	G.703	Ethernet	FDDI	
Spider	X		X		Available
CAMTEC	X		X		Available
Datus	X		X		Announced
Netcomm SW2000	X	X (2 Mbps)	X		Available
Netcomm SW3500	X	X (8 Mbps)	X	X	In preparation
CISCO	X		X		Beta test
Wellfleet			X	X	In preparation
Network Systems		X (34 Mbps)	X	X	In preparation

4.6 Planning backbone networks for LAN interconnection

When using bridges, routers or brouters it is sensible (see Section 4.4.3) to connect the corresponding subnetworks via a backbone network. This backbone network serves as a network for linking the corresponding (sub)LANs. Usually, user stations are not directly attached to the backbone network. If a router is used, the backbone is often called an internet or a transit network. The backbone network and the attached subnetworks may be of the same network type. However, they may also be of different types with different transmission speeds and protocols. Possible network types for backbone networks in the private area include:

* Ethernet: 10 Mbps
* Token Ring: 4 Mbps
* Token Ring: 16 Mbps
* FDDI: 100 Mbps
* DQDB: 140 Mbps

However, if backbone networks have to be implemented using lines provided by public suppliers, for cost reasons, the public lines are usually operated at a considerably lower speed than the attached subnetworks. The German Telekom now provides its own solutions, including, at least in the local area, high-speed lines which are also affordable.

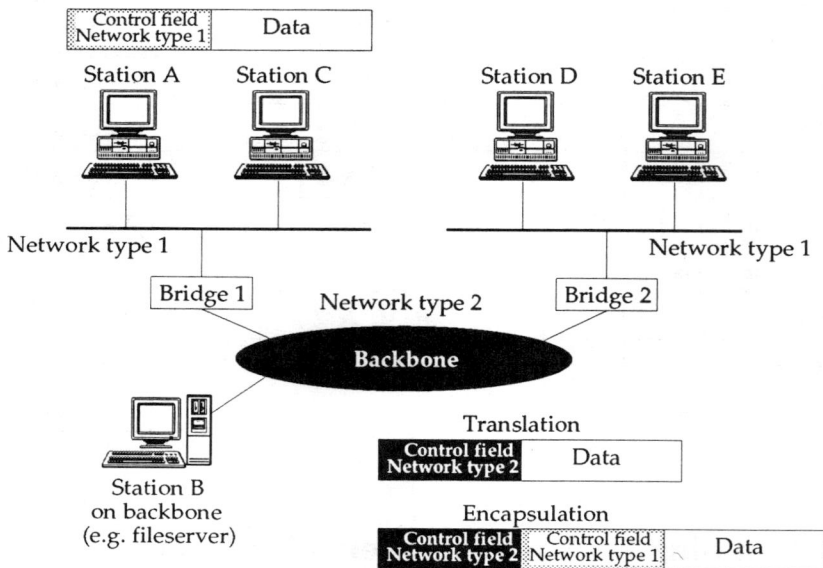

Figure 4.27 Difference between encapsulation and translation.

If the backbone network is of a different type, the subnetworks may be connected in two ways. Either the packets of the subnetwork network type are packed into packets of the backbone-network network type (possibly with fragmentation) and unpacked again on the other side (encapsulation, tunnelling) or there is a translation from the subnetwork packet type to the backbone packet type, and *vice versa* (in other words, a protocol conversion).

Thus, encapsulation is the simpler solution; however, this only permits interworking with local area networks of the same network type on both sides of the transit network, and is often implemented as a manufacturer-specific solution which only tolerates components from the same manufacturer. Translation is the more complicated solution and thus also more lavish and expensive; however, it permits interworking between local area networks of different types and, as a manufacturer-neutral solution admits components from different manufacturers.

If stations are attached directly to the backbone (e.g. FDDI), which may be sensible for computers with a high communications requirement in terms of volume (e.g. file servers), translation may solve the concomitant problem of communication between different network types.

4.6.1 LAN coupling using public services

When connections between LANs have to be implemented over public land, networks provided by the Telekom or other authorized suppliers must be used.

The lines should be dimensioned in such a way that the circuits used for the application to be run on them do not become a bottleneck. The lowest speed for connections between LANs should be around 64 kbps but connecting lines operating at 2 Mbps or 10 Mbps and above may also be sensible for some applications. Normally, these are fixed connections (permanent, physical or virtual connections, leased lines), since data packets may be exchanged at any time (for example, broadcast messages, routing information, network management data). It is not possible to establish a new connection every time since this often takes too long. Switched connections between two LANs are only sensible when large data sets have to be exchanged at fixed times in short intervals.

A prerequisite for the use of the German Telekom services is that the LAN component to be used has a ZZF authorization for the relevant interface. This is not the case for some devices now on the market. In the context of the EC internal market, from 1993, authorization by another European PTT within the EC may replace German authorization.

Of the services provided by the German Telekom, we shall only describe those which meet the above requirements (fixed connections with transmission speeds above 64 kbps).

ISDN

The first implementations of the connection of bridges and routers over ISDN are now available. However, we note that blanket ISDN coverage will only be available from the German Telekom from the end of 1993. Thus, one needs to check whether the location of the LANs involved can be connected to the ISDN. In the ISDN context, semi-permanent connections with a speed of 64 kbps are supplied. The costs are based on distance and are divided into three classes: local area, regional area (distance 50 km) and remote area.

Because of its speed, ISDN may also be a cost-effective way of linking local area networks or remote individual LAN stations at the telephone tariff for short periods only (for example, in order to transmit new price lists, mail, etc.).

On-line links

On-line links are dedicated lines with active network components (for example, modems) which have transmission speeds of up to 2 Mbps (more precisely, 1.92 Mbps). This type of LAN coupling via on-line links is to be preferred when large data sets have to be regularly transferred, since the German Telekom's tariff structure for fixed connections does not depend on the data volume. The tariffs depend only on the distance and the transmission rate. As far as distance is concerned, there are two local area zones (near the local exchange or not), while the remote area is subdivided according to the distance as the crow flies (in km).

Another version involves connections without active network components, which are available with transmission speeds starting from 2 Mbps. These connections are primarily used in or adjacent to the local area and usually consist of bare monomode optical fibres (dark fibre) with DIN connectors. The German Telekom is prepared to rent these circuits on a long-term lease, with no restrictions on transmission speed, on the basis of monthly rental payments, or for a one-off higher payment (to subsidize building costs) and a smaller monthly maintenance fee.

X.25 (Datex P)

The Telekom's Datex P provides permanent virtual connections (PVCs) at up to 64 kbps. The tariff scheme depends on volume and thus costs are difficult to calculate. Since applications in local area networks usually involve the transportation of relatively large data sets (for example, screen-oriented work), because of the volume-dependent pricing structure the costs of an X.25 dedicated line may turn out to be quite high. Thus, Datex P is only recommended for short-term coupling of local area networks in order to reach other computers, directly attached to the Datex-P network, from these networks.

The German scientific network, WIN, which is rented at a fixed price to the German research network (DFN) by the Telekom, is in a special position. More than 250 scientific and research institutions (universities, major research institutions, libraries, company research and development departments etc.) are attached to this network, which uses the X.25 protocol. A connection option with a transmission speed of 2 Mbps is available. The WIN is also used to couple local area networks using routers and for direct connection of computers via OSI protocols. Its transport volume is steadily increasing and amounted to around 180 Gbytes in February 1992.

Future offerings

Dedicated lines at 34 Mbps with the G.703 interface are already available from the Telekom by individual negotiation. Whether these will be affordable in the remote area remains to be seen.

The Telekom's VBN (Vermittelndes Breitbandnetz, switched videoconferencing network), is a fibre optic network with a blanket coverage of Germany. This is primarily used for video communication (video-conferencing). Since its usage is relatively low, it is conceivable that this

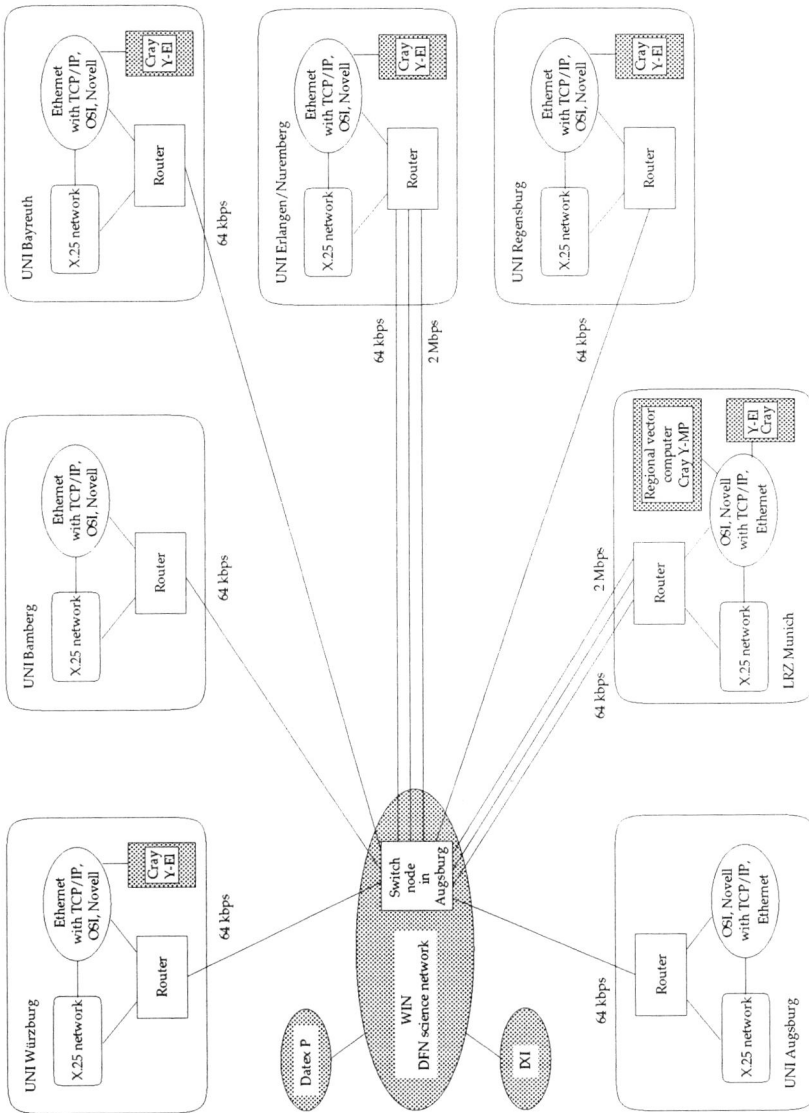

Figure 4.28 WIN integrated network (section of the integrated network of Bavarian vector processors).

network will be opened to permit the connection of local area networks with transmission speeds up to 140 Mbps and higher. This idea is already being tested in pilot schemes.

In addition to making available circuits on which the user determines which protocol is used, the Telekom finally intends to provide backbone networks for LANs in the local area and possibly, at a later date, with a blanket coverage across the country. First trials of backbone networks will take place in Darmstadt (FDDI), Munich (DQDB) and Stuttgart (DQDB). The acceptance of these services, which will also include the operation of the connection components by the Telekom, will depend heavily on the price and on the availability of blanket coverage of Germany.

4.6.2 Fast backbone networks

On private land, backbone networks may be implemented at any time and are not subject to any Telekom restrictions. Such backbone networks should have at least the same, if not considerably higher, transmission rates than the LANs which they are intended to connect. In principle, the following may be used to connect Ethernet LANs via a backbone network: Ethernet itself, Token Ring at 16 Mbps, FDDI and DQDB.

Further developments, such as ATM, Frame Relay, SMDS, Sonet/SDH, etc., which are currently only available as pilot products for connections between routers or bridges will not be considered further here.

Normally nowadays a backbone to connect Ethernet LANs will be either an Ethernet itself or FDDI. Token Ring is ruled out in the Ethernet environment in favour of the Ethernet backbone because of its minor speed advantage and because it is of a different network-type. However, if Token Ring and Ethernet are used to an equal extent within a company, it might also be sensible to use Token Ring as a backbone. Thus, for these reasons, bridges which link Ethernet LANs and Token Ring LANs are not very common in the market.

4.6.2.1 FDDI

At the present time, FDDI is the most common fast backbone for coupling LANs. FDDI (here, we mean FDDI 1) has the following properties:

- Nominal transmission speed: 100 Mbps.
- Data rates of up to 80 Mbps are achievable.
- Ring topologies and star topologies may be mixed.
- A fibre optic transmission medium is used. Implementation on wire circuits (< 100 m) is possible.
- 62.5/125 μ multimode fibre optic cable with wavelength 1300 nm is standard.

- Other types of fibre optic cable are also supported, although with some loss of performance, which is reflected in the permissible distance between two FDDI stations.

- Manufacturer-neutral standard (ANSI X3T9.5 FDDI).

- Fault-tolerant dual-ring topology.

- Overall length of fibre optic cable up to 100 km.

- Maximum distance between two adjacent FDDI stations 1 (2) km.

- Modified Token Ring protocol.

As Figure 4.29 shows, both ring and tree (star) structures are possible. The FDDI standard defines three types of components: concentrators (CON), class-A stations (connection to the dual ring, otherwise known as dual attachment stations (DASs)) and class-B stations (connection to the concentrator, otherwise known as single attachment stations (SASs)). There are two forms of class-A stations (DAS): simple stations and concentrators to which class-B stations (SAS) may be attached. Concentrators may be cascaded in a star shape. An SAS concentrator may also be attached to two DAS concentrators, where only one connection is active at any time (dual homing). This increases the fault tolerance.

Connecting a DAS always requires an interruption of the network operation; an SAS may be connected without interrupting the operation. Should one or more DAS or the ring-shaped fibre optic circuit fail, either the ring remains intact or it is decomposed into several subrings. Should one or more SAS fail (or their fibre optic link) only the SAS involved is (are) uncoupled from the network. Should a concentrator fail, all the stations attached to it are uncoupled from the ring. Structured star-shaped cabling is better reproduced by combining concentrators and SAS; however, in the case of component failure, more devices are affected than for ring-shaped cabling. While the FDDI dual ring is redundant it can only be securely operated if all the devices on the ring are guaranteed to operate perfectly. If this ring leads to end subscribers (for example, an end user's workstation), there is a danger that the whole network may be affected by manipulations on this device. Thus, if possible, ring components should be located in closed areas and reserved for the backbone area of a network. Typical examples of DAS include bridges, routers and brouters for connecting low-speed local area networks and also direct computer connections. SAS may also be subscriber systems (for example, workstations or PCs).

Thus, FDDI may be used in two forms, which may also be mixed:

- as a fast connection between workstations, servers, high-performance computers, etc.;

- as a fast backbone network for local area networks.

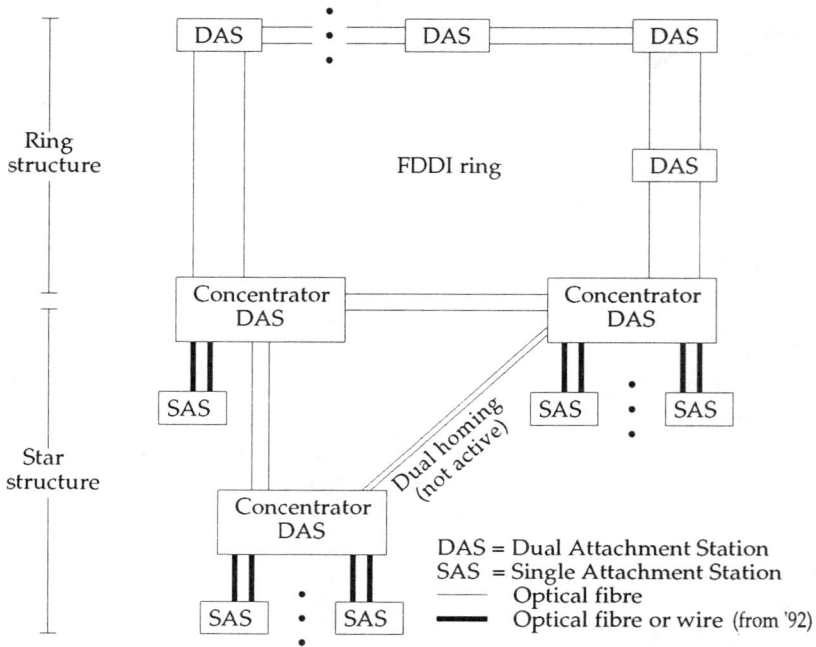

Figure 4.29   Schematic illustration of FDDI configuration.

4.6.2.2 DQDB

DQDB (distributed queue dual bus) was standardized by IEEE 803.6 in the context of the MAN (metropolitan area network) activities, and may also be used as a backbone for connecting local area networks. DQDB is above all preferred by the PTTs of some countries, since here, unlike in FDDI 1, in addition to data communications, speech transmission is also possible (isochronous traffic). DQDB may be characterized as follows:

- Coverage greater than 100 km.
- Distance-independent connection of DQDB networks possible.
- Initial transmission rates of 34 or 140 Mbps; arbitrary rates are in principle possible, since the specification contains no restrictions on the transmission medium or the transmission speed.
- Transmission of both packet-oriented and isochronous information.
- Standardized in IEEE 802.6
- Possibility of migration to ATM since the transmission structures are mutually compatible.

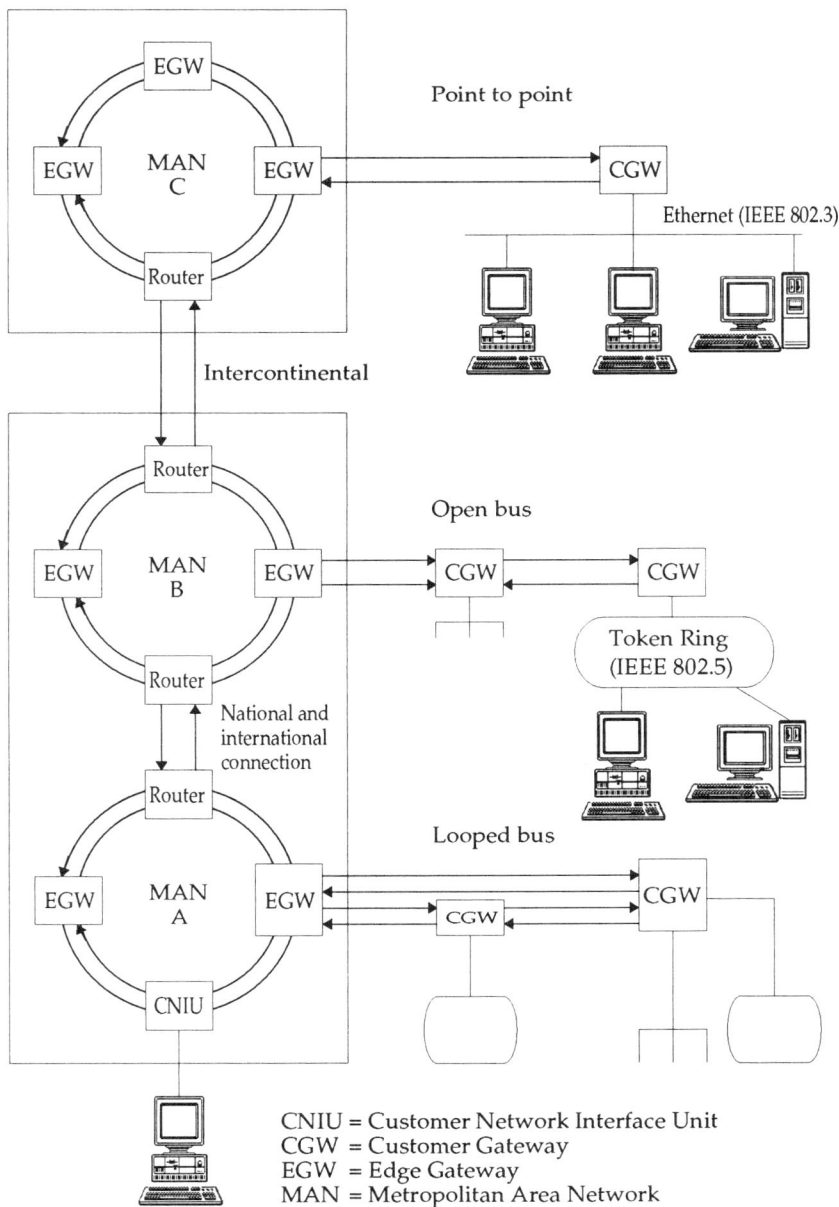

Figure 4.30   DQDB connection and networking facilities (Siemens).

DQDB uses two bus systems running in different directions and permits simultaneous traffic in both transmission directions (full duplex). The individual network nodes (edge gateway (EGW), customer gateway (CGW)) access this bus system concurrently.

Using a distributed queue protocol, it is possible to achieve a maximal network loading, which is not affected either by the network size or by the transmission speed, and to guarantee a fair service to all subscribers on the network. In case of line interruptions there is an automatic reconfiguration facility.

In Germany, DQDB is currently supplied by the Telekom in Munich and Stuttgart in test mode. In both cities, Ethernet LANs belonging to a number of companies and university institutes are coupled via DQDB. A Token Ring interface is also available. The Leibniz Computer Centre is a participant in the pilot project. Here, the CGWs function as remote bridges. The CGWs and the EGWs are administered by the Telekom; thus the user does not need to monitor and manage the backbone network. An impressive demonstration of the interworking of DQDB subnetworks was given at CeBit '92. There are still no direct connections from DQDB to mainframes; thus, DQDB is primarily a connecting network between local area networks. How far DQDB will penetrate the private area as a backbone network remains to be seen; FDDI will remain the market leader in this area for some time.

DQDB could become an interesting offering from the Telekom for fast connection of local area networks belonging to different institutions, just as Datex P is for lower speed networks, provided the service offered and the costs are right for the market. The Telekom has said nothing about the future costs of DQDB.

Chapter 5

Components for connecting data terminals

- Terminal servers

- Connection of PCs and workstations

- Connection of host systems

A network consisting solely of a medium, repeaters, bridges, routers and gateways makes no sense for data communication: it requires the attachment of data terminals which are able to use it as a transport system. Together with Ethernet, which has evolved as a new type of network over the last 15 years, network interfaces have also evolved which are able to convert the existing predominantly WAN- and company-oriented interfaces of data terminals to Ethernet.

Data terminals are taken to include:

- terminals;
- single-user systems (PCs under DOS, UNIX or OS/2, Macintosh computers);
- multiuser systems (UNIX computers, workstations);
- minicomputers (server computers);
- mainframes (special-purpose computers, host systems, vector processors).

These often have interfaces such as, for example:

- V.24 (RS232);
- coax (SNA 3270);
- twinax (IBM 5250);
- PC bus interfaces (AT, XT, EISA, MC);
- minicomputer bus interfaces (for example, VME bus, Q bus, unibus, TURBOchannel);
- channel interfaces for mainframes.

The following requirements may be associated with the connection of data terminals:

- It should be possible to access every available computer system from every data terminal.
- The access must permit interactive operation of every data terminal and, in the case of PCs and workstations, file transfer in both directions should be possible.
- File transfer between the individual computer systems must be possible.
- A common multiple database organization should be supported (server concept).
- It should be possible to implement client–server applications.

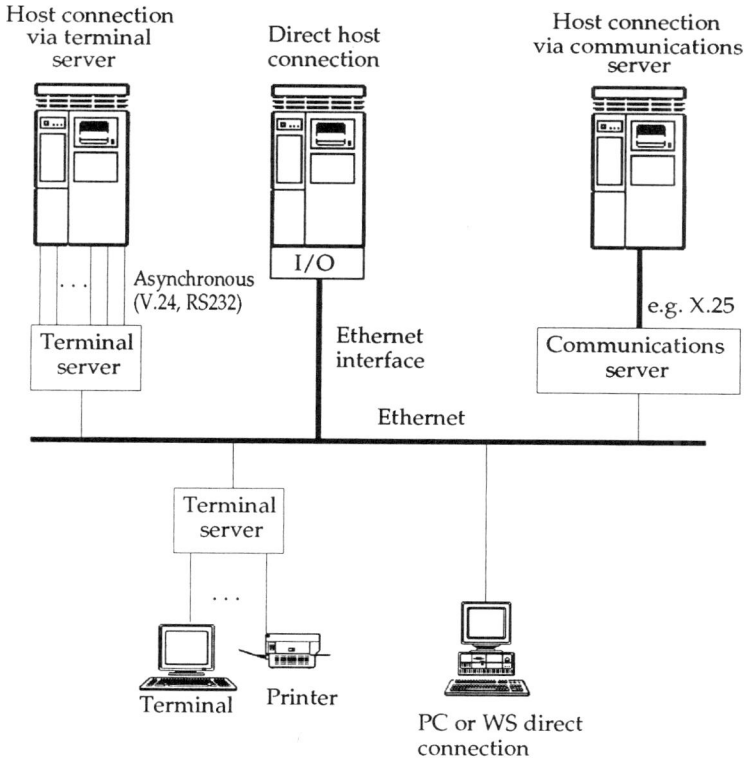

Figure 5.1 Facilities for connecting data terminals to an Ethernet.

In this chapter we shall discuss the following:

- Terminal servers which permit the connection of several terminals (concentrator function) of a given class (for example, ASCII or 3270 terminals) (Section 5.1).

- Slot-in cards for direct connection of data terminals such as PCs and workstations (Section 5.2).

- Bus or channel adapters which permit the direct connection of computer systems to the Ethernet system (Section 5.3).

Network planners will be interested in all components which are not built-in to devices as standard and which therefore have to be procured and selected separately. This chapter will provide some advice.

Early implementations of Ethernet connections used terminal servers on the terminal side and gateways, or even terminal servers, to connect minicomputers and mainframes. This was justified on the following grounds:

- Most existing terminals had no facility for direct connection to Ethernet.

- Direct connection of individual terminals (including PCs) had become too expensive.

- Most minicomputers and mainframes had no connection components for Ethernet; thus, corresponding adapters (gateways or terminal servers) were required.

Because of this architecture some advantages of an Ethernet LAN were either not used or even eliminated. For example, the Ethernet transmission rate of 10 Mbps was not made available, either on the terminal side or on the side of the computer systems, since with the use of gateways and terminal servers, Ethernet was 'choked' (reduced to speeds in the area of 10 kbps) by using other interfaces.

Neither was it possible to make sensible use of other Ethernet facilities such as the broadcast facility at these interfaces. There was also the fact that gateways are predestined to introduce additional delays. In the end, all this led to a slowing of the spread of Ethernet LANs in the initial period.

However, there was a gradual change in this area. This was encouraged by the following developments:

- PCs and higher-grade workstations were increasingly used. It was technically and economically sensible to connect these directly to Ethernet and such a connection facility was offered as a standard, above all in the workstation area.

- Minicomputer and mainframe manufacturers increasingly offered facilities for direct connection to Ethernet for their systems. Thus, in many cases, it was already no longer necessary to use gateways.

However, the implementation of architectures which do not require any adapter components (gateways, converters), means that a universal protocol family should be used between all systems, thus that protocol mapping need no longer take place. This again may be a limiting factor even today, since a mere Ethernet connection facility (hardware) still says nothing about the support for higher protocols.

5.1 Terminal servers

Terminal servers are usually needed to connect 'dumb' terminals to Ethernet LANs. The devices differ according to the connection facilities of the terminals available on the market, which have different interfaces.

5.1.1 Terminal servers for asynchronous devices

Terminal servers for asynchronous connection of terminal devices are components which are frequently used in the Ethernet area. Here, the term terminal server is too restrictive, since these components may in principle be used for all devices which have an asynchronous V.24 (or RS232) port. Earlier, systems using only terminal servers, even to connect computer systems over their asynchronous V.24 ports, were built as Ethernet switching systems. The underlying philosophy of so-called PBX (private branch exchange) systems was adopted. These also provide a switching system at the level of asynchronous V.24 ports. The main difference from PBX systems is that there is no central switching node; instead, the switching is implemented in a distributed fashion by all the terminal servers. These may again be linked via Ethernet LANs.

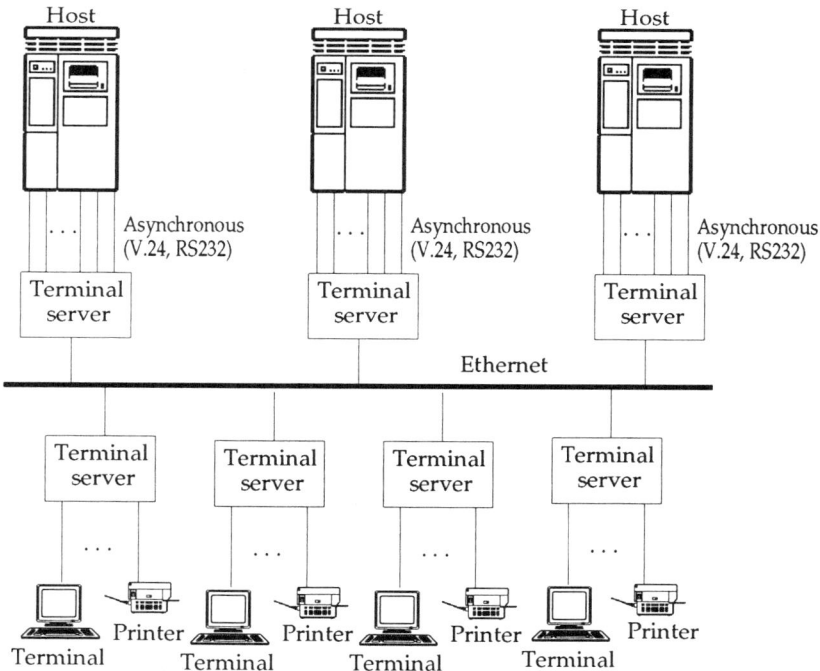

Figure 5.2 V.24 switching system based on terminal servers.

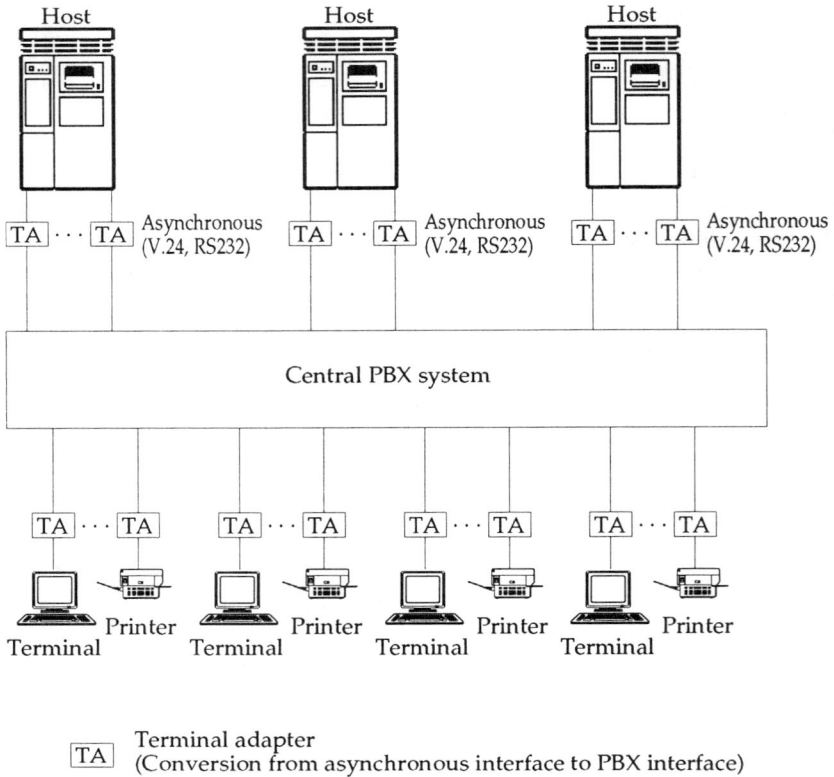

TA — Terminal adapter
(Conversion from asynchronous interface to PBX interface)

Figure 5.3 V.24 switching system based on a PBX system.

The advantages of V.24 switching systems based on Ethernet over PBX systems are:

- A PBX system requires a star-shaped cabling from a central point outwards. This has associated costs, depending on the location. These costs may be reduced by laying an Ethernet LAN, since a very large number of links may be operated over a single coax cable using the multiplex procedure.

- The Ethernet switching system may be extended in very small steps using more and more terminal servers. There may be problems with a central PBX system in this respect.

- The Ethernet system may also be used for other applications, and in particular at higher transmission speeds, while the PBX system is limited by the V.24 terminal switching (transmission rate 64 kbps).

It was precisely the fact that Ethernet could be extended without the need for new cabling which led many users to begin with a pure V.24 switching system based on Ethernet. This completely justifies the existence of such systems, even though as far as their functionality is concerned they may have little new to offer in comparison with PBX systems. In what follows, we shall discuss the most important properties of terminal servers and give a number of criteria for choosing them.

Mode of operation of a V.24 Ethernet switching system

Typical terminal servers now on the market have between 4 and 64 asynchronous ports to which terminals may be connected, provided they have a serial asynchronous V.24 interface. Such a terminal server then operates as follows:

- At a terminal a user is able to initiate connection establishment by entering the address or the symbolic name of any other port of the switching network (port of a terminal server or a computer). If certain conditions are satisfied (port is free, user has the authorization to access it, etc.) a new virtual connection over the LAN to the partner port is created.

- This link is maintained (including secure data transfer, etc.) by protocols which must be transacted by both partners involved. Depending on the choice of these protocols (for example, CDCNet, TCP/IP, DECnet) terminal servers from different manufacturers or only the product from a single manufacturer may be chosen.

- Once the (virtual) connection is established all characters which the user enters at his terminal are transmitted to the partner port over this connection and output there. The same mechanism is used in the other direction.

- The above mechanism would have disadvantages if each character were to be transmitted individually over the LAN in an Ethernet packet of length at least 64 bytes. Thus, the terminal server offers several strategies (data forwarding) whereby several characters may be collected together in a terminal server and only packed into a packet and transported over the network when a certain event occurs (for example, after a certain time elapses or when a carriage return comes from the terminal).

- In addition to pure data transport, terminal servers carry out certain adaptations. For example, the two connected ports may operate at different speeds (speed adjustment) or use different flow control mechanisms.

Application area

Systems which operate in this way may be used to implement the following applications:

- Terminals may call different computer systems.
- Terminal-to-terminal communication is in principle possible.
- Since in most cases not all installed terminals are simultaneously active in a computer system, a system may make fewer (logical) input ports available than would be the case for direct connection (concentrator function).
- For connection establishment, users do not have to use physical addresses, since the individual (logical) ports may be assigned mnemonic symbolic names. Usually, groups of ports (for example, logical ports of a computer or a terminal server, ports of a computer, etc.) may be assigned a single symbolic name (group name).

Selection criteria

When choosing an appropriate V.24 switching system based on Ethernet, the following questions arise:

- Questions relating to the asynchronous ports:
  — What connection speed is supported by the individual ports? Until recently, 9.6 kbps was the maximum available terminal speed. This is no longer the case. There are already terminals (and also terminal servers) which offer speeds of 38.4 kbps and above. However, in the low-speed area current requirements are not covered by all terminal servers (for example, support for 1200/75 bps, as used by videotex terminals).
  — Can the terminal server echo characters?
  — Which parity settings are supported?
  — How many data bits are used per character? This may be of particular importance as far as the connection of older devices is concerned.
  — For which PTT services is there an authorization? This is important as far as the linking of remote terminals is concerned and relates principally to telephone network services such as the support for dial modems.
  — Which V.24 interface signals are supported? This question is important as far as dial-up ports and printer attachment are concerned.

- How many simultaneous connections may be established over each terminal port?

- Is it possible to mix DTE and DCE connections, for example, in order to use the so-called path through facility to reach the V.24 port of a brouter (see also Figure 4.17)?

- Questions on the terminal server architecture:

  - How many ports are available on a terminal server?

  - Which processors are used? How much buffer storage is available? Is the construction modular, in the sense that it can be extended by adding more boards?

  - What is the cost per port of each extension to the terminal server?

- Questions on the protocol layers:

  - Which protocols are used above the Ethernet access protocols? Currently, the following solutions are the most common: TCP/IP protocol family, DEC's LAT protocol, ISO transport and session protocols.

  - When two terminal servers from different manufacturers use the same protocol family, is it certain that interworking is actually guaranteed? This is associated with the fact that additional protocols are needed (for example, to implement the name service or the network management), which are usually company-specific. Currently, the probability that protocols are actually compatible is greatest for the TCP/IP protocol family and for LAT.

- Questions on the performance:

  - What is the overall/net throughput of a terminal server?

  - What is the throughput per port?

  - What is the delay time due to the terminal server?

These questions may serve only as initial reference points. Other questions arise in connection with the operation of these components (for example, configuration, loading of software) in the network, in other words, the network management. These aspects are discussed in Chapter 8.

5.1.2 Terminal servers for 3270 terminals

In addition to asynchronous ASCII terminals, another important class of terminals is that of IBM 3270 terminals and compatible devices. Terminals of this type are attached via a special coaxial cable to a so-called cluster controller. A typical cluster controller may be used to connect up to 32 such terminals. The cluster controller itself is then attached locally directly to an IBM host (or compatible) (with data rates between 1.5 and 2.3 Mbps) or, if it is in a remote location, to a front-end processor (usually of type 37×5) via a normal 4-wire line (with speeds from 9.6 to 56 kbps).

A 3270 terminal server together with an Ethernet LAN offers the following advantages:

- The assignment of a 3270 terminal to a cluster controller (thus to a host) need no longer be fixed; the terminal user may now call the desired host at the network level.

- The relatively expensive cabling between cluster controllers and terminals via coaxial cable (one cable per terminal) may be replaced by the establishment of an Ethernet connection over which multi-terminal connection is supported by the multiplex procedure.

- Ethernet may be used to bridge larger distances with greater speeds, particularly when fibre optic circuits and bridges are used. This may be important in cases where, otherwise, a cluster controller would have to be connected to a front-end processor via a 4-wire circuit.

Of course, when a 3270 switching system based on Ethernet is used certain boundary conditions must be observed. These are largely due to the fact that a 3270 terminal is relatively tightly coupled to a cluster controller, in other words:

- The transmission rate between the cluster controller and the terminal is 2.358 Mbps.

- Each character entered by a terminal user is first transmitted to the cluster controller and then from there back to the terminal (echo mode).

- Most applications in which 3270 terminals are used are screen oriented, in other words, most or all of the screen is rewritten with every transaction. This generates a relatively large volume of data.

In order that a 3270 switching system in the form of terminal servers in the Ethernet LAN can meet these requirements, it must permit a high throughput in the output direction (from the cluster controller to the terminal) and must only exhibit a small delay in the input direction, so that echo characters produced by the cluster controller may be written to the screen without noticeable delay.

The screen size (number of characters per screen) varies according to the model of the 3270 terminal and ranges between 2000 and 3644 characters. In some models, these are supplemented by the so-called extended attribute bytes (EABs) which specify the attributes of each character appearing on the screen in more detail. These EABs must also

Host

Host connection
via terminal
server

3274
controller

. . .

NIU 74
Terminal server

Ethernet

NIU 78
Terminal server

NIU 78
Terminal server

. . .

. . .

Printer

Printer

Terminal

Terminal

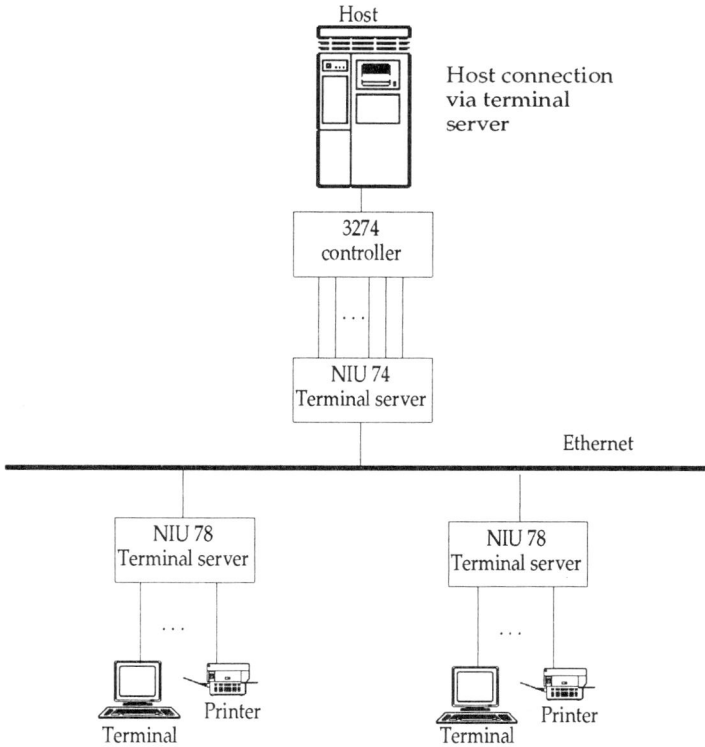

Figure 5.4   Terminal server for 3270 terminals.

be transmitted to the terminal; thus, a full screen write may correspond to transmission of around 7300 characters. When choosing a 3270 switching system based on Ethernet, it is important to carefully check whether IBM or compatible cluster controllers are supported and which class of 3270 terminals is supported. Figure 5.4 shows an example of a 3270 switching system based on Ethernet from Ungermann Bass. At this stage, we must point out that a number of other problems may arise in connection with such 3270 switching systems. Examples include the handling of hard-copy printers which must have a fixed assignment to a controller, or application systems which require a fixed terminal cabling and do not permit switching functions, etc. Thus, the use of a 3270 switching system should be carefully planned.

5.1.3 Combined terminal servers

The solutions described above provide for the construction of a self-contained switching system based on Ethernet either for asynchronous ASCII terminals or for 3270 terminals. However, for many environments, such switching systems represent too great a restriction. This is, in particular, the case when both ASCII and 3270 terminals are present, together with host systems to which both ASCII and 3270 terminals are to be connected. In such environments access from a single terminal (whether ASCII or 3270) to each host present may be desirable.

This leads to the problem of mapping different terminals with their different characteristics on to one another. Within the class of ASCII terminals, the VT100 and the VT220 (both originally terminals from DEC) are generally used as reference terminals. The hope now is that a VT100 or a VT220 should be connectable to an IBM host (or compatible) like a 3270 terminal, and that a 3270 terminal, for example, on a DEC computer should behave like a VT100 or a VT220.

Various products from Bridge Communication (see Figure 5.5) pave

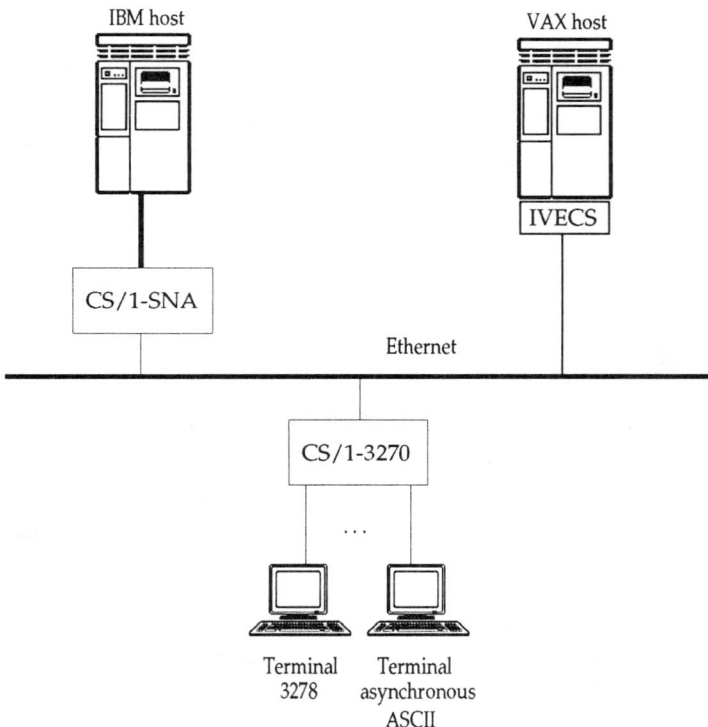

Figure 5.5 Combined ASCII/3270 terminal server.

the way in this direction. The CS/1-3270 terminal server permits (mixed) connection of 3270 and asynchronous terminals. Terminals of both classes may use all facilities of the Ethernet switching system, while 3270 terminals are also able to establish a connection to asynchronous ports and thus emulate a VT100. Thus, 3270 terminals may also work with hosts which only make ports available for asynchronous terminals (for example, a VAX with an IVECS controller card on the unibus and corresponding software).

The counterpart to the above service is also available. The CS/1-SNA server behaves like an IBM 3274–51 cluster controller and may be attached to a front-end processor of type 37×5. In addition, it contains adaptation software which means that it can be called from asynchronous VT100 terminals which then behave like terminals of the 3270 class on the IBM host. Together, both of these components provide a facility for constructing a hybrid 3270/ASCII switching system based on Ethernet.

5.1.4 Products

Despite a reduction in the installation of dumb terminals, terminal servers are still supplied by many manufacturers. The most commonly used protocols on the Ethernet side are TCP/IP and LAT (DECnet). Since these protocols are standardized or published, and because all the protocols needed to operate terminals are present (for example, name server protocols), it is no longer necessary to adopt a closed terminal-server system which uses proprietary protocols from a single company. Mixed terminal servers may be used within a network. Moreover, on the computer side, computers supporting TCP/IP and LAT do not require terminal servers. The products currently available have the following properties:

- On the Ethernet side, TCP/IP and/or LAT are supported. Thus, an alternative choice of the protocols used is often possible.

- Several connections (up to 10) using different protocols (TCP/IP or LAT) may be simultaneously established per port.

- On the terminal side, mainly asynchronous ports, with RJ 45 jacks (space saving) or sub D jacks, are provided.

- The asynchronous interface has access to full modem control facilities and may achieve transmission speeds up to 57.6 kbps; thus it permits the attachment of high-speed dial modems (V.32bis/V.42bis interface).

- Using ROM replacement the devices can also work with other protocols (for example, ISO), or are designed for this.

- The devices are loaded via TCP/IP or DECnet computers, or have a self-load facility.

- There is a parallel interface for operating a printer.

- In addition to the AUI interface for standard Ethernet there is also the BNC interface for Cheapernet.
- The network management may be executed locally or remotely.
- An SNMP agent is built in.
- Interface cards with the terminal server functionality may be built in to a multimedia access centre (see Section 3.6).

The following list (incomplete and uncritical) includes the names of suppliers of terminal servers, although the above properties are not implemented in all products:

- 3Com (Bridge Corp. components)
- CDC (CDCNet components)
- Datability (VCP series)
- Dataco (ScaNet components)
- Digital Equipment (DECserver components)
- EMULEX (Pxx00 series)
- IBM (3174 product)
- Lantronix (EPS and ETS series)
- MICOM/Interlan (NTS series)
- Spider Systems (SpiderPort M250 series)
- Ungermann Bass (Access/One products)

Some of the above suppliers only supply pure TCP/IP and LAT terminal servers, while others supply comprehensive switching systems based on Ethernet. The ScaNet product of the Danish company Dataco is an example of such a comprehensive switching system, which we shall describe. It aims to enable as many different terminal types as possible to communicate with as many computers as possible. In addition to the corresponding terminal servers, powerful terminal emulations are also required. The terminal servers offer facilities for connecting IBM 3270 and 5250 display screens and asynchronous terminals of type DEC VTxxx, SNI, Wyse, etc. On the computer side, gateways provide for the linking to IBM and BS2000 systems and, with protocol conversion to TCP/IP or LAT, to UNIX and DEC systems. Access to public networks is available via the X.21 and X.25 interfaces (see Figure 5.6).

It is worth noting that common protocols, namely ISO protocols, are used between all ScaNet terminal servers and gateways. It is possible to reach the desired computer from all terminals and a terminal mapping is used so that a simultaneous connection to up to four computers may be maintained. Direct connection of PCs via a separate controller card with

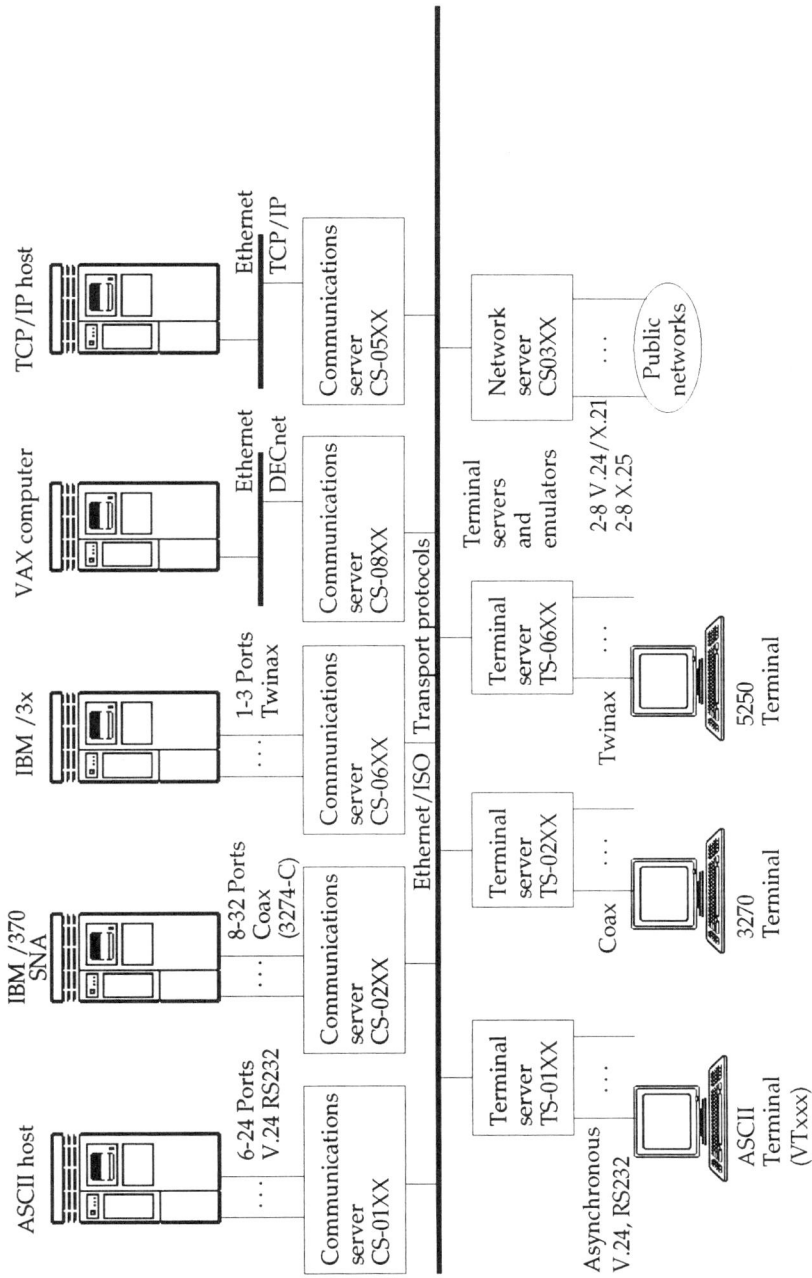

Figure 5.6 Switching facilities with ScaNet.

integration into the ScaNet is possible, as is the linking in of PC networks. Terminal servers and gateways contain a proprietary RISC processor with a performance capability of 33 MIPS. All ScaNet components may be provided with an encryption chip (DESA chip), so that all data on the Ethernet may be securely encrypted.

5.2 Connection of PCs and workstations

5.2.1 PC connection

Increasingly, PCs are being installed instead of dumb terminals in many areas. The following possibilities are available for connecting PCs to an Ethernet-based LAN:

- A standard serial asynchronous PC interface may be used to connect a PC to a terminal server like an asynchronous terminal.
- The PC may be fitted with one of the available 3270 cards and attached to a terminal server like a terminal of the 3270 class.
- The PC may be directly attached to the network by a separately purchased Ethernet controller. This naturally requires appropriate software on the PC to enable it to communicate with the other computers on the network (for example, servers).

In this section, we consider the last possibility in more detail. In principle, all available PC interfaces could be used for connection to an Ethernet controller. However, since the interface must also provide a certain transmission speed, besides the classical PC bus interface, in practice only the parallel interface is used when a bus connection is not available.

Very often, Ethernet controllers based on the parallel interface are used by PCs which, because of the requirements for small size and low weight, do not have a free bus slot. This is primarily the case for portable devices such as hand-held and laptop PCs. Their area of application is related more to mobile use than to permanent integration into local area networks. Remote-area communication (access to local area networks via WAN connections) will play a greater role here than occasional connection to a LAN via these controllers. We shall not discuss these controllers further in what follows; we shall only consider Ethernet controller cards with bus interfaces. As far as bus interfaces are concerned, there are three current bus standards for PCs: the ISA bus (which provides for 8-bit (XT) and 16-bit (AT) slide-in modules), microchannel (MCA) and the EISA bus.

Ethernet slot-in cards (controllers) were originally designed for building PC networks. However, the price of these components has subsequently fallen. Thus, direct connection has become an economically sensible possibility.

Unlike when terminal servers are used, all of the software (switching, name service, transmission protocols) must run on the PC or the Ethernet controller. There exist Ethernet controllers for PCs with or without their own CPUs. Controllers without CPUs usually process layers 1 and 2 of the ISO reference model using dedicated hardware and a LAN chip. Slot-in cards with CPUs also process layers 3 and 4 (thus the whole transport system), while some even process higher levels (for example, cards for manufacturing in the MAP area). Controllers with CPUs may remove the load from the PC; on the other hand, a controller without a CPU with a powerful PC CPU (for example, 80386 at 40 MHz) may operate considerably faster than a controller with its own less powerful CPU (for example, 80186 at 10 MHz). Several years ago the reverse was often true, since the CPUs of controller cards were more powerful than those of PCs; however, in the meantime, the innovative cycle for PCs has been considerably faster than that for controllers.

Removal of the load on a PC, using a separate CPU on the controller may be appropriate in the following instances:

- when the PC is operated as a multiuser computer (for example, with UNIX);
- when the PC is used as a multitasking computer (for example, with OS/2 or NetWare) as a server in a PC network;
- when the PC has to satisfy real-time requirements (for example, in manufacturing).

For standard applications in the office area (single-user operating system, for example, DOS, interactive operation), an Ethernet card without a CPU is fully adequate.

Another factor which may affect the performance is the access procedure used by the PC and controller to access the shared memory. The shared memory may be either on the controller card or in the PC. Figure 5.7 shows the various access procedures.

In the bus-mastering procedure the shared memory (RAM) is in the PC; both the PC CPU and the CPU or the controller unit (ASIC) of the controller card access the memory via the bus. In order to transmit data the control logic of the controller card takes control of the bus (bus master). During this time, the PC CPU may have to wait for the bus. The controller card takes control of the bus using the PC's DMA controller. This may take a little time (microseconds) and may cause delays, particularly for very short data packets.

In the shared-memory procedure, the shared memory is on the controller card. This is a dual-port RAM (DP RAM), since the PC CPU

Bus mastering

```
  PC          ┌─────┐  ┌─────┐
              │ CPU │  │ RAM │
              └─────┘  └─────┘
                  │      ↑  ↑
  Bus    ●─ ─ ─ ─ ┼ ─ ─ ─│──│─ ─ ●
                  │      │  │
  Controller   ┌──────────┐ │
  card         │ CPU/ASIC │─┘
               └──────────┘
```

Shared memory

```
  PC           ┌─────────────┐
               │ CPU    DMA  │
               └─────────────┘
                   │
  Bus    ●─ ─ ─ ─ ─│─ ─ ─ ─ ─ ─ ●
                   ↓    ↓
  Controller  ┌────────┐┌──────────┐
  card        │ DP RAM ││ CPU/ASIC │
              └────────┘└──────────┘
```

I/O access

```
  PC           ┌─────────────┐
               │ CPU    DMA  │
               └─────────────┘
                   │
  Bus    ●─ ─ ─ ─ ─│─ ─ ─ ─ ─ ─ ●
                   ↓    ↓
  Controller  ┌────────┐┌──────────┐
  card        │ I/O Reg ││ CPU/ASIC │
              └────────┘└──────────┘
```

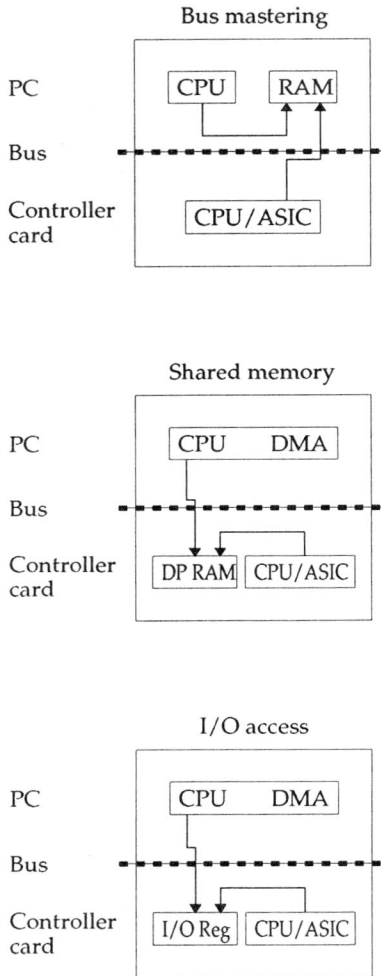

Figure 5.7   Procedures for accessing the shared memory.

accesses it using DMA via the bus and the control logic of the controller card accesses it directly without a bus detour. From the point of view of a PC with the DOS operating system, this memory is an extension of the existing main memory between 640 kbytes and 1 Mbyte. Since this area is often used by other applications (for example, VGA, memory extensions), the usable space is often limited to less than 10 kbytes.

In the I/O access procedure, controller-card registers are addressed as the PC I/O area. The I/O area in a PC is used to address peripherals, which may include a LAN controller card. However, depending on the configuration of the peripheral, the available size of this area is often very limited. Access from the PC is via the DMA controller.

The bus-mastering and the shared-memory procedures are currently the most commonly used methods for accessing the shared memory. Further details are given in Strassacker and Mayer (1992).

The bandwidth of the bus between the controller card and the PC also has a considerable effect on the data transfer rate. Thus, PCs which act as servers should use at least 16-bit, if not even 32-bit (for example, EISA bus), bus cards.

Figure 5.8 shows the schematic structure of an Ethernet controller card with and without a CPU. A built-in on-board transceiver is now taken for granted for all cards. Of course, the card without a CPU also needs some logic in order to be able to process layers 1 and 2 of the Ethernet LAN. This is implemented in the ASIC chip. The card with the CPU usually has a considerably larger memory so that it can process the necessary programs and protocols.

Many manufacturers, such as 3Com (EtherLink series), EXELAN (EXOS series), Schneider and Koch (SK Net series), SMC (previously Western Digital) (Elite 16 series) and DEC (EtherWORKS series) offer whole product families of Ethernet boards. The following criteria may be used when deciding on Ethernet controller cards:

- The on-board processor used (for example, 80X86, 68000), if there is one.

- The amount of RAM available on the controller card.

- 8-bit (XT), 16-bit (AT), microchannel (MC) or EISA bus interface.

- Long or short plugin cards.

- Interfaces for Cheapernet (BNC jacks, on-board transceivers) and/or twisted pair (RJ 45 jacks, on-board transceivers), and/or AUI.

- Free space in which to implement a so-called 'network boot ROM' which allows diskless PCs to be operated over the network.

- Available interfaces and protocols (for example, NetWare, LAN Manager (DOS, OS/2), LAN Server (IBM), DECnet-DOS/PCSA, DEC PATHWORKS, TCP/IP, PC/NFS) (see also Chapter 7).

- Maximum throughput depending on the PC used and test procedures.

- Configurable by hardware switch or via software.

- Availability of similar controller cards from the same manufacturer for workstations.

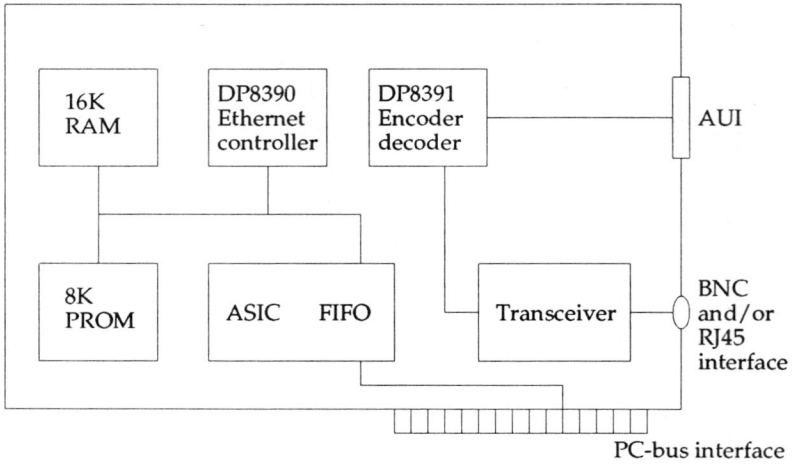

Card without processor (schematic)

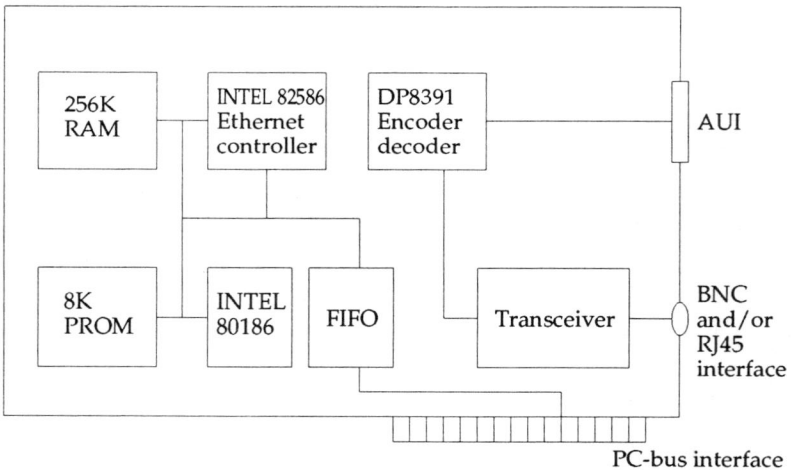

Card with processor (schematic)

Figure 5.8   PC Ethernet controller.

In a heterogeneous system environment, it is particularly important that Ethernet controllers should support several protocol families and that it should be possible to switch to a different protocol without rebooting the PC. Simultaneous handling of several protocol stacks by the controller is also very promising. Thus, for example, when NetWare and TCP/IP protocols are handled simultaneously it is possible to initiate a file transfer from a Novell server (NetWare) to a TCP/IP host from the PC using FTP (TCP/IP protocol family).

Even simple controllers (without CPU) now have a performance capability which is thoroughly adequate for single-user systems. In measurements of the performance capability of controller cards without their own CPUs a file of 1.5 Mbytes was transferred, using FTP on a UNIX workstation, in binary mode from the workstation memory to PC memory. Here, PCs with 80386 CPUs, with a clock rate of 33 MHz, delivered transfer rates of 500 kbps (8-bit XT bus interface) and 750 kbps (16-bit AT bus interface). Translated into the loading of an Ethernet, this gives a value of between 5% and 7.5% for a single file transfer. If several file transfers are executed simultaneously the Ethernet may also reach the stage when a noticeable delay due to overloading is observed. Purely theoretically, for these values, only 20 or 13 (respectively) simultaneous file transfers may be executed at the full speed.

5.2.2 Connection of workstations

Components for connecting workstations are increasingly rarely available as separate products on the market, since workstations and, in particular, those with the UNIX operating system, are fitted with Ethernet interfaces as a standard. These Ethernet interfaces do not usually involve the workstation bus interface; instead, the interface is built into the main board and so may be taken into account when the card is designed. Thus, the restrictions due to the additional bus interface do not apply and higher transmission rates may be achieved. Higher transmission rates may also be attributed to the increased processor performance that workstations offer compared to PCs. Rates of 7.5 Mbps may be obtained in normal operation using FTP (file transfer between two workstation disk drives).

However, if additional Ethernet controller cards are needed for workstations, the same procedure as that described for the PC area is usually used. The connection between the Ethernet controller card and the workstation is established over the corresponding workstation bus system (S bus, VME bus, multibus, Q bus, unibus). The problems and criteria here are similar to those for PC Ethernet controllers. Suppliers of such controller cards include, for example, EXELAN and DEC.

5.3 Connection of host systems

We have already mentioned the problem of host connection in the discussion of the structure of switching systems for ASCII and 3270 terminals. The problem is that until recently, only a few manufacturers, particularly in the mainframe area, supported the direct connection of Ethernet. This meant that, as with terminal connection, special intermediate components had to be inserted to adapt the protocols used in the Ethernet network to the host environment. This shortcoming has now been rectified and almost all new computers which appear on the market are fitted with an Ethernet interface as standard or have a facility for adding on such an interface without great expense using bus and channel interfaces. However, special components are still required for existing computer architectures or special applications.

5.3.1 Channel adapters

Digital Equipment, which together with Xerox and Intel founded the Ethernet movement, was among the first manufacturers to produce a channel adapter. This provided for the direct connection of Digital's VAX systems to Ethernet, using DECnet or TCP/IP protocols for the higher protocol levels. The adaptation to Ethernet involved the use of unibus, Q bus, VAXBI bus or VAX2000 bus slot-in cards.

As a mainframe manufacturer, Control Data (CDC) supplies CDCNet for its Cyber series of computers; this also uses Ethernet-based OSI protocols (up to level 4), although applications which are not standardized by OSI (for example, terminal connection) use proprietary (CDC) protocols. The Cyber host is connected to the Ethernet using a special channel adapter (device interface, DI) on which some of the higher protocols are executed.

On the Cray Y-MP vector processor, the existing VME bus is used to connect a version of the SUN (FEI3) modified by Cray to the Y-MP. The modified SUN then permits access to the Ethernet LAN and transacts some of the TCP/IP protocols.

In addition to these developments, in which company-specific solutions are used to permit access to the Ethernet, access to Ethernet is now available to almost all mainframes via the TCP/IP protocol family (see Section 6.3). Most of these products are manufacturer-specific; however, systems from third-parties, which were forerunners in the early days of Ethernet, are also available.

One example of this is the product from the company Spartacus, which is designed for systems with an IBM architecture. Spartacus markets its own channel adapter for the IBM block multiplex channel on one side and an Ethernet on the other, under the name of K200 Ethernet Control Unit. The K200 executes the Ethernet access protocol and provides the software in the IBM host with an interface for access to Ethernet. The throughput of the adapter is at most 2.5 Mbps. The K200 functions as a

IBM PC
or   RISC/6000
IBM PS/2

IBM 9379
or
IBM AS/400

IBM host
with
IBM 3172

```
┌─────────────┐  ┌─────────────┐  ┌─────────────┐  ┌─────────────┐
│             │  │             │  │             │  │     ╭──AIX──╮│
│             │  │             │  │             │  │ TCP/│ with  ││
│             │  │             │  │   ╭──AIX──╮ │  │ IP  │ TCP/  ││
│ TCP/╭──AIX──╮│  │   ╭──AIX──╮ │  │ TCP/│with │ │  │     │ IP    ││
│ IP  │ with  ││  │   │ with  │ │  │ IP  │TCP/ │ │  │             │
│     │ TCP/  ││  │   │ TCP/  │ │  │     │IP   │ │  │ VM/SP       │
│ PC  │ IP    ││  │   │ IP    │ │  │             │  │ or MVS      │
│ DOS │       ││  │   │       │ │  │ VM/SP       │  ├─────────────┤
├─────┴───────┤  ├───┴───────┴─┤  ├─────────────┤  │ IBM 3172 LAN│
│             │  │             │  │             │  │ Control prog.│
│ LAN adapter │  │ LAN adapter │  │ LAN adapter │  │ LAN adapter │
└──────┬──────┘  └──────┬──────┘  └──────┬──────┘  └──────┬──────┘
       │                │                │                │
───────┴────────────────┴────────────────┴────────────────┴─────────
```

Token Ring or Ethernet

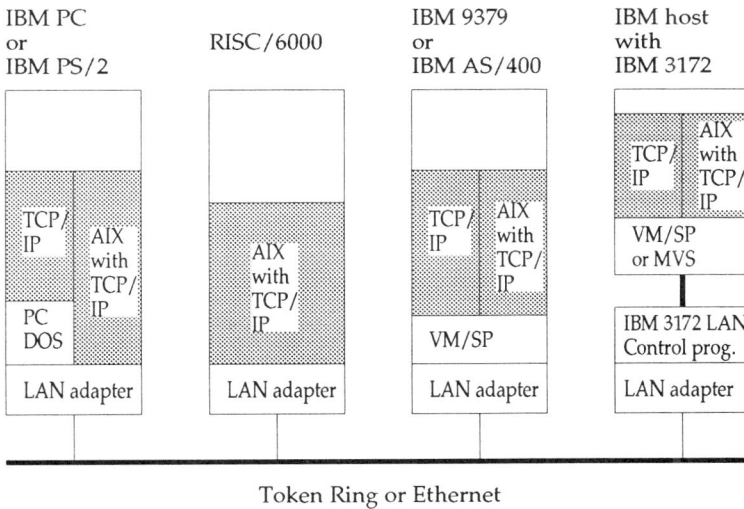

Figure 5.9   TCP/IP in the IBM environment.

standard I/O controller for the System/370 and implements the standard channel architecture. The K200 looks like an independent unit to the IBM host and may be used on the same channel as diskette or tape drives or other devices. In addition, the company provides software for the TCP/IP protocol family which runs under VM.

In the meantime, IBM now offers its own solution for access to Ethernet for its various computer families. Here, TCP/IP is used to provide for as full a range of facilities for communication between heterogeneous systems as possible. Figure 5.9 shows these TCP/IP-based facilities.

The UNIX derivative AIX already contains TCP/IP as a standard. TCP/IP support is available for the VM/SP, MVS and OS/400 operating systems. In the IBM world, the linkage of the classical IBM hosts to Ethernet is via the 3172 controller which may be connected to the block multiplex channel or to the ESCON (fibre optic) channel. Up to four LANs may be connected at the same time, including Token Ring at up to 16 Mbps and FDDI.

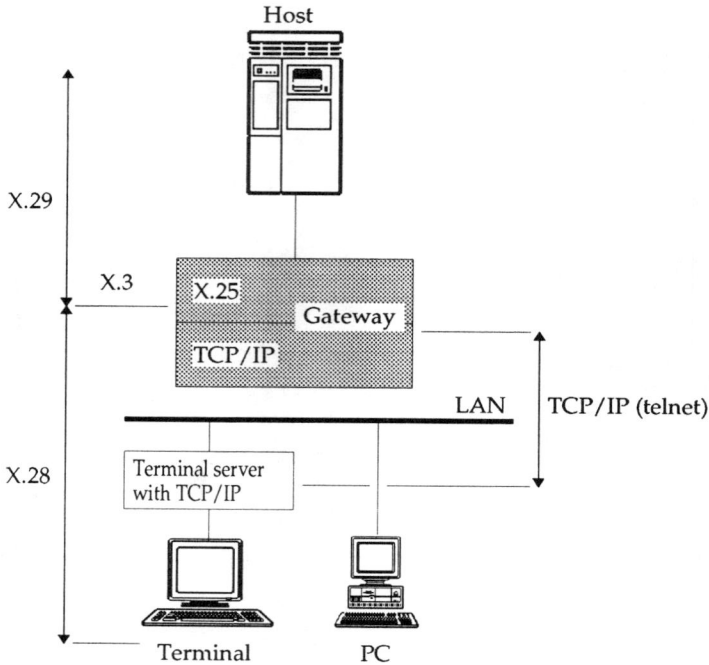

Figure 5.10 X.25 as a basis for connecting computers.

In the meantime, an Ethernet adapter for the 3745 communication-controller series has been announced for the second half of 1992. As a result, the following may be achieved using TCP/IP:

- Implementation of FTP permits file transfer between any systems on which the TCP/IP family is implemented. Additional tools provide assistance for conversion between incompatible file formats (for example, VM files).

- SMTP (simple mail transfer protocol) provides for the exchange of messages and text files between different systems. In the VM/SP implementation of TCP/IP, the PROFS product may also be used for this.

- 3270 terminals attached to the IBM system may establish an interactive connection to other systems.

- ASCII terminals on appropriate terminal servers with TCP/IP support can establish an interactive connection to the corresponding IBM host and behave as 3270 terminals for that host. This is supported by a corresponding 3270 full-screen emulator.

5.3.2 Connection using X.25

Another method for linking Ethernet LANs to mainframes, which is used frequently because of its manufacturer-independent nature, involves the use of an X.25 gateway. X.25, which is standardized by CCITT, was designed as a protocol for connecting computer systems to packet-switched networks; it is very widely used, particularly in Europe. As far as interactive traffic is concerned, it is mainly used with the X.29 protocol. In addition to its widespread use, one advantage of X.25 is that several logical links may be handled over a single computer connection. The transmission rate may be up to 256 kbps.

In the context of local area networks, X.25 is usually used in a form in which the X.25 gateway is configured as an X.3 PAD, so that asynchronous terminals can dial into a host using terminal servers and this PAD (see also Subsection 4.5.3.1). Another protocol, such as TCP/IP, may be used between the X.25 host gateway, the PC and the terminal server. This facility is of course also available for PCs, which are attached directly to the Ethernet. Protocol compatibility with the X.25 gateway is a prerequisite.

We shall not consider other possibilities for connecting existing mainframes to Ethernet (for example, SNA gateway) since, with the ongoing trend towards open systems, direct Ethernet support will increasingly be provided as a standard.

Chapter 6

Higher protocols for Ethernet LANs

- Introduction to the tasks of higher protocols

- CCITT/OSI protocols

- TCP/IP protocol family

- Xerox XNS protocol family

By higher protocols, we mean the protocols of the application system, thus those of OSI layers 5 to 7. They lie above the so-called transport system, in other words, above the functionality of layers 1 to 4 which provides for the secure end-to-end transport of data over the network. This chapter describes the protocols used above the network layer (that is, above the internet protocols). These include transport protocols and higher protocols.

The general tasks of the higher protocols are described in Section 6.1; higher protocols may be said to provide the environment for the development of general communications and network services and also application systems. Later in the chapter, we describe three families of protocols which are important in the Ethernet-LAN context: OSI protocols (Section 6.2), the protocols of the TCP/IP protocol hierarchy (Section 6.3) and Xerox's XNS protocol family (Section 6.4).

6.1 Introduction to the tasks of higher protocols

In a move towards the simplification and unification of the communication of different autonomous systems, ISO (International Organization for Standardization) first began work on a model of the higher protocols at the end of the 1970s.

This resulted in the so-called OSI model (open systems interconnection). This is a reference and architecture model which serves as the basis for further standardization in the communications-protocols area. The value of the model itself lies in the creation of common concepts and terminology and the creation of a mandatory layering and structuring for communication processes between two end systems.

It is assumed that every communication process decomposes into separate subtasks and thus may be transacted in several layers. The individual layers consist of specific entities which belong to the same layer and intercommunicate via protocols. Each layer provides as a whole certain layer-specific services for the layer above, and makes these services available via specific service interfaces. The OSI layer model has 7 layers. We have already described all the sublayers of the lowest three layers (physical, data link, network) in detail. These, together with layer 4, form the so-called transport system of a network. Typical protocol profiles for LAN transport systems were described in Section 4.5.1.

The definition and implementation of suitable protocols for the individual layers requires very similar protocol techniques in each layer. The OSI reference model explicitly names the following:

- Establishment/release of (virtual) connections.

- Multiplexing. In other words, the combining of several virtual connections onto a single connection in the underlying layer.

- Splitting. Here, a virtual connection runs over several connections in the underlying layer.

- Segmentation. In other words, the subdivision of a single protocol data unit into several such units in the underlying layer.

- Blocking. In other words, the creation of a single protocol data unit from several such units in the layer above.

- Detection, correction and reporting of transmission errors.

- Positive acknowledgement of receipt of a complete protocol data unit or negative acknowledgements for non-receipt (for example, after a time interval is exceeded) or incomplete receipt.

- Resetting of virtual connections.

- Control of the source transmission speed by the receiver (flow control).

- Support for expedited data transfer (telegrams).

- Transmission sequencing.

- Addressing of a partner and determination of the route to a partner.

We have already met some of these protocol techniques in the discussion on the LAN-specific layers. Typical protocol parameters which may play an important role, particularly as far as tuning is concerned, include:

- the packet length chosen;
- the acknowledgement procedure used;
- the flow-control method used;
- the timeout values set.

Above the transport system is the so-called application system of a communication network, which consists of OSI layers 5 to 7. These layers involve application-oriented support functions rather than data transport functions; the tasks of these layers are correspondingly different.

Session layer (layer 5)

Layer 5 supports the establishment, structuring and control of sessions. Sessions, which are the logical links of layer 5 entities, are temporary cooperative relationships established for application processes. The session layer provides services for context management (selection of high level protocols, context switching, etc.), interaction management (control and structuring of the session in sections, allocation of authorization for certain actions during a session) and synchronization (definition of checkpoints, in other words, restart and reset functions).

Presentation layer (layer 6)

This provides services which enable the applications to interpret the meaning of the data exchanged; in particular, these are descriptive services which provide for a universal presentation and interpretation of information. These services may be used to convert system-specific encodings of data structures and data presentations (displays) in a heterogeneous environment into a data transfer syntax which is understandable to different partners.

The application of file transfer between two different end systems is a good example of the complexity of the problem in the case of communication of independent autonomous subsystems. The following must be taken into account:

- Different character sets (for example, ASCII, EBCDIC, teletex, videotex).
- Different data formats and interpretations (for example, for representing numbers).
- Different file structures (file records, separators, multifile files).
- Different access mechanisms (sequential, index sequential, random access).
- Different name conventions and access paths within a database.
- Different access rights.

Of course, only some of these tasks are executed in layer 6. Much of this work falls to the application layer protocols.

Application layer (layer 7)

This layer contains the applications in the narrow sense; in other words, the processes which determine the actual semantic content of the communication. Architecturally, these are not prejudiced by the lower layers. In other words, just as a general purpose operating system supports as great a variety of application software as possible on a computer system, so the communication layers 1 to 6 support distributed applications with as few restrictions as possible. Thus, it is impossible to speak of the layer 7 protocol. Instead, a number of the most commonly used applications have evolved for which there exist standards (standards or *de facto* standards) in the form of protocols or data exchange formats. Examples of such standard applications are given below.

File transfer   The protocols support a simple file transfer (e.g. FTP) or cross-system manipulation of virtual file systems (e.g. FTAM).

Remote batch processing   This involves the transfer of job descriptions to another system (job transfer) and the control of the processing (job manipulation).

Message exchange   These protocols range from simple electronic mail mechanisms (SMTP) to electronic emulation of letter post (X.400), including directory services (X.500).

Document interchange   This provides for the interchange of complicated document structures (ODA/ODIF), commercial data structures (EDI standard) and graphical information (CGM, IGES, PDES).

Terminal connection   For example, Telnet, virtual terminal, X-Windows, X.29.

Distributed databases, distributed processing   For example, CCR, TPS, RPC, DTP.

Network management   For example, SNMP, CMIS/CMIP.

Of course, this list can only be cursory.

At present, as ever, different communications protocols from different protocol families are used for different applications and different environments. The protocol families come from the standardization area (ISO, CCITT, IEEE) or from large user groups (for example, ARPA) or they may be so-called *de facto* or industry standards of large or common manufacturers (for example, IBM, Xerox, Intel, Microsoft). Figure 6.1 shows some of the well-known protocol families.

In what follows, we shall consider three major protocol families which are of particular importance in the context of Ethernet LANs. Here, as previously mentioned, we are dealing with layers 4 to 7, since they are often the basis for network programmer interfaces and applications over LAN structures. Standard protocols are indispensable as far as the interworking of subscriber stations in heterogeneous networks is concerned.

The three protocol families described in the following sections, namely CCITT/OSI protocols, XNS protocols and TCP/IP, are incompatible; in other words, LAN stations which support only one of these protocol worlds cannot communicate with subscribers in the other protocol worlds without appropriate gateways.

PC networks and integrated networks of workstations, as described in Chapter 7, are software systems based on LAN structures, which provide all LAN subscribers with a certain application-related functionality network-wide via a unified user interface.

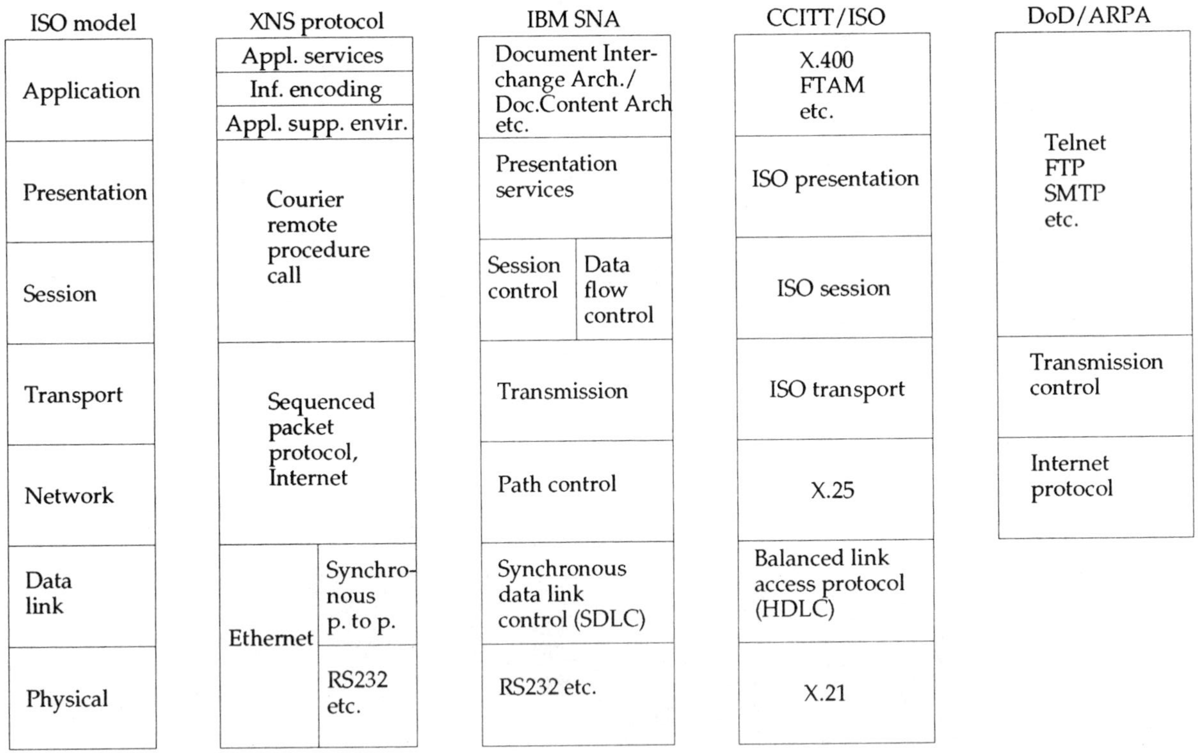

ISO model	XNS protocol	IBM SNA	CCITT/ISO	DoD/ARPA
Application	Appl. services / Inf. encoding / Appl. supp. envir.	Document Interchange Arch./ Doc.Content Arch etc.	X.400 FTAM etc.	Telnet FTP SMTP etc.
Presentation	Courier remote procedure call	Presentation services	ISO presentation	
Session		Session control / Data flow control	ISO session	
Transport	Sequenced packet protocol, Internet	Transmission	ISO transport	Transmission control
Network		Path control	X.25	Internet protocol
Data link	Synchronous p. to p. / Ethernet	Synchronous data link control (SDLC)	Balanced link access protocol (HDLC)	
Physical	RS232 etc.	RS232 etc.	X.21	

Figure 6.1 Illustration of different protocol families.

6.2 CCITT/OSI protocols

6.2.1 Transport-layer protocols

Conceptually, the OSI transport layer only recognizes end systems in the network and not node computers in the transit system, and does not recognize internetting, etc. Layer 4 makes a common transport service available to the application systems (layers 5 to 7), which meets the requirements in terms of cost, throughput and data security (in other words, the quality-of-service requirements).

The transport service uses the following quality-of-service parameters (negotiable or configurable):

- Delay in connection establishment: the maximum time interval between T.Connect.request and the associated T.Connect.confirm.

- Probability of a fault during connection establishment: the number of failed attempts to establish connections which may be attributed to the transport system, divided by the total number of failed attempts to establish connections.

- Throughput: the number of successful transmissions in a given time in the given direction.

- Delay in transit: the maximum time interval between T.Data.request and the associated T.Data.indication, in the given direction.

- Residual error rate.

- Probability of a fault during data transfer.

- Delay in connection release and probability of a fault during connection release.

- Protection of the transport connection.

- Priority of transport connections.

It is the task of the transport layer to choose the network with the corresponding quality-of-service requirements in mind and if necessary to provide any additional quality of service using its own protocol. If this is not possible, connection establishment is rejected.

Thus, the tasks of the transport layer include:

- Connection establishment/release.

- Quality-of-service negotiation.

- Flow control.

- Addressing.

- Data transmission.

• Transmission of priority (expedited) data.

As is the norm in OSI, the transport service is provided via corresponding service primitives (ISO 8072, ISO 8072/1). Figure 6.2 shows the time diagrams for the most important service primitives. A connection-oriented (a) and a connectionless (b) transport service are provided. The service primitives can be specified in more detail using corresponding parameter sets.

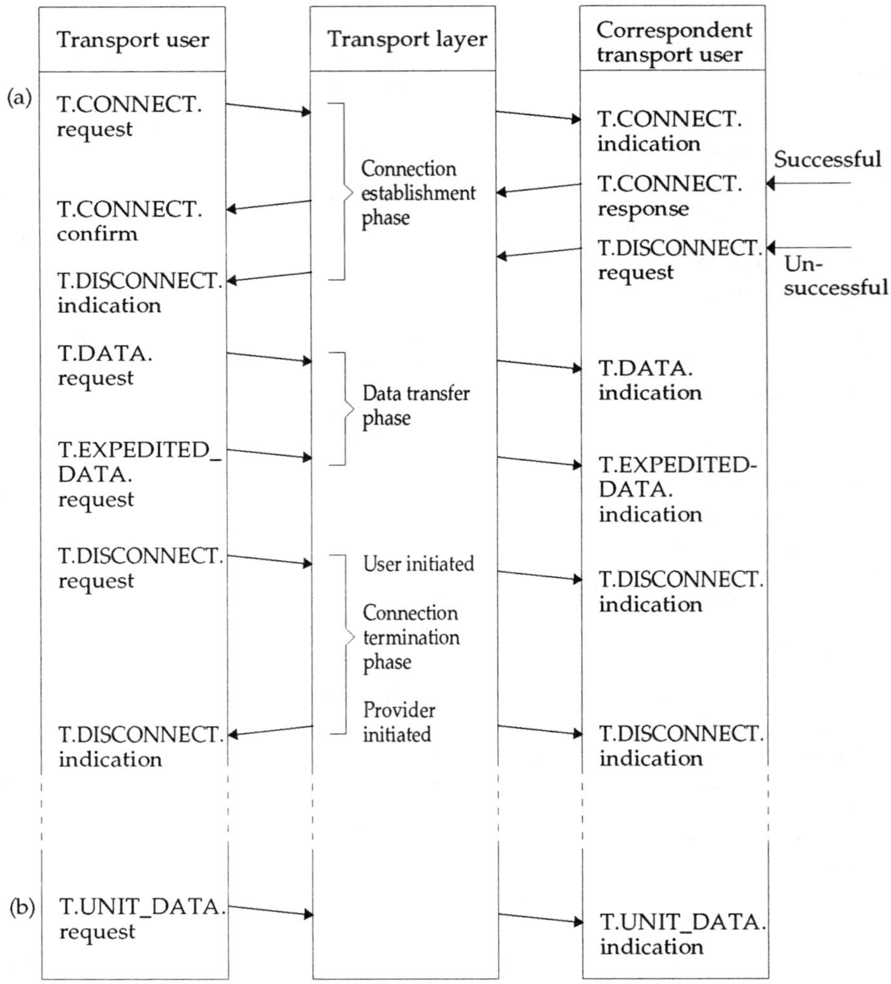

Figure 6.2 Time diagrams for transport services.

In order to provide a common transport service, the transport layer must hide the existence of subnetworks with different network-layer services. The different service types used at layer 4 are implemented as different transport protocol classes, which depend on the layer 3 service.

OSI distinguishes between the following N service types:

N type A   Network connections with a tolerable residual error rate of unnotified errors and an acceptable rate of notified errors. Thus, type A networks are qualitatively high-grade networks with good error-correction intelligence (e.g. X.25 networks).

N type B   Network connections with a tolerable residual error rate but an unacceptable number of notified errors. Type-B networks are networks with a technically high transmission quality with insufficient error correction facilities of their own. Typically, for example, these include local area networks such as Ethernet with LLC type 1.

N type C   Network connections with an unacceptable residual error rate. Here, all the error correction must take place above layer 3. As an example of type-C connections, we cite data communication over international telephone lines.

In order to provide the transport service for the different network types, ISO distinguishes between five different *transport protocol classes* (TP) (ISO 8073):

Class TP0 (simple class)   This is the simplest class and corresponds to CCITT recommendation T.70 which is used in the teletex service. This class was developed for type-A networks.

Class TP1 (basic error recovery class)   This simple error-handling class was developed for type-B networks. It provides mechanisms for minimum quality-of-service controls.

Class TP2 (multiplexing class)   The multiplexing class is based on class 0; however, a flow control mechanism is specified and may be used to multiplex several subscriber connections over a transport connection between end systems. A type-A network is a prerequisite.

Class TP3 (error recovery and multiplexing class)   This class combines the performance features of classes 1 and 2 for type-B networks.

Class TP4 (error detection and recovery class)   This class of protocols provides particularly high error-correction intelligence and is suitable for use with type-C networks.

These details also explain some of the protocol profiles for LAN transport subsystems listed in Section 4.5.1. The transport-protocol classes differ in power; in other words, in the protocol elements (T PDUs) and the protocol mechanisms which they provide. However, a discussion of these differences is beyond the scope of this book. The reader is referred to the relevant literature (e.g. Kerner, 1992; Halsall, 1992).

In what follows, we shall not discuss the OSI protocols of layers 5 and 6 any further. The reader is referred to our comments in Section 6.1 and to the above references.

6.2.2 Application-layer protocols

Even an attempt to provide a detailed description of the application-related layer 7 protocols standardized by CCITT and ISO would be beyond the scope of this book. Sufficient relevant literature already exists (e.g. Beyschlag, 1988; Kerner, 1992; Halsall, 1992).

The underlying model (Figure 6.3) (ISO 9545) is the following.

A distributed application consists of at least two cooperating application processes. Each application process itself has a non-communication-related processing part and a communication part, the so-called application entity, which is of interest here. The latter consists of a user element which executes the application-specific communication part together with standardized application service elements (ASEs) which the user element can use. ASEs contain a specific number of functions to execute certain services. Thus, ASEs represent a 'service construction kit' for the development of distributed applications. The following ASEs have been standardized to date (extract, see Figure 6.3):

- **Association Control Service Element (ACSE)**. This is used to construct associations (cooperative relationships) between application processes and to specify an application context (ISO 8649, 8650).

- **Reliable Transfer Service Element (RTSE)**. This is used to provide for reliable transport of an application protocol data unit within a given time with corresponding notification of errors (ISO 9066).

- **Remote Operations Service Element (ROSE)**. This is used to formulate arbitrary operations on a remote system, where how the operation is to be executed (synchronously, asynchronously) and the response (no response, response only if successful, response only in case of failure, always) can be specified. ROSE represents an extension of the RPC (remote procedure call) mechanism, which is important for the operation of client/server structures (ISO 9072).

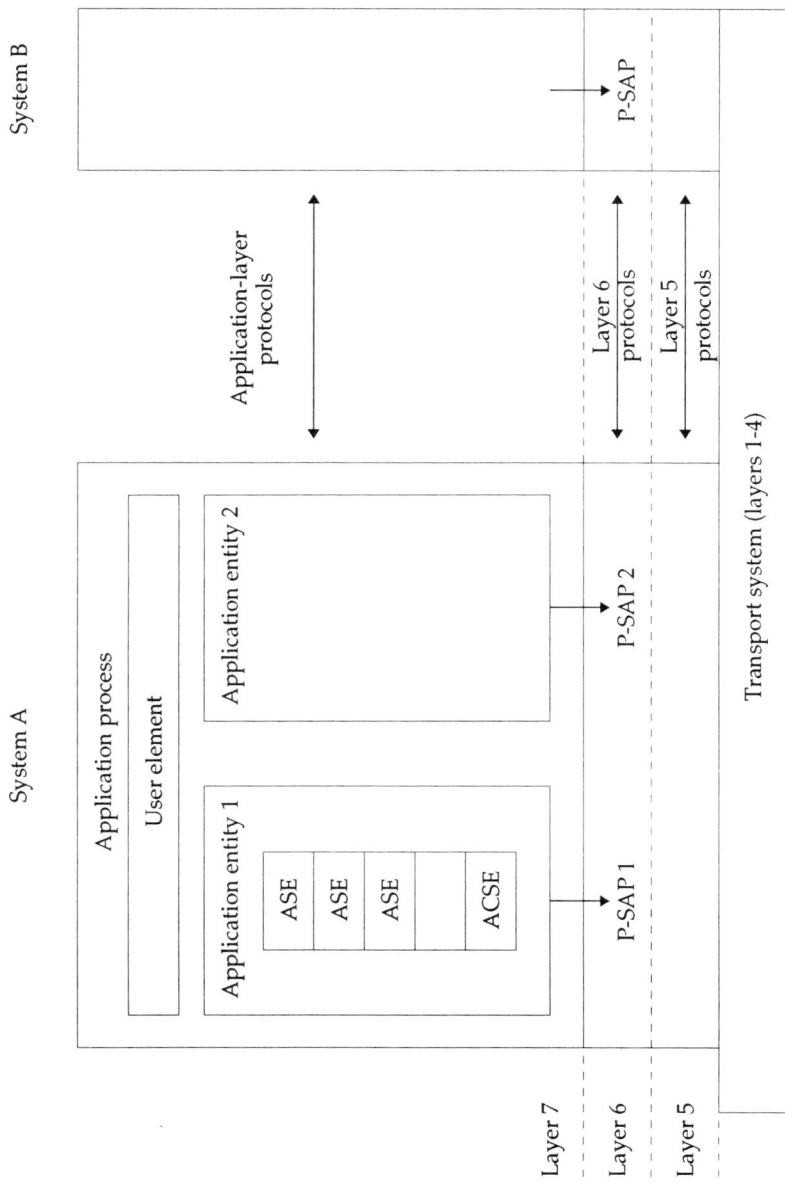

Figure 6.3 Structure of the OSI application system.

System B

System A

Application process

User element

Application entity 1

Application entity 2

ASE
ASE
ASE

ACSE

P-SAP 1

P-SAP 2

P-SAP

Application-layer
protocols

Layer 6
protocols

Layer 5
protocols

Transport system (layers 1-4)

Layer 7

Layer 6

Layer 5

- **Commitment, concurrency, recovery (CCR).** This provides basic services for maintaining data consistency in distributed OSI environments, including sequences of read and update operations in atomic form and use of 2-phase commit protocols. In this context, we mention also TPSE (transaction processing service element) (ISO 9804, 9805).

- **File transfer, access and manipulation (FTAM).** As the name implies, this is more than a pure file-transfer protocol. In fact, it involves the specification of a virtual file system with a tree-like access structure, where the data elements corresponding to the nodes or leaves may themselves be ordered trees. It may be used to define very complicated file structures. The standard provides a wide choice of file and record attributes which may be used to define these structures together with a range of operations. FTAM is available in certain functional profiles from many manufacturers and represents a group of application services which is especially suitable for handling file manipulations in heterogeneous environments (ISO 8571).

- **Message handling system X.400 (MHS).** This wide-reaching CCITT standard defines a model of all the protocols and services for a lavish electronic mail system (ISO 8505). This involves the best-known OSI application software which emulates the full complexity of letter post. Users are represented by user agents (UA) which forward messages to the message transfer system (MTS) via standardized interfaces, for transmission to destination UAs. MTS is a distributed application, which intercommunicating message transfer agents (MTAs) use to deliver messages to the MTA to which the destination UA is known using the store-and-forward principle. The standard specifies a number of application protocols, for example, for communication between two UAs, two MTAs or an MTA and a remote UA. In addition, a number of operations for structuring and manipulating messages are provided for. The 1988 version of X.400 contains mechanisms which make it possible to transmit various document types (for example, DCA, ODA). The X.400 protocol stack is based on ISO transport protocol class 0 (teletex T.70). Closely associated with X.400 is the X.500 directory system, which is a directory and information service designed for networks (ISO 9594).

- **Manufacturing message service (MMS).** This standardizes the exchange of messages in the production area, which are used to control device operations and to monitor and control technical processes (ISO 9506). It is based on an object-oriented abstraction of a device (virtual manufacturing device).

- **ODA/ODIF and EDIFACT.** The specifications of the Office Document Architecture/Office Document Interchange Format

(ISO 8613) and the Electronic Data Interchange for Finance Administration, Commerce and Transport (ISO 9735) define data exchange formats for important application areas.

- **Remote database access (RDA).** This supports access to remote databases from workstations, on a client/server basis.

- **Job transfer and manipulation (JTM).** This supports all the operations needed to execute a batch operation in heterogeneous systems. It is based on a very general concept of jobs (ISO 8831/2).

- **Virtual terminal (VT).** This provides applications with a general device interface, which may be used to describe the presentation of data structures in different device classes in a system-independent way (ISO 9040/1).

The ISO application system protocols are increasing in importance. Their operation has been proved at various multivendor demonstrations. Some of these protocols form a fixed component of the MAP and TOP protocol hierarchies.

6.3 TCP/IP protocol family

6.3.1 Overview

The TCP/IP protocol family already has a very long history: its roots go back to the early 1970s and are closely associated with the beginning of the well-known ARPA network. The ARPA network (ARPAnet) was at that time under construction under the aegis of the (US) Department of Defense (DoD) Advanced Research Projects Agency (ARPA) and was intended as a first computer network for research purposes. Both university computer centres and military installations formed the basis for this network. Part of the ARPA activities gave rise to the TCP/IP protocols as the protocol standard. Even in 1982, 75% of all ARPA computers used these protocols over a wide range of different media. This also soon led to the requirement for many contracts which the US government let to computer manufacturers.

However, a second effect also helped towards the generally acknowledged breakthrough of the TCP/IP protocols, when they became an integral component of the Berkeley UNIX Version 4.2 and conquered the local area network arena. The combination of Ethernet, TCP/IP and UNIX soon became obligatory for many manufacturers of so-called workstations, and remains obligatory to this day. The publishing of all the associated protocols, including the program source code in the form of public domain software, added to the strength of TCP/IP protocols. Thus, it can be said that TCP/IP protocols are available on all of today's important systems.

Trivial File Transfer Protocol (TFTP)	Simple Network Management Protocol (SNMP)	NFS	File Transfer Protocol (FTP)	Simple Mail Transfer Protocol (SMTP)	X-Windows	Telnet protocol (TELNET)	Layers 5-7
		XDR					
		RPC					
User Datagram Protocol (UDP)			Transmission Protocol (TCP)				Layer 4
Internet Protocol (IP) Internet Message Control Protocol (ICMP) Gateway-to-gateway protocols (EGP, IGP, RIP, OSPF)							Layer 3
No special protocols provided. In the LAN area Ethernet is predominantly used							Layers 1 and 2

Figure 6.4 TCP/IP protocol family.

This is true at the lower end for simple PCs and, through typical minicomputers up to mainframes (implementations of TCP/IP also exist for IBM systems) and special computers such as vector and parallel processors. These protocols span a field in a way which might be expected of internationally standardized ISO protocols. For some time, a true TCP/IP boom has been apparent. TCP/IP is viewed as a panacea for the construction of integrated networks of heterogeneous systems.

However, in the USA, the home of TCP/IP, in 1987 the DoD committed itself to a migration within all its networks/projects, so that within a few years only OSI components would be developed and the corresponding networks would be operated using solely OSI services. Exceptions require special justification. The USA civilian authorities (for example, the National Institute of Health (NIH), the National Air and Space Agency (NASA)) and their relevant ministries (for example, the Department of Energy, DoE) have also committed themselves to develop plans for the construction of an OSI-based communications infrastructure in the next few years. The use of ARPANet and/or ARPANet protocols in independent networks based on the same technology (for example, NSFNet) will be gradually reduced. Even the large user associations, MAP and TOP have decided to use an OSI-based infrastructure for the various applications in the production area. However, for the time being, the disappearance of the TCP/IP protocol family from the LAN world and, in particular, from the Ethernet world is scarcely conceivable.

The TCP/IP family includes a number of different protocols. We shall describe the most important of these in more detail. The protocols may be grouped according to the layering of the ISO reference model, see Figure 6.4.

We again stress that the TCP/IP protocol family incorporates standards for the most important applications in computer networks (terminal traffic, file transfer, network management and electronic mail). This also had a considerable effect on its distribution. In the remainder of this section we give a brief description of the most important members of the TCP/IP protocol family. The internet protocol (IP) was discussed in Chapter 4 and SNMP is discussed in Chapter 8.

6.3.2 Transmission control protocol (TCP)

Introduction

The transmission control protocol (TCP) was designed for the construction of a reliable end-to-end transport connection between two systems. Thus, TCP belongs to level 4 of the ISO/OSI layer model and lies directly above the internet protocol. Originally, it was designed for use in packet-switched networks or interconnections of such networks. However, it is in principle well suited for other types of networks. The most important services which TCP provides for its users (application processes) include: connection orientation, sequencing, security against loss, connection monitoring, multiplexing, flow control, transparent data transport and secure connection establishment/release. TCP is in many respects similar to OSI transport class 4. Thus, TCP places quite specific demands on the protocol of the underlying network layer. This must have the ability to:

- transmit messages over an internetwork;
- address each partner uniquely;
- decompose and recombine packets according to the current network conventions;
- transmit certain information about the packet sequence and security features.

These requirements are met by the internet protocol.

TCP service interfaces

In what follows, we shall only describe the interfaces which TCP makes available to its overlying users. With its host-to-host communication, TCP/IP supports the port/socket concept. A host, represented by its various application packages, may be viewed as providing a set of sockets, into which the desired connections, which are linked to input/output ports of the relevant applications by the main software, may be plugged. Some of the sockets and ports are reserved for certain standardized applications (well-known ports), as shown in Table 6.2 in Section 6.3.6.3.

A description of the interfaces between TCP and IP was given in Section 4.3.3.2. The interface upwards consists largely of a set of procedure-like calls with which an application process instructs TCP. In addition to this (synchronous) form of communication, asynchronous tasking between processes and TCP is also possible, in principle. The most important services are:

OPEN Open a virtual connection to a partner (in the active case) or wait until the connection is opened by an arbitrary or a specific partner (in the passive case). A timeout condition may be given.

SEND Deliver a data buffer to TCP for transmission to the other partner. A PUSH flag may be used to force the full data transfer, otherwise the nature of the execution is at the discretion of TCP. An URGENT flag may be used for express packets which must receive priority handling.

RECEIVE Receipt of data from the partner, with entry of the size of the available buffer. TCP informs the client process whether the PUSH or URGENT flags were set by the partner.

CLOSE Release of a virtual connection.

STATUS This service is only of a local nature and its actions depend on the form of the current TCP implementation (in other words, which connection-related status/statistical data is made available).

Connection establishment

Connection establishment between two TCP partners is based on the so-called 'three-way handshake' principle. This mechanism reduces the possibility of the establishment of false connections. The following error situations may arise:

- Simultaneous establishment of a connection by each of the two partners involved.
- Multiple establishment of a connection by the initiator because of a timeout of the first connection-establishment request.
- Unwanted establishment of a connection before the previous connection is released.

Data transfer

Once a connection is established between two partners data packets may be exchanged. Since these could be lost or rendered worthless as a result of errors (checksum test) or overloading of the network, TCP initiates a transmission repeat after the timeout condition expires. This may lead to duplicated data packets, which TCP detects using a special sequence numbering.

Sequence numbering

Each data octet (8-bit byte) transmitted by TCP is assigned a sequence number (of course, this is not transmitted for each octet). This means that, in principle, the receipt of each octet can be confirmed. This is implemented in such a way that the confirmation of octet number n implicitly confirms the receipt of all previous octets. Thus, duplicated segments are detected by the receiver and do not require special treatment. Sequence numbers run from 0 to $2^{32} - 1$, which, of course, requires special treatment in the unlikely but possible event of an overflow of the sequence-number space (for example, if more than 8 Gbytes of data is transmitted during the lifetime of a virtual connection).

Window mechanism

While in other protocols, such as HDLC or X.25 level 3, the transmission window relates to the number of packets still to be transported from the sender to the recipient, because of the sequential numbering of octets, TCP uses a different mechanism. Here, a recipient tells the sender the sequence number of the last octet which it has sufficient buffer space to receive. Unlike the above protocols, this provides for very dynamic management of this window. As soon as a recipient has a higher load and, thus, possibly less buffer space, it can make this known to its partner.

Transmission watchdog

Each data packet transmitted is monitored so that a transmission repeat takes place if no acknowledgement is forthcoming within a given interval (retransmission time). This interval depends heavily on the network type, the dimensioning of the network and the current network load. Too frequent transmission repeats load the network unnecessarily, too long a waiting period decreases the throughput, possibly considerably. Thus, for each data packet, TCP continuously determines the time until the expiry of the acknowledgement period and thus is able to reset the retransmission timer adaptively.

A TCP packet has the header format shown in Table 6.1. The minimum header length is 20 bytes.

6.3.3 User datagram protocol (UDP)

The user datagram protocol (UDP) was defined in order to provide application processes with the direct facility to transmit and thereby fulfil

Table 6.1   TCP protocol header.

Byte no.	Length, bits	Meaning
1–2	16	Source port
3–4	16	Destination port
5–8	32	Sequence number
9–12	32	Acknowledgement number
13	4	Data offset
13/14	6	Reserved
14	1	URGENT flag
14	1	ACK flag
14	1	End of letter
14	1	Reset connection
14	1	Synchronize sequence numbers
14	1	No more data from sender
15–16	16	Window
17–18	16	Checksum
19–20	16	URGENT pointer
21–23	24	Options (optional)
24	8	Padding (optional)

the requirement for transaction-oriented traffic. UDP is directly based on the underlying internet protocol.

UDP does not guarantee to deliver a datagram to the destination partner, neither are any precautions taken against duplication or mixing of a datagram sequence.

UDP has the following simple datagram-header structure:

- Source port (or source address), 2 bytes;
- Destination port (or destination address), 2 bytes;
- Length entry for data field, 2 bytes;
- Checksum over header and data, 2 bytes.

One of the main users of this simple protocol is the internet name server. Other application packages such as SNMP (see below) and NFS are also based on UDP. The latter is discussed in detail in Chapter 7.

6.3.4 Virtual terminal protocol (Telnet)

The aim of the Telnet protocol is to provide a standard method which is as general as possible and permits communication between terminals on the one side and interactive applications processes on the other side. Telnet is based on the TCP transport protocol and uses its connection services.

Overall, Telnet corresponds to ISO layers 5 to 7 (session, presentation and application layers). Telnet is based on three basic concepts:

- the concept of a virtual terminal;
- the principle of mutual agreement of options;
- a symmetric view of terminals and processes.

The virtual terminal

The virtual terminal (VT) is considered as a line-oriented terminal; in other words, input and output is normally structured in lines. It has a printer and a keyboard (imaginary). The 7-bit ASCII character set, embedded in an 8-bit field is used as code. Possible code mappings are purely of a local nature and do not affect Telnet.

Telnet has five control functions which are used to transact standard requirements of a dialogue connection:

- Interrupt process (IP). This process provides, for example, a user with the facility to signal an interruption to an application process.
- Abort output (AO). Most systems provide a user with a facility to abort lengthy terminal output by entering a specific character string. Telnet provides for mapping of this function onto the AO function.
- Are you there (AYT). In many cases, it may be useful for a user to have a control function which he can use to ascertain whether his counterpart (an application process) is still operational.
- Erase character (EC). This control function deletes the last character entered.
- Erase line (EL). This control function deletes the last line entered.

At least the first three of the above functions require immediate transmission to the partner without queueing in the normal data stream. For this reason, Telnet provides a so-called SYNCH signal which is mapped onto the URGENT flag at the TCP interface and forces urgent transmission.

Telnet commands

The term Telnet commands subsumes all protocol elements. They have a common structure within the data stream: the command code (1 or 2 bytes) follows the 'interpret as command' (IAC) escape signal (1 byte).

In addition to the functions described above, the facility to set certain options is of particular interest. The following options are important:

- Binary transmission of data. This permits transparent 8-bit transmission.

- Echo option. This permits character-wise transmission from the terminal to the host and generation of a corresponding echo.
- Suppress go ahead. This may be used in full duplex mode to suppress the 'go ahead signal' which is needed in half-duplex mode.
- Status option. This may be used to query the options which are currently set.
- Timing mark option. This is used to force certain markings in the output data stream.

Connection establishment

A Telnet connection is always based on a TCP connection between a user (TCP) port U and a service (TCP) port S. On every server the well-known port S = 23 is used for Telnet connections.

6.3.5 File transfer protocol (FTP)

The file transfer protocol (FTP) is used to permit shared use of files of several systems and file transfer between different systems and to simplify the administration of files on different systems. FTP is based on the TCP transmission protocol and the Telnet interactive terminal protocol.

FTP is best explained using the following model:

- A user is connected to the so-called user protocol interpreter (UPI) via a local user interface.
- When the service is required by the user the UPI establishes a Telnet connection to a server protocol interpreter (SPI).
- The UPI transmits FTP commands to the SPI over this connection. These commands specify the nature of the desired file transfer (character presentation, transmission mode, file structure, desired file operation, for example, fetch file, store, append, delete, etc.).
- The file transfer itself is then executed over a separately established connection between a server transfer process (STP) and a user transfer process (UTP).

In a variation of this model, it is also possible that the user may be a subscriber to a third system from which he initiates a transfer between two other systems.

Character presentation

FTP may be used to transmit both character-encoded information and binary data. In both cases, the user must be able to specify the form in which the data is to be stored on the destination system.

As in the case of Telnet, a 7-bit ASCII character code packed into 8-bit octets is used to transmit character-encoded information. Since such characters are stored in different ways on different systems (for example, on a PDP 10, 5 7-bit characters are stored in a 36-bit word; for MULTICS, 4 9-bit characters are stored in a 36-bit word; in the /370 architecture, 4 8-bit EBCDIC characters are stored in a 32-bit word; for CDC-NOS, 10 6-bit characters are stored in a 60-bit word), the sender and the recipient must carry out a local conversion between their character presentation and that used for the transmission.

However, special agreements must also be made when transmitting binary information. For example, transmission from a system with 32-bit words to a system with 60-bit words, requires a specification of how the individual words are to be stored (for example, left-justified in the 60-bit word or consecutively using all 60 bits of words in the destination machine). Other agreements relating to formatting (printer control, tabs, etc.) are required for text files. FTP provides basic services for these problems.

File structure

The problem of selecting the file structure has precedence over that of the character presentation. FTP has three basic file structures:

- the whole file is viewed as a byte stream with no additional structure;
- a file consists of a sequence of records;
- the file has the most complicated structure of an index sequential file.

If one file type is mapped onto another by the transfer (for example, byte stream onto record structure), the details of the mapping are specified by the user (for example, how ends of lines are marked).

Transmission modes

One other consideration as far as file transfer is concerned is the choice of a suitable transmission mode. FTP has three different transmission modes:

- **Byte-stream mode.** This mode is independent of the file structure (not to be confused with the byte-stream file structure). The file is transmitted as it is, without the creation of special blocks and without compression. Record marks are represented by an EOR (2-byte control character for end of record). The transfer is deemed to be complete when an EOR is received.
- **Block mode.** A file is transmitted in the form of individual blocks.

Each block is prefixed by a length entry and a descriptor. The latter includes entries about EOR marks and also provides help for a possible restart of the connection.

- **Compression mode.** In this mode, several consecutive repeated octets may be compressed. The compression involves prefixing the character concerned by the number of repeats.

Error handling and restart

FTP takes no precautions against data corruption. This task falls to the underlying TCP. However, in the block and compression transmission modes, measures are taken to cater for a transmission restart. This involves introducing checkpoints during the transmission which may be referred to if a restart is needed. This is particularly sensible when long files have to be transmitted and it is not highly unlikely that one of the components involved will fail.

FTP commands

FTP has a number of commands which are initiated by the user and transmitted by the UPI via the Telnet connection to the SPI. The most important of these are:

- Commands for access protection, including standardized transmission of user IDs, passwords and accounting numbers (unencrypted on the network).
- Commands for transmission parameters, including entry of the desired data presentation, file structure and transmission mode.
- Service commands, including entry of the desired service (store, delete, rename, transmit directory, alter working library, etc.).
- Special services, including all services relating to the delivery of electronic mail.
- Connection establishment. An FTP control connection is established between an arbitrary user port and the server port 21 using TCP.

Implementation

A complete implementation of FTP may be extremely complicated. However, so that it is possible to implement at least simple file transfer for a low cost, a minimum environment is defined in which the ASCII-non-print file type, the byte-stream mode and the stream and record structures are specified.

6.3.6 Further protocols

6.3.6.1 Simple mail transport protocol (SMTP)

SMTP is the internet standard for the distribution of electronic mail. It is text-oriented and based on TCP. A message consists of a head and a body. The head contains among other things: the date, the reference, the recipient, the sender, recipients of copies, etc.; the user is prompted to define these entries. The body typically consists of free ASCII text. Messages with several recipients on a single destination host are transmitted once to the destination and distributed there. Functionally, SMTP is inferior to X.400.

6.3.6.2 Simple network management protocol (SNMP)

SNMP is the protocol which is used to transport management information between an SNMP agent and an SNMP management station (Figure 6.5).

The agent is located in a network node (for example, router, bridge, terminal server, host) and is responsible for collecting relevant management data from the node, which is stored in the management information base (MIB). Examples of this information include: timers, counters, addresses and protocol parameters. The agent responds to SNMP enquiries from the manager, which query or set the MIB values. The latter is responsible for the control of the node. In addition, the agent may transmit a so-called trap message when certain events occur. SNMP is very important for the LAN management. We shall return to this in Chapter 8.

6.3.6.3 Other protocols

The protocols listed in Table 6.2 represent only a cross-section of the ARPA protocol family. All protocols are described in documents known

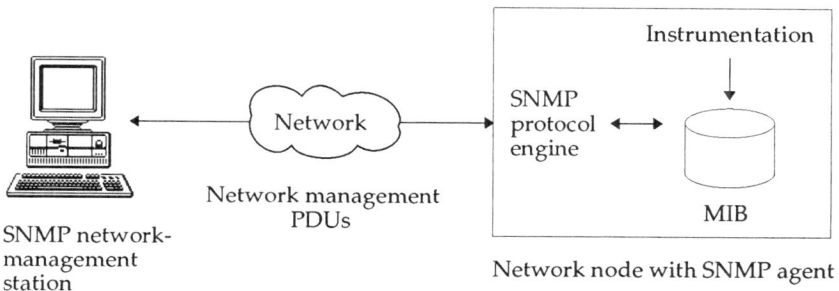

Figure 6.5   SNMP management model.

Table 6.2 TCP/IP application protocols.

Protocol	Description	RFC	Well-known port
ARP	Address resolution protocol		
AUTH	Authentication service	931	113
BOOTP	Bootstrap protocol	951	67, 68
ECHO	Echo protocol	862	7
FTP	File transfer protocol	959	20, 21
GRAPHICS	Graphics exchange protocol	493	
MPM	Exchange multimedia protocol	759	46
LDP	Load debugger protocol	909	
LPR	Line printer daemon protocol	1179	514
NFS	Network file system	1094	2049
NNTP	Network news transfer protocol	977	119
RJE	Remote job entry	407	
RLP	Resource location protocol	887	39
SMTP	Simple mail transfer protocol	1157	25
STATSRV	Sending gateway statistics	996	95
TELNET	Remote terminal protocol	854	23
TFTP	Trivial file transfer	783	69
UDP	User datagram protocol	768	
X	X-Window system	1198	6000

as RFCs (Request for Comments). These may be called up via FTP from the internet host NIC.DDN.MIL. To do this, one must sign on under the user name 'anonymous' with the password 'guest'. The call is by command 'get RFC:RFCnn,txt' where nn is the identifying number of the RFC. An overview of the overall documentation may be obtained using the command 'dir RFC:RFC-INDEX'.

6.4 Xerox XNS protocol family

6.4.1 Overview

With its development of the Ethernet procedure in the 1970s, Xerox became the founder of local area networks. Xerox's aim was to make local area networks and the associated technology (concepts of workstations and dedicated servers) usable for office automation. For more than a decade, Xerox has been one of the largest users worldwide, operating an integrated network of local Ethernets. This was facilitated by the definition and implementation of a whole series of additional protocols, including application-layer protocols based on the Ethernet standard. Many of these protocols are important outside the Xerox world and have become a type of *de facto* standard (for example, XNS protocols are used by Novell networks under the names SPX and IPX). This is particularly true for the lower protocol layers (internet and transport protocol) and also for some application protocols (for example, interpress protocol). The XNS protocol family includes a number of protocols, which are shown in Figure 6.6.

Xerox uses these protocols as the basis for extensive office communication and automation systems. Both proprietary products and products from other manufacturers are used in these systems. The protocol definitions for the whole of the XNS protocol family are published and may be obtained from Xerox Systems Institute in Sunnyvale, CA 94086 for a small fee.

6.4.2 Sequenced packet protocol (SP)

The sequenced packet protocol (SP, sometimes also called SPX) of the XNS protocol family provides a reliable transport connection between two end systems. It belongs to ISO layer 4. SP is largely based on the internet protocol of the XNS family (see Section 4.3). It provides users with the following services: connection orientation, sequencing, security against loss, flow control and transparent data transport.

SP is packet oriented and the packets exchanged are packed into an internet-protocol datagram. Thus, SP places fewer demands on the internet protocol than, for example, TCP (TCP requires that IP should have a facility to fragment larger packets and transmission of such large packets is unprotected).

SP service interfaces

SP may make several different interfaces available to its users, depending on the current implementation: the byte-stream interface, the packet-stream interface and the so-called reliable packet mode.

While the first interface hides packet boundaries completely from the SP user and thus may take advantage of any favourable local circumstances for each computer system (buffer size, transfer mechanism), in both the other cases all packets are delivered as transmitted. In addition, in the third case, packets are also delivered even though the sequence may not be preserved. This naturally makes more work for the SP user (sequencing). In principle, all end systems which implement SP may communicate with one another regardless of the interface chosen.

Packet format

SP distinguishes between packets and system packets. Both types have the same basic structure. The former are used to transmit data, the latter are

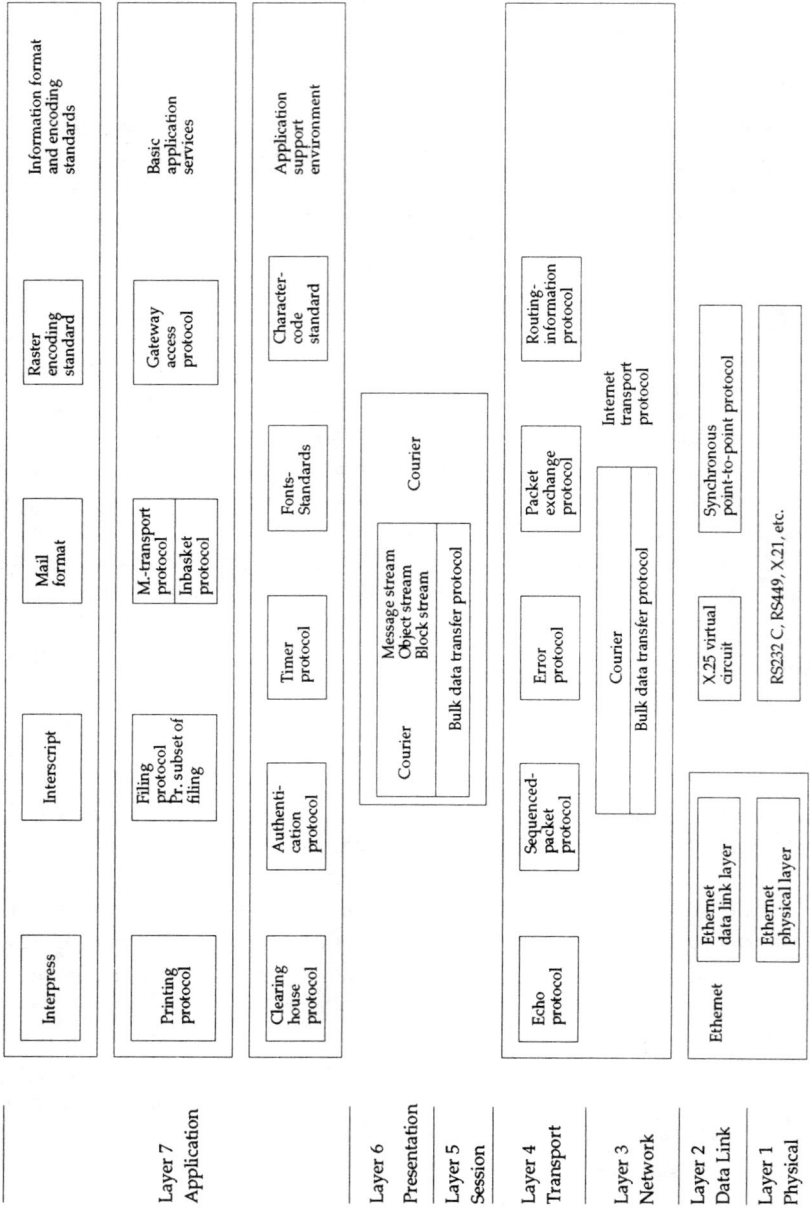

Figure 6.6 XNS protocol family.

used for connection management and other administrative tasks. Various bit fields in the protocol header identify the exact function of a packet.

If 'send acknowledgement' is set, the partner is forced to explicitly send an acknowledgement for a data packet. A system packet for which send acknowledgement is set may thus be used as a polling mechanism (for example, to check that the partner is active). The attention field identifies a data packet as being particularly important. It is used to indicate a telegram (expedited data), where it is imperative that the recipient should attempt to accept the packet. Thus, the data field of this packet may only be one byte long. The 'end of message' field is used to structure a packet stream. The sender is able to close a sequence of packets with a packet in which the 'end of message' field is set. Of course, this identifier must be transmitted to the recipient by the SP entity.

Structuring of the data stream

A sender may also identify the packet of a data stream using the so-called data-stream field. This field may only be arbitrarily set by higher protocols and enables them to structure the data stream without accessing it directly. For the SP protocol, while this field is a component of the protocol it has no meaning (is not evaluated). One possible application for an interactive terminal protocol would be, for example, to separate text and graphics data in this way (this is usually done using escape sequences within the data stream).

Connection identifier

Every packet contains a source and a destination connection identifier (16 bit). Together with the internet address (network, host and socket number), these uniquely identify a connection. Different incarnations of the same connection between two partners are distinguished by different connection-identifier pairs. The connection identifier plays an important role in connection establishment (see below).

Sequence numbering

Packets in each direction are assigned increasing sequence numbers (16 bit). These are used for sequencing, to detect duplicates, for security against loss and in acknowledgements. When a connection is established the sequence number counter is always set to 0.

Acknowledgement numbers

There is a fixed relationship between acknowledgement numbers and sequence numbers. A recipient uses this to tell a sender which packet

Table 6.3   SP packet header.

Byte no.	Bits	Meaning
1	1	System packet flag
	1	Send acknowledge flag
	1	Attention flag
	1	End-of-message flag
2	8	Data-stream type
3–4	16	Source connection ID
5–6	16	Destination connection ID
7–8	16	Sequence number
9–10	16	Acknowledge number
11–12	16	Allocation number
ff.		Data

sequence number it expects next, in other words, which packet it has just received.

Allocation numbers

The allocation number is closely related to the acknowledgement number. A recipient uses this to tell the sender the packet sequence number up to which it is able to receive packets. This mechanism is used for flow control; thus, it is based on packets rather than on data octets, as in TCP. Nevertheless, a rigid window need not be used since the recipient can adjust the difference between the acknowledgement number and the allocation number to suit its local conditions (for example, availability of buffers).

Connection establishment

On connection establishment, the sender transmits a system packet to the recipient which contains its own connection identifier, together with the sequence number 0. The recipient replies to this with another system packet containing its connection identifier and the foreign connection identifier. Thus, the connection is uniquely specified. Possible errors and how they are handled will not be discussed in further detail here.

Every SP packet has the structure shown in Table 6.3

Comparison of TCP and SP

In what follows, we give a brief comparison of the two transport protocols, the sequenced packet protocol (SP) and the transmission control protocol (TCP) (Table 6.4).

Table 6.4   Comparison of TCP and SP.

Feature	SP	TCP
Flow control	On packet basis	Based on sequence numbers per byte
Window technique	Dynamic	Dynamic
Packet header length, bytes	12	24
Connection ID, bits	16	16
Connection establishment	At higher level	3-way handshake
Retransmission timer	Adaptive	Adaptive
Expedited data	Yes	Yes
Checksum	Optional	Mandatory

Even at the level of the transport protocol, there are scarcely any differences, except for checksums, which, in the case of TCP, create more work for both the recipient and the sender (but also provide increased security). One other difference is that TCP allows the recipient more freedom to allocate its buffer sizes; if the recipient actually uses this option, the sender must continuously adapt to this by choosing suitable packet lengths.

In summary, it can be said that the main differences between the protocol families are not at the level of the transmission protocols, but at the level of the application protocols. We also note that the transport protocol defined by ISO (at least the class 4 protocol) is superior to the above two transport protocols as far as the handling of system errors is concerned (error recovery).

6.4.3 Courier: remote procedure call protocol

One of the most frequent operations as far as the construction of distributed systems is concerned is the interrogation of a server by a client with a subsequent response from the server. Such an operation is often called a transaction. The underlying mechanism is a procedure call, similar to those of higher-level programming languages. The Courier remote procedure call protocol provides generally applicable basic elements for just such applications.

Of course, Courier is not suitable for all applications in distributed systems (file transfer is a counterexample). As far as its suitability is concerned, there are restrictions for transaction-oriented traffic, since Courier is based on the use of virtual connections rather than datagrams alone. Thus, if the reaction-time requirements are very high, Courier may not be suitable. Courier uses the following model. A client executes a remote procedure call, which is transmitted over the network to a passive element, the remote program. The latter executes the function specified and then transmits the results of the function call together with possible error messages to the caller (client).

Courier itself has three layers. The lowest layer establishes a virtual connection, which is a reliable, sequence-preserving, flow-controlled, bidirectional communications channel. It uses the sequenced packet protocol for this. The transmission involves data blocks with the length being a multiple of 16 bits (block stream).

The middle layer of the Courier protocol is associated with layer 6 of the ISO layer model. It provides a standard presentation of various data types and thus permits the transmission of so-called object streams to each partner. Thus, typed data objects may be transmitted and (equally importantly) interpreted by the partner as such. The basic types available include Boolean, cardinal, integer and string. These basic types may also be used to form higher types, such as fields, sequences and records.

The highest layer of the Courier protocol is then responsible for the procedure call mechanism itself. At this level a so-called message stream is transmitted. Four different message types are defined: call, reject, return and abort. Thus all the aids needed to avoid calling non-local procedures are available.

One good example of the use of Courier would be a file management system which is operated on a special non-local file server. This could provide procedures for opening files, reading, writing and closing files.

6.4.4 Interpress document description language

The interpress document description language is an important XNS application protocol. It concentrates on a special application area, namely the device-independent description of individual print pages and whole documents for printers which use the raster principle (where a whole page is composed of individual points or pixels, which may also be individually selected). Originally, interpress was also intended to support the creation of documents (editing); however, this was soon rejected. Thus, it is only used for the final presentation of a print document for the purposes of printing.

The simplest way of supplying raster printers with information is to forward a bit map of the final page. However, the disadvantages of this solution are clear:

- The creator of the document has to take into account the number of pixels (raster density) of each printer.
- The dataset to be transmitted is very large (over a million bits per page, even in compressed form).
- The host system on which the document is generated must know the raster representation of all characters in all available fonts.

- Operations such as rotation or distortion of individual objects cause problems.

For these reasons, the design of interpress followed another path. Interpress may be compared with a programming language which is used to describe individual pages and whole documents, in other words, a document description language. The content of an individual page may be described in three ways:

- by textual description of characters;
- by geometrical representation of objects (vector graphics);
- by a pictorial description (raster graphics).

In addition to describing individual pages, it must also be possible to compose whole documents (printing on both sides, paper size, special batch instructions) and to carry out administrative tasks in a multiuser environment (document identifiers, author names, storage locations, etc.). Interpress also provides assistance for this.

For reasons of efficiency, the interpress syntax is chosen in such a way that automatic processing is easily accessible (binary pattern). This form is naturally difficult for people to understand, thus there exist aids which convert interpress documents into a form which is easy to read. We shall not discuss the individual language elements of interpress in further detail here.

6.4.5 Comparison of the TCP/IP and XNS protocol families

The protocol families which until now have frequently been used to construct Ethernet internetworks in a world of heterogeneous systems are TCP/IP and XNS; TCP/IP is now the more common. In the long term it is probable that these two families will be threatened by appropriate ISO protocols. Even now, a number of products exist which already implement ISO protocols in Ethernet internetworks.

TCP/IP is the older of the two protocol families and was not originally designed for use in LAN internetworks. Both protocol families have the same root, namely research activities at Stanford University. Thus, it is no surprise that, conceptually, at level 3 they are not very different. Both assume datagram-oriented communications networks. In fact, this is very different from the ISO protocols which, even at this level, are originally based on mainly connection-oriented communication.

Unlike TCP/IP, XNS was strictly designed for use in local area networks (and Ethernet, in particular). This is reflected in the differences in the care with which the two protocols treat error protection for the transmitted data. TCP/IP has checksums at the level of the transport protocol, XNS does not. This is one frequent reason why TCP/IP implementations are viewed as being generally less powerful (from the point of view of the achievable throughput) than comparable XNS implementations. In fact, because of the mandatory calculation of checksums, TCP/IP has more work to do than XNS. In view of the high technical transmission quality of modern LANs, this is an important factor. However, the most important difference between the two protocol families must be in the objectives which they each seek to realise.

From the beginning, the task of TCP/IP was to support communication in heterogeneous computer networks. The main problems to be solved related firstly to terminal access to different computer systems and secondly to file transfer between these systems. This is naturally reflected in the protocols defined. The two most important application protocols of TCP/IP were initially Telnet and FTP. Xerox, on the other hand, as a manufacturer of network office automation components, began from a somewhat different system environment. In this environment, conceptually expressed in terms of a distributed system based on (relatively homogeneous) workstations and various servers (in particular, file and print servers for processing office documents), other problems are the centre of attention. This meant that the main application protocols created by Xerox (for example, Courier, interpress or printer integration) were more typical of office communication.

On the other hand, a virtual terminal protocol (for terminal access) and a usable file transfer for a heterogeneous system environment are completely missing from the XNS world. For this reason, we now have the following situation. Although office automation was greeted with euphoria, it has not gained as great a foothold as was once expected. On the other hand, the problems of a heterogeneous environment were, and to some extent still are, far from solved. However, considerably more attention has been given to these problems in recent years, probably because the benefits of their solution were more visible. Because of this situation, the TCP/IP protocol family has recently come noticeably to the fore, while the XNS protocols are more in the background than might have been predicted some years ago.

As far as the construction of heterogeneous system environments is concerned, only TCP/IP or OSI protocols are worth considering. While XNS bears the stamp of Xerox company politics, the evolution of the protocols of the TCP/IP world is strongly influenced by the user community. The facility for making new proposals to the internet authorities via the RFC mechanism and the possibility of rapid user testing using public domain software have stimulated the spread of the TCP/IP family even further.

Chapter 7

PC networks and integrated workstation networks

- Application programming interfaces

- PC networks

- Distributed systems in the UNIX world

This chapter is devoted to a number of important applications developed as a result of the new possibilities offered by local area networks. The main characteristics which distinguish local area networks (e.g. Ethernet) from previous network types (e.g. multilevel star networks with BSC or SDLC interfaces) are the high transmission rates available to individual stations and the access of many stations to a shared medium. The network transfer time decreases to the same order of magnitude as the time taken to access local resources (disks and other peripherals) and, in addition to the traditional single point-to-point connections, it is now easy to implement more complicated forms of communication such as 1-to-N, N-to-1 or N-to-M relationships. These conditions have led to the evolution of PC networks and computer networks with distributed applications.

Section 7.1 contains separate discussions of the application programming interfaces for the DOS and the UNIX worlds. These are important prerequisites for the implementation of integrated networks of PCs and workstations. Section 7.2 is concerned with PC networks; it includes an introduction to the most important representatives (Novell NetWare, Microsoft's LAN Manager, Banyan Vines) followed by a number of general criteria for choosing such systems.

In Section 7.3, we switch to the next most important world after the PC world, namely that of distributed systems composed of interconnected workstations, where the latter are primarily UNIX based. The NFS (network file system), RFS (remote file sharing system) and AFS (Andrew file system) applications are used to show how distributed applications may be implemented in the UNIX world. While in the case of PC networks, Ethernet plays an important role but is not the only network concept worthy of consideration, it has an indisputable claim to leadership in the UNIX world. However, we also note that many questions relating to the construction of such systems are not Ethernet specific.

7.1 Application programming interfaces

Application programming interfaces (APIs) are service interfaces which may be accessed by user programs at which network services may be called. These interfaces are very important because they provide a way of separating communication services from processing services. Since there are various potential users of communication functions (system kernel, system processes, application programs) which each require different network services, at a corresponding level of abstraction, different interfaces to different logical and procedural levels are also desirable. The 'height' of an interface (in other words, the level of abstraction) may be determined by comparison with the ISO model. APIs may be used to develop user programs independently of the underlying network technology. Although many products also provide APIs within the transport system, we shall only consider APIs in the application system. In so doing, we must distinguish between the DOS world and the UNIX world.

7.1.1 MS-DOS systems

7.1.1.1 NetBios

In August 1984, IBM announced NetBios (network basic input/output system), originally in the context of the introduction of the IBM personal computer network adapter. Immediately it was announced, NetBios was recognized as being far more than just another of the many interfaces specified for PC-DOS or MS-DOS 3.1. This was the first time that a manufacturer had defined and advertised an interface between an operating system and a network. There is now an internet standard ('RFC-compliant NetBios' RFC 1001/2) which discusses the interworking of NetBios implementations from different manufacturers.

Here is a brief overview of NetBios (Figure 7.1).

- NetBios originally described the interface between MS-DOS and an arbitrary transport system.
- NetBios carries out the functions of OSI layers 1 to 5, without specifying the protocols of the individual layers.
- Other manufacturers are able to offer the NetBios functions with their own preferred protocols and transmission media at a common interface.
- The NetBios interface is now available in both MS-DOS systems and UNIX systems.
- NetBios emulators are also available for other systems.

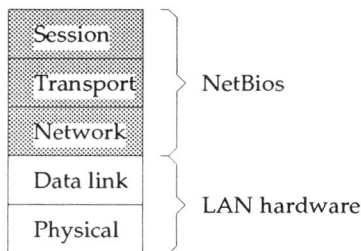

Figure 7.1 NetBios and the layer model.

Table 7.1   Network control block (NetBios).

No. bytes	Meaning
1	Command field
1	Return code
1	Local session number
1	Name number
4	Message buffer address
2	Buffer length, bytes
16	Call destination name
16	Your source name
1	Receive timeout value
1	Send timeout value
4	Post address (not-wait only)
1	Local network adapter number
1	Command completion code
14	Reserved

Functionality   From the point of view of applications, NetBios implements the first five layers of the OSI layer model; in other words, the transport system including the session layer. It makes the following services available to application programs:

- a reliable datagram service;
- the facility to establish virtual transport connections;
- the management of symbolic names for end addresses, so that application programs do not need to handle network addresses.

Thus, several virtual connections may be simultaneously established and maintained by MS-DOS application programs. This, of course, makes it possible to implement network applications with multiuser capabilities.

NetBios also supports the use of several symbolic names by a single MS-DOS system, which enables a system to carry different services.

Implementation details   As in the Bios interface, NetBios functions are addressed using software interrupts. This involves the use of the interrupt '5C' and the input of a 'network control block', NCB. The values in the control block specify the desired function in more detail. The NCB has a uniform structure (see Table 7.1). The following functions are available:

- General services.
    - RESET. Reset the network adapter and clear all session connections and symbolic names.

- — CANCEL. Interrupt an outstanding function.
- — STATUS. Query the status of the adapter.
- — UNLINK. This is used in conjunction with the 'remote program load' (RPL) facility.
- Name-management services.
  - — ADD NAME. New symbolic names up to 16 characters long may be introduced. Up to 16 different names per system are permitted. The name must be unique within the network.
  - — ADD GROUP. In contrast to the above function, names introduced by this function may be used as group names; in other words, they need not be unique in the network.
  - — DELETE. Delete a name.
- Connection-control services.
  - — CALL. Establish a session connection to a partner.
  - — LISTEN. Wait for another partner to establish the connection.
  - — HANGUP. Release a session connection.
  - — SEND. Data transmission.
  - — CHAIN. Data transmission with chained buffers.
  - — RECEIVE. Wait to receive data from a specific system.
  - — RCV ANY. Receive data on any session connection.
  - — STATUS. Query the status of all active sessions.
- Datagram services.
  - — SEND DATAGRAM.
  - — BROADCAST. Transmit a message to all stations which are ready to receive a datagram.
  - — RCV DATAGRAM. Prepare to receive datagrams.
  - — RCV BROADCAST. Prepare to receive broadcasts.

We also note the following facilities and/or restrictions:

- Up to 32 sessions may be maintained.
- Every function call has a wait/no-wait option which specifies whether the caller should wait for the function to be evaluated in full (wait) or continue its work subject to notification when the function is completed (no-wait).
- When the no-wait option is used a timeout condition may be formulated.

- Up to 32 function calls may be queued.

Name management An application may choose its own symbolic name and make it known in the network via the NetBios interface. In the case of the IBM implementation of the PC network, the following algorithm is used:

- The application passes the name to NetBios.
- NetBios initiates a broadcast containing this name.
- Each station receiving this checks to see whether it has already assigned this name and returns a corresponding acknowledgement.
- In the positive case the chosen name is entered in the NetBios name table.

However, use of the IBM implementation of NetBios in an internet environment (a LAN internetwork) may involve problems. As far as the management of symbolic names is concerned, the implementation provides for a fully distributed system because every network subscriber is solely responsible for managing its assigned names (in the form of tables in the network adapter). This means that the network broadcast mechanism must function well when a search for a name is involved. Moreover, in an internetwork of several local networks this search for a name must extend over all subnetworks which, depending on the underlying internetwork technology, may lead to considerable expense.

7.1.1.2 MS-DOS 3.1

In what follows, all statements about MS-DOS 3.1 also apply to later versions. While NetBios, as a relatively general interface to (local area) networks makes a general communication mechanism available to different operating systems, MS-DOS 3.1 provides the (operating-system-specific) interface between the application program and a PC network. It is the intention of MS-DOS 3.1 that typical and very common network applications should access and manage shared files. In order to provide these applications with a common basis, general system services have been created to permit file access and manipulation in a network environment. These special services of MS-DOS 3.1 may be regarded as services of level 6 of the OSI layer model. Thus, they are ranked above NetBios.

In order to provide a common data management service, the earliest PC networks based on DOS Versions 1 and 2 had to trick DOS so that they could initiate system calls and if necessary transport them over the network to a server. The latter then read or wrote to the disk and returned the result over the network. The available system calls were at a very low device level (sector write and read) so that these networks were more appropriately

Table 7.2 MS-DOS handle function calls.

AH reg.	AL reg.	Definition
3D		Open file with sharing specified
44	09	Is device redirected
44	0A	Is handle local or remote
44	0B	Change sharing retry count
59		Get extended error
5A		Create temp file with unique name
5B		Create new file
5C	00	Lock byte range
5C	01	Unlock byte range
5E	00	Get machine name
5E	02	Setup printer control sharing
5F	02	Get assign list entry
5F	03	Redirect device to net
5F	04	Cancel redirection

referred to as 'device sharing', rather than 'file sharing'.

MS-DOS 3.1 is different in this respect. It provides system calls which may be viewed as file management services rather than device function calls (for example, create or open a file). In the DOS terminology they are called 'Extended (handle) function calls'. Table 7.2 gives a brief overview of all handle function calls.

We now describe the two most important handle function calls, 'extended open' (3D) and 'lock/unlock file access' (5C) in more detail.

The extended open DOS function call provides for a file to be opened with entry of the required access characteristics for multiuser access. The following access modes may be specified: read access, write access and read/write access. The following modes are available for multiple access by a number of users: compatibility mode, deny read/write (exclusive), deny write mode, deny read mode, and deny none mode. Thus, it is possible to construct environments in which one application reads and alters a file while others may read the file at the same time. When extended open is used, users must state how they themselves wish to use the file and how other application programs may use it.

The group of lock/unlock file access DOS function calls permit the cross-synchronization of the read and write calls to the same file by a number of users. This is achieved using a locking mechanism which provides for the locking of a subarea of a file (record, byte area) against other accesses during a specific processing sequence.

It can certainly be claimed that MS-DOS 3.1 was one of the most important standards which various manufacturers used in their implementation of a network operating system. This is particularly true for areas in which the emphasis is on shared data management. Here, MS-DOS 3.1 provides powerful basic services. The development of more extensive functionality (user management, security concepts, etc.) then falls to the overlying applications.

7.1.2 UNIX systems

UNIX is dialogue oriented and has multiuser and multitasking capabilities. Thus, it is more suitable as a basis for distributed applications than MS-DOS. In addition, all UNIX versions incorporate a range of communications services. These are mainly accessible to the user via two interfaces: a command interface and a programmer interface (interprocess communication).

At the command level, the command 'mail' may be used to exchange messages between two users. Here, the addressing is by user and system names and is thus location independent. The commands 'uuto', 'uupick' are 'uucp' are also available for the transfer of larger files. 'uuto' may be used to transmit files to another computer where they will then be called at a later time from a spool area by the addressed user using the command 'uupick'. These services protect against attacks on the initiating computer since the data is only transmitted and cannot be requested from other points. 'uucp' is a command which is used to transmit data between two computers in an arbitrary manner. The transmitted file is copied directly into the addressed file tree. This request may be issued by either of the two computers involved or by another computer. The command 'uux' may be used to execute commands on a remote computer. The commands described all run asynchronously, in other words, the user initiates the job and is not informed about its completion. Finally, 'cu' provides for simple remote dialogue. After selecting the remote computer and a line to this computer the user is received by the terminal process of the remote computer and may then operate from his local workstation as if he were attached to a local machine.

In addition, from UNIX 4.3 BSD, synchronous commands for file transfer (rcp), remote job execution (rsh) and user-friendly remote dialogue (rlogin) will be provided. Unlike the above services, these are based on TCP/IP.

At the program level, all UNIX versions provide the signal mechanism and so-called pipes for process communication. Signals lead to the interruption of the process or to the execution of actions specified by the user. 'Pipes' permit unidirectional logical connections between two processes. However, these two communication mechanisms are not suitable for general interprocess communication since they operate locally between specific ('related') processes.

General interprocess communication is however available in the

UNIX BSD family and from version 3 of System V; processes may exchange data with any other processes in the network in either a connectionless or a connection-oriented mode. The communication mechanisms of the two versions of the system, which are mutually incompatible, are abstracted from the underlying protocol and thus provide a service interface. In practice, TCP/IP is very often used for connection-oriented communication.

Overall, UNIX services form flexible base services for complicated communications applications. They are directly available to users and are also included in numerous network operating systems and distributed file systems which we shall discuss later. The RPC mechanism, which is important for distributed applications, is also discussed later.

7.2 PC networks

The starting point for PC networks is the requirement that resources should be made directly available to a place of work and that, in addition, a number of workstations should be able to share resources. This may be necessary for economic reasons or because of technical system-related professional constraints (work using shared data). Various PC network concepts have been implemented to comply with these concepts. The first development involved three stages. The first forms of a PC network were characterized by a shared use of storage media and other peripherals. The server made disk capacity (disk sharing) and printer capacity (device sharing) available. The second generation of PC networks is characterized by file serving and multiuser applications. Users may share applications and data. The third stage provides for the distribution of applications across various computers (distributed application). Communications services, for example, in the form of electronic mail, are also provided. In addition, communication with other networks and PC–host coupling are also important. Finally, PC networks must be incorporated into the overall DP scheme.

7.2.1 Structure of a PC network

A PC network consists of several functional units. These include:

Servers

One or more servers make resources (for example, files, laser printers, CD drives, CPU power) available to the network subscribers; they represent the central resources in the network. A server system may or may not be exclusively devoted to execution of the server function (dedicated server). If a server system is operated in the non-dedicated mode, in addition to providing the server functions it also acts as a normal workstation.

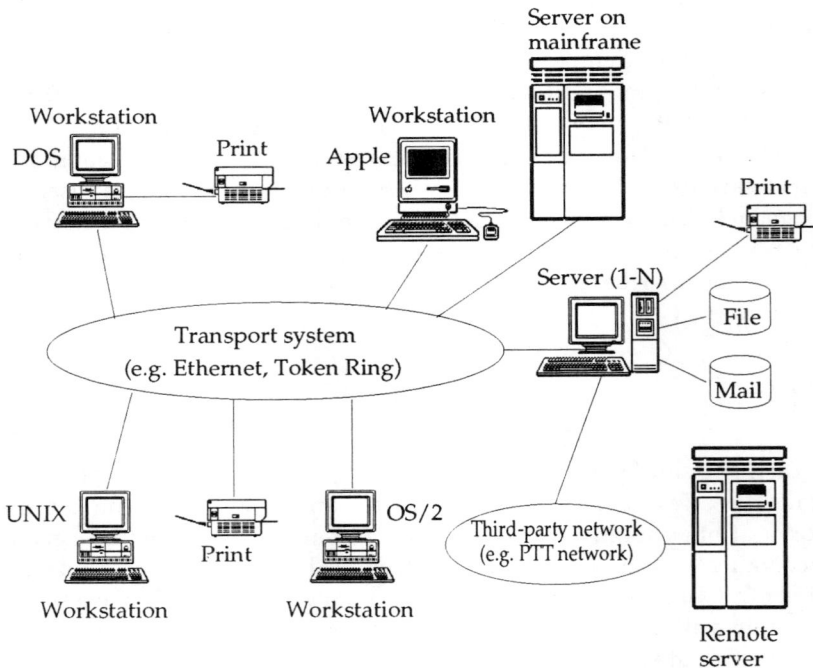

Figure 7.2   Schematic diagram of the structure of a PC network.

Another version involves the operation of a workstation in the peer-to-peer mode in which only some of the resources of the workstation are made available to other workstations. Usually, several peer-to-peer workstations are present in a network, sometimes all workstations operate in the peer-to-peer mode.

Workstations

A workstation (also often referred to in the context of PC networks) is an independent workstation computer with its own operating system (for example, DOS, OS/2, UNIX). Sometimes a workstation is not fitted with a hard disk or a diskette drive (diskless workstation), in which case the operating system is loaded by the server. The workstation is the interface between the user and the PC network.

Transport system

The transport system connects the server with the workstations. High transmission rates are demanded of the transport system, since, for example, access to a server disk should not take significantly longer than access to a local disk. In addition, the transport system must be able to cater for 1-to-N connections (1 server to N workstations). These requirements may be met by local area networks, and, in particular, by Ethernet. In addition, the transport system includes the corresponding computer interface cards (see Section 5.2) and the components used to build the networks on which the transport system is based (see Chapters 3 and 4).

Network operating software

The network operating system controls and regulates the access to the network resources. The server software may be based on a separate server operating system (for example, Novell) or run as an application over a suitable standard operating system (for example, OS/2 or UNIX). Software for operating the PC network must also be installed in the workstation (for example, shell, redirector).

7.2.2 Novell NetWare

Novell NetWare, which is a leading network operating system for the PC area, was introduced in 1983 and has evolved steadily since then. Its extent and functionality are such that to discuss them would go beyond the scope of this book. The reader is referred to the relevant literature for details. Novell's market share is currently greater than 60%. In 1991, a cooperation agreement was even concluded with IBM, previously one of the strongest competitors in the PC network market, which included the operation of NetWare by IBM.

The main features of NetWare are:

- The file server is not based on DOS (single tasking system), as in older PC networks with NetBios, but is implemented with Novell's own operating system (multitasking system), directly above the PC hardware. In this way, a substantially higher performance capability is achieved.

- NetWare contains important components as far as a network-wide user management and other security requirements are concerned.

- NetWare can be implemented on a variety of different networks with different network cards (this naturally includes Ethernet).

- An internetwork of local area networks (which may also be of different types) is supported.

- As far as data security is concerned, there exist facilities for duplicating both disks and whole file servers (fault tolerance) and for archiving on external data carriers.

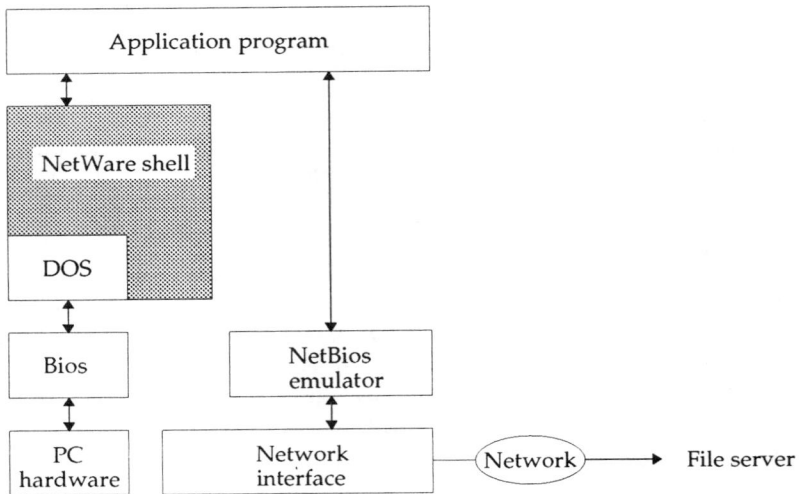

Figure 7.3   NetWare shell in a workstation.

Workstations

Workstations using MS-DOS 3.1 and newer versions may be operated. A 'network interface shell' developed by Novell generates the connection between the user and the network, otherwise the standard version of DOS is unchanged. However, NetWare shells are also available for computers with OS/2 and MS-Windows 3.x and for Macintosh workstations. Commands for the following areas are available to the user:

- Receipt and transmission of messages from and to users (user groups) on other workstations.

- Facilities to login to and logout from a file server, including the use of a password, the definition of a prologue which runs automatically after a login and a mechanism for changing the password.

- Various commands which enable the user to set the access rights of other users to his own files and directories.

- Commands for addressing the print server and querying its status.

Servers

In principle, a PC which runs as a file server may also be used as a normal workstation. This is possible because the file server software does not run as a standard DOS application but as an extension of DOS with direct hardware access. On the one hand, this increases the performance capability of the file server while on the other hand it makes it possible (particularly for small networks) to introduce a file server at a low cost.

Commands available for operating the file server include:

- Various services to monitor and control the printer queues.

- Commands to introduce or remove magnetic tapes or alternate disks and commands to initiate backup of the hard disk.

- Various user-management services.

- Status indicators and commands to monitor file-server activities.

Measures to increase the speed in the file server include:

- Directory caching of all the directory information in the server RAM cache, so as to avoid time-consuming disk searches.

- Directory hashing with a considerably more effective procedure for searching within the directory used.

- The whole of the RAM cache is used for file caching of the latest information required.

- Elevator seeking is used in which requests to access the hard disk are sorted so as to avoid moving the read/write head unnecessarily.

- The hard-disk formatting and file storage are implemented in a faster way which does not conform to DOS.

Administration

NetWare has very distinctive user management and access protection systems. The overall management falls to the system administrator. Each user may have his own user ID, which is requested together with a password (the length and period of validity of the password and the maximum number of attempts to enter it correctly may be preset) on login to the file server. In addition, each user is assigned a so-called user profile, which defines which network resources (for example, file space and printers) this user is permitted to use. This may be used, for example, to reserve individual devices for specific user groups. In addition, it specifies the directories and subdirectories to which the user has access together with his access rights to these directories (read, write, etc.). A user's access to the network may also be restricted to specific times and specific terminals. The work of the system administrator is further supported by the fact that it is possible to form user groups which have a common profile. The system administrator can also assign access rights to the queue operator (management of the output queues), the console operator (management of the server), the user account manager and the workgroup manager (for example, for deletion and inclusion of user groups).

The access of the administrators to the server, which may be protected by password, may be either direct (locally) or over the network (remote). In addition, an accounting facility for services such as storage and connection time is also available.

Internetworks of several LANs

The facilities of NetWare are also available in an internetwork of several local area networks. Up to 4 or 16 networks may be connected via a server. If this number is exceeded, a dedicated PC is needed to connect the local area networks together via suitable network adapters. Bridge software then runs on this PC, which ensures that the various types of protocols are mutually compatible. In particular, this may be used to create an internetwork of different types of local area networks (for example, Token Ring and Ethernet). At the user level, the fact that an internetwork of local area networks is involved is hidden.

Fault tolerance

Novell provides a number of procedures to increase the fault tolerance of the file server. The most important of these are:

- Duplication of the FAT (file allocation table) and the directory. Both the directory and the FAT are duplicated in different areas of a disk.

- Check read and hot fix mechanism. After a write procedure, a check read of the same area is executed for comparison with the data in the RAM. If it appears that a sector of the disk is defective the data is stored in an area reserved by the installation (hot fix).

- Disk shadowing. It is possible for a file server to refer a controller to two independent disk subsystems. The data is stored on both disks. If one disk should fail, the other disk is automatically switched in.

- Channel shadowing. Here, in addition to the disks, the controller is also duplicated. An increase in speed may be achieved if in read operations, both disk systems are read in parallel and the first data found is processed.

- Transaction updating service. It is possible to define points at which an action is completed and a disk storage operation is required. This protects against inconsistencies in database systems.

- UPS monitoring. This involves intelligent deactivation, controlled by NetWare, using an uninterruptible power supply (UPS). If there is a power failure, the network subscribers are informed and if the emergency power supply fails the data and the server hard disk are protected.

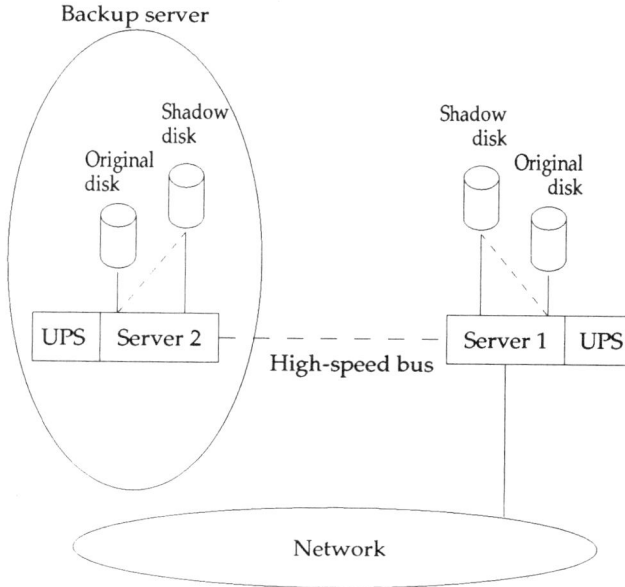

Figure 7.4   Fault tolerance – NetWare measures.

- Server shadowing. This involves both duplicated disks and duplicated file servers. These should be connected by a separate high-speed link so as not to generate an additional loading of the network. This was announced by Novell in 1986; an implementation has been available since the first quarter of 1993.

Linkage to NetWare

NetWare offers a number of add-on products with the facility for connection to WAN circuits. These may be used as follows:

- PCs or terminals may be asynchronously connected to the Novell network over dedicated or switched lines (access server).
- Foreign computers may be reached asynchronously from the Novell network (NetWare asynchronous communication server).
- Two Novell networks may be linked together asynchronously (asynchronous bridge).
- Two or more Novell networks may be linked together via X.25 (X.25 bridge).

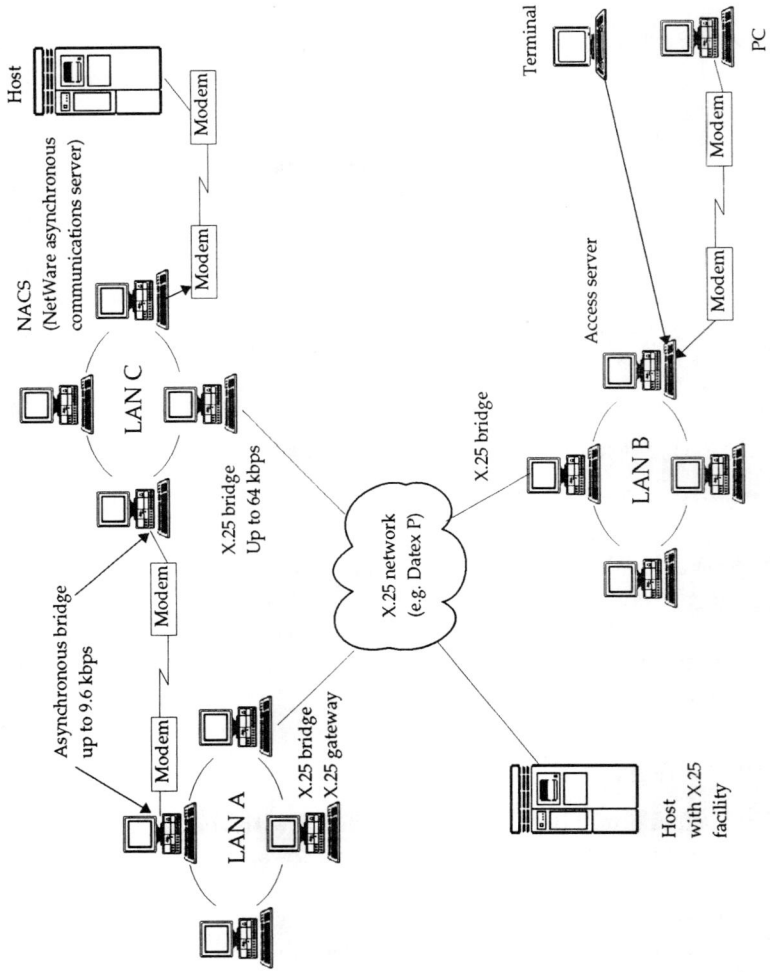

Figure 7.5 Linkage of WANs to NetWare.

- Foreign computers may be reached from a Novell network via X.25 (X.25 gateway).

Various types of NetWare SNA gateways may be used to link a Novell network into the IBM SNA world. The following possibilities exist:

- Remote linkage.
- High-speed remote linkage.
- Token Ring linkage.
- Coax linkage.
- Coax/mux linkage.

Similarly, facilities are available for linkage to IBM 5250 networks (IBM system /3X, IBM AS/400).

Opening to the rest of the DP world

The aim here is integrate the various system worlds, such as:

- PCs with DOS, Windows or OS/2
- Macintosh computers
- workstations and minicomputers with UNIX or UNIX derivatives
- mainframes with proprietary operating systems

into an overall DP structure, which may have very many levels. The task has become somewhat easier in recent years, since the number of proprietary operating systems is decreasing and the number of open operating systems is increasing (down sizing). The majority of computers now reaching the market (for example, vector and parallel computers) now use UNIX or UNIX derivatives and even large manufacturers such as IBM (AIX) and DEC (ULTRIX) are opening up to the world of UNIX systems. In addition, suppliers of a large range of applications have recognized that the only chance of survival is to integrate as many system worlds as possible (open APIs).

One subsidiary aspect is the shared use of data, which does not explicitly have a short lifetime or which is not purely related to a single workstation. The main reasons cited for central data management are consistency considerations, and simplification in the areas of data security and archiving. Usually, mainframes and minicomputers which have already been in use for a long time, and on which maintenance of the previous data will continue, are used for this or a special high-performance file server system is installed in the computer centre.

Novell realized the importance of opening the PC network to the rest of the DP world at an early stage. From the beginning, NetWare has had a built-in NetBios emulation, so that applications based on this interface may also be used under Novell.

NetWare for VMS was an early example of a product. In NetWare for VMS the Novell server runs under VAX/VMS on DEC VAX computers. Thus, the VAX computer becomes another server for a PC network. PC users can now use the resources of the VAX, where the data on the VAX is stored in the VAX's own data format. The same user IDs and passwords may be used for NetWare and for VMS. Equally, the same files may be used under both NetWare and VMS. In addition, terminal emulation software in the PC may be used to address the VAX directly.

Another step was the strategic product Portable NetWare which offered interested manufacturers of minicomputers the chance to implement the NetWare server functionality on their platforms. Currently, Portable NetWare is operated by Altos, Data General, Interactive Systems, HP, NCR, Prime and Unisys (among others), while products from IBM, Pyramid, Stratus and Sun have been announced.

However, the implementations of some of these products show that even though more powerful processors are used in the platforms of some of these companies, the server performance is often lower than that of a PC with an 80386 or 80486 processor using Novell's operating system, which is extremely well-tailored to the server requirements. However, such 'third-party' solutions are not supplied for their high server performance but in order to provide PCs in the Novell network with access to the DP world corresponding to the basic operating system used by the server (for example, UNIX). Thus, a workstation may access the UNIX server transparently, while the latter operates simultaneously as a NetWare server. Through the NetWare virtual terminal software the user has access to all UNIX applications and files. UNIX users again have access to NetWare files.

It is also possible to introduce one's own applications into the NetWare world in the form of NetWare loadable modules (NLMs). NLMs run as tasks, parallel to the operating system on the file server.

Other steps towards a general opening of the system follow from the NetWare support for TCP/IP, NFS, SNMP and NetView. For details of this the reader is referred to the relevant literature. Figure 7.6 shows the protocol support provided by NetWare. Here, the open data link interface (OPI) is offered as a common interface for network adapter cards and NetWare streams is a common interface to the applications.

With these add-on products and facilities, the term PC network is no longer justified. Not only PCs under DOS, but also PCs under OS/2 and Windows, and Macintosh PCs can now share the use of one or more file servers, where the latter may be implemented on computers with NetWare, OS/2, VMS (DEC), UNIX or VM (IBM). Thus, files and also resources such as printers, CD-ROMs, etc. in the PC, DEC, UNIX and IBM worlds may be shared via file servers.

NetWare services and server applications					
NETWARE streams					
XNS (IPX, SPX)	NetBEUI	TCP/IP	Apple Talk (AFP)	SNA	OSI
ODI (Open data link interface)					
Ethernet	Token Ring	Arcnet	. . .		SDLC

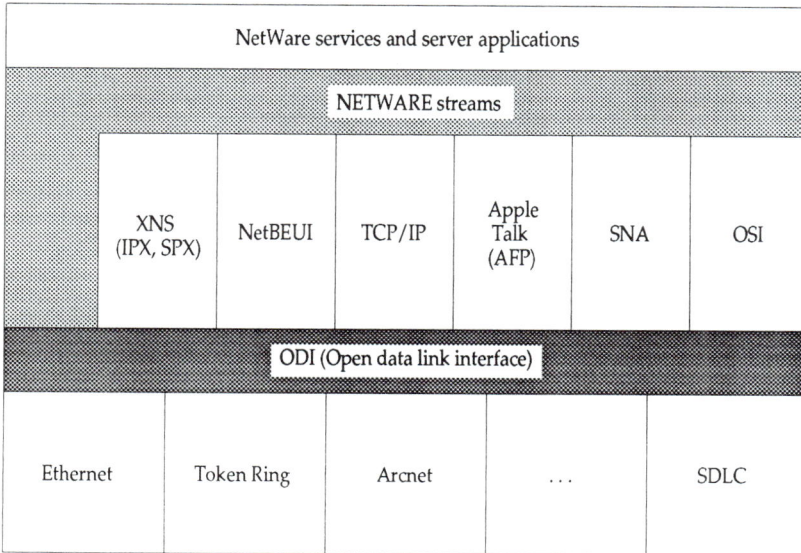

Figure 7.6   Protocol support provided by NetWare.

Product range

Novell delivers NetWare software in various modules, depending on the functionality required. The most important of these are (status – February 1992):

- **NetWare 286 v2.2**. NetWare v2.2 is designed for small-to-medium size companies, workgroups or departments. The cost per server depends on the number of connections: 5, 10, 50 or 100 users may be served simultaneously. The server may be operated in dedicated or non-dedicated mode. The server must be at least a PC with an 80286 processor and 2.5 Mbyte of RAM. Faster processors such as the 80386 and the 80486 are operated by NetWare v2.2 in the 80286 mode.

- **NetWare 386 v3.11**. NetWare v3.11 is tailored to the 80386 and subsequent processors and makes full use of their capabilities. This provides for a clear increase in performance. This version is intended for large company-wide PC networks. Here too, the cost depends on the number of servers used and the maximum number of connections which may be simultaneously active (5, 20, 50, 100, 250).

- **Netware Lite**. Netware Lite has been on the market since 1991 and is intended to cover the low-cost PC network area, in which the peer-to-peer principle is often used. Here, each PC may be both a server and a workstation. Any PC may make files and peripherals available to any other PC. NetWare Lite is only available for PCs based on DOS 3.x and above and its cost is determined on a per PC basis. It is suitable for small networks with up to 6 PCs. Of course, it does not have all of the properties of NetWare described above. If an extension of the network or integration into it of non-DOS computers is planned for a later date, NetWare v2.2 or v3.11 may be a better choice, since their futures are more certain. In general, we note the following about peer-to-peer networks:

The advantages are:

— Fast, problem-free installation of small LANs.

— Savings on additional hardware since the servers are not operated in the dedicated mode.

— Inexpensive to purchase.

The disadvantages are:

— The low performance of the server functions, since these are based on DOS.

— The limited connectivity, which is mostly restricted to DOS computers.

— The danger that data may become confused and difficult to control if the data to be shared is held on several file servers.

NetWare add-on products   Based on NetWare, an extensive market for NetWare-compatible products, ranging from interface cards for PCs (also from Novell) to applications which run in the server (for example, mail), has developed.

7.2.3 Microsoft LAN Manager

Until now, the development of the LAN Manager has been closely related to the development of OS/2. Microsoft and IBM jointly developed the basic version of OS/2, and the LAN Manager was to be based on this. IBM in its further developments has moved away from Microsoft and occasionally markets OS/2 under the name BS/2 and the LAN Manager under the name LAN Server. Microsoft has developed the LAN Manager further in conjunction with 3Com and has attempted to market this product via OEMs. 3Com was also one of the first companies to market the LAN Manager under the name 3+Open. Since 3Com pulled out of the PC-network market, Microsoft has tried to market the LAN Manager product directly. Since the LAN Manager in the server is based directly on the OS/2

Table 7.3 Overview of the functionality of NetWare v2.2 and NetWare v3.11 (taken from Datacom's NetWare guide). * denotes items which are optionally available as separate products.

	NetWare v2.2	*NetWare v3.11*
Supports PC-/MS-DOS 3.x	Yes	Yes
Supports PC-/MS-DOS 4.0	Yes	Yes
Supports PC-/MS-DOS 5.0	Yes	Yes
Supports MS-Windows 3.0	Yes	Yes
Supports OS/2 v1.3	Yes	Yes
Supports Apple Macintosh	Yes	Yes*
Supports UNIX/NFS	No	Yes*
Supports OSI FTAM/TP4	No	Yes*
SPX/IPX	Yes	Yes
NetBios	Yes	Yes
DOS named pipes	Yes	Yes
OS/2 named pipes	Yes	Yes
TCP/IP	No	Yes
AppleTalk	Yes	Yes*
Decentralized print service	Yes (VAP)	Yes (NLM)
Backup service	Yes (VAP)	Yes (NLM)
Dynamic configuration	No	Yes
Workgroup management	No	Yes
Password encryption	Yes	Yes
Asynchronous remote bridge	Yes	Yes
Resource accounting	Yes	Yes
Improved security	Yes	Yes
UPS monitoring	Yes	Yes
NetWare name service	Yes*	Yes*
Remote management facility	No	Yes
Bus support	MCA, ISA	EISA, MCA, ISA
User configuration	5, 10, 50	5, 20, 50, 100, 250
Max. hard-disk size	2 Gbyte	32 Tbyte
Max. file size	256 Mbyte	4 Gbyte
Max. no. open files	1000	100 000

operating system its success is closely related to that of OS/2. Microsoft is attempting to decrease this dependence in that in the future, it is to base the LAN Manager on Windows NT. In addition, LAN Manager server systems based on UNIX computers are increasingly being marketed by OEMs. After this rather unfortunate start, with version 2.1, a product is now available which may be considered to be a competitor with the market leader NetWare. We shall only describe those functions of the LAN Manager which are very different from the functions of NetWare.

Servers

As previously mentioned, the LAN Manager requires OS/2 (from V1.2) as a prerequisite for its server functions. Here, OS/2 facilities such as its multitasking capability, protected mode and HPFS (high performance file system) are used to increase the speed. The use of OS/2 requires a large memory in the server (at least 9 Mbytes of RAM and 80 Mbytes hard disk). Support for multiprocess servers (two processors) should be possible. In addition to the well-known NetBios interface which may also be used for interprocess communication over the network (see Section 7.1), another interface 'named pipes' is available, which is more effective, more powerful and easier for the developer to implement. This may be used to implement server schemes, for example, with an SQL database.

Workstations

Currently computers with DOS (from version 3.3), MS Windows or OS/2 (from version 1.1) with corresponding software may be connected to a single

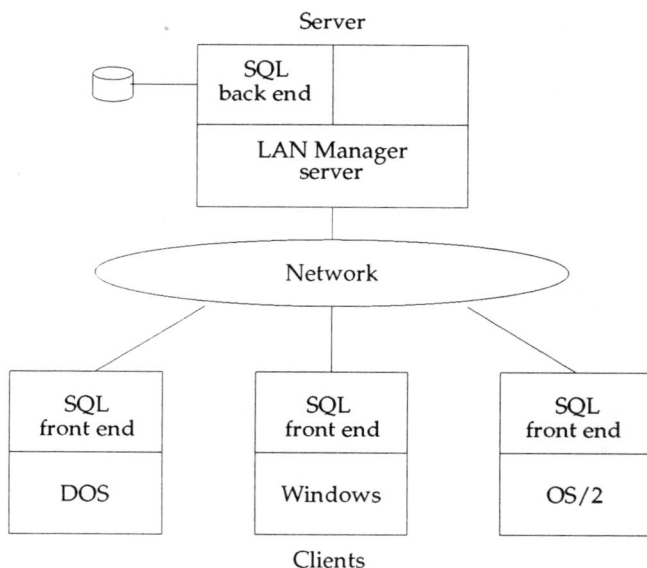

Figure 7.7   Client–server scheme with the SQL database.

network using the LAN Manager. It is also possible to link in Macintosh computers.

Peer servers

Workstations which use OS/2 (from v1.2) may act as peer servers. Stations with the peer-server software have unrestricted facilities for interprocess communication. This means that, for example, SQL servers may be implemented on these. In addition, they may make files, printers and communications adapters available to other users.

Administration

In addition to administrative facilities similar to those provided by NetWare, several servers may be combined into a domain. Thus, it is possible to bring together the overall user and group management at a single point. This has the advantage that the user has only to give one password for all resources in the domain; in other words, the user does not have to login to every server. This facility also exists for NetWare, but is only available through a relatively expensive add-on product (NetWare name service).

A copy function permits selective copying of files from one server to another at set times. Thus, important files may be held on various servers and thereby protected against failure of a server. Moreover, with a user-friendly distribution of new software versions and programs it is possible to reach all servers in a domain.

Opening to the rest of the DP world

Implementations, known under the name LAN-Manager/X, are available which are based not on OS/2 but on UNIX. Products are available from NCR, SCO, SNI, Bull and HP (among others). Linkage to NetWare is possible, so that workstations may be simultaneously connected to LAN-Manager and NetWare networks. Access to SNA environments is possible via the DCA/Microsoft communication server and VMS may be accessed via DEC PSA.

With its personal computing systems architecture (PCSA) and the PATHWORKS software, DEC has offered its own solution for linking the PC, UNIX and DEC worlds. Servers with VMS, ULTRIX or OS/2 may make their services available to workstations with DOS, OS/2 or Macintosh operating systems. The workstations have access to the file, disk, printer, mail and remote boot services of the server(s). A server under VMS permits the exchange of data between VMS and PC users. The disk service stores DOS files on the disk of the VMS server. A server under ULTRIX also permits connection to NFS. Servers under OS/2 provide access to the LAN Manager. Simultaneous access to NetWare and PATHWORKS servers is possible from DOS workstations.

An add-on product may be used to permit access from the LAN Manager PC network to TCP/IP hosts via Telnet and FTP. Linkage into network management systems is possible using SNMP or NetView.

7.2.4 Banyan Vines

Banyan first brought its networking operating system, Vines (virtual networking software), to the US market in 1983. From the beginning, Vines was designed for networking large numbers of PCs based on a single operating system within larger companies. The emphasis was attached not only to local area networks, but also to networks connecting different sites.

Banyan only moved into Europe in 1986. Currently, Banyan is mainly used by large companies which set great store by the networking of large numbers of servers in different locations. Moreover, the introductory price for Vines was so high that users of small PC networks found the option prohibitive until now. However, the price has now been adjusted to match that of the market leader, Novell. In what follows, we shall only describe those features of Vines which are very different from NetWare.

Servers

The operating system on which the server software is based is a special AT&T version of UNIX. UNIX is used even when the server is implemented on a PC with an Intel 80X86 processor. In the future, there will be a move to SCO-UNIX. UNIX and Vines require a large amount of RAM (4 Mbytes) and hard-disk (80 Mbytes) storage. Servers may be operated with up to eight processors simultaneously using Vines/SMP (symmetric multiprocessing). Currently, however, there only exist servers with two processors (for example, Compaq Systempro, ALR Powerpro).

Workstations

A workstation using Vines may have DOS, MS-Windows 3.x or OS/2 as operating system. Under DOS, the driver requires up to 115 kbytes of memory. Currently, only limited support is available for Macintosh and UNIX computers.

Global name management system

All components of the Vines network are incorporated in the Street Talk global name management system, which is based on the X.500 standard. Vines components may be services (e.g. mail service, 3270 gateway), file areas or users. Each component is automatically allocated a name. The name is associated with attributes (e.g. rights and a password). These are stored in a database which is distributed across the network as a whole.

This database provides for the introduction of newly defined objects into the network without reconfiguration. Street Talk names have a hierarchical three-level structure (Object@Group@Organization) and thus permit unique identification of objects in complicated networks. The names are stored hierarchically; in other words, there is a directory of organization names with corresponding subdirectories. In larger networks this information may be distributed over several servers. Not least because of Street Talk, these complicated networks are user-friendly as far as management is concerned, since when the Street Talk information is altered (for example, introduction of a new server via a switched connection), there is an automatic exchange of information between servers.

Facilities for communication

Banyan supplies an intelligent communication adapter card (ICA) especially for communication in the WAN area, for which an 80286 processor on the card itself permits the implementation of up to six different connections. In terms of protocols, asynchronous communication, synchronous communication (HDLC, SDLC) and X.25 are supported up to transmission speeds of 64 kbps. Table 7.4 lists possibilities for implementation using the ICA card. The card is installed in the existing servers and an additional gateway computer is not required.

Transparent server/server coupling is possible over standard or high-speed LANs, over dedicated or switched connections and over packet-oriented data networks (X.25 and IP networks).

It is very easy for the user to call host computers from the Vines network using Street Talk names, since the hosts themselves have corresponding names. The user simply calls the name, without knowing how the connection is implemented (for example, via several servers and remote lines). The following terminal emulations are supported for host connections: asynchronous, BSC/IBM 3270, SNA/IBM 3270.

Table 7.4 Possibilities for implementation using the ICA card.

ICA protocol	Vines communication services
Asynchronous	Asynchronous host connection PC dial in (remote PC) Server/server connection via switched line
SDLC	3270/SNA host linkage
HDLC	Server/server connection via dedicated lines
Datex P	Server/server connections via private and public data networks (X.25 connection)

Table 7.5 Banyan Vines product range (status – December 1991).

	Vines/286	Vines/386 Team	Vines/386	Vines/486	Vines/SMP
Number of users	5–30	3–10	5–50(+)	20–250(+)	30–500(+)
Computer supported	80286	80386	80386	80486	80386/486
Storage requirement min/max, Mbyte	4/16	N.A.	6/16	8/48	8/250
Available options					
E-mail, PC print, dial in, etc.	X	X	X	X	X
Server/server LAN	X		X	X	X
Server/server X.25		X	X	X	X
TCP/IP support			X	X	X
SNA gateways, max. sessions	32	32	96	96	96
Advanced 3270 with HLLAPI, APA		X	X	X	X
LAN adapters, max.	2	4	4	4	4
Serial communication (ports)	6	6	12	12	12

Product range

Various versions of Banyan Vines are available; the details of these are given in Table 7.5 (status – December 1991).

In summary, the strengths of Banyan Vines can be said to relate mainly to the internetworking of PC networks in the WAN area and to the linkage of external computers. Anyone who is planning this and can do without some of the features and further facilities of NetWare should take Vines into consideration.

7.2.5 Selection criteria

In what follows, we discuss some of the selection criteria which may be used to decide between available individual network operating systems. While the list is by no means complete, it may nevertheless serve as a guide.

The choice of a network operating system depends essentially on the following factors:

- The computers which are to be used as workstations.
- The computers which are to be used as file, database or communications servers.
- The performance of the server computers.
- The facilities for connecting high-speed peripheral devices to the server computers.
- The security at the various levels.
- The extensibility and the performance capacity of the network.
- The facilities for connection to foreign host systems and workstations.
- The facility for including electronic mail, facsimile, telephone and ISDN connections.

Server computers

Assuming that we are concerned with the implementation of network operating system software for LANs on a central server computer, the following conditions are important.

- The server must contain an implementation of a file system which can provide for fast and (at the same time) secure access to the applications and data, which may be simultaneously used by all stations.
- The server must provide for efficient control of all data input/output operations. This may be achieved using various caching mechanisms.

The intermediate storage of data in the RAM (file caching), for example, prevents unnecessary access to the hard disk.

- The server operating system should make full use of the computational and addressing facilities of the CPU used. In high-powered applications, it should also be possible to use multiprocessor servers.

- It must be possible to connect and operate high-grade peripherals (for example, hard disks with a high storage capacity, backup drives, CD ROM drives).

- It must be possible to integrate various LANs in the server computer and to connect to the WAN world.

- It must at least be possible to integrate the server computer into a central network management system (for example, SNMP, NetView).

Security

Since server computers and the managed data on them are central resources which may be accessed simultaneously by many users, the availability of these and their protection against misuse are important. The following considerations are helpful:

- Uninterruptible power supply at the server-computer hardware level; redundant data management with duplicated or shadowed hard disks, automatic backup or even duplicated servers.

- On the workstation side, diskless stations which may be loaded by remote booting.

- Restriction of access to the server via logon with user names, passwords, station addresses and timeouts.

- Security procedures at the volume, directory and file levels using different user (group) access rights.

- Security at the application level in multiuser operation using file, record and semaphore locking together with transaction control.

Installation

This covers all the activities involved in preparing the system for use. This includes, for example, the entry of user IDs and passwords, the initialization of the server including the preparation of shared files (can existing directories be used without modification?), and the installation of the individual workstations. Important criteria include the time required and whether the installation may be executed statically or dynamically.

Management tasks

It should be possible to monitor many aspects of an operational network operating system locally or over the network (remote). This begins with a check as to which objects (files, printers) are reserved for which users. In addition, it should be possible to check that individual servers are operational and, if necessary, to start these up without disturbing the rest of the network. It may also be interesting to determine which workstations are being used by which users. This may be extended to the question of a facility to provide usage and accounting statistics. The manner in which new users, workstations or servers are introduced to or removed from the distributed system is also important.

Maximum network size

The maximum network size naturally depends heavily on the applications required. In addition, many details of the implementation also play an important role. PC networks with around 100 or more stations may now be used.

Performance of PC networks

It is virtually impossible to give a global overview of the performance capability of PC networks. The reasons for this include the variety of system environments which must potentially be considered, and the rapid release of changed hardware and software versions.

However, we shall give a number of values which, by way of example, illustrate the differences between individual network operating systems (from PC Professional 9/91). An Ethernet configuration was measured, Western Digital (WD) 8- and 16-bit and Novell (NV) NE2000 adapter cards were used and the file server was a Compuadd 333T (80386 processor at 33 MHz).

The measurements were carried out using a server and four workstations. Each station randomly accessed data records of size 1 kbyte of a server file of overall size 100 kbytes, in which the data was altered each time. The values given in Table 7.6 are relative, in the sense that higher values represent better results.

From the test results, it is striking that the performance of the LAN Manager is considerably higher when cards from different manufacturers are used than when cards from the same manufacturer are used in the server and in the workstations. Table 7.7 gives a comparison of the three products described for PC networks.

The comparison does indicate differences, however, these mainly relate to maximum values which, in reality, are rarely reached. Overall, we note that, at least as far as the leading network operating systems

Table 7.6 Performance measurements for network operating systems with adapter cards.

Network operating system	Adapter card	Value
LAN Manager stations	WD cards	0.28
LAN Manager stations	NV cards	0.18
LAN Manager server LAN Manager workstations	WD card NV cards	1.10
Novell v3.11 stations	NV cards	1.22
Novell v2.2 stations	NV cards	1.16
Novell v2.2 stations	WD cards	1.24
Vines stations	WD cards	0.33

are concerned, the times of major differences both of functionality and of performance are past.

7.3 Distributed systems in the UNIX world

After the discussion of PC networks, we next consider distributed systems in the UNIX world. The main difference, as far as the system concept is concerned is as follows.

In the case of PC networks, in general, single-user workstations are connected to various server systems over a network. Thus, conceptually, there is a clear division between workstations and server systems.

When UNIX systems, in which individual systems (usually multiuser systems) are linked, the picture is usually somewhat different. Here, each system acts as a workstation (client) and as a server, simultaneously. One important goal when internetworking these networks is to create a network-wide distributed file system. In what follows, we shall use the Network File System (NFS, Sun), the Remote File System (RFS, AT&T) and the Andrew File System (AFS, Carnegie-Mellon University) to illustrate the associated intentions.

7.3.1 Network File System (NFS)

Sun's Network File System (NFS), which was developed in 1984, is designed to implement a common file management (file sharing) in a network consisting of different computer systems with a wide range of operating

Table 7.7 Comparison of network operating systems.

	NetWare v2.2	NetWare v3.11	LAN Manager	Vines
Servers				
Basic operating system	Proprietary	Proprietary	OS/2	UNIX
Disk format	Proprietary	Proprietary	HPFS, FAT	UNIX
Network cards in server (max)	4	16	8	4
RAM storage requirement	2 Mbyte	4 Mbyte	9 Mbyte	4 Mbyte
File systems				
No. open files (max)	1000	100 000	32 000	999
No. disks per server (max)	32	1024	No max	7
Disk storage (max)	2.2 Gbyte	32 Tbyte	2199 Gbyte	5 Gbyte
Max. file size	255 Mbyte	32 Tbyte	2199 Gbyte	No max
File over several disks	No	Yes	No	No
Security				
Shadowed disks	Yes	Yes	With HPFS	No
Access controlled by date and time	Yes	Yes	Yes	Yes
Password encrypted on network	Yes	Yes	Yes	Yes

Table 7.7 *(continuation).*

	NetWare v2.2	NetWare v3.11	LAN Manager	Vines
Network size				
Max. connections per server	100	250	1000	No max
Management				
Fault and status files	Yes	Yes	No	Yes
Display faulty network packets	Yes	Yes	Yes	Yes
Display network faults	Yes	Yes	Yes	Yes
Display open files	Yes	Yes	Yes	Yes
Display users logged in	Yes	Yes	Yes	Yes
Display current server load	Yes	Yes	No	Yes
Printers				
Printer spooler	Yes	Yes	Yes	Yes
Modification by users	Yes	Yes	Yes	Yes
No. printers supported	No max	No max	9	10
Print on workstation printer	Yes	Yes	OS/2 stations only	Yes

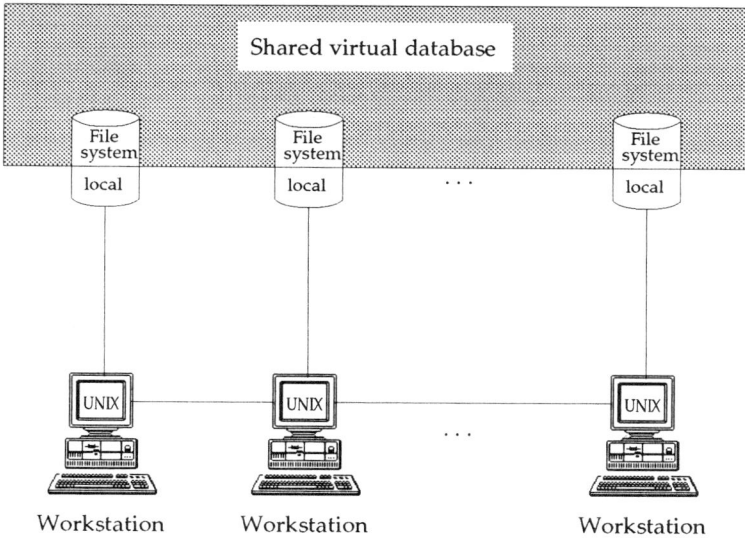

Figure 7.8   Integrated network of UNIX workstations.

systems. The associated interfaces and protocols have been published by Sun. NFS was incorporated as a standard with the TCP/IP protocols in SunOS (a UNIX BSD derivative). Since 1989, NFS has also been a built-in component of AT&T's UNIX System V. Other implementations exist for a number of operating systems, including MS-DOS (PC-NFS). Thus, in UNIX environments, NFS has become a standard. NFS provides transparent access to the files on a server, where, according to design criteria, the access speed for the server disk should be at least 80% of the access speed for the local disk. Thus, diskless workstations may also be used in the network. NFS is based on the protocols of the TCP/IP protocol family, but extends upon the facilities of FTP and Telnet in that it also permits record-wise access to remote files. FTP, on the other hand, only provides for a complete file transfer.

In addition, NFS generalizes the original UNIX mount command to foreign remote file systems. The user is allowed to see directories and files of one or more remote computers as part of his own local logical file system. System calls to this virtual file system are checked before execution to see whether they are to be sent to the local file system or as a message to a remote file system to be processed in a server. The access to the virtual file system is transparent to the system call. Thus, NFS implements a distributed file system.

Because of the available communications performance, the facilities

1. Initial situation

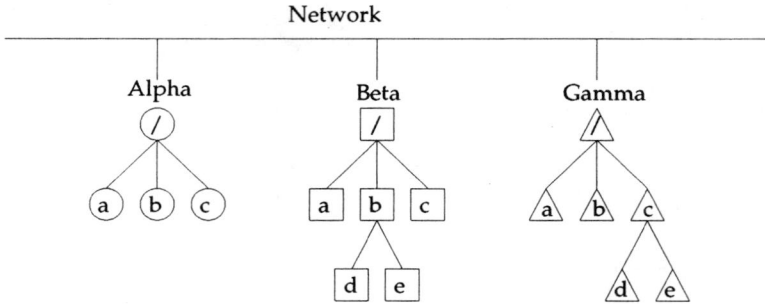

2. After the 'mount' commands on the systems Alpha and Gamma

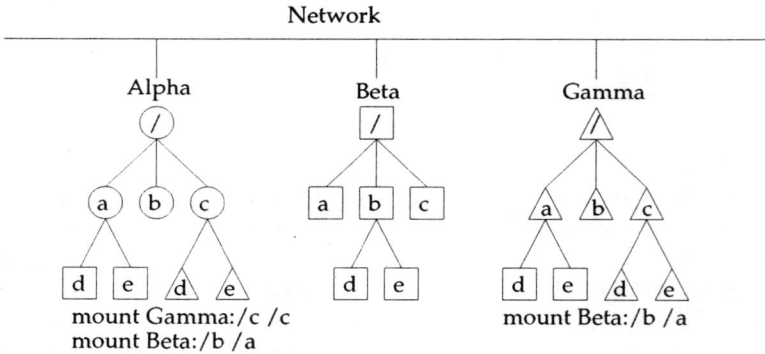

Figure 7.9 Mount process.

provided by NFS can only be sensibly used in networks with high transmission rates. Thus, the combination of NFS with Ethernet LANs is particularly important. NFS is less suitable for applications which operate over low-speed WANs (for example, 64 kbps) since, because the network transfer rates are far lower than the disk transfer rates, perceptible bottlenecks may occur in the network.

Various protocols form the basis for an NFS implementation. Table 7.8 shows how these protocols fit into the OSI layer model.

The transport protocol used is not TCP/IP but the simpler, connectionless and thus more effective UDP (see Section 6.3.3).

Table 7.8   NFS protocol layering.

OSI	NFS layer protocols		
Application	NFS, Mount, NIS (YP)		
Presentation	XDR		
Session	RPC		
Transport	UDP		
Network	IP		
Data link	CSMA/CD	Token	Token
Physical	Bus	Bus	Ring

Key: NFS   Network File System
      NIS   Network Information System
      YP   Yellow Pages
      XDR   External Data Representation
      RPC   Remote Procedure Call
      UDP   User Datagram Protocol
      IP   Internet Protocol

Remote procedure calls (RPCs) come under OSI layer 5. They were specifically designed for NFS and are semantically similar to the normal synchronous procedure calls of programming languages. Remote procedure calls are a very powerful (hardware- and software-independent) tool for specifying and transmitting function calls in a network, supplying these calls with parameters and causing them to be executed on a remote server. The server then transmits the result of a call to the initiator (client). Security-related weaknesses of RPC (for example, the transmission of unencrypted data on the network) have now been removed with the definition of 'secure RPC'.

The External Data Representation standard (XDR) corresponds to the presentation layer of the OSI layer model and specifies the permitted formats for data being transmitted. It solves problems due to differences in hardware and data presentation formats. XDR also covers a library of conversion routines which provide for adaptation of the various formats. This library is specific to each destination system.

The NFS application services of OSI layer 7 specify operations which are needed to access a hierarchical file system via a network. They recognize directories, files and bytes within files as standard elements. In addition to the NFS service functions the mount service is another application layer program. This links the remote file system of the server into a logical local

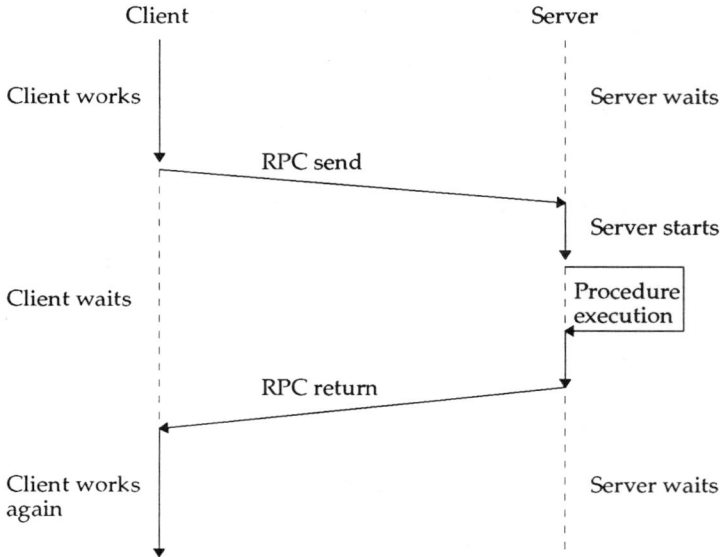

Figure 7.10 Remote procedure call.

file system of the client. Mounting does not involve data transmission, nor does it involve conversion from different data formats. A problem arises as a result of the different file-name conventions for different operating systems. For example, in DOS all file names are in upper case, while upper and lower case are permitted under UNIX. Many UNIX file names cannot be represented under DOS, however this is circumvented in NFS by the use of special characters. One other application-layer service is the so-called Network Information System (NIS), which was previously known as Yellow Pages (YP) (this name had to be altered because of copyright problems). NIS is a directory service. A prerequisite for proper authorization of access to server resources in NFS is that identical user IDs and user numbers are used on both computers (client and server). It would be very expensive to maintain this information about users without automatic matching. NIS provides for a considerable simplification. One computer in the network is identified as the NIS master and maintains a central user file. NIS programs in the individual computers ensure, by communicating with the NIS master that the required information is available locally. The NIS service is not limited to the management of user information, but may also be used for central network-wide management of general information (e.g. internet addresses, Ethernet addresses) in the form of tables.

7.3.2 Remote File Sharing system (RFS)

AT&T's Remote File Sharing system is another implementation of a network-wide file system. It is a component of UNIX Version V Release 3, and as such is intended to connect UNIX systems. Unlike Sun's NFS, which is designed with the construction of a heterogeneous system with shared databases in mind, RFS is only important for the (homogeneous) UNIX System V world. RFS permits network-wide access not only to files of any type, but also to special devices (which are handled like UNIX files) and 'named pipes'.

The most important design objectives of RFS were:

- Transparent access. The standard UNIX interface was to be preserved; in other words, as far as the user is concerned, there was to be no difference between local and remote file access.

- Semantically faithful. The semantics of previous (local) file operations were to be preserved; in particular, file and record locking of non-local files was also be possible.

- Compatibility. Existing applications should also be able to access non-local files without re-translation.

- Independence from the network. RFS was to be designed in such a way that it would be cleanly separated from the underlying network. In particular, it should be possible to run it over both LANs and WANs, without modification.

- Portability. As far as possible, RFS code was to be hardware independent. This was intended to provide for fast and simple portability to other systems.

- Performance pattern. Because of the fact that every access to non-local resources generates a significant overhead, the number of accesses to the network was to be minimized.

RFS is based on the so-called client–server model, in which each client system requests a service which is provided by a server system. The assignment of the client and the server refers to a specific job relationship. In another job relationship, this assignment may be exactly reversed. RFS does not permit diskless workstations or clients only (for example, DOS PC).

An RFS network may be viewed as a network of several file management systems (which are located on every computer in the network). A so-called name server ensures that the individual objects (files) in this overall system are callable and may be distinguished by name. The name space is divided into domains and has two levels. Each domain has a central name server which ensures that the symbolic names are unique within the domain. When a connection is established between a client and a server system the name server is involved. It is responsible for determining the location of the carrier system in which the desired file is to be found. In the next step a so-called 'remote mounting' procedure is used to incorporate the target file in the client's file hierarchy. From this point, the file is indistinguishable from a local file as far as users or application programs are concerned.

The UNIX system calls of the kernel (streams and remote system calls) are used for communication between client and server. When, for example, such a call addresses a file on a remote system a so-called 'request message' is generated and sent there; this carries with it all the information needed for the processing as a whole. The actual processing of the system call is followed by a 'response message' which transports the result back to the initiator.

In order to achieve the desired independence from the network used, clear interfaces must be defined between RFS and the network and the required network functions must be defined. Here, unlike in NFS, connection-oriented connection between a client and a server machine was chosen. Moreover, various different job relationships may be handled over an existing connection using the multiplex procedure.

One particular problem of distributed systems is the question of access protection and secure access. How does a user prove his identity and his authorization to access a certain file? How can a server machine trust a check of a user's identity carried out on a client machine? Firstly, each client machine must prove its identity to the server machine. This can be done using a special password. At the user level the UNIX security concept is extended to the network environment and the user ID of a user on a client machine is mapped onto another user ID on a server machine. Thus, different levels of access authorization are possible on different machines.

7.3.3 Andrew File System (AFS)

Like NFS and RFS, the Andrew File System (AFS) is also a distributed file system. It was developed by Carnegie-Mellon University and is currently marketed as a commercial product by Transarc Cooperation. AFS is intended for an integrated network of a large number of workstations and PCs, which may extend not only over the LAN area, but also over the WAN area. AFS has been chosen as the distributed file system by the Open Software Foundation (OSF) in the context of the Distributed Computing Environment (DCE).

OSF is an association of almost all important DP manufacturers which was founded in 1988 (it now has more than 280 members including IBM, HP, DEC and SNI) which aims to develop strategic guidelines and standards for common interoperable system environments. Important achievements of OSF to date include a common UNIX-based operating system (OSF/1) and the graphical user interface (GUI) OSF/MOTIF. DCE is not a new network operating system but a collection of proven concepts and products for creating future networked client–server environments. Similar plans are in hand for a Distributed Management Environment (DME).

AFS has the following notable features:

- A common global name space. Users always address files with the same path name, regardless of the computer used. This provides for fully transparent access to local and remote files, including those in other cells; the actual location of the file is not known to the user.

- Caching on the client side. File-system management information, and also, if necessary, file fragments are held by the client. Firstly this reduces the network load; secondly, when the data is held locally, use may be made of the faster access to the local disk. The consistency of the data in the cache is maintained by management of state information.

- Division into cells. Areas with servers and clients which are managed by a single organization may be divided into cells, for each of which a system administrator, who manages, monitors and maintains the cell, is responsible. (This corresponds to a domain concept.)

- Security. This is increased by encrypting passwords in the network and monitoring file access based on verified user IDs. In addition, all data relevant to authorization and authentication lies in a secure cell server (Kerberos). For example, an individual login process is necessary for access to AFS.

- Availability. For reasons of security and reliability, several copies of data are kept within a cell (replication). Only read access to duplicates is available. In the case of failure, the tasks are dynamically redistributed by the server. AFS has a built-in backup system which provides for the generation of consistent material without interruption to the system.

- Implementation in the UNIX kernel. The most important functions are implemented in the UNIX kernel. On UNIX systems this provides for true transparency, high performance capability and good portability.

Clients and servers are connected by RPC (not the same as NFS RPC). The cache manager on the client corresponds to the protocol exporter on the file server. Access to data is synchronized by a token mechanism. The existing physical file system on the file server, which is called an episode, is based on logical partitions which are configured independently of physical partitions and which represent management entities for replication, reconfiguration and backup. AFS is based on an extended virtual file system which is in

AFS client			AFS server	
User applications		RPC calls	Token manager Host module Replication server	Fileset server BOS server
System calls			System calls	Protocol exporter
Virtual file system			Virtual file system	
Cache manager	Local file system		Cache manager	Episode file system

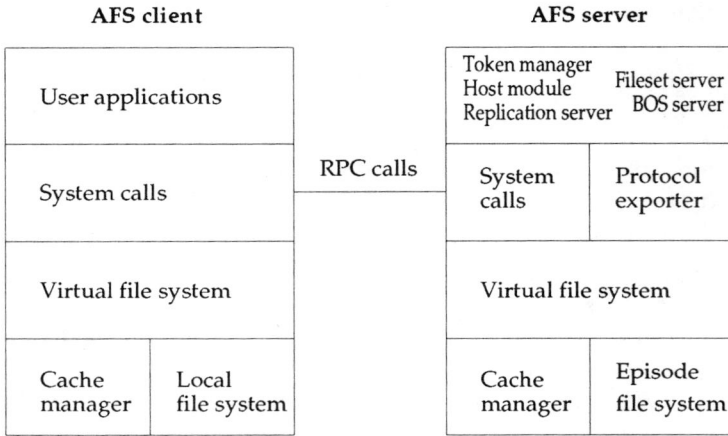

Figure 7.11   AFS architecture.

principle compatible with that of NFS. At the level of operations, it is possible to create gateways to other distributed file systems (AFS/NFS translator); however, the safeguarding of the security functions is a problem.

7.3.4 Evaluation

Any evaluation of the above distributed file systems, NFS, RFS and AFS, must be made against the background of the computers, operating systems and networks involved.

NFS was developed by Sun as an operating-system-independent tool. Over 100 different manufacturers now offer NFS on UNIX systems (BSD and System V), UNIX derivatives (for example, XENIX, ULTRIX, AIX) and non-UNIX systems (for example, MS-DOS, DEC VMS, IBM VM) for all possible computers (from PCs to mainframes). The files are incorporated in a virtual file system which thus does not support all UNIX operations (for example, access to remote devices, file locking, file appending). NFS is primarily suitable for LANs; as far as use in WANs is concerned, only a limited recommendation can be given, because of the high communications requirements. NFS also has a weakness in the security area, since the remotely attached file system depends on the security system of the remote machine. Thus, if access authorization is handled carelessly, it is easy for third parties to gain unauthorized access to data. There is no comprehensive protection system, since this is almost impossible because of conceivable

Table 7.9 Comparison of NFS and RFS.

	NFS	RFS
Manufacturer	Sun	AT&T
Year introduced	1985	1986
Functionality	Network file system	Distributed file system
	Remote execution	
	NIS	
	Diskless workstation	
Transparent access to remote files	Yes	Yes
Access to all types of files	No	Yes
	(all except special files and named pipes)	
Server system semantics conserved	No	Yes
Type of connection	Datagram	Virtual circuit
Stateless protocol	Yes	No
File and record locking	In future (records)	Yes
Authentication mechanisms	Yes, user and machine	–
File caching	Server + client	Server
Operating system independent	Yes	No
Implementations	Most UNIX systems, MS-DOS, VMS, VM	UNIX V
Architecture independent	Yes	Yes
Transport system independent	Yes	Yes
Name service	Distributed via NIS	Central

285

reciprocal mount processes. Thus, a typical NFS system does not have a tree structure but is a root system with many references. However, because of its broad distribution, NFS is currently the predominant distributed file system. Together with PC-NFS, it forms a good link between the PC-DOS and the WS-UNIX worlds. For example, NFS has been used for some years at several sites to supply software to DOS PCs, where the server is a UNIX system, on which full use is made of UNIX's good file protection mechanisms.

Because of its design, RFS is restricted to UNIX System V environments. However, there, it is so fully embedded in UNIX that differences between local and remote files are only visible when problems with the network or the remote server arise. Thus, RFS is best suited for systems with UNIX System V; however, it is not possible to integrate a computer with a different operating system (including UNIX BSD). Moreover, AT&T has not published its protocol for RFS and the licences are expensive. RFS appears to be the loser in the race with NFS – even AT&T supplies its UNIX System from Version 4 with RFS and NFS. Table 7.9 gives a comparison of RFS and NFS.

AFS may be viewed as the secret victor over NFS. OSF's decision against NFS and in favour of AFS may result in an undreamt of increase in AFS implementations in the forthcoming years, despite the current broad distribution of NFS. Differing in some respects from NFS, AFS has the following features:

- The formation of names for directories and files is consistent over all systems.
- Coherent system management is available from anywhere in the system.
- It has a protection and access control mechanism.
- The availability of the data is high.
- It has an extensive granularity even for very large configurations, without a significant loss of performance.
- It is also suitable for the WAN area.
- It has a gateway to NFS.

AFS is currently available on IBM, HP, Sun, DEC and NeXT computers; it is being developed for other systems.

Chapter 8

Operational aspects and network management

- Planning LANs

- Cabling strategies

- Network management architectures

- Tools and devices for operational support

- Operational aspects in LANs

- Ethernet LANs at the Leibniz Computing Centre

The final chapter of this book deals with aspects which concern the network provider, namely network planning, the selection of products and the operation of the network. Many of the questions considered are in no way specific to Ethernet; most of the topics covered in what follows are relevant to a larger class of networks. However, the LAN-specific experience which forms the basis for the following sections was predominantly gained on Ethernet LANs.

The comments on LAN management relate principally to typical questions which arise in relation to the planning and operation of LAN communication infrastructures for all areas of DP provision; thus, larger networks are to the fore in our considerations. When a single PC network consisting of a small number of homogeneous PCs is connected over an Ethernet LAN, many of the problems are irrelevant.

Section 8.1 is concerned with planning aspects. It includes an explanation of the embedding of LANs in DP-service structures and discusses the analytical steps which are needed when planning networks as a communication infrastructure. It ends with a further discussion of the criteria for choosing LAN components.

Section 8.2 is devoted to cabling strategies. This takes account of the need for transmission-related integration; in other words the ability to operate different logical networks over a single physical cable structure.

Section 8.3 is concerned with standardized network management architectures as a prerequisite for integrated network management systems. The architectural approaches of ISO, IEEE and internet are described. The latter, together with the SNMP management protocol, is particularly important in the practical application of LANs.

Section 8.4 describes the facilities provided by various network management tools, ranging from devices for monitoring the Ethernet cable structure to integrated network management systems.

Section 8.5 contains a detailed discussion of the operational aspects of LANs. These are presented for the various functional areas of network management.

The chapter ends with a description of the very extensive communication structures of the Leibniz Computer Centre (LRZ), which is the environment in which the authors of this book gained their experience of LANs.

8.1 Planning LANs

CCITT defines the network planning task as follows:
'Network planning is the continual interactive process of

- monitoring the current network characteristics

- understanding environmental constraints/considerations
- forecasting future needs and technology
- evaluating technical opportunity
- creating the most appropriate, consistent and coordinated plans on a long-, medium- and short-term basis
- modifying plans based on results of actual implementations

in order to provide ongoing cost-effective and timely communication service to users.'

This definition makes it quite clear that network planning is an interactive process. Moreover, it states that networks are only one subsystem of an institution's overall system concept, although they are also of infrastructural importance. The company objectives are paramount; there is strong interaction between the organizational structure (structural organization, operational organization) and the underlying model of information flow within the company.

The planning relates not only to the network and its topology, the physical and logical network structure (whence the cabling structure, the network components and the protocol hierarchies), but also to the embedding in the other DP-service structures and the technical operational scheme (whence the monitoring procedures, the operating of the network and the management tools).

8.1.1 Embedding of LANs in DP-service structures

Only in the rarest of cases is it possible to plan a network in a void or to devise a network for a self-contained application. The embedding in and the interworking with other DP-service structures, together with the consideration of organizational structures, constitute further requirements on local area networks.

The structural and operational organization affects how distributed tasks are coordinated within a company; this has a decisive influence on the distribution of CPU capacities, storage capacities, server functions, applications, data, I/O devices and workstation systems and the extent to which these are decentralized. This distribution in turn has a direct effect on the network planning because it determines the traffic volumes, the topology, the installation costs and the operational requirements.

The overall service area of a company is divided into subareas, which may be based on:

- Organizational subdivision (for example, group, department, area).
- Spatial subdivision (for example, building, building complex, separate site).

- DP hierarchies (for example, departmental computers of various capacities, servers with different ranges of functions).

These subdivisions may lead to service levels with a layer-specific DP service. Thus, multilevel service schemes develop. Examples of service levels include:

- In the production environment:
    — Field level: sensors, actuators, DNC machines, robots.
    — Process/device-control level: process and test monitoring, procedure management, process control technology.
    — Production- or laboratory-control level: logical, technical and business-management tasks.
    — Company level: execution of administrative, business-management and company-political tasks.
- In the university environment:
    — Level 1: user workstations.
    — Level 2: decentralized local shared services (servers assigned to a group or a department, expensive I/O devices, departmental DP systems).
    — Level 3: area of computer centre hosts, central database, central server.
    — Level 4: high-performance computers (large mainframe, vector computers), archive server.

These examples show not only that the computers corresponding to different levels are very different, but also that the level-specific communication requirements may also be very different in terms of:

- The nature and frequency of the data transfer (transaction characteristics).
- The nature of the data to be exchanged (signals, dialogue, files, reports, graphics).
- The extent of real-time requirements.
- The requirements relating to linkage of the stations (for example, device interfaces).
- Connection structures, topology, installation requirements.

This may result in different network structures for the corresponding layers, for example:

- Industrial network (industry bus, field bus).

- PC network (Ethernet, Token Ring).

- Minicomputer network, integrated network of workstations (Ethernet, Token Ring).

- Mainframe network (for example, SNA).

- Terminal network (for example, NET/ONE).

- Computer centre network (backend network, for example, Ultranet, FDDI).

The subnetworks (the networks corresponding to the individual service levels) have different HW interfaces, transmission rates, protocol profiles and network services.

The necessary interworking of the different service areas (Figure 8.1) gives rise to requirements on:

- Switching services.

- I/O routing.

- The concentrator function.

- Interfaces to PTT services.

- Interfaces to manufacturer networks, PBXs.

- Shared services, server functions.

- Security aspects (separation of subareas, formation of closed user groups).

Subareas often contain LAN segments or multisegment LANs. For the junction between subareas of the same level, it is advisable to use separating network components such as bridges, routers or brouters. Extensive subareas may be used, for example, for backbone solutions. Depending on their size, these may be independent management domains.

Local area networks should be sufficiently modular that, within a certain environment, they are open to alterations during the lifetime of the network, which may involve:

- Introduction of network subscribers.

- Introduction of new application areas and information types.

- Alteration of the network load.

- Internetworking.

- Movement of network subscribers and components.

This wish list affects the capacity of transmission media and the network access units and the hierarchy of the protocols used (or those which may be used).

Access to external networks

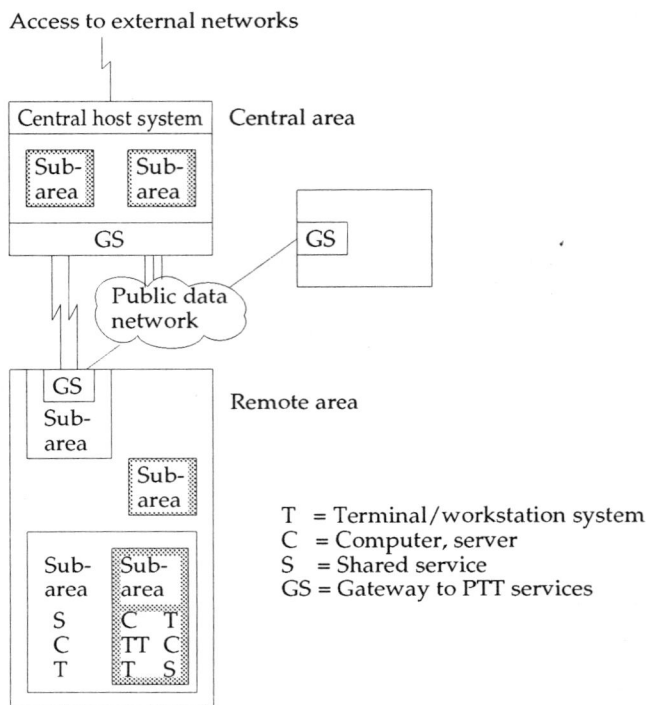

Figure 8.1   Subdivision of the service area into subareas.

8.1.2 Preparatory analyses prior to using a LAN

The following analyses should be carried out as essential subtasks of the planning of all larger networks.

8.1.2.1 Analysis of applications

Here, the qualitative information flows, the network users and the network services implied and anticipated by the application-related requirements should be listed. The analysis of the applications describes the purposes for which the network is used. Determination of the profiles of application-related requirements is important to the choice of the right network technology. This stock-taking involves answering the following questions:

- Which subtasks are currently covered by which procedures? Which should be covered in the future?
- Which points and which members of staff require which information?

- What are the organizational and communication-related connections and interfaces between departments/areas?

An application profile is described in terms of breadth, volume and robustness (Neumair, 1986).

The breadth of a profile defines the range of the applications which are to be supported, for example:

- Classical office work (for example, dealing with correspondence, electronic mail, diary management).

- Commercial DP (for example, transfer of material data, production data, stock data).

- Technical DP (for example, process monitoring, control and logging of measurement and weighing processes).

- DP management (for example, remote loading of software, data saving and archiving).

The volume of a profile defines the numerousness of the applications and their distribution over time; this is outlined by the following questions:

- How many potential users are there?

- How many users are there normally?

- Which applications are seldom used, which are frequently used?

The robustness of an application profile is determined by the capacity- and security-related requirements imposed by the applications. Examples here include:

- To what extent can loss of data be tolerated?

- How flexible can the reaction of an application to a network fault or outage be?

- What are the data protection requirements?

- What are the fault detection requirements?

This task must also involve:

- a high-level description of the applications to be executed over the LAN, including, for example:

    — integrated networks of workstations with a shared laser printer and a gateway to public data networks,

    — file transfer between data acquisition stations and the central data management system,

- — rapidly accessible document archiving for associated word processing systems,
- — interactive access to various host computers,
- — backbones to link PC clusters and networks;
- a description of the direct network users, including, for example:
    - — asynchronous terminals,
    - — PCs with integrated controllers,
    - — a specific database system,
    - — a file transfer program,
    - — a gateway,
    - — a host computer,
    - — a monitoring facility,
    - — a network monitor station;
- a description of the network services, including:
    - — transport services,
    - — network management services,
    - — server performance,
    - — data protection aspects,
    - — user interfaces.

This exercise may be used to derive a service architecture. This involves the development of a clear view of how the tasks should be distributed across the LAN being planned and any relevant existing communications networks. The result may be a preference for a particular application-oriented LAN or a more transport-oriented LAN.

8.1.2.2 Analysis of locations with communication needs

The aim of this section is to derive structural diagrams such as Figure 8.1. These are used to determine the spatial distribution of network users and that of closed user groups, organizational units, building complexes, postal boundaries, etc.

This information serves as an important basis for the following decisions:

- choice of topology;
- location of terminals and computers;
- arrangement of server facilities (shared resources);
- cabling structure;

- gateways to PTT services;
- arrangement of access-protection components (for example, filters, encryption devices, accounting devices);
- location of switching devices, repeaters, bridges, routers.

8.1.2.3 Quantitative assessment of needs

Following the previous steps, a statement about the information types and the transaction characteristics is required.

Examples of information types include: text, binary data, vector graphics, raster graphics, digitized speech, hi-fi audio information, moving pictures (video), etc. Thus, it is important to determine the types of information to be transmitted since different information types impose different requirements on the network as far as the transmission bandwidth, the storage, the real-time processing, the switching technology and the fault-handling are concerned. For example, (on-line) transmission of speech requires a special frequency band and a low delay; however, as a consequence of the high redundancy of speech and the physiological properties of the ear the reliability and error-rate requirements are lower than those for data transmission. Video data requires a far higher transmission rate (10^7–10^8 bps) than data dialogue (10^4–10^5 bps) or facsimile (10^6 bps) transmission.

The transaction characteristics cover the volume- and time-related distribution of the interactions arising from the communications relationships handled over the LAN (number of subscribers, connection type, operating mode, interaction frequency, type and volume of information per interaction, time requirements).

These differ greatly for, for example, the following applications: dialogue, data entry, batch applications (RJE), measured data acquisition, information systems (information retrieval), teleworking, file transfer.

The transaction characteristics may normally be specified using only very approximate values. Using a list of devices and applications which access the network directly, an attempt should be made to give a rough estimate of typical, application-specific message lengths (for example, screen contents, file sizes, transport segments, etc.). Next, the transfer rates for all relevant pairs of network users and applications should be determined (average values, peak loads).

These figures may be used to determine the traffic load requirements for each subscriber and thus for the network stations via which the subscribers access the LAN. The sum of the peak loads of all subscribers is an upper bound for the network load and provides a guide to the bandwidth required, assuming that the peak loads occur at the same time.

An optimal layout for a DP system can only be designed with respect to a specific load situation. The determination of the load to be carried by the system is a very complicated task. Very often, it is impossible to give a clear definition of the load for an individual user and the system layout has to take into account a number of very different load situations (daytime or night-time operation, regular weekly or monthly system loads). Thus, the flexibility of the system design in respect of possibly very different situations plays a major role. There are various approaches for characterizing load situations.

Specification of the system/network performance in the form of a description of the potential performance is closely related to the specification of the system/network load, although, conceptually, these should be clearly distinguished. The required performance must always relate to the previously defined loads.

The most popular performance indicators are:

- Throughput (channel, port, total rate, network).
- Delay (system response time, round-trip delay, connection-establishment time, switching time, waiting times in network components).

We note that these may be conflicting target quantities. Maximization of the throughput is not always equivalent to minimization of the delay.

8.1.2.4 Terminal analysis

This is used to determine the types and numbers of devices to be connected to the LAN (terminals, workstation systems, servers, host computers, real-time computing peripherals).

Since, in general, it cannot be assumed that all subscriber devices have built-in LAN access units (e.g. Ethernet controllers), they may have to be attached to independent network access units (e.g. terminal servers, network interface units (NIUs)). Thus, when analysing terminals, one must also determine the interface characteristics (connectors, pin assignment, procedures supported, parameters such as data rates, parity, etc.).

8.1.2.5 Cable-path analysis

Following the analysis of the spatial distribution of communication needs favourable cable paths must be determined. Bearing in mind the required bandwidths, one must check the extent to which existing cables may be used. For this, cable types and electrical and mechanical characteristics, etc. must be determined. The restrictions for the installation must be investigated. These relate to the rooms for the network components and data terminals, cable shafts, positions for outlets, amplifiers, taps, transceivers and head ends, and to the distances involved. Electromagnetic interference, for example, on paths through production areas, or climatic conditions may lead to requirements in terms of shielding properties or sheath composition.

One should also check the minimum radii of corners for laying purposes and the distances to be bridged.

This analysis determines possible cable paths and thus alternative topologies. On this basis, one can check whether the desired network connections lead to restrictions on the choice of the LAN. Moreover, not all LANs support all topologies. In addition, different system restrictions apply to the individual forms of LANs (for example, relating to maximum segment lengths, numbers of segments, overall connection lengths, number of repeaters, distance between MAUs and controllers, minimum distance between subscriber branches). Finally, the cable-path analysis is the basis for the assessment of cabling costs, which depend less on the cable type than on the laying costs.

An example of recabling of a building is discussed in Section 8.2.

8.1.2.6 Analysis of other restrictive conditions

Other determining factors which influence the network planning and the choice of products include:

- Protection of existing investments (for example, compatibility requirements for SW versions, interfaces and services).
- Availability: MTBF/(MTBF + MTTR).
- Data protection requirements.
- Reserve capacity, provision for expansion.
- Cost restrictions relating to procurement, migration or running costs.
- Cost of migration (for users, providers). This relates to the replanning of procedures, adaptation of the organization, training, documentation.
- Technological developments, market trends, standardization.

The planning for the introduction of the LAN ends with invitations to tender for the LAN and the selection of the LAN. This involves (at least) the following points:

- **Operational verification**. The new network may alter operations. For example, other communication mechanisms and external data carriers may be inapplicable, software must be adapted.
- **Adaptation of the organizational plan**. The introduction of a network creates new responsibilities, for example, for the operation of the network, monitoring, maintenance, training, documentation and reporting.
- **Planning of the introductory training**. This includes the generation of training documents (documentation, operating

manuals) and the implementation of a training programme. The acceptance of the network may be influenced by careful planning.

- **Planning of the physical network installation.** Some questions have already been discussed in Section 8.1.2.5. ECMA (ECMA, 1990) has produced a useful guide especially for Ethernet LANs of type 10base5 (standard Ethernet). Nemzow (1992) is also useful. IEEE 802.7 and Hudson and Taylor (1986) contain useful advice about the installation of broadband networks.

- **Development of a HW/SW operating scheme.** This includes:
  — classification of network components according to the risk that they will fail and specification of fault-tolerance mechanisms;
  — definition of monitoring procedures;
  — problem management;
  — inventory and documentation management;
  — reporting;
  — the HW/SW maintenance scheme;
  — selection of management tools;
  — specification of management applications.

- **Planning for the acceptance test.** This includes:
  — preparation of a functional and performance test;
  — development of test and load programs;
  — provision of suitable measurement arrangements;
  — detailed specification of reproducible test operations;
  — agreement of the associated logging of results and faults, including the evaluation of these (for example, relative contribution to the overall system down time).

Overall, in the planning for the introduction of the LAN, attention should be paid to the following apparently trivial points:

- Large networks should be introduced in stages.
- Timescales should not be unrealistic. Specific introductory plans should not become a rigid maxim.
- Changes to the plan and improvisation of details should be encouraged.

It is often worth considering a pilot project to introduce new network schemes and network technologies. This offers the following advantages and possibilities:

- The information flow model on which the network planning is based may be improved.

- The usage/load profile may be verified.

- The acceptance and the training costs and/or the migration costs can be tested or better estimated.

- Cost/risk analyses may be carried out with greater accuracy.

- The list of requirements may be refined or modified.

To keep the costs of the pilot project down a clear pilot objective should be defined and a short duration for the pilot project should be specified. The subscribers chosen for the pilot project should be representative of a typical group for that part of the network.

8.1.3 Choice of LAN components

The above analytical steps may be followed by the LAN selection phase. An invitation to tender or testing of a product can only be successful at a justifiable cost if the requirements for the LAN are accurately defined during the planning phase. Only then is it possible to list the set of selection criteria to be considered and divide it into classes according to priority.

The selection of a LAN, particularly when the LAN is an important architectural component of a company's communication infrastructure, is more difficult than the selection of a computer system. Here is a list of some of the criteria which may vary from LAN to LAN: medium, signal structure, topology supported, network access, connection services, adaptation services for device interfaces, gateway services, network management services, application-related services, performance pattern, data protection, data security, operational security, extensibility, availability on the market, conformance to standards, acceptance/training costs.

In this book, we have discussed the criteria for evaluating Ethernet components in a number of previous chapters. Table 8.1 lists the most important areas.

When choosing LAN products, the following are also important:

- **Conformance to standards**. Which standards or standard profiles are supported (subsets)? Are functions which deviate from the standard and add-on functions identified separately?

- **User friendliness**. The use and handling of the services should be made as simple as possible using suitable mnemonic names for the services, callable help functions, intelligible error messages, menu trees and facilities enabling experienced users to bypass user prompts.

- **Network management**. The complexity of the operational aspect of computer networks is often underestimated. Thus, the management functions provided in the LAN components are of crucial importance. We shall discuss this later. Management functions were also covered in the earlier discussion of components.

- **Product background**. Even when a product satisfies all technical requirements, the product background should also be taken into consideration. Here, the following points are important:

  — Available options (HW/SW) and accessories.

  — Granularity of the product range.

  — Deliverability. How long has the product been on the market?

  — Product area. Are there other suppliers? Add-on products? Does the product have a promising future?

  — Quality and coverage of the documentation.

  — Reference installations, distribution of the product.

  — Maintenance alternatives.

  — Advice.

  — Prices (component prices, minimum configuration, installation, SW licences, SW maintenance, HW maintenance).

  — Technological developments, market trends.

  — Conformance to the most important standards.

8.2 Cabling strategies

8.2.1 The problem

For some time, changes in the way in which cabling for the purposes of in-house communication is undertaken have been taking place in large companies and organizations. The previous procedure may be termed a strategy for network-technology-dependent cabling according to need. Network-type- and device-dependent connection cables and interface points were only provided to a small extent. On the whole, cabling was only undertaken to meet requirements (as necessary). The cost effectiveness of this procedure decreases as the need for new interface points increases.

Thus, more and more, attempts are being made to implement a

Table 8.1   Evaluation of LAN components.

LAN components	Section in which selection criteria are discussed
(1) Basic components	
— Ethernet-LAN types	3
— Standard Ethernet incl. thick coax, repeater, transceiver	3.1
— Cheapernet incl. thick coax, repeater, transceiver	3.2
— Optical transmission system	3.3.1
— Fibre optic cable	3.3.2
— Fibre optic connection technology	3.3.3
— Twisted pair systems	3.4
— Transceivers	3.1.2, 3.1.3
	3.2.2, 3.2.4,
	3.4.3
(2) Linking elements	
— Repeaters	3.1.4, 3.1.5
	3.2.5
— Bridges	4.4.2
— Routers	4.4.2
(3) Connection elements	
— Ethernet controller	5.2.1
— Terminal server	5.1
— PC connection	5.2.1
— Channel adapter	5.3.1
(4) NM tools	
— Line monitoring devices	8.4.1
— Protocol monitoring devices	8.4.2
(5) Application systems	
— PC networks	7.2.5
— Distributed file systems	7.3.4

complete cabling, which has the following properties:

- The greatest possible flexibility as far as terminal attachment is concerned.
- The maximum possible independence from the LAN access technology.
- The greatest suitability for transmission of different types of information (data, speech, images).

- Flexible extensibility.
- Bandwidth reserves.

Of course, this approach requires a very accurate view of the services which will be provided in the future by a complete cabling system, together with rather more deliberate integrated planning than in the past. We shall outline this cabling problem using the example of site-wide cabling.

Designing a scheme for site-wide cabling means:

- No site-wide cabling of individual systems, but an integration of as many applications as possible on a single suitable medium.
- The cable network must cover the present and future needs of a site (in terms of interfaces and bandwidth).
- The cable network should be capable of acting as a backbone network to link subnetworks (possibly specialized) on a site-wide basis.

Thus, the planning aspects involve:

(a) The data types to be taken into account (data, speech, video).
(b) The transmission capacities.
(c) The planned device connections.
(d) The distances to be bridged.
(e) The macro and micro structure of the service area (connecting buildings, within a building).
(f) The lots of the existing cable.
(g) Possibilities for extensions.
(h) Security aspects.

Only after taking into account all these aspects is the planner able to select components of the cabling structure such as:

- **Network technology.** Broadband LAN, Token Ring, Baseband Ethernet, ISDN, PBX.
- **Cable type.** CATV 75 Ω, Coax 50 Ω, twisted pair (UTP, STP), fibre optic cable.
- **Cable components.** Connectors, wiring closets, splitters.
- **Transmission components.** Amplifiers, frequency converters, repeaters, bridges, star couplers.
- **Network connection components.** Taps, modems, transceivers, MAUs.
- **Device connection components.** Controllers, NIUs.

On (a) and (b)

If it is necessary to transmit data, voice and video over the same medium broadband technology (almost any transmission rates may be achieved, depending on the frequency subband) and fibre optic systems should be considered. It is also possible to combine voice and data with a rate of 64 kbps using PBXs, although 64 kbps is already often an inappropriately low rate for current data terminals. However, a true ISDN interface (S0) is not always available inwards; there is often a mapping onto 2-wire lines over a non-standardized company-specific interface, so that for the end user, parallel data and voice traffic over a single line is often not possible. Data traffic at up to 10 Mbps is possible for the Ethernet baseband technology over coax (50 Ω), Cheapernet, twisted pair or fibre optic cables.

On (c) and (d)

Corresponding interface support for the network components is not available for all cable types. Often, one has to find a third-party manufacturer. The number of terminals connected depends not only on the network technology but also on the cable type used.

Example – Ethernet

- Type 10base5: 100 stations per 500 m segment, 2.5 m minimum distance between taps.

- Type 10base2 (Cheapernet): 30 stations per 185 m segment, 0.5 m minimum distance between taps.

Example – IBM Token Ring

- Cable type 1: Maximum distance between stations and distribution panels 100 m, maximum distance between distribution panels 200 m, up to 12 distribution panels and 260 stations per ring.

- Cable type 3: Maximum distance between stations and distribution panels 45 m, maximum distance between distribution panels 120 m, up to 2 distribution panels and 72 stations per ring. With repeaters a distance of 750 m may be bridged using a copper cable and 2000 m using fibre optic cable.

On (e)

Not all forms of topology are supported by all products. For example:

- IBM Token Ring supports physical stars (the star nodes are the wiring closets).

- Broadband networks support a tree structure.
- Ethernet supports a bus structure.
- Fibre optic cables and StarLAN each support a multilevel star topology.
- Twisted-pair cables support a star topology.

In summary, the technical trends may be characterized as follows:

- Increasing digitization.
- Increasing bit rates.
- Further diversification of the transmission procedures.
- Decentralization of the switching intelligence.
- Further penetration of optical fibres.

As the bit rate increases, so does the dependence on the transmission-related properties of the cable both for the transmission function itself and for the reciprocal effects of copper wires in the same cable and in the adjacent cable on each other. We note that the application area for coaxial cable is shrinking as the application area for fibre optic conductors and symmetrical lines (here, predominantly telephone cables) is extended (Pattay, 1989).

However, in addition to transmission-related requirements on the cabling structure, there are also operational requirements. These include differences in the lifetimes for different cabling areas, the creation of different logical network structures on a physical cabling structure, ease of fault location, security against unauthorized access, etc.

8.2.2 Structured cabling

As previously mentioned, a structured cabling should if possible support various logical network topologies and various transmission and access procedures for high bit rates. At the same time, only one physical network, in other words, shared cabling, should be used. This consists of cable lines and concentration points, where wiring closets, patch fields, network components, etc. may be implemented. If one chooses a hierarchical cabling with a star-shaped physical topology, then it is not difficult to configure the wires into a logical bus, ring, tree or star topology.

Structured cabling means:

(a) Dividing the whole site into cabling areas.

— Area I: Cabling between buildings (site backbone, primary area).

— Area II: Rising lines within buildings to connect storeys

(building backbone, secondary area).

— Area III: Horizontal cabling of storeys (workplace cabling, tertiary area).

— Area IV: Room cabling (workplace cabling).

(b) Specification of transition points between the areas.

— Transition point I–II: transition into a building.

— Transition point II–III: transition to a storey.

— Transition point III–IV: transition into a room, possible transition points to existing cabling.

The transition points may mean a change of medium or a change in the network technology, for example:

— Transition from optical fibre to coax cable.

— Transition from broadband to baseband technology.

— Transition from LAN to WAN technology.

— Transition from a PC network to a mainframe network.

The following assignment of cable systems to areas is in principle conceivable:

— Optical fibre: Area I.

— Broadband: Areas I, II.

— Twisted pair: Areas III, IV.

— Thin Ethernet: Areas III, IV.

For the transition points use of star couplers (transition points I/II, possibly II/III), hubs (transition points II/III, possibly III/IV) and separating components (bridges, routers, brouters) suggests itself.

Because of the importance of the cabling structures, standard approaches have also been followed for some time, for example:

- DIN/VDE AK 715.3.

- EIA/TIA Standard 586 (1): Commercial building telecommunications wiring (1991).

- ISO/IEC JTC1/SC25/WG3: Study on generic cabling for information technology.

- CEN/CENELEC: The design and configuration of customer premises cabling. (1) ISDN implementation.

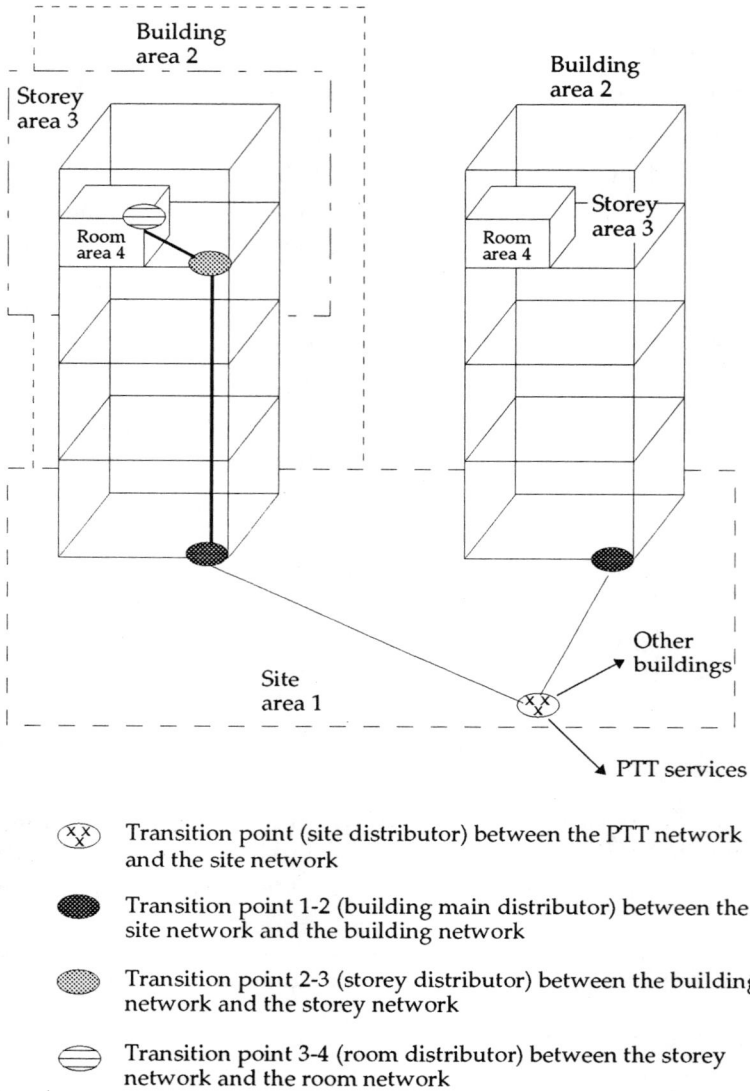

Figure 8.2   Structured cabling.

ISO/IEC specifies the following requirements:

- The life expectation of a cabling system should be at least 10 years.

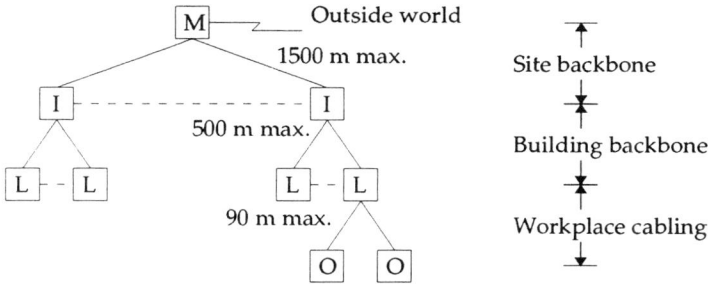

M = Main node (site distributor)
I = Intermediate node (building distributor)
L = Local node (storey distributor)
O = Information access point (terminal)

Figure 8.3   EIA/TIA cabling standard 586.

- It must be possible to implement the following interfaces on the cable system: S−0 bus, S_0 point to point, PBX cabling, Token Ring (4/16 Mbps), Ethernet 10base5, Ethernet 10baseT, Ethernet 10baseF, FOIRL, FDDI, X.21, V.11, V.24, V.28.
- Minimum bridgeable distances should be 3 km in the primary area, 500 m in the secondary area and 100 m in the tertiary area.

The ISO document is based on the previous work carried out by EIA/TIA (see Figure 8.3), which included the following recommendations:

(a) **Primary area.** 62.5/125 μ fibre optic cable with attenuation 3.75 dB/km for $\lambda = 850$ nm at 160 MHz and 1.5 dB/km for $\lambda = 1300$ nm at 500 MHz. For broadband applications, 75 Ω coaxial cable may be used. Monomode fibre optic cable or 50/125 μ or 85/125 μ multimode fibre optic cables are the second choice. The primary area may have length up to 1500 m to incorporate the site backbone. The transition point to the PTT network is called the main node, that to the building network is called the intermediate node.

(b) **Secondary area.** Naturally, it is possible to use the same cable as in the primary area. In addition, 50 Ω coax cable according to IEEE 802.3, 4-pair 100 Ω UTP cable (24 AGW), and 2-pair 150 Ω STP cable according to IEEE 802.5 are possible. Another possibility is 25-pair 100 Ω UTP. The distance from the intermediate node to the storey distributor (local node) must be at least 500 m.

(c) **Tertiary area.** Like the secondary area, but 50 Ω thin coaxial cable may also be used. The individual cables of the workplace cabling must be able to bridge a distance of at least 90 m. While fibre optic cable to the workplace is provided for as an option, it will only become interesting in the future when appropriate terminal interfaces are more common.

For the connector system, the EIA/TIA standard provides for 8- pin RJ 45 connectors the 100 Ω cable and BNC connectors for the Ethernet coaxial cable. For the 150 Ω cable the self-locking hermaphrodite connectors of the IBM cable system are specified. ST type connectors are proposed for fibre optic systems.

8.2.3 A cabling example

In this section, we shall not describe and discuss all conceivable complete cabling strategies, but give a single example of how, under certain assumptions, such a complete cabling can be undertaken.

These assumptions are the following:

- The complete cabling should not consider voice/telephone traffic. Thus, no attempt will be made to integrate voice and data services, as far as the cabling is concerned.

- Transmission of moving images is not supported.

- Ethernet should be used as a global network access procedure. Thus, it should be possible to integrate all forms of data communication based on Ethernet.

- The site is assumed to be a complex in the PTT juridical sense; in other words, all the cabling must be implemented on private land. The site contains a number of individual buildings. Each building has several storeys with a number of rooms.

- The connection density should be one connection per room. Technically, there should be a facility for using additional components to connect several devices in one room.

- No particular spatial concentration (location) of data streams is defined.

Based on these assumptions, it is possible to design a cabling structure which provides for a wealth of room connection points.

To obtain a more structured problem we subdivide the cabling topology into several hierarchical levels.

Level 1   Cabling between buildings.

Level 2   Vertical rising lines within buildings, cabling between individual storeys.

Level 3   Horizontal cabling of a storey, cabling within the storey of a building.

Level 4   Room cabling, cabling within a room.

The individual cabling levels should be cabled independently. If a suitable transition point is defined the planning and the implementation may also be carried out independently.

The above requirements are now satisfied by the choice of the following cable system and network components.

Level 1 (connections between buildings)   A cable system based on fibre optic cables is proposed for use between buildings. Physically, the connections between the buildings should be laid out using fibre optic cable and/or a corresponding number of fibres so that both a star-shaped (possibly even multilevel star shapes) and a ring-shaped network topology may be implemented with the cable structure. Thus, Ethernet may be used for the site backbone and a later transition to FDDI is also possible. A fibre optic cable should consist of from 6 to 12 fibres (for later extensions).

Transition point 1–2   The transition from the building to the network which connects the buildings is via a bridge or brouter and the corresponding media interfaces. These make it possible to implement traffic separation and so keep traffic which is local to the building within the building and lock out traffic which is not intended for the building. In addition, the filter facility may be used to suppress unwanted traffic.

While fibre optic cabling is unquestioned for level 1, we shall discuss alternatives for levels 2 to 4.

Version 1 for levels 2 to 4

Level 2 (building rising lines)   A vertical Ethernet segment with the standard coaxial cable technology is used to connect the individual storeys together.

Transition point 2–3   The connection between the cable system of a storey and the rising lines is implemented via local repeaters. If required (possible separation of the traffic within a storey), separating components (for example, bridges) may also be used here.

Version 1 is shown schematically in Figure 8.4.

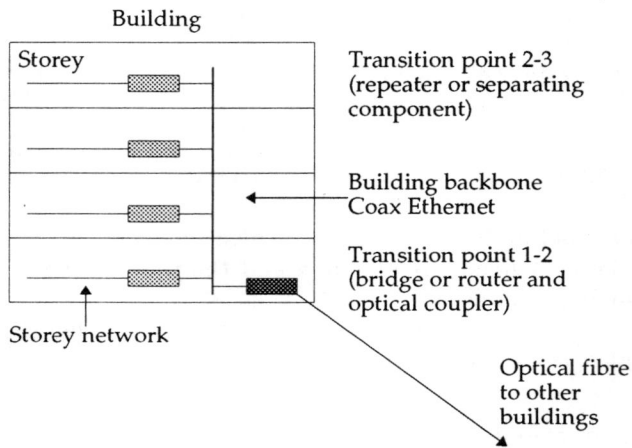

Figure 8.4 Building cabling, version 1.

Version 2 for levels 2 to 4

Level 2 The storey cabling begins directly in a star coupler, which is the transition point from level 1 to level 2. Current active star couplers have interface cards for fibre optic conductors, standard Ethernet coaxial cable, Cheapernet cable and twisted cable. An active star coupler as a central cabling node may be used as the starting point for storey cabling of a complete building. The repeaters used in version 1 as transition points from level 2 to level 3 may be dispensed with. This implies not only lower costs but also the removal of active network components or possible sources of faults.

Version 2 is shown schematically in Figure 8.5.

For versions 1 and 2, one conceivable solution for levels 3 and 4 is the following:

Level 3 (storey cabling) Within a storey, one or more Ethernet standard cables are laid in such a way that the cable passes through all the rooms for which connections are planned.

Transition point 3–4 A standard transceiver is installed in each room which permits connection to the storey cable.

Level 4 (room cabling) The cabling within a room is via a standard transceiver cable. If several connections are to be implemented in a single room, multitransceivers are used which permit the connection of up to 15 Ethernet stations (per multitransceiver).

Building

Storey

Transition point 2-3
(star coupler, multimedia
access hub)

Transition point 1-2
(bridge or router and
optical coupler)

Ethernet Coax
Cheapernet Coax
Twisted pair

Optical fibre
to other
buildings

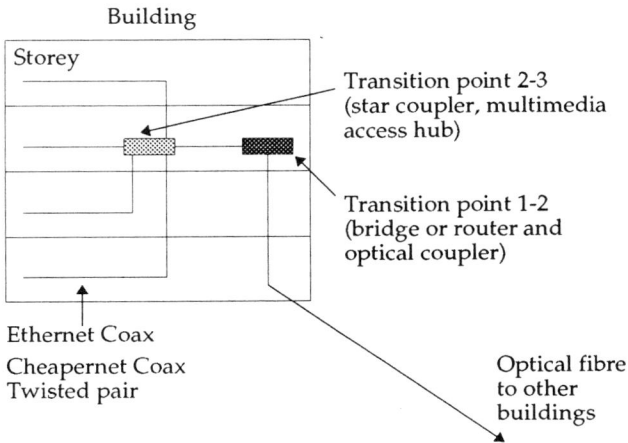

Figure 8.5   Building cabling, version 2.

Version 3 for layers 2–4

In view of the trend towards applications requiring increasingly high bit
rates (visualization, windows technology, moving pictures) and the trend
towards faster device interfaces, in the long term, building cabling as shown
in Figure 8.6 has a promising future.

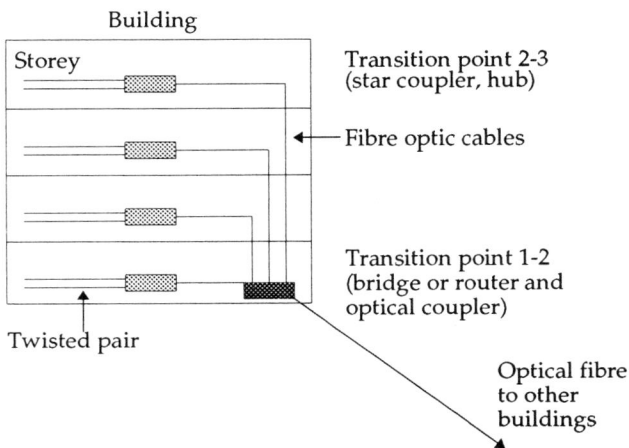

Building

Storey

Transition point 2-3
(star coupler, hub)

Fibre optic cables

Transition point 1-2
(bridge or router and
optical coupler)

Twisted pair

Optical fibre
to other
buildings

Figure 8.6   Building cabling, version 3.

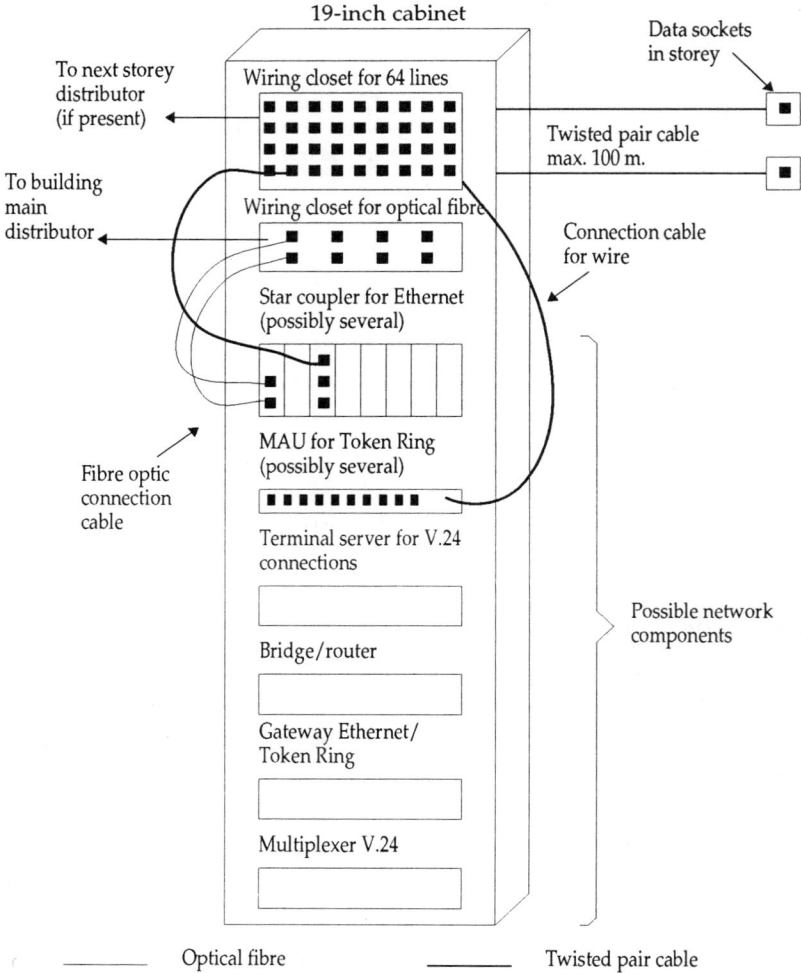

Figure 8.7   Storey distributor (basic structure).

From the building main distributor (transition point 1–2) which is identical with the building transition point for the site cabling, fibre optic cables lead outwards in a star shape to all the storey distribution panels (transition point 2–3). A star- shaped twisted-pair cabling (preferably STP) leads from the storey distribution panel to the individual rooms, where the distance should not be greater than 100 m.

The centrepiece for the maintenance and configuration of the physical cable structure is the storey distributor. This is usually a 19-inch cabinet (see Figure 8.7) which holds wiring cabinets for fibre optic and twisted-pair conductors together with active connection elements and servers. Because of its infrastructural importance a UPS should be used. So that the necessary ventilation can be estimated, we give the following estimates of the power consumption of network components: star coupler 70 W, terminal server 250 W, bridge 70 W, brouter 250 W, multiplexer V.24 120 W, 10baseT hub 70 W.

The cost of a cabling system is composed as follows:

- Cable costs
- Laying costs
- Costs of distributors and amplifiers
- Costs of the network interface points
- Device connection costs
- Software costs
- Maintenance costs and management tool costs.

In a complete cabling, network interfaces and device connection account for the lion's share.

To reduce the costs in the case of new buildings, at level 3 a complete system of empty pipes leading from the storey distributors may be retained, so as to provide for cabling as necessary at a later date.

Overall, the following recommendations should be observed:

- Existing networks and cabling should be used whenever possible.
- New cabling should only be installed where it is currently needed.
- New cabling should imply structured cabling.
- Cabling should be coordinated on a site-wide basis.
- A pilot project is advisable for large projects.

8.3 Network management architectures

8.3.1 Approaches to an integrated network management

Network management includes all the precautions and activities needed to guarantee the effective and efficient use of a communication system. Thus, network management is oriented towards operational objectives and concerns personnel, procedures, programs and technical systems. It covers planning, operation and control aspects together with the consideration of organizational forms.

The specific form of a network management scheme depends on a

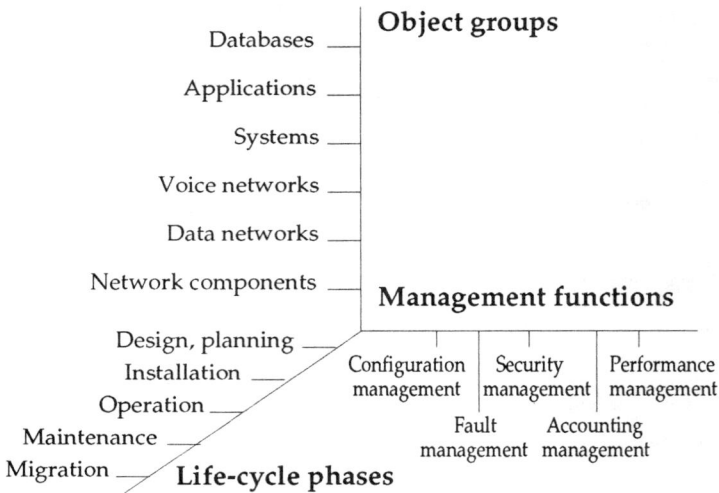

Figure 8.8   The dimensions of network management.

number of influencing factors. These include the objectives of the network, the network services which must be guaranteed and the quality-of-service parameters. We would also cite the physical network structure and the logical structure determined by the protocol hierarchies which is also shaped by the information types supported and the communication-related characteristics of the application. Finally, the organizational and operational structure of the network provider (private or public) and of the network users also determine the network management.

The complexity of the network management task in today's large networks is a result of the variety and multiplicity of the components to be managed, the heterogeneity of interfaces, protocols and system software, the broad spatial distribution and the involvement of different areas of responsibility. The integration of services in multiprotocol networks, integrated networks and subnetwork structures, together with the necessary support for distributed applications, increasingly complicate network management. The latter means that the once normal division between system, network and application management already appears artificial in many places. As Figure 8.8 shows, complicated management is a result of a number of different factors.

Complicated network management (NM) is only possible under computer control. If it is to be an integrated network management, it must be based on a standardized network management architecture. Such an architecture must satisfy the following requirements:

- Integration of communications architectures and network types.
- Integration of management functional areas.
- Integration of organizational and temporal aspects.
- Support for distributed applications and common programming and operator interfaces.

Finally, there must be a common concept for a management database.

Today we are still some way away from realizing the vision of integrated network management in a heterogeneous environment, although the need for standardized network management architectures has been perceived and recognized. This is shown by the architectural approaches of OSI, internet and OSF. Numerous network management systems are available on the market, but they are not yet integrated in the sense of the above requirements:

- In the absence of standards, many manufacturers have developed their own solutions for their component world.
- The systems on offer are generally restricted to the management of individual network components rather than that of the communication network as a whole.

In large heterogeneous networks this leads to a situation which is characterized by:

- A multiplicity of very different interfaces which the operating staff must learn to handle. These interfaces differ both in their mode of operation (syntax) and in their functionality and capability (semantics). One consequence of this multiplicity of protocols is the associated high degree of specialization of personnel.
- Isolated redundant applications, since each manufacturer implements management functions individually and cooperation with systems from other manufacturers is not provided for.
- Isolated redundant data sets for storing management-related information, which must all be created and maintained by the network provider.
- A functionality which is incommensurate with the complexity and size of present day networks. By way of example, we cite the necessity of a complete, up-to-date and consistent documentation of a communication network or the need for automation in the area of fault management.

One important step towards a solution of these problems may be described by the keyword *integration*. The aim is to make management functions available to the network provider in a uniform way, independently of the network technology and the manufacturer.

Even though *the* integrated network management system is not yet available, the network provider can and should endeavour to introduce steps leading towards an overall management system. Such steps might be:

(1) **Spatial concentration of the (heterogeneous) management systems.** The multiplicity of physical interfaces of the NM systems is retained.

(2) **Integration of operator consoles.** Access to the (heterogeneous) NM systems from a single dedicated point (graphics terminal with windows surface). The multiplicity of logical interfaces of the NM systems is retained.

(3) **Integration of surfaces (user interfaces).** As in (2), however, all the applications are addressed via a common surface. This requires a manufacturer-independent representation of the network.

(4) **Integration of applications.** The extraction and uniform handling of certain NM applications leads to the concept of the manager of managers. This step requires a certain common understanding of management data.

(5) **Integration of information.** The management systems are based on a manufacturer-neutral information model, which may be used to establish an NM object library. Examples of such libraries include internet's MIB I/II and the library of the OSI NM Forum.

Integration as in step (5) is the most far reaching. This facilitates a uniform management for heterogeneous systems. In the end, this implies that the network and system management are based on network management architectures. The design of network management architectures is based on the specification of certain submodels.

The *information model* is central. It includes the schemes for describing network management information and, in particular, for describing managed objects as an abstraction of the real network resources which are actually to be managed and controlled. Here network resources may include both HW components and SW modules. The modelling paradigm (for example, entity–relationship model, object-oriented approach, variable approach) of the information model has a formative influence on the overall NM architecture. The *organizational model* specifies both the actors in the NM architecture and their roles. Even the definition of domain concepts comes from here. The *communication model* defines the schemes for exchanging management information between the actors. The specification of the management protocols together with

Spatial integration   Heterogeneous computer network
(components from various manufacturers)

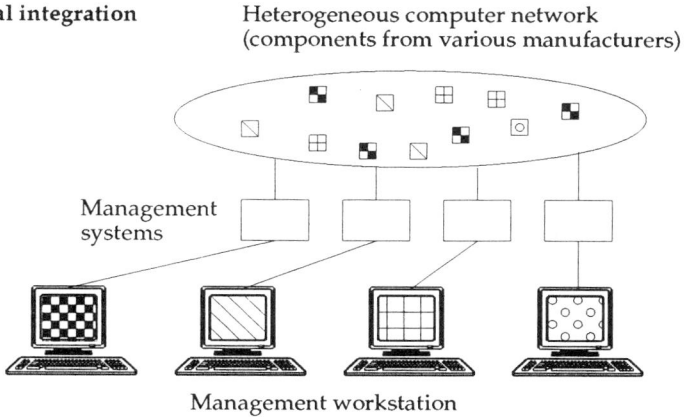

Management
systems

Management workstation

**Operator console
integration**   Heterogeneous computer network
(components from various manufacturers)

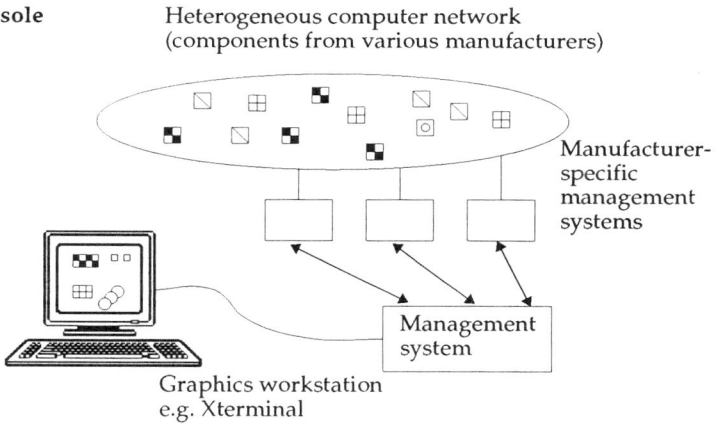

Manufacturer-
specific
management
systems

Management
system

Graphics workstation
e.g. Xterminal

Surface integration

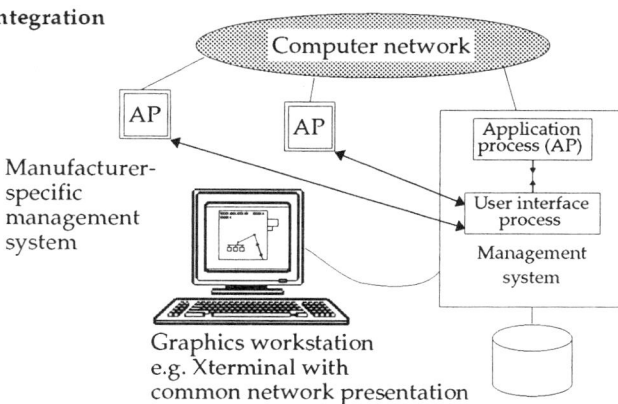

Computer network

AP

AP

Application
process (AP)

Manufacturer-
specific
management
system

User interface
process

Management
system

Graphics workstation
e.g. Xterminal with
common network presentation

Figure 8.9   First integration steps for an NM solution.

the selection of managed objects and the encoding of management information belong in this area, as does the support for this special communication by an underlying communications architecture. Finally, the *functional model* divides all the management tasks into management functional areas and attempts to specify general (generic) management functions.

Well-known network management architectures include:

- OSI network management
- Internet management
- OSF distributed management environment (DME)
- Telecommunications Management Network (TMN)
- IBM's NetView.

The above architectures differ, sometimes considerably, in the models used (Hegering, 1991a).

As far as Ethernet LAN management is concerned, only the first two architectures are currently important, the OSI management, because the LAN-related IEEE management schemes are based on it and it is the more comprehensive architectural approach, and the internet management, because almost all LAN components now on the market understand the SNMP protocol. We shall discuss these two architectures in the next two sections.

8.3.2 OSI and IEEE management

We shall not discuss the OSI network management architecture in detail since currently, as far as the practical use of LANs is concerned, it does not have the importance to which it will be entitled in the future as a result of its flexible and powerful schemes. For a detailed description, see Kerner (1992) or Black (1992).

OSI information model

All management activities are concerned with the administration, control and monitoring of management resources. These may be modelled using a standardized description context which is specified by the *information model*. OSI is distinguished by an extensive model in which the chosen approach is an object- oriented description. Resources are described as objects (managed objects, MO). In the object-oriented approach an object is viewed as an instantiation of an object class, the properties of which also determine those of the object. A class of objects may be defined to be a subclass of a superclass and thus inherits all the properties of the superclass(es). The properties may then be refined or extended.

Classes of managed objects (MO classes) are described in terms of:

- attributes, or characteristic properties of the MO which are visible outside the MO boundary;

- operations and actions which may be used to manipulate the whole or part of the object;

- notifications which provide for asynchronous reporting of the resource represented by the MO;

- the behaviour of the MO as the result of an operation.

Thus, an MO represents the abstract view of a real resource. Management involves the execution of operations such as create/delete MO, action, get/add/remove/replace/set attribute_value on the MO boundary.

The syntactic description of an MO class involves a template language based on the use of ASN.1 macros. Figure 8.10 shows an example of a section of the description of a LAN hub, in which use is made of the facility to refer to description macros which are defined elsewhere.

OSI, IEEE, OSI Network Management Forum and other groups have since modelled a number of resources, including resources in the LAN area, in this way. The results are in the form of MO catalogues or MO libraries; in addition, more recently, with the specification of new Ethernet standards, all relevant objects have been described in this way (IEEE, 1991). The conceptual repository in which all MOs of a system are stored is called a *management information base* (MIB). The sources of the contents of an MIB are shown in Figure 8.11.

The structure of an MIB is determined by the inheritance tree of the MO classes and by the explicitly specified MO containment tree (of containment relationships between MOs). The latter is also used for name binding. The containment tree may be used to describe complicated composite managed objects (for example, a hub has several slot-in cards, the latter have several ports).

OSI communications model

The purpose of management is to manipulate resources in a manner which is oriented towards operational objectives. For this, management information must be exchanged between the cooperating open systems.

The OSI communications model has three different management categories: the *systems management* (SM), the *layer management* (LM) and the *layer operation*. These terms are explained by Figure 8.12.

The ISO NM architecture does not specify how the three NM categories interwork. Even the nature of the interworking with the local management (for example, the operating system) remains open. This is understandable from the point of view of the communications model (in

Hub   MANAGED OBJECT CLASS
                            DERIVED FROM ISO/IEC 10165-2: Top;
                            CHARACTERIZED BY:
                                BEHAVIOUR DEFINITIONS
                                ATTRIBUTES   HubID GET,
                                                        NumberOfRelays GET,
                                                        RelayActive GET,
                                                        HubGroupCapacity GET,
                                                        TimeSinceHubSystemReset GET,
                                                        HubResetTimeStamp GET,
                                                        HubHealth GET,
                                                        GroupMap GET
                                OPERATIONS
                                    ACTIONS   ResetHubSystemAction,
                                                        ResetHubAction,
                                                        ExecuteSelfTest1Action,
                                                        RelaychangeoverAction
                                    NOTIFICATIONS
                                                        Hub Health,
                                                        GroupRelayConfigChange,
                                                        ProprietaryExtensionAlarm:
                            REGISTERED AS   iso(1)std(0)iso8802)csma(3)hubmgt(18)objectclass(0)
                                               hubobjectclass(X);

Hub Name   NAME BINDING
                            SUBORDINATE OBJECT CLASS   Hub
                            NAMED BY SUPERIOR OBJECT CLASS   ISO/IEC 10165-
                                                                 2:System;
                                WITH ATTRIBUTE   HubID;
                                BEHAVIOUR   HubBehaviour
                            REGISTERED AS   iso(1)std(0)csma(3)hubmgt(18)namebinding(3)
                                               hubname(X);

HubID ATTRIBUTE
                                WITH ATTRIBUTE SYNTAX   IEEE802CommonDefinitions.uniqueIdentifier,
                                MATCHES FOR   Equality;
                                BEHAVIOUR   HubIDBehaviour,
                            REGISTERED AS   iso(1)std(0)iso8802)csma(3)hubmgt(18)attribute(4)hubid(X);

Remark: TOP is superclass in the inheritance tree
                  SYSTEM is superclass in the containment tree

Figure 8.10   Templates for the MO class hub (section).

other words, the standardization), although, from the point of view of the
implementor it is unsatisfactory. All NM categories have access to MIB
information.

Management
applications
(policies, algorithms, models,
management solutions)

Network user
(directories, QoS-info)

Network provider
(organizational info, network
inventory, versions, life-cycle)

Management
applications

MIB content

Top-down

Bottom-up

Resources

Communications
protocols

Network components

Manufacturers

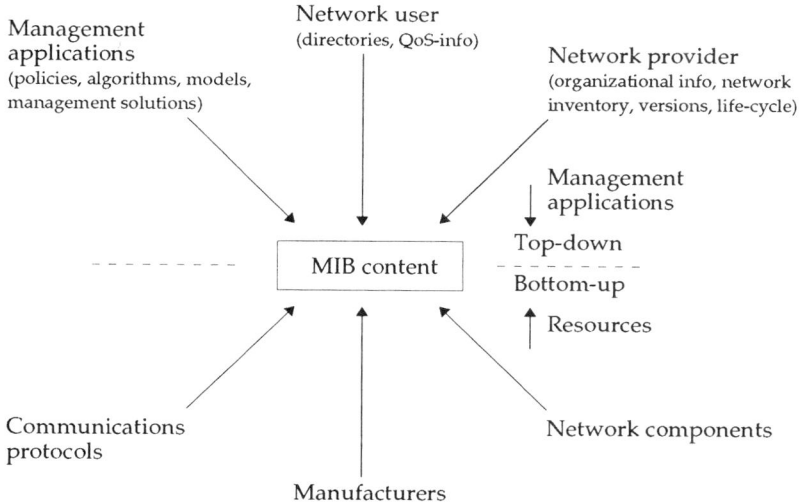

Figure 8.11   Sources of managed objects.

The systems management is concerned with the overall management of cooperating systems. It is apparent in distributed management applications (system management applications, SMA), which involve cooperation between corresponding SM application processes (SMAP).

Management induces asymmetric relationships, thus, for a specific application, an SMAP may have the role of manager (managing system) or the subordinate role (agent system). The roles may change and SMAPs with various roles may coexist in an OSI system.

The communications-related part of the NM application is the *systems management application entity* (SMAE) which exchanges management information with SMAEs of other systems via appropriate NM application protocols (systems management protocols). This is the normal type of management communication in the OSI NM architecture; it requires the full OSI functionality of the system (in other words, all seven layers) as a prerequisite.

The OSI NM architecture supports this exchange of management information (see Figure 8.12) between the NM application processes, which is executed via the SMAE, with specially developed *Common Management Information Services* (CMIS) and a corresponding *Common Management Information Protocol* (CMIP) (ISO 9595, ISO 9596). Figure 8.13 shows the embedding of CMIS and CMIP in the architecture of OSI layer 7.

CMIS is used to access and manipulate (remote) MOs and may also be used to operate on the whole MIB information tree. CMIS is a

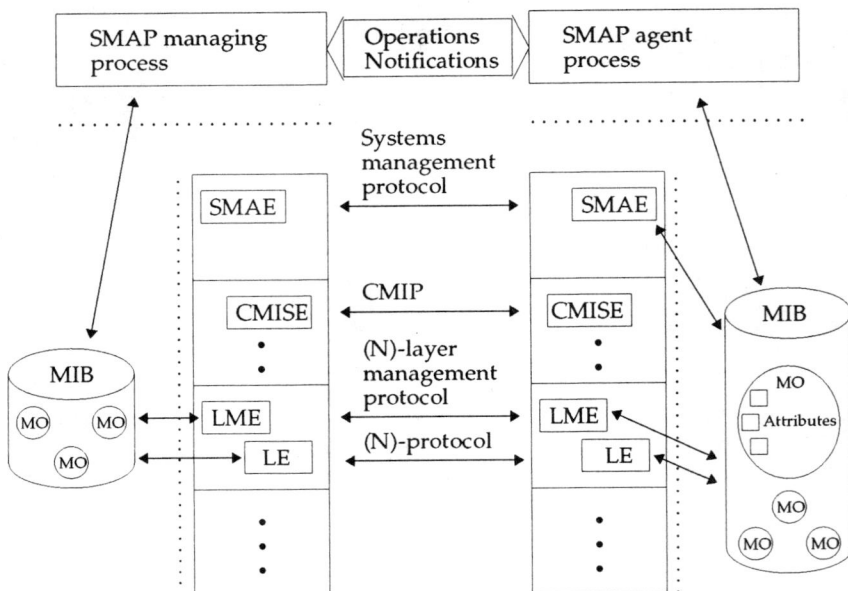

MO   = Managed Object
MIB   = Management Information Base
LE   = Layer Entity
LME   = Layer Management Entity
CMISE = Common Management Information Service Entity
CMIP   = Common Management Information Protocol
SMAE = Systems Management Application Entity
SMAP = Systems Management Application Process

Figure 8.12   OSI communications model.

connection-oriented service which uses the services of ACSE for connection management.

CMIS supports the following groups of services:

- **Association management.** INITIALIZE, TERMINATE, ABORT.

- **Execution of operations.** M-GET (to read MO attributes), M-SET (to set or modify MO attributes), M-ACTION (to initiate an MO action), M-CREATE (for dynamic introduction of an MO), and M-DELETE (for dynamic deletion of an MO).

- **Event reporting.** M-EVENT-REPORT (to transmit an MO notification).

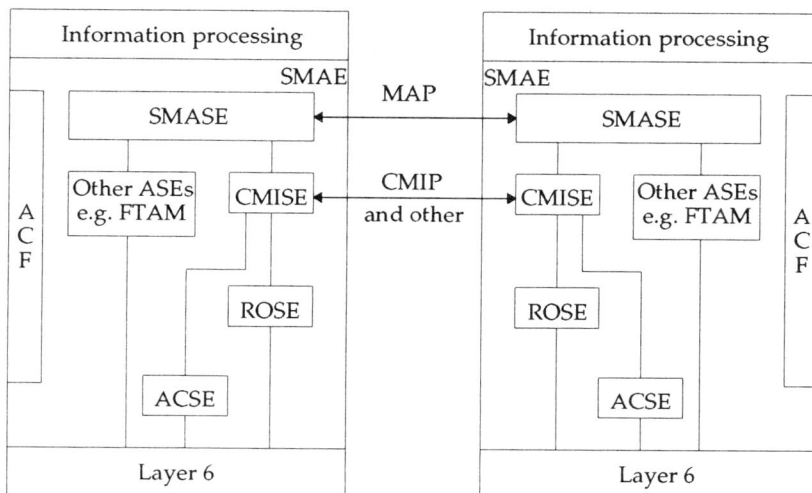

ASE	= Application Service Entity
ACF	= Association Control Function
ROSE	= Remote Operations Service Entity
ACSE	= Association Control Service Entity
SMASE	= System Management Application Service Entity
MAP	= Management Application Protocol

Figure 8.13   Embedding of CMIS/CMIP in the OSI communications architecture.

Some of the services are confirmed services, others may be unconfirmed. Additional services are under discussion. A list of the many parameters of these services would go beyond the scope of this book.

In CMIS/CMIP, the selection of MO and the passing of parameters to an MO, together with the structure of the protocol data units (CMIP PDUs), are naturally closely based on the OSI information model and reflect its flexibility and facilities. The mechanisms for selecting managed objects are of interest. Objects are identified by names, where, because of the containment hierarchy, it is assumed (name binding) that the objects are hierarchically ordered in the MIB, according to their names, in the form of a management information tree. For each service CMIS then provides for:

• The specification of a set of MOs relevant to this service call in the form of a subtree of a given depth. This facility is called *scoping*.

• Selection of certain objects from this set using *filters*. A filter consists of one or more statements about the presence or value of MO attributes.

- Entry of synchronization conditions when accessing several MOs (for example, atomic, best effort). For example, in the first case, a check is made to ensure that the operation can be executed for all target objects.

In addition, for certain services it is possible to request several confirmations as a response (multiple reply). This facility makes sense, since using scoping, subtrees in the object hierarchy may be addressed as candidates for a management operation.

The *layer management* concerns functions, services and protocols which are specific to a single layer and do not require the services of higher OSI layers. Examples of such layer-specific management functions include loop tests (for layer 1), the exchange of routing information (for layer 3), loading-protocols for software (for example, at level 2).

Although the OSI NM architecture explicitly includes the layer management as a category, this area has received very little attention from ISO (except for protocols for exchanging routing information). However, in the context of the introduction of LAN and MAN technologies, a number of specifications for layer management are included by the IEEE in the 802.X standards.

A communication entity of the layer management is called an (N)-layer management entity (LME), the corresponding protocol is the (N)-layer management protocol.

Of course, management information and management functions are also components of the normal layer management (protocol management or layer operation) which we met in the preceding chapters. Examples include window sizes and timers or the test frame in HDLC and the RESET-PDU in X.25, other protocol parameters for the phases of connection establishment and release and fault information.

A means of recognizing the management-related protocol elements as such would naturally be desirable. The need for this has recently been recognized and is already being taken into account in the development of more recent protocols (for example, FDDI, DQDB).

IEEE management

The IEEE management architecture makes extensive use of the concepts of the OSI network management. This concerns, in particular, the use of the OSI information model, which is specified in the ISO 10165 standard (structure of management information, SMI).

In the nature of things, the IEEE LAN/MAN management (IEEE, 1991) concerns layers 1, 2a and 2b. Typically, the corresponding network components (modems, repeaters, bridges, etc.) are not provided with a full layer 7 functionality in the OSI sense, and management activities are often required when subfunctions are absent. Thus, the systems

LMMU   LMMS LMMPE LMMS   LMMU   Managed object
                                          boundary

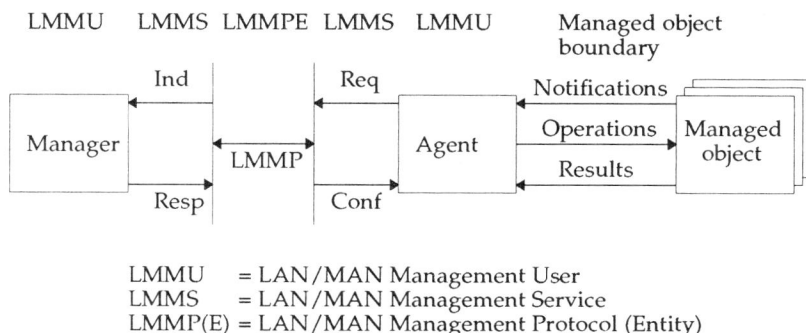

LMMU   = LAN/MAN Management User
LMMS   = LAN/MAN Management Service
LMMP(E) = LAN/MAN Management Protocol (Entity)

Figure 8.14   IEEE LAN/MAN management model.

management preferred by OSI is not appropriate and a layer management is more suitable. This means that a layer-specific management protocol for LANs must be designed so that management applications may be located directly above lower LAN protocol layers, and that local interfaces between LAN protocol entities and the layer management must be defined. LAN-specific managed objects and attributes must also be defined. All this work is being carried out by the IEEE. Figure 8.14 shows the LAN/MAN management architecture, while Figure 8.15 shows the LAN/MAN communications model.

The connectionless LLC service (type 1) in the confirmed/unconfirmed versions is the chosen basis for the management protocol. There are many reasons for this. Firstly, many applications have a lower data-integrity requirement and already include acknowledgement at the application level. Secondly, real-time applications in the management area cannot afford the overhead of a connection management.

Because they are based on the same OSI information model, both CMIS and LMMS (LAN/MAN management service) have the same basic functionality; in addition, LMMP (LAN/MAN management protocol) uses the PDUs and procedures of the CMIP specification. Thus, CMIP and LMMP may coexist in the same manager or agent system, and it is easy to construct proxy managers which act as relays between CMIP- and LMMP-based services.

The convergence protocol entity (CPE) is used to overcome the differences between the LLC type 1 and the LMMP services. CPE is responsible for detecting duplicates, losses and sequence violations and for handling the abstract syntax of the management information, etc. Thus, the functionality of layers 3 to 6 needed for LMMP must be implemented.

CMIP   LMMP

	CMIP		LMMP
7	CMISE/ROSE and ACSE		CMISE/ROSE (=LMMPE)
6	Presentation		Convergence protocol entity (CPE)
5	Session		
4	Transport		
3	Network		
2	LLC/MAC		LLC/MAC
1	Physical		Physical

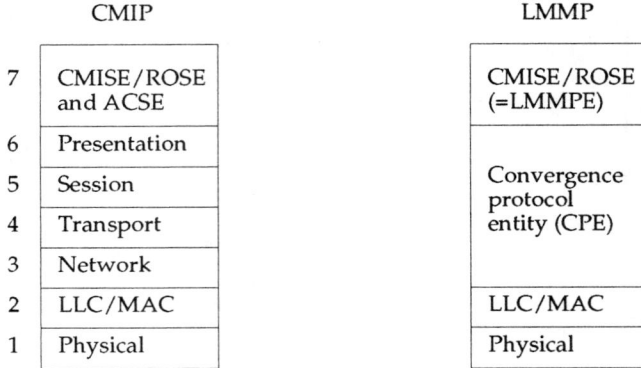

a. Comparison of CMIP and LMP

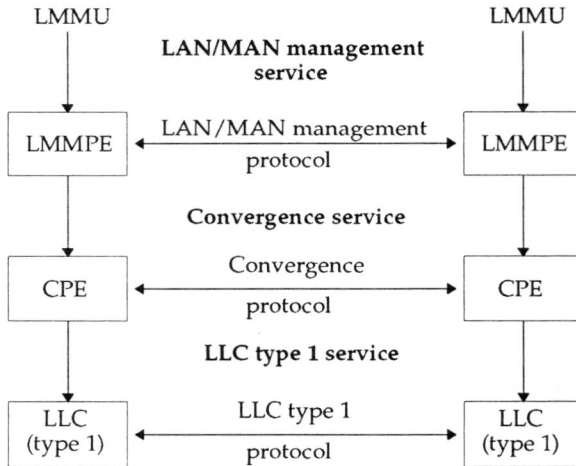

LMMU   LMMU

LAN/MAN management service

LMMPE ← LAN/MAN management protocol → LMMPE

Convergence service

CPE ← Convergence protocol → CPE

LLC type 1 service

LLC (type 1) ← LLC type 1 protocol → LLC (type 1)

b. Implementation of LMMS

Figure 8.15 LAN/MAN communications model.

The IEEE 802.1B documents describe the LMMS, LMMP and CP services and protocols and the specifications of the associated managed objects.

IEEE P802.3K/D4 describes the managed objects of an Ethernet hub. These include the hub itself, its ports and port groups, the indicators, the status values, the operations which may be initiated, the error-message and event indicators, counters, etc.

Finally, the IEEE 802.1E standard of 1990 describes the system load protocol with the information block (bit pattern) directly above the LLC between a load server and the loadable devices; in other words, the memory of a LAN network component which is used for the purposes of transporting a bootstrap load process.

We shall not discuss further details of the IEEE management documents here.

8.3.3 Internet management with SNMP

The internet management system in the TCP/IP world is based on a simplified management architecture. While OSI is essentially based on peer systems, Internet uses the concept of a *Network Management Station* (NMS) to introduce a ranking (Figure 8.16). The network manager is an application resident centrally in the NMS which collects and evaluates data from the network nodes (managed nodes, agents). Nodes may be either so-called host systems such as workstations, PCs, terminal servers or printers (whence DTEs), gateway systems such as IP nodes, or network components such as bridges, hubs and multiplexers. NMSs and nodes communicate in a kind of master/client relationship via a simple management protocol, the *Simple Network Management Protocol* (SNMP). In principle, the NMSs have the active role, while the nodes exercise a passive role.

Databases representing the managed objects of each node type are implemented in the agents. Each database is an MIB View, in other words, a section of the *Internet Management Information Base* (IMIB), which is a uniform, protocol-independent data repository.

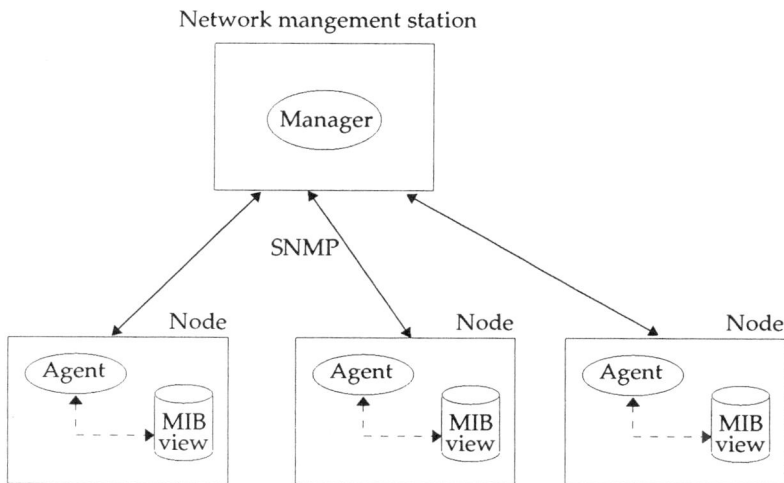

Network mangement station

Manager

SNMP

Node   Node   Node

Agent   Agent   Agent

MIB view   MIB view   MIB view

Figure 8.16   Internet management model.

The information model upon which the Internet MIB is based is much simpler than the OSI information model. Although managed objects also exist for internet, they are not based on an object-oriented approach, with the formation of classes, inherited features, refinement, allomorphism, etc. There are no generic object classes, and there is no subdivision according to attributes or attribute groups. Management information is described by simple abstract data types. In this sense, the objects are the smallest accessible units. This gives rise to a flat object world with structured addressing; registration and containment hierarchies are specified in the same tree structure. Internet objects may be identified using the registration tree (Figure 8.17). For example, the system description (sysDescr) has the identifier 1.3.6.1.2.1.1.1. or mib.1.1.

Internet uses the standard MIB (MIB I), which defines more than 114 objects combined into eight groups (RFC 1066); there is also the extended MIB (MIB II) with more than 170 objects, experimental MIBs for new network technologies, etc. The object libraries are constantly being extended. In particular, use of the model permits the incorporation of manufacturer-specific MIBs into the registration tree. This leads to a new heterogeneity in the object world, though the management information may be transported using SNMP.

The scheme for defining an internet object has the following frames:

- Name (object descriptor, object ID).
- Syntax (syntax of data type modelling the object).
- Definition (informal description).
- Access (for example, read only, read/write, not accessible).
- Status (mandatory, optional, obsolete).

The syntax for the object types uses only simple ASN.1 types; an object type macro may be used to facilitate type definitions. The number of predefined types (including network address, internet address, counter, gauge, time ticks and opaque) is considerably smaller than in OSI. A detailed comparison of the OSI and internet information models may be found in Hegering (1991b).

SNMP is used to transport the management information. The protocol has five protocol data units: GetRequest, GetNextRequest, SetRequest, GetResponse and Trap. These elements may be used to query and set values in the agent MIBs and to send certain alarm messages. The latter are sent using traps, which agents use to notify the NMS that predefined events have occurred (for example, LinkDown, LinkUp, ColdStart, AuthenticationFailure). As described in Chapter 6, SNMP is based on UDP. Figure 8.18 (from Terplan and Voigt, 1991) shows the SNMP architecture.

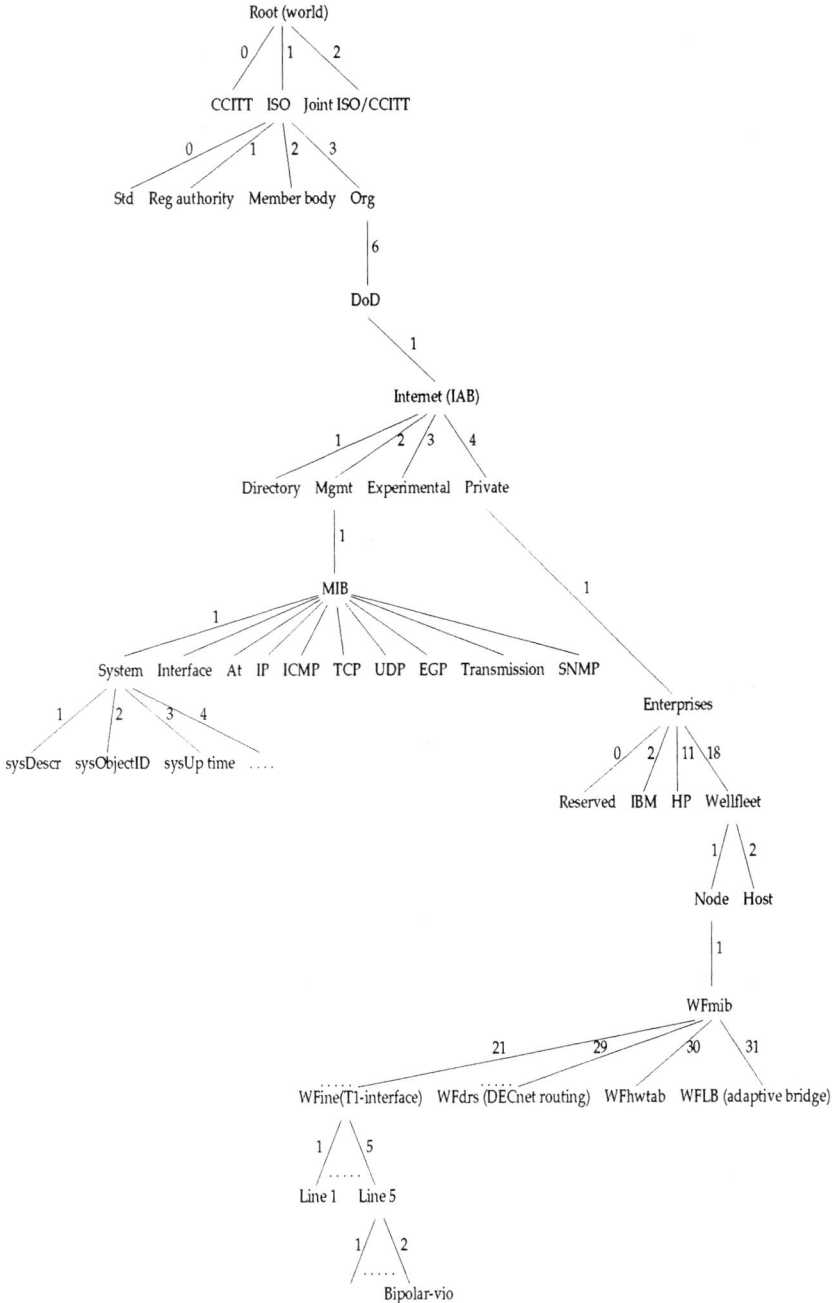

Figure 8.17   Internet registration tree.

```
     SNMP client                           SNMP server
      (Manager)                              (Agent)
```

| SNMP user interface |
| SNMP application |

| SNMP Traps | SNMP Get (next) Set Get response |

```
 <————>  SNMP
         protocol
```

| SNMP server |

Authentication		Authentication
UDP		UDP
IP		IP
HW / drivers		HW / drivers

| Version | Community name | PDU |

SNMP message

| Request ID | Error status | Error index | Variable name | Variable value |

Get response PDU < 484 Bytes

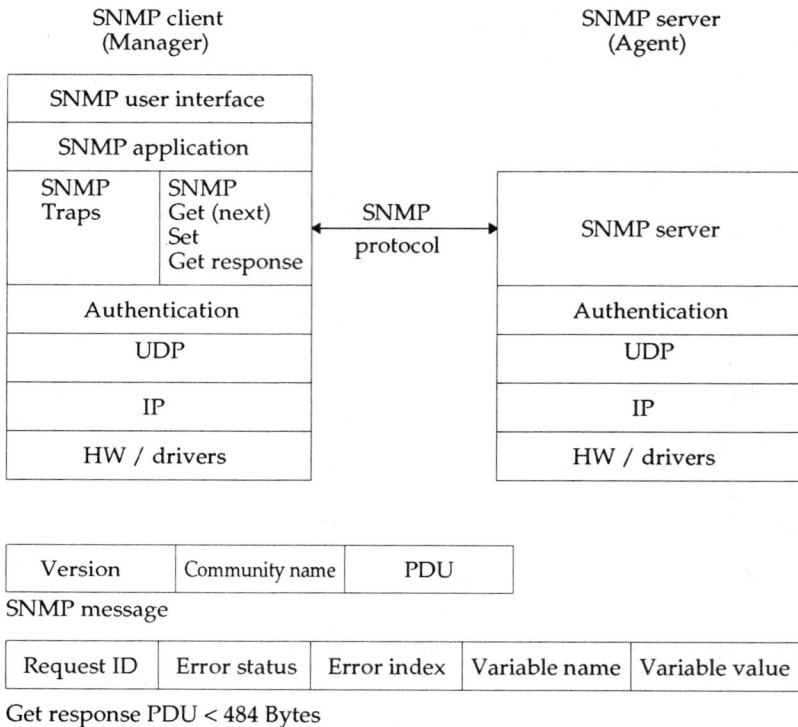

Figure 8.18   SNMP architecture.

The internet management system monitors and controls the network by polling the devices. The data is evaluated in the NMS. If the polling rate is very high or there are many agents in the network, this type of procedure may lead to non-negligible overloading of the network. Here, the OSI management system with its more powerful object structures, dynamic objects, discriminators, filter mechanisms, scoping, etc. provides more flexible facilities.

However, the internet management system together with SNMP also has quite considerable advantages:

• The simplicity of the concept has led to very rapid implementations.

• The CPU and storage requirements are small. Thus, an SNMP management system may be implemented even in simple LAN components.

• There are many products on the market. Hosts, PCs, terminal servers, bridges, routers and hubs support SNMP and the internet MIBs.

- An increasing number of management applications are based on SNMP. A number of products are available (see Section 8.4.2.2), and these will spread rapidly in the near future as the number of UNIX workstations and LANs increases.

In the long term, OSI NM is undoubtedly the better architecture, and from the network provider's point of view offers a more suitable architectural approach for large heterogeneous networks. However, in the LAN area, in practice, only an SNMP-based management system is available today.

8.4 Tools and devices for operational support

In this section we shall describe components and systems which may be used to support the operation of an Ethernet LAN. LAN problems may occur at all levels of the ISO model, from the lowest (hardware) level to the application level. Some supporting tools are more concerned with the hardware-oriented lower levels of a network, whereas others cater more for higher protocols and application software. Because of the varied nature of faults and the complexity of LANs, there are no devices available that can handle all the faults which may occur at all levels of a network. Multimeters, time-domain reflectometers and transceiver testers, which are discussed in the first part of this section, may be used to test hardware-oriented network components such as the different Ethernet transmission media and transceivers. Protocol analysers and network management stations which are considered subsequently are mainly used to test software-controlled network components such as bridges, routers and gateways and their protocols.

Whether it is worth purchasing individual devices of this type depends heavily on the size of the network and on the variety of the protocols used. Unlike some manufacturer-specific homogeneous networks, LANs often consist of a large number of different hardware and software components, which naturally increases the complexity of the problem to be solved. The relatively high purchase prices and maintenance costs of diagnostic components of this type must be weighed against the frequency of faults and the resulting breakdown situations. Many of the devices also require trained operators. For example, if one wishes to investigate the behaviour of the protocol between two stations on the Ethernet, while a protocol analyser will pick out the corresponding data packets, the analysis must be carried out by staff members acquainted with the protocol, unless an intelligent protocol-error-analysis program, possibly based on an expert system, is available. Usually, 'full equipping' with such devices is only worthwhile for very large networks. However, in any case, a procedure for handling maintenance and faults should be put in place in all LANs and corresponding agreements taken out with companies with the appropriate competences. For example, if a PC network based on Ethernet is installed in a lawyer's chambers, after the installation of the Ethernet LAN, the supplier should also measure the cable electrically and in a communications engineering sense check the operation of the PC network; additionally, the company should guarantee to trace and eliminate faults within an agreed time of their occurrence.

8.4.1 Devices for monitoring the Ethernet cable structure

In this section, we shall describe devices which may be used to monitor and check the operation of hardware-oriented Ethernet components such as Ethernet media, transceivers, repeaters, etc. This includes indicator lights, multimeters, time-domain reflectometers and transceiver testers. Usually, the devices are only needed for the installation and preventive maintenance of the cable structure; sometimes, however, they may also be used to diagnose medium-related transmission faults.

8.4.1.1 Indicator lights

Although indicator lights in the form of lights of various different colours or LEDs are not actually autonomous instruments for monitoring the operation of the network, they may, nevertheless, provide valuable information about faults in the network. Moreover, these are often contained in the network components at no additional cost. When a decision is to be made between components from different manufacturers (for example, transceivers), the number of indicators should also be an important criterion in the decision. If check lights are comprehensively present in all the important components of an Ethernet LAN this may provide valuable help in the detection of faults. In the case of Ethernet, indicator lights are commonly available for SQE, transmit data, receive data, collision and ready to receive for various components. While these check lights cannot provide exact information (for example, the number of collisions per second) the frequency of blinking or a single absence of an indicator (assuming that the light is not itself defective) may provide the first hint of a fault. Thus, it is possible to detect, for example, the overloading of a segment or an individual station, failure to receive data or halted transmission of data and to determine the general operational status of a component. Since these possibilities relate primarily to functions up to layer 2, as many as possible of the components which deal with these layers should be provided with indicators. These include controller cards (with on-board transceivers) in the data terminal, all forms of transceivers, multitransceivers, multiport repeaters, repeaters, interface cards in bridges, etc.

Table 8.2 Electrical values for various Ethernet installations.

Resistance	Minimum	Maximum
Ethernet V2.0	17 Ω	72 Ω
IEEE 802.3 (10base5)	17 Ω	72 Ω
Cheapernet (10base2)	17 Ω	72 Ω
Twisted pair (10baseT)	16 Ω per 100 feet	30 Ω
Voltage	Minimum	Maximum
Ethernet V2.0	−0.7 V	0.7 V
IEEE 802.3 (10base5)	−0.7 V	0.7 V
Cheapernet (10base2)	−0.7 V	0.7 V
Twisted pair (10baseT)	0 V	17 V

8.4.1.2 Multimeters

The multimeter (or multitester, volt and Ohm-meter) may be used to measure the voltage, amperage or resistance of an electrical conductor. This device may be used to determine whether the permissible values for Ethernet are adhered to. Table 8.2 lists the permissible values for various versions of Ethernet. If the values are not adhered to, for example, a break in the cable, a short circuit, a cable which is not terminated by resistors or damage to the outer conductor, may be deduced. The multimeter is an inexpensive and simple device for diagnosis of a network problem in layer 1. It is small and easy to handle. It is primarily used to check an Ethernet medium after the initial installation to see that it has been correctly laid. However, while it can indicate a fault, it cannot locate faults in the way that the time-domain reflectometer can. Its use presents problems during the continuous operation of the network since the terminating resistor on the cable must be removed for measurement and thus the whole coax segment is unusable during the measurement.

8.4.1.3 Time-domain reflectometers

The time-domain reflectometer (TDR) may be used to:

- detect malfunctions such as short circuits, breaks, chafing and kinks in the cable;
- determine the number of interface points (transceivers) and their relative distances;
- locate faults (which the multimeter cannot do).

This is a combined device consisting of a signal generator and a device

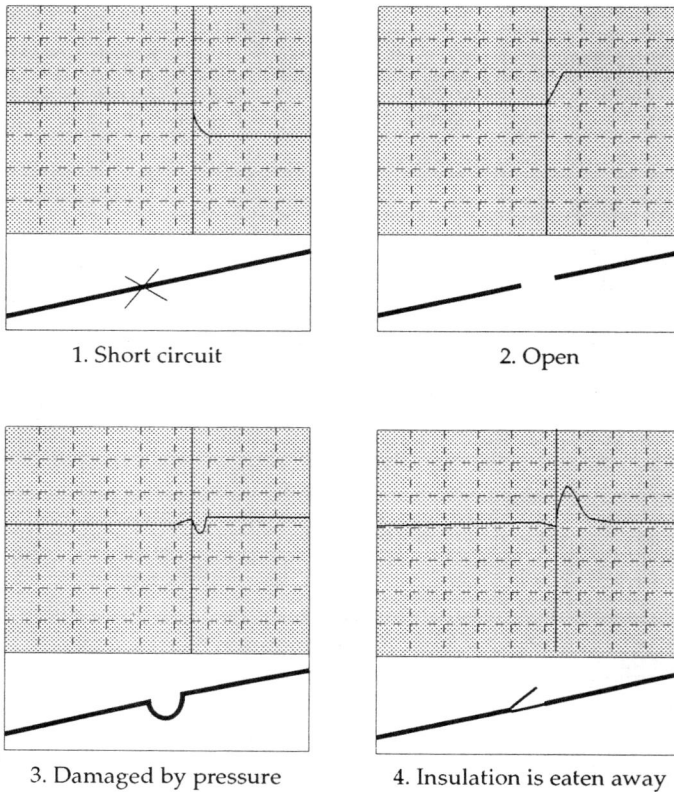

1. Short circuit

2. Open

3. Damaged by pressure

4. Insulation is eaten away

Figure 8.19   Typical measurement results from a time-domain reflectometer (from Terplan and Voigt, 1991).

to measure the voltage, which may be used for flat-conductor, coaxial or twisted-pair cables. The measurement principle of the TDR is based on the fact that most cable defects cause a change in the impedance characteristics of the medium. If there is a fault in a cable to be checked, part of the test pulse will be reflected at the point of the defect. The nature of the fault can be determined from the shape of the reflected pulse (if the device permits this, see also Figure 8.19). The position of the defect may be determined more or less accurately (depending on the device) using a distance indicator on the measuring device (for example, screen, paper printout, digital display). Corresponding optical time-domain reflectometers (OTDRs) also exist for optical media.

Measurement using a time-domain reflectometer should be carried out after every new installation of an Ethernet medium by the company which laid it and supplied as documentation (for example, on paper). This not only provides information about laying faults (for example, kinks in the cable) but also acts as a reference measurement which could be useful in later searches for faults. Simultaneous documentation of the actual path of the cable through the rooms greatly simplifies later location of faults when these occur, since the length reading from the TDR does not indicate the actual position of the fault. Some TDR devices may also be used for measurement without interrupting the operation of the network.

8.4.1.4 Transceiver testers

A transceiver tester may be used to monitor the correct installation and mode of operation of a transceiver and the attached transceiver cable. Unlike a multimeter, a transceiver tester may be used to check that a transceiver with a vampire clamp into the core of the yellow Ethernet cable has been correctly installed. In addition, the receive and transmit functions and the so-called heartbeat (or SQE) may be checked. It is also possible to check the transceiver cable to ensure that is it operational (pin-wise in some models) and that it is properly lodged in the transceiver. These devices are usually inexpensive and provide a fast and exact indication of the successful installation of a transceiver which, if carried out improperly, could lead to faults in the whole coax cable segment.

8.4.2 Devices for monitoring Ethernet protocols

In addition to checks that the hardware-oriented network components are functioning correctly, the protocols which run on these must be investigated and analysed in order to guarantee smooth operation of an Ethernet LAN. This is carried out using independent portable devices (mostly based on PCs), known as LAN analysers or protocol analysers, which are used for protocol encryption, statistics and load simulation. Similar functions are also built into so-called platforms, which are independent network management systems (NMSs) with an extensive functionality, and which are usually implemented on workstations under UNIX. Since, as a result of increased data communications volumes and for security reasons, local area networks are increasingly being divided by bridges and/or routers, the network provider is no longer able to monitor all the network traffic and thus also the error behaviour from a central point. For example, the CSMA/CD procedure relates to a single collision domain. Thus, either an analyser must be purchased for each subnetwork or a single portable analyser must be used locally when faults occur.

Another solution involves so-called monitor boxes or PODs, which act as facilities for delivering network data to the central monitor, where the latter has the same functionality as a LAN analyser. Usually, no single one of these three possibilities (illustrated in Figure 8.20) is capable of providing a solution to the problem on its own.

Use of a LAN analyser

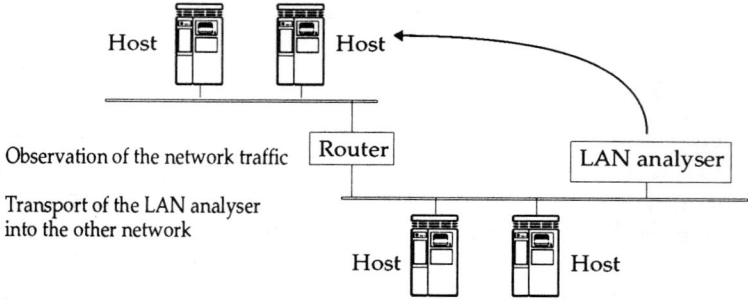

Observation of the network traffic

Transport of the LAN analyser into the other network

Use of monitor systems

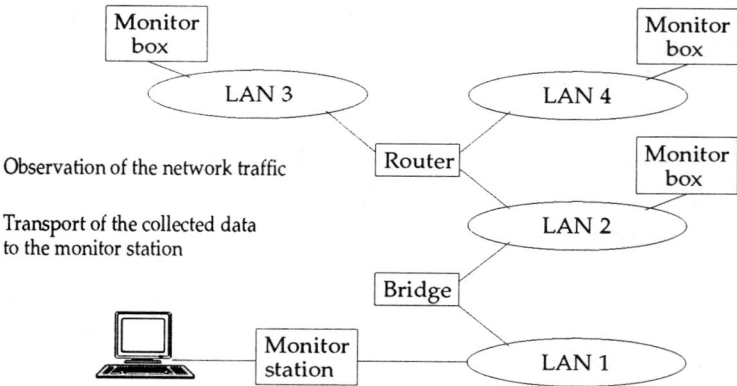

Observation of the network traffic

Transport of the collected data to the monitor station

Use of a network management system

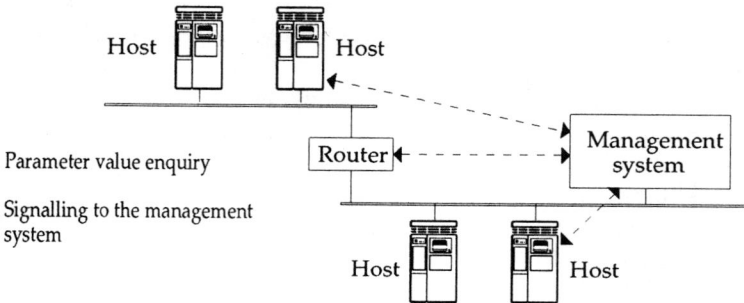

Parameter value enquiry

Signalling to the management system

Figure 8.20 Possibilities for network monitoring.

If the number of subnetworks increases sharply (for example, Ethernet internetworks with more than 150 subnetworks have been reported) the installation of LAN analysers or PODs in each subnetwork is no longer affordable. Of course, a single LAN analyser for such a large number of subnetworks will not be sufficient either. Thus, other possibilities must be sought. One possibility, for example, is that the components such as bridges and/or routers which separate and at the same time connect the subnetworks should collect such management information and deliver it to a central network management station. In practice, this may now be achieved using SNMP agents in components which deliver their data to a central SNMP network management platform. However, in comparison with the insertion of LAN analysers or PODs in every subLAN, the facilities of the SNMP solution are considerably poorer since the number of generally defined parameters of the standard MIB is so small that this information is far less than that available locally to LAN analysers. These problems could be solved by the definition of manufacturer-proprietary subMIBs, but the compatibility with other components would be lost.

8.4.2.1 LAN analysers

A LAN analyser is defined to be an independent, portable diagnostic tool which is primarily used to analyse the packets on an Ethernet LAN. It may be used to acquire, decode and analyse data packets and also to simulate data packets. Occasionally, subfunctions such as those of the time-domain reflectometer or the multimeter are built into these devices. In addition, higher-grade devices support not only Ethernet but also a number of other interfaces in the LAN area (e.g. Token Ring, FDDI) and the WAN area (e.g. X.25, V.35, Frame Relay), so that all transition components between these areas (e.g. gateways or routers) may be tested using a single device.

Such devices are often based on PC extensions. This approach involves a HW extension of the PC communications interfaces and special protocol evaluation software which is often supported by higher level programming languages. Examples of LAN analysers (far from complete) include HP's LAN Protocol Analyser 4972 A, Rohde and Schwarz's Ethernet Test Probe LAS0.7, the Spider Monitor from Spider Systems, LTR's Network Quality Analyser (NQA), Excelan's LANalyser EX 5000, Network General's Sniffer System, the Protolyzer from ProTools and Wandel and Goldermann's DA-30. Depending on the functionality, the prices for these devices lie in a broad range.

By way of example, Figure 8.21 shows the possible use of a LAN analyser (here, the NQA LAN analyser) to record the load on an Ethernet LAN over a period of 25 minutes. The number of packets per second (top row), the percentage loading per second (middle row) and the number of collisions per second (bottom row) are shown.

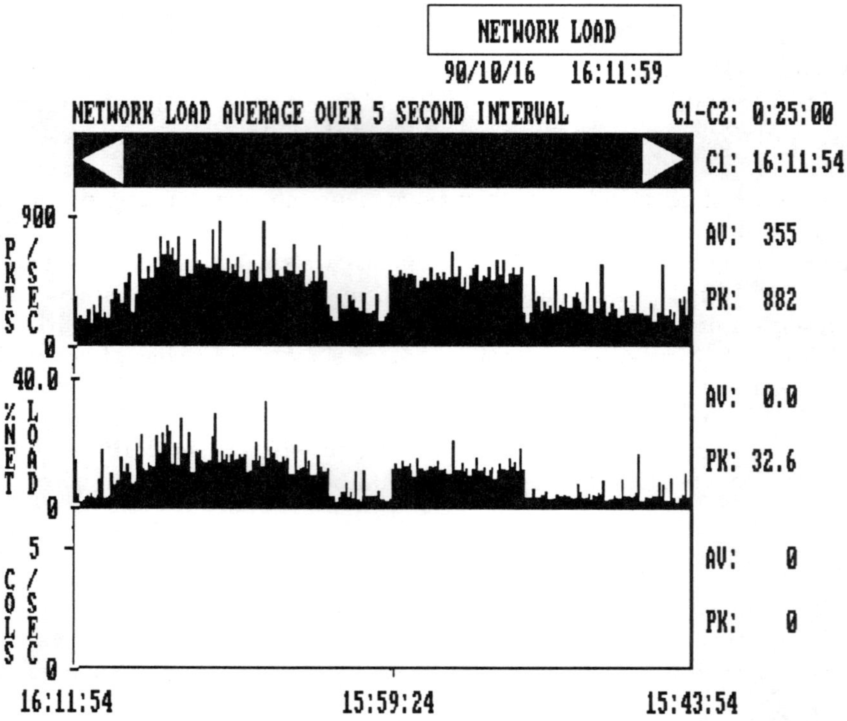

```
                    ┌─────────────────────┐
                    │    NETWORK LOAD     │
                    └─────────────────────┘
                     90/10/16   16:11:59
   NETWORK LOAD AVERAGE OVER 5 SECOND INTERVAL        C1-C2:  0:25:00

   ◄                                        ►         C1:  16:11:54

   900                                                AV:   355
   P /
   K S
   T E                                                PK:   882
   S C
     0

   40.0                                               AV:   0.0
   % L
   N O
   E A                                                PK:  32.6
   T D
     0

   5                                                  AV:    0
   C /
   O S
   L E                                                PK:    0
   S C
     0
   16:11:54            15:59:24            15:43:54
```

Figure 8.21   Loading of an Ethernet recorded using the NQA LAN analyser.

The following may play an important role in the choice of such systems:

- Portability (size, weight, laptop or standalone device).
- The size of the memory used to record the data traffic.
- The number and fineness of the filters for controlling the recording of the data packets, and the extent to which these may be chained.
- The presentation of the evaluated data (hex dump or text representation).
- The number of possible protocol interpreters, including those for higher layers (for example, for TCP, IP, IPX, X.400, X.500).
- The performance capability of the device itself, as far as the ability to record all the data traffic without packet loss (even when an Ethernet is almost fully loaded) is concerned.

- The user prompting and the access protection on certain functions (for example, load generation).

- The facility for generating network loads and predefined data packets.

- The performance capability of the statistical functions provided (for example, connection matrix, error rates, network loading, long-term recording).

- The printer connection for documentation of the data.

- The possibility of remote operation, for example via dial modems (outband) or remote login (inband).

- The number of network interfaces supported both in the LAN and WAN areas.

New products and improvements of existing LAN analysers appear regularly on the market; these are often described and evaluated in relevant professional magazines and journals.

LAN analysers are important tools for network management, above all in relation to error isolation and performance optimization in networks with heterogeneous components. Currently any embedding in network management systems (NMS, see next section) is either impossible or inadequate. Often, data collected by the LAN analyser cannot be evaluated by a given NMS or information available in an NMS (for example, computer IDs) cannot be transferred to the LAN analyser.

8.4.2.2 Network management systems

Unlike LAN analysers which passively pick up and evaluate traffic passing on the LAN and actively transmit data packets to the LAN, network management systems are devices which, based on common protocols and presentation surfaces in the network management area, permit interworking between the network components and the devices attached to the network. They actively fetch standardized management information from the components, or have this information deliberately signalled to them, and support a user-friendly operation of the network. In Section 8.3, we gave examples of standardized network management architectures including the OSI network management system with CMIP and the SMI object library and the internet management system with the protocols SNMP and CMOT and the object libraries MIB I and MIB II. In addition, it should also be possible to integrate other management procedures from the WAN area and from the non-standardized company-specific area into the network management systems.

Next we describe requirements and selection criteria for these network management stations (Valta, 1992).

These include:

(1) Basic properties of a NMS such as:
- The number of protocols supported (e.g. SNMP, CMOT, CMIP, IEEE 802.2, MAP, TOP, X.25, DECnet, etc.).
- The number of object libraries supported (e.g. Internet MIB I and II (and successors), experimental MIBs, manufacturer MIBs, object libraries based on OSI SMI or OSI/NM Forum, manufacturer-specific libraries, etc.).
- The extensibility of the object libraries, since these are highly dynamic. Here, the extension method is important (dynamic or static, with or without compiler); if a compiler is used, the nature of the description language is also important (e.g. RFC 1155 – description, OSI templates, NM Forum templates).
- The granularity of the solution. Can the NMS consist of several communicating core systems? Is there a hierarchy of subsystems? Which protocol is used for intercommunication?
- The linkage to other foreign NMSs such as IBM NetView, DEC EMA, HP OpenView.
- The linkage to other necessary systems such as cabling documentation systems, directory and mail systems.
- The storage of the network-related data, distinguished according to the nature of the data storage (files only, object-oriented database, relational database. etc.), the scope of the information (see also Section 8.5.1) and how the data is to be accessed (by applications or by direct database interface).

(2) Scope of the application-related functionality, including:
- Interrogation of the object variables, individually or in fixed or definable groups.
- Continuous monitoring of object variables with facilities to start, end or standardize a message or a display type, to store a message, including over a long period, and to carry out correlation with other measurement points.
- Write access to object variables with the facilities to access individual attributes, groups of attributes and groups of objects and to carry out consistency checks.
- Event handling with facilities for definition, notification, long-term storage and evaluation of events.
- State monitoring with facilities to define states, associate states with events and introduce and react to changes of state.
- Incorporation of a trouble ticket system (TTS).

— Selection of components via standard services such as Telnet, X.29 and rlogin.

— Configuration change.

— Incorporation of other management applications, for example, from the manufacturers of special components.

(3) Facilities of user surfaces, including:

— The basic prerequisites determined by the main software used (X11, Motif), the colour or monochrome display, possible non-graphical interface facilities (for example, commands, menus) and the possible use of X.Terminals.

— The structure and management of the network presentation (also called the map), which may be built up using text and graphics editors with various degrees of user-friendliness, automatically (discovery function) or based on network data.

— The hierarchical ranking of fixed and/or variable maps.

— The representation of network components by graphics symbols, which may be fixed or self-defined.

— The possibility of a realistic representation, for example, for hardware components, cabling and topography.

— Visualization of changes of state using predefined colours for generic logical units.

— The definition of views for different users and different ways of looking at a network.

— The possibility of simultaneous use by several users, by LAN administrators, LAN operators and LAN maintenance engineers.

(4) Facilities for creating one's own network applications, which are determined by:

— The programmer interfaces for communication, the user surfaces, the databases used, etc.

— The user-friendliness of the programmer interfaces, which depends, for example, on the programming language, the complexity of the service, documentation, test facilities and program libraries.

(5) Other criteria such as:

— Security criteria, for example, provision of a separate user administration system with layered protection of the individual functions.

— The time-related costs associated with installation, map generation, extensions, network data acquisition, understanding the product and the concepts involved.

— Availability of the products, support and sales.

— Costs, including subcosts for various functions, discounts, maintenance, training and manuals.

— Future developments including the date and scope of new versions.

The selection criteria already give an overview of the possible functions of an NMS. The market is at present still very heterogeneous and very confused. Thus, the OSF is working on this problem and is attempting to establish a common platform for system and network management by the definition of a Distributed Management Environment (DME). The first results of an operational version are not expected until the end of 1993. An introduction to this is given in Heigert (1991) and OSF (1992).

NMS which satisfy many of the above requirements are usually based on UNIX workstations. Here, the GUI is often based on X-Windows/Motif. There is a clear separation between the object managers (if there are any) which implement the connections to the real network components to be managed and their objects and the applications which edit the data in the NMS. SNMP and CMOT are the most frequently used management protocols. The languages C and C++ are often provided for the development environment. However, we note that in most NMSs only the values of the variables are made available; the evaluation of these values is often left to the user who must then program appropriate network applications for this purpose himself. Figure 8.22 shows the schematic structure of such an NMS for the example of the HP OpenView Network Management Server.

The cost of the software for an NMS can be very high. This naturally depends on the functional scope of the NMS software. To this must also be added the cost of the workstation hardware, which is also not small, since large, high-resolution, colour display screens are used.

Examples of NMSs include (the list does not claim to be complete) the HP OpenView Network Management Server, Sun's SunNet Manager, Cabletron's Spectrum product, DEC's DECmcc, the DualManager from NetLabs, the NMC3000 from Network Managers and the LAN Systems from Hughes.

These products differ in terms of the hardware environment needed, the functionality of the GUI, the number of available applications and their functionality, the availability of object managers, the cost of generating new applications and object managers and, naturally, the procurement and operation costs.

It is not easy to choose a specific NMS. On the one hand, the continuous and rapid evolution of products causes problems, while on the other hand, it is often impossible to compare products in a real network environment since this would require a costly adaptation procedure.

User interface

X11
OSF Motif

Database

HP OpenView Windows		Communications	Data management services	Database management system	DB
Applications					
Object Manager			Event management services		DB
Infrastructure					

SNMP	CMOT	CMIP
UDP	TCP	OSI
IP		

Communications protocols

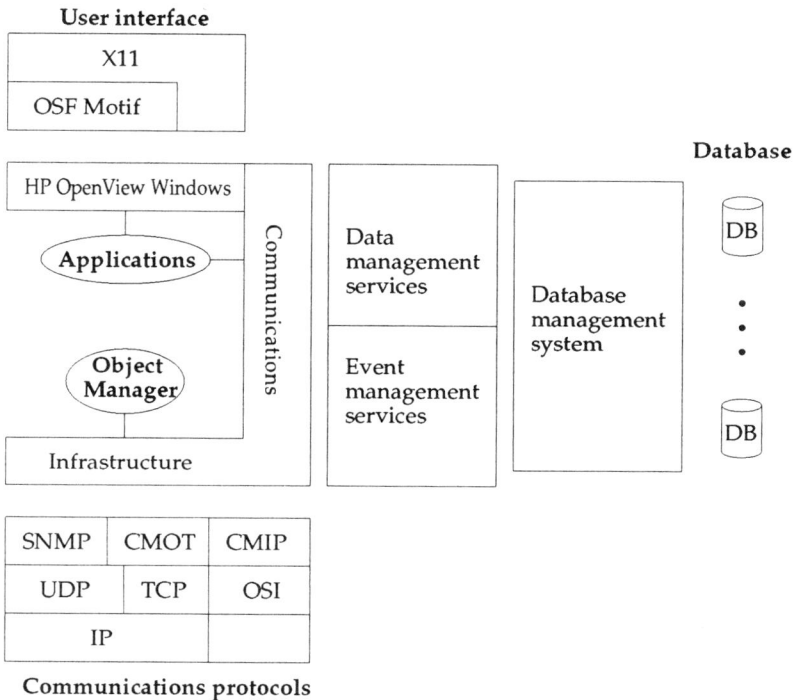

Figure 8.22 Schematic structure of a network management system (based on the example of HP OpenView).

In addition, product presentations (for example at trade fairs) are often not very informative.

The available NM products for non-manufacturer-specific networks are still inadequate. In particular, the range of NM applications offered is still thin and often limited to a more-or-less user- friendly network monitoring with read access to components, status monitoring, definition and monitoring of thresholds and graphical display of messages. Incorporation of network components which support SNMP is unproblematic. But SNMP-based systems cover only a small part of the needs. They are too internet- and LAN-oriented, the underlying paradigms are consciously kept simple and are inappropriate for management of larger, more complicated, heterogeneous networks. OSI products, which may be conceptually more appropriate, are only now reaching the market. However, even the availability of good OSI-based platforms does not solve the whole NM problem. Only the network provider can realize the full potential of NM architectures through the specification of NM applications and specific management databases. This requires a fundamental analysis of management procedures, information flows, network components, management databases and appropriate goal-oriented management policies. This type of top-down development of specific NM systems was not necessary for homogeneous networks and places new demands on many providers. The results of the analysis must then be mapped onto the platforms in accordance with the architecture paradigm. This means firstly the modelling of resources and NM algorithms and then the development of object managers and proxy agents, etc. Even though the NM architectures are still partly in a state of flux, network providers and network users should be involved with them *now*.

As described above, integrated management systems do not initially result in great progress as far as the functionality they offer the network provider is concerned. However, they provide a facility for accessing standardized management information over standardized interfaces, and thus form a sensible basis for the creation of management applications to meet current and future requirements.

The boundaries between network management, the system management of distributed systems (for example, extended WS clusters on a client–server basis) and the management of distributed applications are becoming increasingly blurred. Thus, managed objects are becoming more and more complicated. A flexible restructuring of management information, in the form of an adaptation to the specific operational environment (customizing) is required. This results in the need for powerful information models with flexible structuring concepts (for example, inheritance, allomorphism, containment, relationships). The monitoring of large networks with many autonomous components requires event mechanisms and easy object selection. The incorporation of organizational structures requires domain concepts.

These arguments already suggest that more complex and powerful management architectures (for example, OSI NM, OSF DME, ODP) point the way ahead. Thus, the Leibniz Computer Centre, which currently uses SNMP management on a large scale is now in the throes of intensive preparation for the more complicated architectures.

8.5 Operational aspects in LANs

The operational and management aspects of an Ethernet may be divided into functional areas analogous to the ISO proposals for network management:

- Configuration management

- Fault management
- Performance management
- Security management
- Accounting management.

Figure 8.23 shows the relationship between the individual functional areas.
In the following sections we shall consider these aspects from the point of view of an Ethernet LAN. Much of what is said also applies to the operation of networks in general and, in particular, to the operation of other types of LANs. The objective of each of these subaspects must be to achieve a highly stable network operation and to guarantee the necessary quality of network services. The operation of an Ethernet LAN may sometimes become very complicated as a result of:

- the large number of components used;
- the spatial distribution of the components;
- the heterogeneity of the hardware and software components used;
- the different responsibilities for the components (personnel from different companies);
- the different responsibilities for the partially independent subLANs.

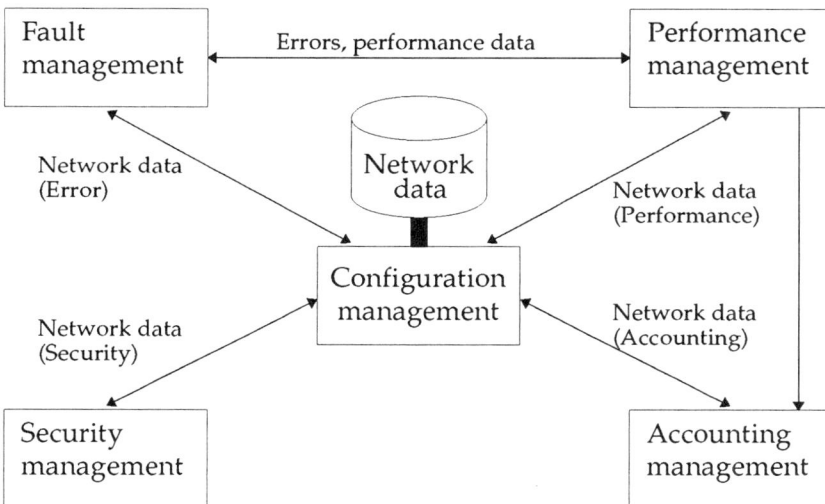

Figure 8.23   Relationship between the network management functional areas.

Table 8.3 Assignment of functional areas of LAN management to people.

Functions	LAN operator	LAN administrator	LAN analyst	LAN maintenance
Configuration management				
Management of network data		x		
Changes		x		
Name and address allocation		x		
Cable documentation				x
Fault management				
Status monitoring	x			
Receipt of error notifications	x			
Fault diagnosis	x	x	x	
Tests		x	x	
TTS management	x			
Performance management				
Definition of performance indicators			x	
Measurements			x	
Tuning			x	
Data-protection management				
Threat analysis		x		
Implementation of measures		x		
Accounting management				
Cost recording		x		
Allocation of costs		x		
Monitoring of SW licences		x		
LAN planning				
Planning			x	
Market monitoring			x	
Component tests		x	x	
Implementation				x

The distinction between central and decentralized control of the network is common in all domains. Central control is usually sensible for computer networks belonging to a single provider; in other words, when required, it should be possible to address all network components (stations, terminal servers, servers, bridges, routers, gateways) from one point in the network. This should also be possible over network boundaries, for example, via bridges, routers or brouters, and should include functions such as remote loading, status requests, restart, configuration, etc. However, the central control should not rule out a local control, which is indispensable for maintenance and test purposes.

Status requests should be possible both locally (for example, using function light indicators) and over the network from a central network management station (see Section 8.4.2). Status requests should provide information about the state of the network components as a whole, about boards and ports and also about the current state of device connections and about configuration parameters and the activity of connections, etc.

In large LAN networks (for example, at the LRZ), various personnel profiles describing the levels of training of staff members to whom the functional areas of network management may be assigned have been developed. Table 8.3 lists these profiles.

Of course, this assignment may be different for smaller LANs; among other things, all the functions might be combined in a single person. Another solution is to task another company with this job (outsourcing), which should not be a bad solution for a relatively small network with a large number of heterogeneous components.

8.5.1 Configuration, network documentation

The functional area of configuration in the network management context includes the management of the physical and logical configuration, the monitoring and manipulation of the network operation and the management of the associated documentation.

Network database

While the PCs in a PC network which is installed in only a small number of adjacent rooms, can still be inspected visually, this will not be possible for extensive local area networks such as those installed in universities and large companies. The task of network configuration and control can only be carried out with correspondingly extensive, accurate and current network data. Thus, one important basic tool of the network management system should be a database containing all relevant data about the network components to be managed and configured. First approaches to determine the structure and the content of such a network database are contained in the ISO and internet standard documents (see also Section 8.3). Currently, network databases are often based on the combination of very different files. Figure 8.24 illustrates this. A network database should include:

- The network device documentation, including:
  - Location (room, building, address, operating company, position in the room, telephone number at the location).

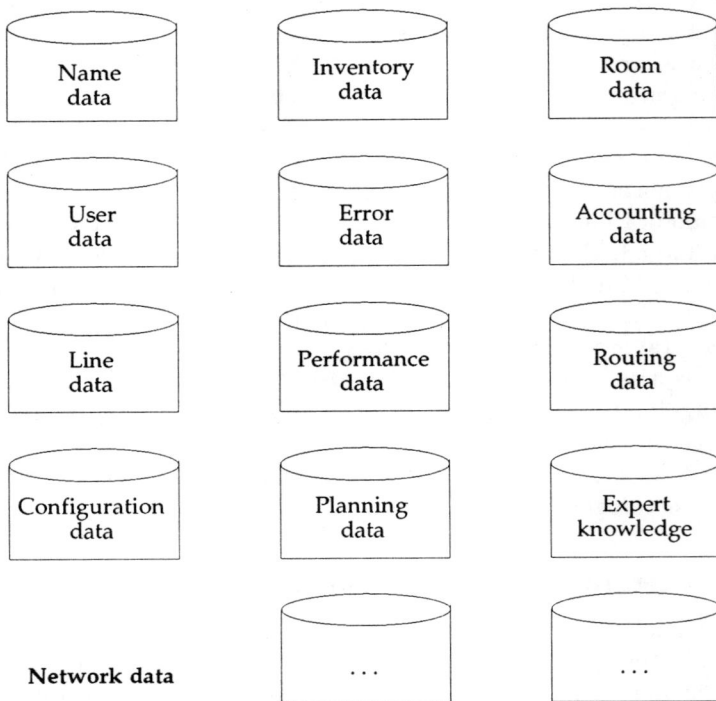

Figure 8.24 Components of a network database.

— Properties (type, manufacturer, operating system, hardware fittings).

— Responsible persons (name, telephone number, area of responsibility).

— Network interfaces (connection controller, connection hardware, connection protocol with names and addresses).

- The line documentation, including:

— Position (start point, end point, length, course).

— Properties (cable type).

— Responsibilities (in-house or PTT line).

— Links to the distribution panel.

- The topological documentation, including:

— The topological course of the network media.

- — Accurate room and building plans.
- The fault documentation (possibly the trouble ticket system (TTS)), including:
  - — fault type
  - — time of the fault
  - — removal of the fault.

This network data should be integrated into a single database and be callable from as many points of the network as possible by various members of the network provider's staff (LAN operators, LAN maintenance engineers, LAN administrators, LAN analysts). In addition, there should be a connection to other services supporting the network operation. For example, it should be possible to extract lists of the assignment of names to addresses (MAC addresses) from the database and play these into LAN analysers in order to avoid laborious typing of this data into the analyser. There should also be a connection to the network management station and to the trouble ticket system.

Control and configuration

Control and configuration in local area networks is often complicated by the fact that different components must be looked after by different manufacturers. No common operator interface has yet been built. Thus, the aim should be to integrate the management aspects of all these systems. Corresponding approaches to integration were discussed in Section 8.3.

Provided the functionality of LAN network components does not simply depend on the adjustment of a few hardware switches; in order to set the possible choices of parameters for supported interfaces and protocols, the components are configured by altering software (parameters). The adjustment of parameters to actual operational situations is called *configuration*.

These parameters include:

- Protocol parameters (message lengths, window size, timers, priority, etc.).
- Parameters relating to the connection of devices to terminal servers (device type and class, procedure, bit rate, parity, etc.).
- Entries for routing and bridge tables, name servers and directory databases.
- Filter parameters for bridges (addresses, protocols, manufacturer, links, etc.).
- Parameters for router connection circuits (interfaces, speed, flow-control procedures, etc.).

- Spanning tree parameters of a bridge (priority of the bridge, etc.).

As part of the network management activities, OSI is also attempting to develop standards for the configuration interface; however, standardization is a long way off. Thus, the configuration of individual LAN components differs according to:

- The position at which configuration takes place.
- The storage used for configuration.
- The time at which configuration becomes valid.
- The GUI of the configurator.

(1) **The position at which configuration takes place.** The system configured (target system) is not always the same as that on which the configuration is carried out. This may be for technical reasons, for example, because the configuration requires editors and macroprocessors which are not available on the target system. However, it may also be for security or organizational reasons and may depend on whether configuration files can be remotely loaded. Configuration may be carried out:

    — in the network component itself (for example, via an ASCII terminal with VT100 terminal emulation attached to the V.24 interface);

    — in a network component for any other network component from the same manufacturer;

    — in a dedicated station (network management station) for all network components.

(2) **The storage used for configuration.** Here too there are various solutions. If the data is held on diskette or hard disk in the network component, the configuration may be carried out very quickly by changing diskettes. This is not the case when the data is stored in an EPROM; moreover, in this case, because of capacity restrictions the scope of the configuration parameters is smaller, which may also affect the flexibility. Use of flash EPROMs could mitigate these restrictions.

(3) **The time at which configuration becomes valid.** If every reconfiguration operation is associated with a load process (in other words, an interruption of service), the configuration is said to be static. Dynamic configuration permits changes to the configuration data during continuous operation. Thus, conceivable times at which the new operational parameters may become valid include when a new component is loaded, when a component is restarted, and when one of the component ports involved is restarted.

(4) **The GUI of the configurator.** The quality of the GUI depends on the extent to which individual parameters may be changed quickly and the extent to which the network administrator is freed from having to play around with the individual parameters of a large number of devices, for example by facilities such as the ability to define device profiles, configuration variants or configuration profiles which apply to whole groups of devices. The user-friendliness is also improved by corresponding documentation of the configuration data, which should, if possible, also be suitable for supporting the network control. The need for special protection of the configurator and configuration files against unauthorized use is discussed in Section 8.5.4. The types of access protection range from doing without passwords to the possibility of establishing areas of responsibility for configuration by using separate network-global, component-local and function-specific passwords.

The *system generation* (in other words, the generation of new software modules or versions for LAN components) also forms part of the operation of the LAN. Since the LAN components in general do not have access either to local peripherals or to a convenient programming environment, the following possibilities are available:

*   The new version is delivered in a PROM; the PROM must be exchanged.

*   The linked software is delivered as object code on diskette. Read stations are used to load the software into the main memory.

*   The new software must be generated from SW modules delivered on a separate computer system (network monitor station, host, PC), which must have access to corresponding cross software.

Some LAN suppliers only provide these programming environment aids on particular computer systems; a fact which must be taken into account in relation to costs when purchasing the LAN. The components are then loaded over the network from the disk of this computer system.

Decentralized loading and configuration do not require a central configuration/generation station. This is certainly a cost advantage as far as small LANs are concerned. However, such procedures are no longer practicable for large networks. Since the variety of interfaces and the range of available transport services are also increasing, the configuration software is becoming more and more extensive. It no longer seems sensible to hold this software in a decentralized way on each component. Thus, there is a tendency for manufacturers of functionally powerful LAN components (e.g. brouters) to carry out the configuration process centrally, for example, on a PC or a workstation with a connection to the LAN.

8.5.2 Detection and correction of faults

Fault management is taken to mean the detection, isolation and correction of faults. In local area networks, fault management is often not carried out as a precaution but only when a fault occurs, even though the LAN has now become a central element of a DP service. Moreover, many measuring instruments (see Section 8.4), which can only cover individual fault handling subfunctions, complicate the work of those involved with their different user surfaces.

A fault may be defined to be a deviation from set operational objectives or network functions, where these are defined. Messages about faults are usually transmitted either by the network components themselves or by the network users. Possible sources of faults include:

- Data transmission paths (for example, transceiver cables, thick Ethernet, thin Ethernet, twisted-pair cables, fibre optic cables, PTT connection circuits).
- Network components (for example, transceivers, repeaters, bridges, star couplers, server computers, data terminals).
- Network-component software.
- Inadequate interface descriptions (indirectly).
- Operating errors.

Faults or problems should be detected as soon as possible, preferably before they are reported by users, using network-status monitoring and alarm messages. In status monitoring, continuous measurement generates a large amount of information, the transmission, recording and evaluation of which results in a considerable overhead unless the information is processed by intelligent filtering. However, an almost continuous measurement provides quite accurate information about the first occurrence of a fault, which may later be hidden by other fault- related phenomena, together with long-term information, for example about the loading of a network. Sporadic messages may be used for problems of an analytical nature and functional faults; however, they do not provide data for network planning and monitoring. With the help of filters and thresholds, alarms instead of mass data and routine messages can report the most important matters to the operating staff.

Problems may often be processed in four stages. Simple problems (for example, dead device, wrong user entry) may still be dealt with by fault-reporting centre (user service, help desk). By restarting network components and notifying the PTT or maintenance companies LAN operators can handle faults such as device stoppages, line faults, and interface defects. LAN specialists are consulted regarding faults in components for which they are responsible (for example, configuration errors, routing problems).

Finally, in the case of more acute software and hardware faults in network components, recourse to the appropriate manufacturer or supplier may be necessary.

One valuable aid is the entry of reported faults in a DP supported fault report system (trouble ticket system, TTS). Thus, for example, it is possible to avoid duplicated processing of faults, to determine correlations between faults, to document the correction of faults, and to report a current fault status (including for users).

Other important prerequisites for successful fault finding and correction are a precise knowledge of the hardware and software components of the network (network documentation), the presence of fault correction procedures, the use of appropriate measuring instruments (see Section 8.4) and a sufficient level of knowledge amongst the network maintenance staff.

Thus, fault handling involves the following steps:

- Fault detection.
- Fault isolation (assignment of the fault to a fault source).
- Reproduction of a fault.
- Documentation of the fault.
- Analysis of the cause of the fault.
- Correction of the fault.
- Preventive maintenance.

Ready-made procedures, decision matrices and flow diagrams provide for considerable savings of time and expense in diagnosis. Detailed examples are given by Datapro, Miller (1989) and Nemzow (1992). We shall not describe these here. Naturally, all this must be related to the topology, the architecture and the transmission media of the LAN to be managed. Such elaborate procedures may then form the basis for future expert systems.

Organizational prerequisites for fault management include:

- Telephone connections to the sites where data terminals and network components are installed.
- Device identifications which are clearly visible to the users (these should not only identify the device but also include advice on how to isolate the fault).
- Devices should be accessible outside the normal service hours.
- There should be a specific procedure for informing all user groups concerned.

8.5.3 Performance aspects

The term performance management covers the recording of data in order to evaluate and improve the performance capability of the network resources.

Previously, the discussion of the performance capability of local area networks all too often referred only to the performance which was achievable at the lowest protocol levels (medium, signal structure, access strategy), while comparisons were restricted to only a few situations or special loads. In Ethernet, however, the performance pattern is heavily affected by the length of paths between stations, the packet length and the number of stations which wish to transmit. Thus, for a small number of stations and large packets, the performance limits may be reached at 85% loading, while for large numbers of stations and small packets, the limits are reached for a loading of from 25% to 30%. Thus, measurements and performance considerations should always relate to real networks.

In the meantime, there has been a change in the network management philosophy. As far as network operation is concerned, attention is no longer directed primarily towards the performance capability of the Ethernet in limiting situations or towards the attached terminals. Instead, it can now be assumed that the performance of the attached terminals is such that precautions must be taken to prevent the occurrence of limiting situations. Bridges and routers may be used to configure an Ethernet LAN according to the load. This problem was discussed in Section 4.3.3. Whilst previously the question was how to implement the load on the Ethernet, the question now, particularly for large LANs, is often how to remove the load from the shared Ethernet LAN and separate it into several subLANs.

However, one should not completely neglect to study the performance capability of Ethernet components. The network performance visible to the end user (useful data rates, network delay) is an important performance criterion, which is determined by product-conditioned architectural differences in the Ethernet components involved (controllers, bridges, routers, terminal servers), the protocols used within a protocol family, and the limitations of the individual stations (for example, PCs, workstations). In addition, the current network configuration, the application and the traffic characteristics play a large part.

As far as the attached stations are concerned, the performance is affected by the hardware (for example, CPU speed, main-memory size, memory access times), the operating system (for example, page size, allocation of priorities, I/O organization) and the way in which the communications software is linked in to the operating system. As far as the controller cards are concerned, factors include not only the distribution of protocol functions over the modules and the buffer management, but also organization of the interfaces between controllers and other devices (see Section 5.2).

In the experience of users, the useful data rates, determined by the network architecture and the protocol hierarchy, often fall far below 50% of the nominal data rates offered. Much performance capability may be lost in the mapping of the protocol layers onto one another. This includes not only the CPU cost of the mapping but also the protocol overhead, the copying of buffer contents between protocol entities and the fragmentation or blocking of message units. Thus, higher network services such as virtual terminal (Telnet), file transfer (FTP) or electronic mail, internetworking and transport protocols (XNS, TCP/IP) may affect the Ethernet frame length in different ways, and so make the use of the actual Ethernet layers more or less efficient. Thus, for example, XNS permits a maximum data field of 600 bytes, while IEEE 802.3 allows for a frame length of 1500 bytes. For some measurements, the observed FTP transmission rate has been found to be only 40% of the underlying TCP transmission rate.

One should take this into consideration when choosing LAN components and seek guarantees on the performance. Of course, these can only be valid if it is possible to carry out measurements to prove them. The following questions may be helpful in this respect:

- What is the useful data rate of a port, a board, a controller?
- What is the maximum achievable useful data throughput over a bridge, a router, a brouter or a gateway?
- For which network access protocols or network-internal protocol levels can parameters such as block and window sizes, transmit- and receive-buffer sizes and priorities be influenced? Can some of this tuning be carried out dynamically?
- What is the throughput of specific protocol layers?

A consideration of performance requires performance measurement. Performance measurement is needed to check assured performance guarantees and to facilitate the analysis of bottlenecks in the network operation. Aids to performance measurement include load generators and software and hardware monitors.

In addition to the tried and tested stop watch, software monitors (e.g. LAN-connection monitors or measuring programs in the hosts/PCs), which use the measurement resources contained in the generation programs (e.g. counters, time stamps, etc.), or hardware monitors may be used as measuring monitors. An early example of a software monitor based on the 'standard user' measuring technique is the PERGAMON product, which is described in detail in Marquard et al. (1987).

Other examples of measuring aids include the well-known and often installed command of the UNIX world, 'ping', or its later derivatives (for example, isiping) with which, using the ICMP protocol of the TCP/IP protocol family, the user himself may poll other TCP/IP computers. The

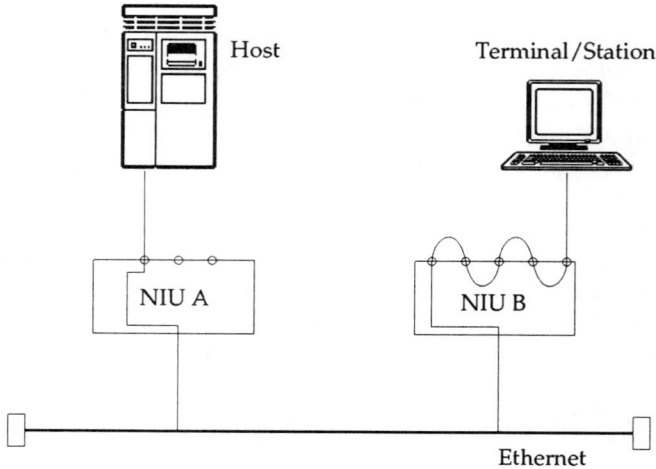

Figure 8.25 Generation of a load for a terminal server.

'pinged' computer replies to the packet of predefinable length with an echo packet of the same length. Thus, for example, turn-around times to other different computers in the network may be estimated. In general, we note that, both in the UNIX and TCP/IP worlds, there are a number of freely available (public domain) software products which support various measurements on an Ethernet (for example, the matrix of communications relationships). Such products are also available for OSI protocols (for example, OSI-ping).

LAN analysers provide another means of determining the performance of an Ethernet (see Section 8.4.2) and may be used for continuous or discrete measurements. Interesting quantities here include the percentage loading of the network, the packet-size distribution, the number and type of defective packets per unit time, the number of active stations and the communications relationships between stations. These devices are also suitable for load generation. Other possible load generators include, for example, continuous output from a host computer, automatic dialogue in workstation systems, etc. Figure 8.25 shows how relatively simple resources may be used to generate a load for a terminal server.

Next we describe a number of results which have been obtained using the measuring aids outlined above. The performance values were often obtained on the extensive LAN of the Leibniz Computer Centre of the Bavarian Academy of Sciences (LRZ), the configuration of which is described in Section 8.6. The examples show that the performance aspects certainly have a role to play as far as practical operation is concerned. We also note that statements about the performance capability must perforce be seen in the context of the specific test environment. We again stress that the results here are only intended to indicate orders of magnitude. In addition, they depend on each product version and on the test environment, and thus, in particular, on the behaviour of the other LAN subscribers.

Propagation-time delays

Measurements of the turn-around time were carried out on the extended LRZ network using the 'isiping' product of the TCP/IP protocol world, as described above. Terminal servers on the CDCNet (Terminal Device Interface, TDI) at various locations in the LRZ network were 'pinged' from a Sun. The values obtained are shown in Table 8.4.

In the first example, the TDI and the Sun are directly connected via a single multiport transceiver. In the second example, the TDI and the SUN are connected via the Ethernet backbone network with 2400 m of fibre optic cable, 1 bridge, 2 routers and 3 star couplers. In the third example, the TDI and the SUN are connected via a 2 Mbps transmission circuit of length 20 km with 1 bridge, 3 brouters and 2 star couplers. Finally, in the fourth example, the TDI and the SUN are connected via a 64 kbps transmission circuit with 1 bridge, 1 TDI and one star coupler. As one might expect, the speed of the transmission circuit, the distance between the two components and the size of the echo packet affect the turn-around time. The minimum values are most important as far a judgement of the actual propagation time is concerned. The maximum and average values are affected by the instantaneous loading of the components involved. Nevertheless, taking the average values, except in the last case of the 64 kbps transmission circuit, the values lie in an acceptable range. The results also show that difficulties may be encountered with applications (for example, NFS) in local area networks which run over 64 kbps circuits, since the expected response times (for example, acknowledgement of packet receipt) cannot be adhered to.

Throughput for file transfer

Throughput rates for file transfer between different computers over an Ethernet LAN have been reported by various sources. The rates vary depending on the transmission protocols and the Ethernet controllers used, but are interesting enough to earn a mention here.

For DECnet protocols, using VAX computers, rates of up to 7.5 Mbps for transfer from memory to memory and 2 Mbps for transfer from disk to disk have been observed.

For the FTP protocol of the TCP/IP protocol world, rates of 1.5 Mbps between the disk memory of a Sun workstation and that of a PC 386 and 3 Mbps between two CDC Cyber computers are achievable.

Table 8.4 Turn-around times in the LRZ network.

Type of LAN circuit to the 'pinged' computer	Packet size	Turn-around time (in μs)		
		Minimum	Average	Maximum
10 Mbps constant,	64	7	8	218
5 m distance	1.008	14	14	94
on same multitransceiver	1.508	20	25	351
10 Mbps constant,	64	11	18	395
2400 m distance	1.008	24	31	471
several connection components involved	1.508	34	46	486
2 Mbps connection circuit for remote bridge	64	14	18	269
20 000 m distance	1.008	34	39	299
several connection components involved	1.508	50	56	346
64 kbps connection circuit for remote bridge	64	43	46	276
1500 m distance	1.008	291	300	420
several connection components involved	1.508	436	444	591

Rates up to 1.4 Mbps are achievable using Novell NetWare (back up of PC disks on to server PC disks) for PC-to-PC communication between MS-DOS computers.

These figures already show that a single application on the local area network, which is made available to the user as a standard service, may easily occupy 10% of the network capacity of the Ethernet. The measurements show that currently the limiting factors are the disk access speed and the CPU power (above all for PCs). Since these values are being continuously improved, in the near future, it will be possible for a single connection to occupy the whole capacity of Ethernet. In these applications (file transfer), because of the large Ethernet packets (on average over 1000 bytes), the effect of the delay due to the CSMA/CD procedure is relatively small, since, per unit time the possible collisions as a result of the CSMA/CD algorithm contribute relatively little.

Overall network loading

At the LRZ, the network load is continuously determined and recorded using LAN analysers. A clear increase in the network load has been observed in this way. At the end of 1989, the following values were obtained for the whole of the LRZ network (see Section 8.6) without using separating components such as bridges or routers.

A network activity of some 300 active connections, the majority of which were interactive applications, generated an Ethernet load of between 5% and 40% for a measurement interval of one second, up to 17% for a measurement interval of 20 seconds and an average daily load of between 3% and 7%. A maximum of 1400 packets per second was observed. Of all Ethernet packets, 75% were shorter than 128 bytes (which means a high CSMA/CD-algorithm rate) and only 1% were longer than 1 kbyte. No noticeable disturbances of the terminal traffic were observed during this period.

Two years later, at the end of 1991, the overall LRZ network was divided into four subnetworks using brouters. Observations were then taken for the subLAN covering only the LRZ building, and the following results were obtained.

A network activity of some 100 active connections where, now, in addition to screen-oriented (e.g. X-Windows) interactive applications, some of the applications included file transfer (e.g. FTP) and distributed file systems (e.g. NFS), a load of up to 60% was observed for a measurement interval of a second, with a load of up to 40% for a measurement interval of 20 seconds and a daily average load of around 4%. Up to 1500 packets per second were observed. As a result of the changed applications, the average packet length was considerably greater. Disturbances were sometimes noticeable in the interactive traffic during a file transfer. Figure 8.21 shows such a file transfer which may lead to disturbances for other applications.

The two sets of measurements show that, despite the subdivision of the network and the small number of simultaneous applications in the subnetworks, the network load has nevertheless increased considerably as a result of changes in the nature of the applications.

Höns and Köpke (1987) studied the limiting load of an Ethernet of the GMD (Gesellschaft für Mathematik and Datenverarbeitung, German Society for Mathematics and Data Processing). The network did not even break down for network loads of over 90%. Blocks were also transmitted in this saturation phase, for which Ethernet handled all stations fairly. A load of 60% was given as a generally critical threshold.

As previously mentioned, when network-separating components (bridges, routers, brouters) are used, network overloads may be avoided. Errors in the initial dimensioning of the network cannot be corrected by tuning measures alone. However, there exist planning and modelling tools for finding the correct LAN dimensioning and some of these may also be used to tune the performance during continuous operation. Examples of such packages include LANNET II.5 from C.A.C.I, LANSIM and LAN A I from Internetix and BONes from Comdisco (Terplan and Voigt, 1991).

8.5.4 Security aspects

Security measures in local area networks depend very heavily on the requirements of individual network providers and the attached computers. Installation of security measures should always be preceded by a risk analysis to specify the requirements. The aims of the security measures should then be:

- no divulging of information to unauthorized persons;
- no falsification of information to deceive those authorized to receive it (spoofing);
- no possibility for users to deny use to those with the necessary authorization;
- data integrity.

Security measures may be divided into those which concern the network and those which concern the computers attached to the network. In what follows, we shall discuss the security problem for local area networks, and Ethernet LANs in particular. We shall not discuss the problem of the security of the computers attached to the network (for example, virus protection, stations with no permanent local storage facilities) in further detail. After describing possible security threats, we discuss measures to counter these dangers.

Ethernet itself does not take any precautions to provide for increased security; it is a simple, open, physical medium. The main security loopholes in Ethernet are a result of the open architecture, the use of the broadcast principle for communication, the ease with which new stations may be attached, the lack of physical security and the ease with which transmission may be disrupted.

Security threats may include passive attacks on the network in which the traffic on the network may be listened in to and recorded. This is easy to do, since Ethernet LANs are diffusion networks with standardized layers 1 and 2. Thus, every station on the network is able to hear and evaluate all CSMA/CD frames and all data link frames, provided it is fast enough. This facility is used by LAN analysers. Software is also available (including for PCs and workstations, some of it public domain software) which may be used to record and evaluate foreign Ethernet data packets. One example in the PC area is the network monitor software LANWatch from FTP Software which runs with many popular controller cards. The functionality corresponds extensively to that of LAN analysers, without the need for additional hardware components in this case. A further example from the workstation area is the program 'nnstat' which is available on many UNIX systems. Another way of listening in to the overall Ethernet traffic is to record the electromagnetic emission from copper cables (for example, UTP cable for 10baseT). The data which is obtained by eavesdropping may be used, for example, to identify subscribers, to read passwords and data which are not encrypted on the network and to analyse traffic flow.

Undesirable 'black' stations may connect to the network using vampire clamps, the free ports of a multitransceiver or the Cheapernet wall outlets without being noticed, since these methods do not involve an interruption of service. Instantaneous fault signals will *de facto* be handled like collisions, short frames or other transmission errors.

Active attacks on the network, in which the data on the network is altered include the repetition, delaying, introduction, modification or deletion of certain data. In addition, the crippling of the network, for example, by load generation (e.g. continual broadcasting of connection requests) by a LAN analyser, and the feigning of a false identity, for example of a server (e.g. by replying more rapidly to a name-server query or by inserting an existing MAC Ethernet address using software) belong to this category.

Other dangers to the security of a network which must also be reckoned with include unintended possibilities such as the breakdown of active or passive network components, transmission errors, misrouting of information, and operating faults.

The above threats may only be reduced by combinations of a number of graded measures. Such measures should be designed to prevent passive attacks, to detect active attacks (in practice, these cannot be prevented) and to circumvent unintended events. However, one should always bear in mind that the largest potential threat is from people. Research has shown that people were (maliciously) involved in more than two thirds of security failures. Measures exist at the physical and logical levels, and organizational measures are also available.

Measures at the physical level may include:

- Untappable media (e.g. fibre optic cable) could be used instead of copper cable.
- Cable conduits, free ports (e.g. on multitransceivers), and network wiring closets together with the active components they contain (e.g. star couplers, bridges) could be made inaccessible.
- Regular measurements could be taken using TDRs to detect unauthorized transceiver connections.
- The network could be monitored using LAN analysers to detect unknown MAC addresses.
- LANs could be separated using bridges, routers or brouters.
- Redundant active (e.g. bridges) or passive (e.g. a second trunk line) network components or parts of these (e.g. parts of the power supply system) could be installed.
- A star-shaped cabling could be used, since in this case, unlike in a bus structure, only one device is attached to a line. This could then be used by intelligent hubs for security measures.

Measures at the logical level include:

- Access to the network and to the resources provided could be controlled. This control may be divided into the following subaspects: uniform user interfaces, identification, authentication, authorization, confidentiality, secrecy, and anonymity. Here, particular attention should be paid to the facilities for dialling into the network over WAN networks (e.g. telephone modems, X.25 access).
- Communication relationships could be separated and routed using filters in bridges, routers and brouters.
- Passwords should be used intelligently.
- Appropriate procedures (e.g. public- or private-key encryption) could be used to encrypt data passed between terminals (e.g. use of the overall frame).
- Empty network traffic could be generated to complicate traffic-analysis attempts.
- The network traffic as a whole could be monitored to detect irregularities.

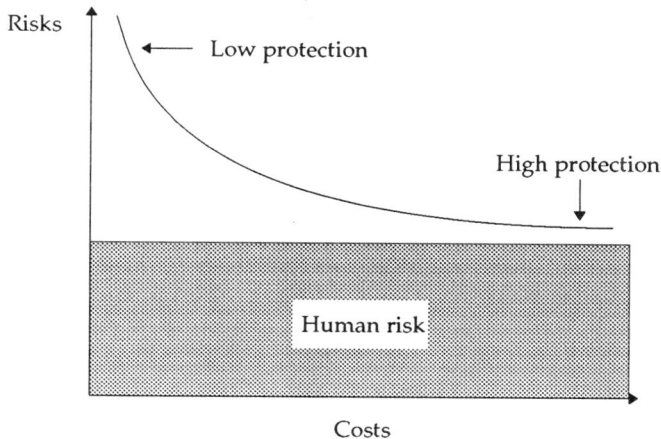

Figure 8.26   Relationship between costs and risks for security measures.

The following organizational measures may be appropriate:

- Access to the tools of the LAN administrator (e.g. LAN analysers) and to network components (e.g. routers) could be restricted (e.g. using passwords) and monitored.

- Data could be altered within the security measures (for example, password changes, names of servers, telephone numbers).

The above measures cannot of course be complete. The LAN provider should carry out a risk analysis in order to decide which measures to implement and how. Finally, there is a close relationship between the increase in costs and the risks offset by the manufacturer. Figure 8.26 illustrates this.

8.5.5 Accounting

Accounting management involves the determination of the usage of the network resources and the passing on of the costs to those responsible. Accounting is increasingly important as far as local area networks are concerned. However, current LAN products have practically no accounting facilities. Thus, LAN costs are usually estimated and treated as general costs. The increased integration of LANs into more global communication infrastructures (access to remote computers, commercial database services, servers in local area networks, PC networks, internetworking, use of remote repeaters, LAN–WAN coupling) demands increased usage- and user-dependent accounting facilities for LAN services. When one faces up to the fact that communication costs now amount to 50% of a total

EDP budget, it becomes even more important, particularly for larger companies, to assign the costs to those responsible. However, one should also realize that recording of and accounting for the services of a LAN and its attached computers are much more complicated and expensive tasks than that of accounting for the resources of an individual central computer. The requirements that no user should be able to enter the system illegitimately or to leave the system without the resources he has used being recorded, are usually essentially met by multiuser mainframes, but not by workstations or in local area networks. At the same time, the sharp growth in the numbers of distributed systems increasingly requires usage- and user-oriented accounting facilities.

The implementation of an accounting system, the way in which the accounting parameters are recorded and the distribution of the costs, etc. is a management decision. This may be influenced by company policies because the ratio between the expense of recording costs and their usefulness must be assessed.

After the fixed and variable costs of all components (for example, cabling systems, connection components such as bridges and routers, PTT connection circuits, communications servers) to be included in the accounting have been recorded, the costs must be allocated to those responsible. Here, all degrees of refinement are conceivable as far as the recording of costs and their distribution to those responsible is concerned. The more refinement there is, the more expensive and cost-intensive the accounting procedure becomes.

The basic usage parameters which may be recorded include:

- The number of packets transmitted.
- The duration of the connection.
- The bandwidth of the connection.
- The location of the other communication partner (for example, over WAN or PTT circuits).
- Conversion costs for gateway services.
- Reservation of server resources.
- Use of software products.

Accounting arrangements include:

- Proportional accounting for departments.
- Accounting for attached stations.
- Static accounting for users (for example, monthly accounting).
- Dynamic accounting for users (for example, running debiting of charges above a preset limit).

The requirement for user-oriented accounting is closely associated with the facilities for user identification (Hegering and Chylla, 1987) since only identifiable users can be charged. User identification can also be used for access protection as a security measure.

No tailor-made accounting system is yet available; the network provider must decide whether he wishes to install such a system, and if so, how. A detailed discussion of this may be found in Rhodes (1991). Tools which may be helpful when implementing an accounting system include the accounting systems in PC-network servers (for example, Novell), software systems for monitoring software licences and distributing software (e.g. SiteLock from Brightwork) and LAN analysers (e.g. recording of the communication relationships and station activities).

8.6 Ethernet LANs at the Leibniz Computer Centre

In what follows, we shall describe an example of a large Ethernet LAN configuration, namely that of the Leibniz Computer Centre of the Bavarian Academy of Sciences (LRZ). The LRZ has been involved with local area networks for a long time and, in particular, with Ethernet. It deployed one of the first Ethernet installations in Germany. In this instance Ungermann Bass's NET/ONE was used based on Ethernet Version 1.0. Already in 1983, one of the first test reports in the German language was issued by the LRZ.

As the regional university computing centre for Southern Bavaria the LRZ is responsible for providing all universities in its catchment area with a DP service which cannot be provided in a decentralized fashion, for example, with PCs and workstations. Thus, currently (December 1992) the installations in the service area with computer capacity located centrally in the LRZ building comprise:

- a CDC Cyber 2000 mainframe under the NOS/VE operating system;
- a Cray Y-MP8/8128 vector computer under UNIX;
- a CDC CD 4680;
- three clusters of six high-performance HP 750 workstations each;
- some 100 workstations (PCs, Suns, MACs, Next, etc.).

These computers are interlinked by an FDDI network, which is connected via a brouter to the many-branched communications network in the Munich catchment area. The network is used by the computers in the institutes of the Munich universities for communication amongst themselves and with the central computers in the LRZ and for remote communication. Remote communication is covered by connections to WIN, IXI, Internet and Datex P (see also Figure 4.28). A smaller part of this communications network is still an X.25 network based on PTT leased-lines, the main part is a local area network based on Ethernet.

In the LRZ network, the following cabling strategy is used for the buildings to be supplied. Between buildings on an adjacent piece of land (e.g. the Garching campus), because of the distance and for protection against lightning, the cable is made of optical fibres. The connection with the fibre optic circuits is provided in the buildings by star couplers to which Ethernet cable segments (yellow cable) are then attached, which usually lead through all rooms, storey by storey. Figure 8.27 is a schematic illustration of this for the Garching campus area.

Depending on the premises, the Ethernet coaxial cable is laid either in window-sill conduits, in the floor (sometimes under a false ceiling) or in individual cable bridges. Exceptionally, the cable is even fixed to the wall using cable clamps. Use of Cheapernet is only provided for an institute's own local area networks in nearby rooms. When there is heavy local traffic on institute networks (for example, workstation cluster with servers under NFS), these are linked in by bridges or routers as separate subnetworks. Ethernet based on 10baseT is at present only used in areas in which the existing wire-lines must be used for this, since recabling is impossible. The use of 10baseT in new buildings to be erected is under consideration.

When PTT services are needed to connect the Ethernet islands in the Munich local area, depending on the tariffs and the traffic volumes, on-line connections with speed 64 kbps or 2 Mbps or even monomode fibre optic circuits (dark fibre) are used. Currently nine such fibre optic circuits with a transmission speed of 10 Mbps are rented from the Telekom for a monthly fee. The extension to 27 locations in the Munich area is in preparation, for which a 12-year agreement for use of 140 Mbps fibre optic circuits for a large one-off payment and small monthly maintenance fees has been reached with the Telekom.

Until the end of 1989, the LRZ Ethernet LAN was operated in an unstructured way without deploying a backbone network with bridges or routers. Because of the traffic load, structuring was and still is necessary (see Section 8.5.3). This was carried out using brouters (see Section 4.4), in such a way that the backbone network only connects the brouters to one another and is currently also based on Ethernet.

Figure 8.28 shows the segmentation of the LRZ Ethernet by brouters. The segmentation was carried out according to parts of buildings. As a saving and to simplify matters, a brouter was not installed in every building. Where possible, multiport brouters were installed. The brouters implement routing for the TCP/IP, DECnet and IPX/SPX (Novell) protocol worlds, while all other protocols are handled by the bridge function.

Data terminals are connected in two ways. Existing devices without Ethernet capabilities (alphanumeric displays (for example, VT100), graphics displays, printers, plotters) are attached via existing wire lines to the nearest terminal servers, which support the TCP/IP, CDCNet and

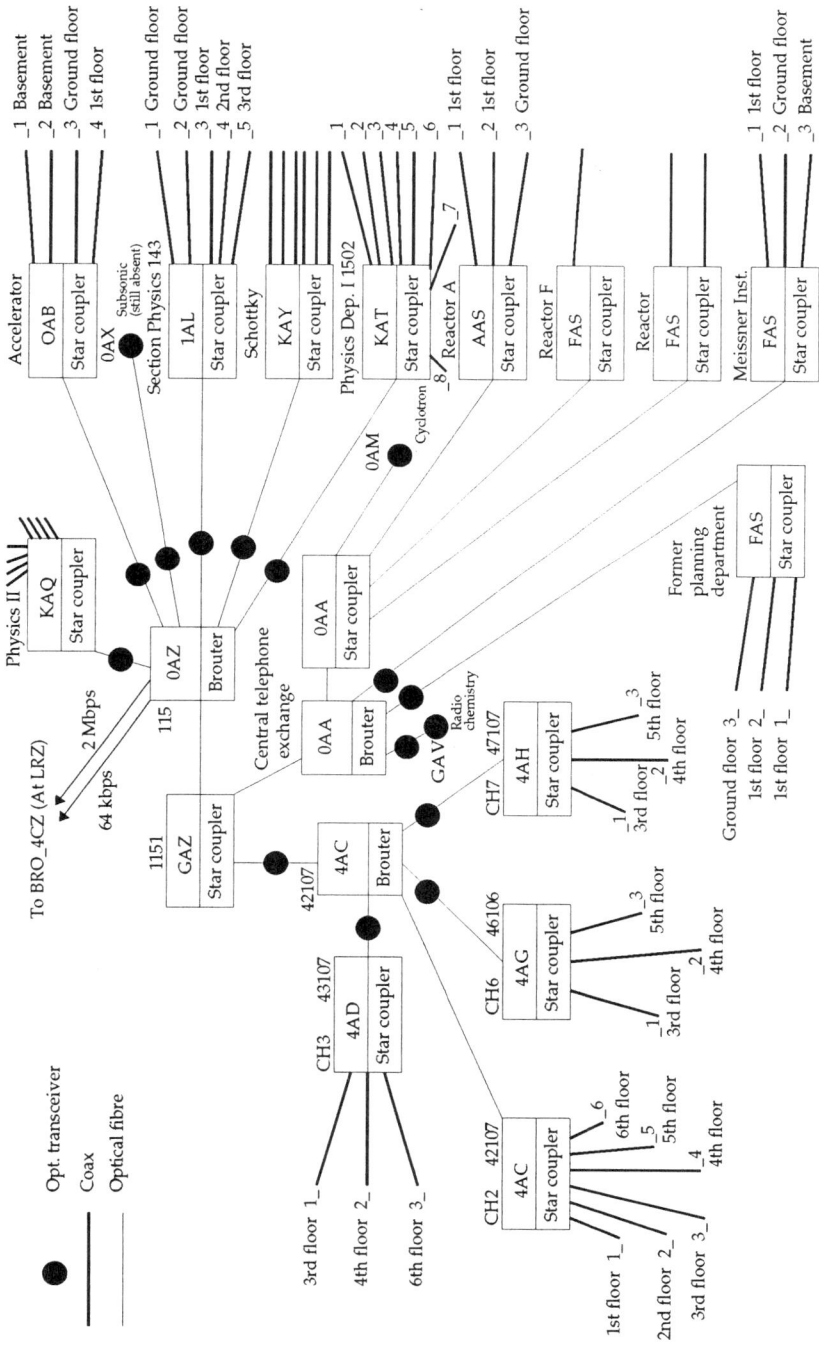

Figure 8.27 LRZ Ethernet integrated network (Garching campus).

367

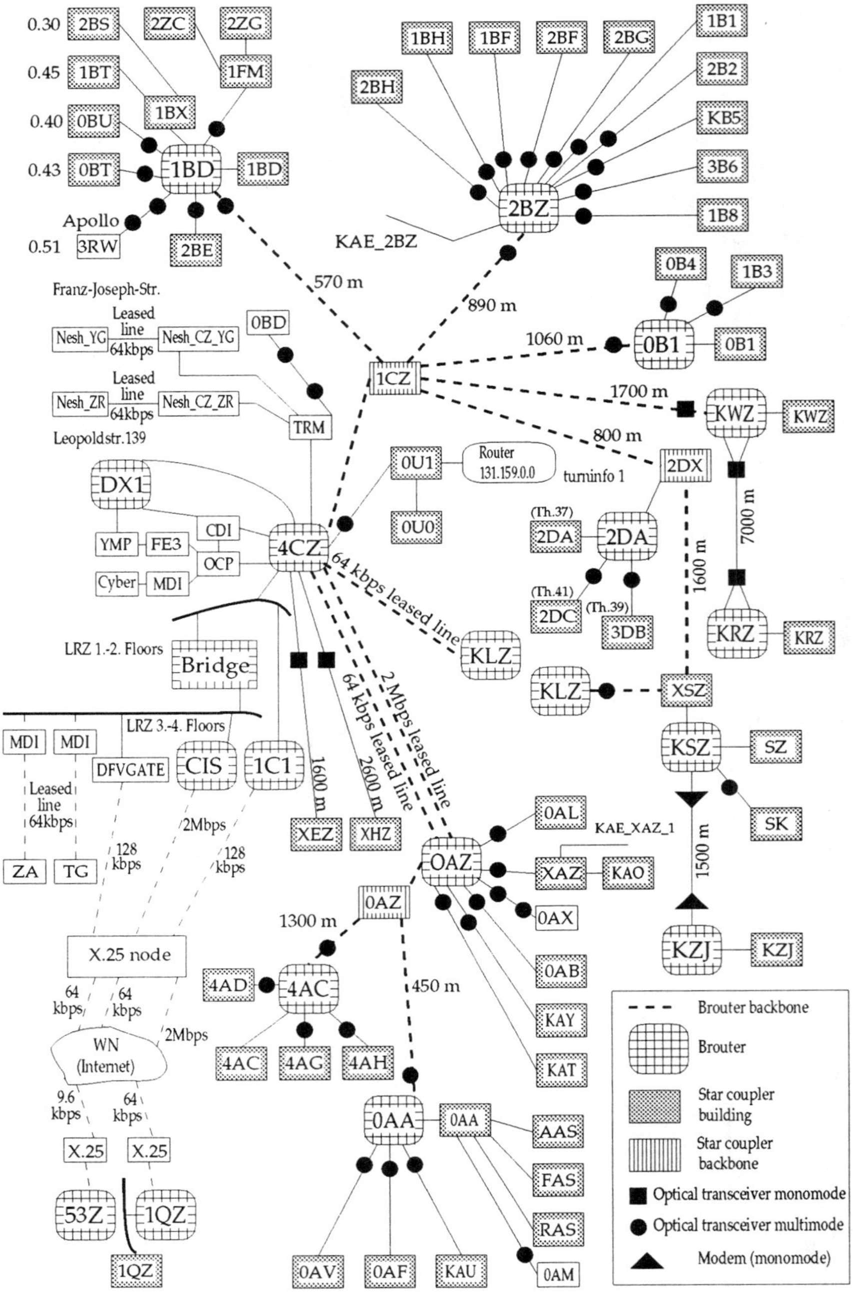

Figure 8.28 LRZ Ethernet integrated network.

DECnet protocols on the LAN side. The number of new non-Ethernet devices installed is decreasing sharply. PCs are connected via a variety of slot-in cards which may be operated with or without their own processors, in parallel or in series (by rebooting the Ethernet card) and with various higher protocols. High-grade computers (for example, workstations, minicomputers) may be connected using the Ethernet interface which is already fitted as a standard in these computers.

The central computer services of the CDC Cyber installation under NOS/VE may be accessed over Ethernet via TCP or over the mainframe network architecture CDCNet; access to the UNIX-based CRAY vector computer, the CDC 4680 and the HP workstation clusters is via TCP/IP.

The LRZ Ethernet currently comprises the following parts (May 1992):

- approximately 22 000 m of coaxial cable (yellow cable);
- approximately 45 000 m of fibre optic circuits (including Telekom circuits);
- 52 active star couplers;
- 35 bridges in the institute area;
- 16 brouters for the backbone network;
- 10 hubs for 10baseT Ethernet;
- 55 terminal servers.

This Ethernet is divided into over 170 logical and physical subnetworks. Currently, over 2500 Ethernet (MAC) addresses are recognized in the LRZ network.

In addition to the above protocols, TCP/IP and CDCNet, which are needed to access the central DP server in the LRZ building, the OSI, DECnet, Novell (IPX, SPX) and AppleTalk protocol families are also used, where TCP/IP (around 70%), Novell (around 20%) and CDCNet (around 5%) predominate.

In general, when constructing Ethernet LANs with such heterogeneous components and end subscribers, as in the case of the LRZ network, one must distinguish between the terms *tolerance* and *compatibility*.

Tolerance means that the products from different manufacturers may coexist on the same Ethernet network without interfering with one another. A prerequisite is that the components should have different Ethernet (MAC) addresses, since all protocol families use the same protocol up to the MAC layer. In the case of Ethernet this is guaranteed by the worldwide central allocation of Ethernet addresses by Xerox. Tolerance does not mean that these components are able to communicate with one another.

Compatibility means that the higher protocols of the different components above the MAC layer are also identical. Only then is intercommunication possible. Products which use TCP/IP protocols are a good example of this.

All the components used in the LRZ network tolerate one another. As previously mentioned, the TCP/IP, CDCNet, DECnet, Novell (PC network) and AppleTalk protocol worlds are used on the Ethernet network without interfering with one another. A transition through gateways is only possible under certain circumstances. In the LRZ network, gateways between TCP/IP and CDCNet, Novell (Pegasus) mail and SMTP mail, SMTP mail and X.400 mail, TCP/IP and X.25 and CDCNet and X.25 are provided.

The following points should be noted with particular reference to the operation of the LRZ network (insofar as they were not already covered in Section 8.5):

- The large number of heterogeneous network components and attached computers does not currently admit a common network management system; it is still necessary to work with different company-specific systems. If possible, the components are monitored using SNMP.

- The independence of the connected institutes means that additional computers may be connected without the LRZ being informed at a sufficiently early stage. Thus, the network documentation often lags behind the current state.

- The stability of the network is gratifying. Breakdowns and faults (both in the hardware area and in the software area) only affect the subLANs concerned, since bridges and routers largely provide for fault separation.

- The overall network must be constantly adapted to the changing traffic loads. The number of subLANs is increasing relentlessly. In the Ethernet feeder area an annual increase of up to 20% in the traffic volumes is assumed.

The ongoing development of the LRZ network in the next three years is aimed towards:

- a blanket provision (in other words, LAN connections in all rooms) to all university buildings of a high-speed network, based on an in-house network investment programme (the Munich universities have more than 100 000 students);

- increased use of Telekom fibre optic circuits in the Munich local area with no restrictions on speed;

- an increase in the transmission speed of the backbone network from

10 Mbps (Ethernet) to 100 Mbps (FDDI);

- the linkage to remote area communications with a high transmission rate (2 Mbps–WIN, or later 34 Mbps–DQDB).

Abbreviations

ACSE	Association Control Service Element.
AFOS	Active Fibre Optic Segment.
AFS	Andrew File System.
AGW	American Gauge Wire.
ANSI	American National Standardization Institute.
API	Application Programming Interface.
ARPA	Advanced Research Projects Agency.
ASE	Application Service Element.
ASN.1	Abstract Syntax Notation One.
ATM	Asynchronous Transfer Mode.
AUI	Attachment Unit Interface.
bps	Bits per second.
BSC	Binary Synchronous Communication.
CAD	Computer Aided Design.
CATV	Cable Television.
CCITT	Consultative Committee for International Telegraphy and Telephony.
CCR	Commitment, Concurrency, Recovery.
CD	Compact Disk.
CEN	Comité Européen de Normalisation.
CEPT	Comité Européen d'Administration des Postes et Télécommunications.
CGW	Customer Gateway (DQDB).
CIM	Computer Integrated Manufacturing.
CMIP	Common Management Information Protocol.
CMIS	Common Management Information Service.
COS	Cooperation for Open Systems.
CP	Convergence Protocol.
CPE	Convergence Protocol Entity.
CRC	Cyclic Redundancy Check.
CRV	Coding Rule Violation.
CSMA/CD	Carrier Sense Multiple Access/Collision Detection.
DARPA	Defense Advanced Research Projects Agency (US).
DAS	Dual Attachment Station.
DCA	Document Content Architecture.
DCE	Data Communications Equipment.
DCE	Distributed Computing Environment.

DFN	Deutsches Forschungsnetz (German research network).
DI	Device Interface.
DIX	DEC/Intel/Xerox.
DL	Data Link.
DMA	Direct Memory Access.
DME	Distributed Management Environment.
DoD	Department of Defense (US).
DP	Data Processing.
DQDB	Distributed Queue Dual Bus.
DSI	Distributed System Interworking unit.
DTE	Data Terminal Equipment.
DTP	Distributed Transaction Processing.
ECMA	European Computer Manufacturers' Association.
EDI	Electronic Data Interchange.
EGP	Exterior Gateway Protocol.
EGW	Edge Gateway.
EIA	Electronic Industries Association.
ENV	European Prenorm.
FCB	File Control Block.
FCS	Frame Check Sequence.
FDDI	Fibre Distributed Data Interface.
FIFO	First-In-First-Out.
FO	Fibre Optic.
FOIRL	Fibre Optic Inter-Repeater Link.
FOMAU	Fibre Optic Medium Attachment Unit.
FTAM	File Transfer, Access and Management.
FTDM	Fixed Time Division Multiplexing.
FTP	File Transfer Protocol.
FWHM	Full Spectral Width Half Maximum.
GUI	Graphical User Interface.
HDLC	High-level Data Link Control.
HW	Hardware
ICA	Intelligent Communication Adapter.
ICMP	Internet Control Message Protocol.
ID	Identifier.
IDP	Internet Datagram Protocol.
IEEE	Institute of Electrical and Electronic Engineers.
IGP	Interior Gateway Protocol.
IHL	Internet Header Length.
IP	Internet Protocol.
IPX	Internet Packet Exchange.
IRL	Inter-Repeater Link.
ISDN	Integrated Services Digital Network.
ISO	International Organization for Standardization.
IXI	International X.25 Interconnect.
JANET	Joint Academic Network (UK).

JTM	Job Transfer and Manipulation.
kbps	Kilobits per second.
LAN	Local Area Network.
LAT	Local Area Transport.
LD	Laser Diode
LED	Light-Emitting Diode.
LLC	Logical Link Control.
LM	Layer Management.
LMMP	LAN/MAN Management Protocol.
LMMS	LAN/MAN Management Service.
LMMU	LAN/MAN Management User.
LRZ	Leibniz-Rechenzentrum (Leibniz Computer Centre), Munich.
MAC	Medium Access Control.
MAN	Metropolitan Area Network.
MAP	Manufacturing Automation Protocol.
MAU	Medium Access Unit.
Mbps	Megabits per second.
MDI	Medium-Dependent Interface.
MHS	Message Handling System.
MIB	Management Information Base.
MIPS	Million Instructions Per Second.
MO	Managed Object.
MTA	Message Transfer Agent.
MTBF	Mean Time Between Failure.
MTTR	Mean Time To Repair.
NAP	Network Access Protocol.
NAP	Network layer Access Point.
NCB	Network Control Block.
NFS	Network File System.
NIS	Network Information Service/System.
NIU	Network Interface Unit.
NLM	Network Loadable Module.
NM	Network Management.
NMS	Network Management System.
NRZ	Non Return to Zero.
ODA	Office Document Architecture.
ODIF	Office Document Interchange Format.
OEM	Original Equipment Manufacturer.
OS	Operating System.
OSF	Open Software Foundation.
OSI	Open Systems Interconnection.
OSPF	Open Shortest Path First protocol.
OTDR	Optical Time Domain Reflectometer.
PAD	Packet Assembly Disassembly.
PAD	Padding bits.
PBX	Private Branch Exchange.

PC	Personal Computer.
PCSA	Personal Computing Systems Architecture.
PDU	Protocol Data Unit.
PFOS	Passive Fibre Optic Segment.
PICS	Protocol Implementation Conformance Statement.
PLS	Physical Layer Signalling.
PMA	Physical Medium Attachment.
PROM	Programmable Read Only Memory.
PVC	Permanent Virtual Circuit.
RAM	Random Access Memory.
RDA	Remote Data Access.
RF	Radio Frequency.
RFC	Request for Comments.
RFS	Remote File System.
RIP	Router Information Protocol.
RISC	Reduced Instruction Set Computer.
RJE	Remote Job Entry.
RM	Reference Model.
ROM	Read Only Memory.
ROSE	Remote Operations Service Element.
RPC	Remote Procedure Call.
RPC	Root Path Cost.
RTD	Round Trip Delay.
RTSE	Reliable Transfer Service Element.
SAP	Service Access Point.
SAS	Single Attachment Station.
SDH	Synchronous Digital Hierarchy (SONET).
SDLC	Synchronous Data Link Control.
SFD	Start Frame Delimiter.
SMB	Server Message Block.
SMDS	Switched Multi-megabit Data Service.
SMI	Structure of Management Information.
SMTP	Simple Mail Transport Protocol.
SNA	Systems Network Architecture.
SNMP	Simple Network Management Protocol.
SONET	Synchronous Optical Network.
SP	Sequenced Packet Protocol.
SPF	Shortest Path First.
SPAG	Standard Promotion and Application Group.
SQE	Signal Quality Error.
SRT	Source Routing Transparent bridge.
STA	Spanning Tree Algorithm.
STP	Shielded Twisted Pair.
SW	Software.
TAP	Terminal Access Point.
TCP	Transmission Control Protocol.

TDR	Time Domain Reflectometer.
TIA	Telecommunications Industries Association.
TMN	Telecommunications Management Network.
TOP	Technical and Office Protocols.
TPSE	Transaction Processing Service Element.
TTS	Trouble Ticket System.
TTY	Teletype interface.
UA	User Agent.
UDP	User Datagram Protocol.
UMD	Unscrambled Mode Delimiter.
UPS	Uninterruptible Power Supply.
UTP	Unshielded Twisted Pair.
VBN	Vermittelndes Breitbandnetz (German switched videoconferencing network).
VDE	Verein Deutscher Elektrotechniker (Association of German Electrical Engineers).
VT	Virtual Terminal.
WAN	Wide Area Network.
WIN	German science network.
WS	Workstation.
XDR	External Data Representation standard.
XNS	Xerox Network System.
YP	Yellow Pages.
ZZF	Zentrale Zulassungsstelle Fernmeldewesen (German central telecommunications authorization authority).

Bibliography

Bibliography for Chapter 1

Boell H. P. (1989) *Lokale Netze*. McGraw-Hill, New York

Bux W. (1981). Local-area subnetworks: a performance comparison. *IEEE Trans. Comm.*, COM-29, 1465–1473

Göhring H.-G. and Kauffels F.-J. (1992). *Token Ring: Principles, Perspectives and Strategies*. Addison-Wesley, Wokingham

Hammond J.L. and O'Reilly P.P. (1986). *Performance Analysis of Local Computer Networks*. Addison-Wesley, Reading, MA

IEEE Std. 802-1990: Overview and Architecture. IEEE New York. ISBN1-55937-052-1

Kauffels F.-J. (1991). *Lokale Netze – Systeme für den Hochleistungs-Informations-transfer* 5th edn. Datacom-Verlag, Bergheim

Spaniol O. (1982). Konzepte und Bewertungsmethoden für lokale Rechennetze. *Informatik-Spektrum*, 5, 152–170

Stallings W. (1988). *Local Network Technology* 3rd edn. IEEE Computer Society Press, New York

Suppan-Borowka J. and Simon T. (1986). *MAP-Datenkommunikation in der automatisierten Fertigung*. Datacom-Verlag, Pulheim

Bibliography for Chapter 2

Crane R.C. and Taft E.A. (1980). Practical considerations in Ethernet local network design. In *Proc. 13th Hawaii International Conference on System Sciences*, 166–175

DIX (1980). *The Ethernet – A local area network, data link layer and physical layer specifications*, Version 1.0. DEC, Intel, Xerox

ECMA *Local area networks–CSMA/CD baseband*

ECMA 80 (1984). *Coaxial cable system*, 2nd edn.

ECMA 81 (1984). *Physical layer*, 2nd edn.

ECMA 82 (1984). *Link layer*, 2nd edn.

IEEE Std. 802-1990: Local and Metropolitan Area Networks, Overview and Architecture. ISBN 1-55937-052-1

IEEE Std. 802.2-1987 (ISO 8802-2-1989): Logical Link Control

IEEE Std 802.3-1985 (ISO 8802-3-1989): Local Area Networks Part 3: Carrier Sense Multiple Access with Collision Detection, Access Method and Physical Layer Specifications

IEEE Std. 802.3 a,b,c,e-1988: Supplements to CSMA/CD Access Method and Physical Layer Specifications (corresponds to ISO 8802-3-1990)

IEEE Std. 802.3i-1990 (ISO 8802-3-1990-Supplement): Section 13: Multisegment Baseband Networks: Section 14: Type 10baseT

IEEE Std. 802.3h-1990: Layer Management

IEEE Project 802: Draft Supplement to ANSI/IEEE Std. 802.3-1988: Section 15, 10baseF; Section 16, 10baseFP; Section 17, 10baseFA. P802.3J/D6-D9, 1991

IEEE Std 1802.3-1991, CSMA/CD Conformance Test Methodology

IEEE Draft Standard P 802.1B. LAN/MAN Management, July 1991

IEEE Std 802.1E-1990. System Load Protocol

IEEE Draft Recommended Practice 802.1F. Guidelines for the Development of Layer Management Standards. May 1991

ISO/IEC 8802-2/DAD1: Logical Link Control, Addendum 1: Flow control techniques for bridged local area networks, 1988

ISO/IEC 8802-2/DAD2: Logical Link Control, Addendum 1: Acknowledged connectionless-mode service and protocol, Type 3-Operation, 1990

ISO IS 8802-2: Local Area Networks – Logical Link Control, 1987

ISO 8802-2/DAD1: Local Area Networks – Logical Link Control, Addendum 1: Flow Control Techniques for Bridged Local Area Networks, 1988

ISO 8802-3/DAD2: Local Area Networks – Logical Link Control, Addendum 2: Acknowledged connectionless mode Service and Protocol, Type 3-Operation, 1990

Metcalfe R.M. and Boggs D.R. (1976). Ethernet: distributed packet switching for local computer networks. *Comm. ACM*, 19(7), 395–404

Shoch J.J., Dalal Y.K., Redell D.D. and Crane R.C. (1982). Evolution of the Ethernet local computer network, *IEEE Computer*, 10–27

Bibliography for Chapter 3

Lambert T. (1991). Drahtlose LANs. Steht die nächste Workstation vor der Tür? In *Verkabelung*, Datacom special, 190–197

Mathias C.J. (1992). Wireless LANs – the next wave. *Data Communications*, March 1992, 83–87

Bibliography for Chapter 4

Bauerfeld W. and Heigert J. (1987). Gateways–Struktureller Überblick *DATACOM*, 9 (part I), 12 (Part II)

Borowka P. (1992). *Brücken und Router*, Datacom-Verlag, Bergheim

Bradner S.O. (1992). Ethernet bridges and routers – faster than fast enough. *Data Communications*, February 1992, 58–69

Comer D.E. (1991). *Internetworking with TCP/IP. Vol I: Principles, Protocols, Architecture. Vol II: Design, Implementation and Internals.* Prentice-Hall, Englewood Cliffs, NJ

Holleczek P. and Kleinöder J. (1991). Beurteilung aus der Praxis *DFN Mitteilung,* 25, June 1991 and *26/27,* November 1991

IEEE Std 802.1D-1990: Media Access Control (MAC) Bridges

Perlman R. (1992). *Interconnections – Bridges and Routers in OSI and TCP/IP.* Addison-Wesley

Bibliography for Chapter 5

McClimans F.J. (1992). *Communication Wiring and Interconnections.* McGraw-Hill, New York

Naugle M.G. (1991). *Local Area Networking.* McGraw-Hill, New York

Bibliography for Chapter 6

Beyschlag U. (ed.) (1988). *OSI in der Anwendungsebene.* Datacom-Verlag, Pulheim

X.400ff: Message handling Systems (CCITT)

X.500ff: The Directory (CCITT)

Glaser G.M., Hein M. and Vogl (1990). *TCP/IP.* Datacom-Verlag, Bergheim

Halsall F. (1992). *Data Communications, Computer Networks and Open Systems,* 3rd edition. Addison-Wesley, Wokingham

ISO 8505 Message Oriented Text Interchange System (4 Parts)

ISO 8571 File Transfer, Access and Management (4 Parts)

ISO 8613 Text and Office Systems–Office Document Architecture and Interchange Format (8 parts)

ISO 8649/50 Association Control Service Element. Service Definition/Protocol Specification

ISO 8331 Job Transfer and Manipulation Concepts and Services

ISO 8832 Specification of the Basic Class Protocol for Job Transfer and Manipulation

ISO 9066 Reliable Transfer (2 Parts)

ISO 9072 Remote Operations (2 Parts)

ISO 9506 Manufacturing Message Specification (2 Parts)

ISO 9545 The Directory (8 Parts)

ISO 9735 Electronic Data Interchange for Finance, Administration, Commerce and Transport (EDIFACT)

ISO 9804/5 Common Appplication Service Elements–Commitment, Concurrency and Recovery

Kauffels F.-J. and Suppan J. (1992). *FDDI–Einsatz, Standards, Migration.* Datacom-Verlag, Bergheim

Kessler G.C. and Train D.A. (1992). *Metropolitan Area Networks.* McGraw-Hill, New York

Kerner H. (ed.) (1992). *Rechnernetze nach OSI.* Addison-Wesley

Strassacker P. and Mayer H. (1992). Technische Eigenschaften von LAN-Kommunikationsbaugruppen. *DATACOM*, 4, 94–96

Xerox (1985). *Xerox Network Systems Architecture: General Information Manual and Protocol Descriptions*

Bibliography for Chapter 7

Freed L. and Derfler F.J. (1992). *Guide zu NetWare*. Ziff-Davis, New York

Göhring H.G. and Jasper E. (1993). *PC–Host Communications. Strategies for Implementation*. Addison-Wesley, Wokingham

Görner B. (1991). *Novell NetWare leichtgemacht*. Markt und Technik

Habermaier M. (1991). *Unix in lokalen Netzen*. Oldenbourg-Verlag

Kauffels F.-J. (1991). OSF DCE–der Weg zur verteilten Datenverarbeitung. *DATACOM*, 6

Kersten H. and Weinand M. (1991). *Sicherheitsaspekte bei der Vernetzung von Unix-Systemen*. Oldenbourg-Verlag

Krödel M. (1991). *Der LAN-Manager in der Praxis*. Markt und Technik

Lanzatella T.W. An Evaluation of Andrew File System. Cray User Group Meeting 1991

Server Software. PC Professional, September 1991, p. 289–316

Santifaller M. (1991). *TCP/IP and NFS: Internetworking in a UNIX Environment*. Addison-Wesley, Wokingham

Sheldon T. (1991). *Novell NetWare 386. The Complete Reference*. Osborne/McGraw-Hill, New York

Bibliography for Chapter 8

Black U. (1992). *Network Management Standards*. McGraw-Hill, New York

Datapro Research Corp.: The LAN Trouble Shooting Sequence. NM 50-300-101, Delran, USA

Datapro Research Corp.: Network Management Information Service. Issue 2: LAN and Internetworking Management

ECMA (1990). *Local Area Networks. Planning and Installation Guide for CSMA/CD 10 Mbit/s Baseband LAN Coaxial Systems*, TR/26, second edition, June 1990

Garbe K. (1991). *Management von Rechnernetzen*. Teubner-Verlag, Stuttgart

Hegering H.-G. (1991a). Architekturansätze für ein heterogenes Netzmanagement. *PIK*, 4, 245–246

Hegering H.-G. (1991b). Die Problematik einer Management Information Base (MIB) für ein integriertes Netzmanagement. *Informatik–Forschung und Entwicklung*, 6, 171–185; alternatively: How to find significant management information in a heterogeneous network environment. In *Proc. Joint SAIEE/CSSA Int. Sym. Network Management*, Univ. Pretoria, Rep. South Africa, 27–29 May 1991

Hegering H.-G. and Chylla P.: Benutzeridentifikation und Abrechnungsdienste in einer verteilten Systemumgebung. In *Kommunikation in verteilten Systemen*, RWTH Aachen, 16–20 February 1987, Series Informatik-Fachberichte Nr. 130, Springer-Verlag; alternatively: Access Control as Part of LAN Management. In *Proc. 4th European Fibre Optic Comm. and LAN Conf. (EFOCLAN)*, Amsterdam, June 1986, pp. 205–214

Heigert J. (1991). OSF DME–Kein klarer Gewinner. *DATACOM*, 11

Höns G. and Köpke F. (1987). Ethernet unter Hochlast. *DATACOM*, 10, 28–33

Hudson B. and Taylor B. *Implementing a Broadband LAN*. NCC Publications, Manchester

IEEE Draft Standard 802.1B. LAN/MAN-Management. P802.1B/D19, July 26, 1991

IEEE Draft Supplement to Std. 802.3. Layer Management for Hub Devices, Section 19. P802.3K/D4. August 6, 1991

RFC 1155: Structure and Identification of Management Information for TCP/IP-based Internets

RFC 1156: Management Information Base for NM of TCP/IP-based Internets

RFC 1157: A simple network management protocol SNMP

ISO 7498-4: OSI-Reference Model, Addendum 4: NM Framework

ISO 10040: OSI-Systems Management Overview

ISO 10164: OSI-Systems Management Functions

ISO 10165: OSI-Structure of Management Information

Kauffels F.-J. (1992). *Network Management: Problems, Standards and Strategies.* Addison-Wesley, Wokingham

Kerner H. (ed.) (1992). *Rechnernetze nach OSI.* Addison-Wesley

Lüschow S. (ed.) (1991). *Verkabelung*, Datacom special, 2

Marquard R., Mues D., Olsowsky G. and Suppan-Borowka J. (1987). *Ethernet Handbuch.* Datacom-Verlag, Pulheim

Miller M.A. (1989). *LAN Troubleshooting Handbook.* M&T Books, Redwood City

Nemzow M.A. (1992). *The Ethernet Management Guide–Keeping the Link* 2nd edn. McGraw-Hill, New York

Neumair H. (1986), Anwendungsevaluation – Einordnungshilfe aus Anwendersicht. In *Lokale Netze. State of the Art 2/86*. Oldenbourg-Verlag

OSF (1992). OSF Distributed Management Environment (DME) Architecture. Open Software Foundation.

Pattay, W. von: Verkabelungsstrategien für Inhausnetze. SYSTEMS 89, GI-Fachseminar

Rhodes P. (1991). *LAN Operations: A Guide to Daily Management.* Addison-Wesley

Rose M.T. (1991). *The Simple Book. An Introduction to Management of TCP/IP-based Internets*, Prentice-Hall, Englewood Cliffs, NJ

Terplan K. and Voigt C. (1991). *LAN-Management.* Datacom-Verlag, Bergheim

Valta R.F. (1992). *Netzmanagementstationen – Vergleichende Darstellung.* Leibniz Computer Centre Internal Report

Index